Pop: Truth and Power at the
Coca-Cola Company

Pop

TRUTH AND POWER AT THE COCA-COLA COMPANY

Constance L. Hays

arrow books

Published by Arrow in 2005

7 9 10 8 6

Copyright © Constance L. Hays, 2004

Constance L. Hays has asserted her right under the Copyright, Designs and Patents
Act, 1988 to be identified as the author of this work.

First published in the United States by Random House Inc. in 2004

Arrow
The Random House Group Limited
20 Vauxhall Bridge Road, London SW1V 2SA

Random House Australia (Pty) Limited
20 Alfred Street, Milsons Point, Sydney
New South Wales 2061, Australia

Random House New Zealand Limited
18 Poland Road, Glenfield
Auckland 10, New Zealand

Random House (Pty) Limited
Endulini, 5a Jubilee Road, Parktown 2193, South Africa

The Random House Group Limited Reg. No. 954009

www.randomhouse.co.uk

A CIP catalogue record for this book is available from the British Library

Penguin Random House is committed to a sustainable future for
our business, our readers and our planet. This book is made from
Forest Stewardship Council® certified paper.

Printed and bound in Great Britain by Clays Ltd, Elcograf S.p.A.

ISBN 978 0 09 947257 5

For John
and
for the brave

There's the fruits of promotion now;
there's the vanity of glory;
there's the insanity of life!

Herman Melville, *Moby-Dick*

Contents

Preface

COCA-COLA BEGAN SIMPLY, as so many things do. Filled with sparkle and democratically priced, it was as American as baseball, as accessible as jazz. It cost a nickel, which almost anyone could afford. Before long, it was everywhere.

It originated in a time of turmoil, as an antidote cloaked in innocence. It was marketed vigorously upon a willing public. And in its essence there is conflict.

A swallow of Coca-Cola is both sweet and tart. A single formula joins together elements as commonplace as table sugar and as exotic as the cola nut. It began as a drink, as dark as night, and became an experience, flowing over time and place, linked by memory to the meal on the table and the company at hand. Over more than a hundred years it came to be seen as a constant amid change, a rock standing against the tide.

It was the most ubiquitous soda, sold at every grocery store and luncheonette and stadium across the land. It was the drink of the people, but it also possessed an odd power, a power that lifted it above other soft drinks. Much of that was the work of the Coca-Cola Company, where salesmanship was everything. But there was also, after a little while, a romance that developed between this soft drink, born to an America still repairing itself after the Civil War, and the people who bought it. 'We love our Coca-Cola,' they would say. And that was true.

The Coke story begins near the close of the nineteenth century, before the Wright brothers launched their plane from the dunes at Kitty Hawk. It continues through war and peace, boom times and recessions, coasting along through the Gilded Age and the Marshall Plan, outlasting Prohibition and Reaganomics, becoming a relic of the Great Depression as well as the great bull market. Cast in small relief against everyone else's highs and lows, enduring everything that history handed to it, Coca-Cola provided brief, carbonated, affordable interruptions—simple moments of pleasure, as the company liked to say—in the daily struggles and routines of life. It could be adapted to fit almost any market condition and made to seem appropriate for almost any occasion.

It was just a soft drink, after all.

At the same time, to the men in charge of Coke it was virtually limitless in its prospects. From the start they held it up as an elixir brimming with promise, a 'brain tonic' that would ease the headaches of a South enduring Reconstruction. As the Depression settled in they harnessed Santa Claus to their cause, creating for him a new image that always included a bottle of Coke – 'a luxury you can afford' – in his glove. World War II gave them cause to festoon their product with the Stars and Stripes. Later they made Coke go hand in hand with the quest for world peace.

Through relentless advertising, clever marketing, and sometimes plain old luck, Coke came to stand for the glamorous, prosperous, flag-waving side of America, the part that always looked forward, not back. The soldiers fighting the good fight drank Coca-Cola, and so did presidents and rock stars and other heroes Americans might imagine themselves to be.

The men of Coke could have found themselves pouring all their effort into an unresponsive nation, but people returned the affection. First they loved Coke because it was something new and different, and maybe because it did indeed cure what ailed them. Later they regarded it as a comforting souvenir of eras that had come and gone. It stood for a simpler time, when silos held nothing but corn and when Berlin and the Bay of Pigs were only places on a map. Coke was still the same as it had been a long time ago, when they were young.

But love was worth only so much within the Coca-Cola Company, where executives lived in a state of constant agitation. They were hugely ambitious, driven to capture as much of the world as they could for Coke. Their thoroughly modern business ran independently of the climate, the calendar, and the clock. They developed a lust for power, and consequences barely figured in their plans.

They rapidly conquered America, then repeated the performance across the planet. By 1981, the Coca-Cola Company was a ninety-five-year-old colossus pumping soda to practically every shoal and rain forest and concrete-paved corner on earth. At home, Coke stood for all-American notions like free enterprise and runaway success. Abroad, it was even more intoxicating: a bottle of optimism, the liquid substitute for liberty. Governments might come and go, but Coke would always find a way to be for sale in the cafés and the bus stations, its curvaceous image visible as the smoke cleared, beckoning toward the American way.

Around the world, Coke crossed the line between consumer product and object of desire. It imprinted itself upon cultures everywhere, appearing in movies, in literature, in paintings and sculpture, and in the lyrics of songs. Well before the Coca-Cola Company marked its one hundredth anniversary, all kinds of people could see that Coca-Cola possessed an image that exceeded the sum of its parts. It was Marilyn Monroe and the Statue of Liberty in a single package, tantalizing and familiar all at once, the world's best-known brand.

The men running the Coca-Cola Company in 1981 recognized Coke's awesome power. But they were sure they could improve on it. The first century of Coke had had its high points, but so much had been sloppy, undisciplined, or left to luck—unpredictable forces no one could trust. So they planned a future that they would control from top to bottom, in their company's best interests—a future that would be far different from the reality they knew.

First, though, they needed a revolution.

The Coca-Cola empire of that moment bore little resemblance to the original Coca-Cola Company that began in 1886. At first, Coke was served only at marble-fronted soda fountains. But it was the self-starting Coca-Cola bottlers who fanned the public's affinity for a product that was neither essential nor especially good for them. They made it portable, and they made it easier to get. And they changed the Coca-Cola Company.

They were independent businessmen who built factories right in the middle of dusty, impoverished towns. Inside, they turned Coke syrup into soft drinks; outside, they put up signs that read, DRINK

COCA-COLA. They became the owners of machinery that everyone could see and began to wield authority that everyone could feel. The bottlers took Coca-Cola afield, out of the cities and towns and into the farmland and the coal mines and the rest of rural America—to all the places where there would never be a soda fountain. They guessed right—that Americans craved convenience as much as they craved that sugary soda. Taking in a nickel for every bottle of Coke they sold, they wound up better off than anybody else around. They towered over small-town life, serving as mayor, heading up the Chamber of Commerce. But first and foremost, they were Coca-Cola bottlers. That was an identity, not just a job.

By the 1920s, a quarter century after the first bottle of Coca-Cola was created, more Coke was being sold in bottles than at soda fountains. The bottlers were indispensable, and life was more difficult for Coke. The company owned the brand; the bottlers owned the markets, splintered all across America, each with a personality of its own. The bottlers were exceedingly powerful, the closest thing to an equal that the company would ever know. Coke needed them and depended on them, but it could not control them. In Atlanta, a fire of resentment began to burn. It would never go out.

The bottlers existed, according to the prevailing theory inside the Coca-Cola Company, only because one of Coke's leaders had suffered an extraordinary lapse in judgment. And for nearly as long as there was Coca-Cola in bottles, breaking the bottlers' hold would be a strategic priority for a parade of senior executives at Coke. They wanted to go back and start over. They tried, and failed, again and again.

But in 1981 an extraordinary group of men took charge of Coke and began laying the foundation for a new and improved version of their company. Five years later, a century after the first Coca-Cola was served, they had come up with yet another plan for a brand-new bottling system, one that would be more subservient to Coke. This time, they got their wish.

Reinventing the bottling business was the start of a shimmering universe that they designed for themselves. They would bring everything about Coca-Cola under the supreme control of Atlanta and transform the company into a more sustained, efficient, and lucrative force than anything the business world had ever seen. With that victory over the bottlers in hand, Coke began a march down a new path, one intended to shower all glory and power upon the Coca-Cola Company. The *new* Coca-Cola Company.

It would be a complex journey, buoyed by egos, punctuated with triumphs and molded by secrecy.

And it began with a vision, of a world of Coke.

Pop

Chapter One

The Road to Rome

ON A BRIGHT FALL morning in 1994, Doug Ivester, the recently anointed president of the Coca-Cola Company, was driving himself to Rome, Georgia, spinning north along the interstate, the steel-and-glass towers of Atlanta receding behind him as the landscape became an uneven blanket of pines.

Ivester had his day all planned out. Like plenty of Coke executives before him, he had a certain fixation with Hollywood – the glitter, the lights, the adjustable distance between image and reality. And now he was going to star in his own short film, which he had already named *The Road to Rome*.

He had borrowed a sport-utility vehicle and hired a camera crew. Husky and hawk-nosed, he had dressed down for the occasion in a V-neck sweater and left his usual silk necktie at home. He aimed the boxy car toward Rome, pulling over every so often at all kinds of places to ask whether they served Coca-Cola.

It became an exercise in frustration, if you happened to be the second-highest-ranking executive at the company that owned the Coca-Cola brand. The cameras trailed Ivester at every stop, recording the scene at a karate studio where the flustered owner apologetically explained before the inquiring lens that he didn't sell Coke, and at the Kennesaw Mountain tourist attraction, where there was no Coke, either. In his reedy North Georgia twang, Ivester kept asking everyone in his path the same apparently simple question: What if people coming to these places wanted a Coke? What if they finished training for their black belt, looked around for a way to quench their thirst, and realized there was no place nearby to get their hands on a Coke?

There was only one right answer in the script that dictated: They'd be disappointed. So would hundreds, no, r of other people across the globe, in all of the other places where Coke still wasn't for sale in every possible nook that it could be sold. The message of the film – that even right in its own backyard, a place presumably already saturated with Coke, the Coca-Cola Company still had plenty of room to grow – was an ongoing theme inside the company. And Ivester was going to make sure Coke got every last bit of that growth.

There would be no Oscars for *The Road to Rome,* which was completed on a modest budget that year and screened before limited audiences – Wall Street analysts mostly, and here and there a Coke bottler. But it was remarkable nevertheless, articulating something beyond the typical corporate statement of purpose. It was a graphic guide to the mentality of the Coca-Cola Company and the mind of the man who now occupied its second-highest position: a man who believed fervently and unremittingly in the supremacy of Coca-Cola.

That the drink was more than a century old and was still not being sold absolutely everywhere hounded Ivester. People close to him claimed that he could not sleep at night if he knew that a store somewhere in the depths of the nation, any nation, was not selling Coca-Cola. Maybe it was the pizza parlor in Omaha that Warren Buffett, the legendary investor and Coke director, visited one day with his grandson, only to report back that it served nothing but Pepsi. Ivester made it his personal project to get the Pepsi out and the Coca-Cola in; within weeks, he had made the change. Maybe it was a country like Vietnam, where for years American business had been prohibited. Awaiting the day the embargo might end, Ivester had a plane loaded with Cokes and signs and other equipment intended to capture the new market. In 1994, a few hours after the State Department gave American companies the green light to invest again in Vietnam, the Coke plane took off. It was on a mission to restore the business that politics had inconveniently halted almost twenty years earlier.

Like many of the people at his company, Ivester had a relentless faith in the drink's appeal for people of all ages, races, cultures, and economic profiles. To him, if Coke was on the shelf, or in the vending machine, or in the dispenser down at the 7-Eleven, then that's what people would buy. But still, even in tried-and-true

Coke country, like the hills of Georgia – the part of America where Ivester himself grew up – there were plenty of places that didn't stock it. And the key to filling in all those holes, to completing the program put forth by legions of Coke men culminating with Ivester, was to seal the gaps between the Coca-Cola Company and its historically feisty and independent bottling system.

The Coca-Cola Company was 108 years old on the morning that Ivester set off for Rome, and it was already the biggest soft-drink company in the world. Nineteen ninety-four was its greatest year yet. People drank Coca-Cola morning, noon, and night in the United States, where Coke had gotten started. In many places Coca-Cola stood in for coffee as the way people began their day. It had replaced milk and fruit juice in many lunchboxes, even in baby bottles in some places, if everything you heard was true. Ivester liked to predict that one day, along with red wine and water goblets, a formal table setting would have to include a broad-shouldered Coca-Cola glass.

That was just one of Ivester's goals. And he usually got what he wanted. Over the previous decade, he had transformed Coke from a nodding institution into a sleek and ultra-competitive global champion, envied and imitated by dozens of other American companies. Along with two colleagues, Roberto Goizueta and Donald Keough, he had created a monolith that tapped skillfully into emerging markets and pumped unexpected growth out of old ones. They had turned a well-known brand-name soda into a money machine, an ice-veined fountain jingling with cash. As Ivester drove along the road to Rome, Coca-Cola was the best-known product in the world. The company was selling Coke at the rate of 850 million eight-ounce bottles a day, or 310 billion bottles a year. Stacked one on top of another, a year's worth of global Coke sales would create a tower reaching nearly all the way to Mars. Fourteen months of sales would get you all the way there.

But that was not enough for Ivester.

Like Goizueta, he wanted the consumption of Coke to keep on growing. Now that Keough had retired, it was just the two of them, and they aggressively promoted the company's prospects, touting the opportunities to sell ever more Coca-Cola worldwide before an impressed Wall Street. The Coca-Cola Company was all about growth, the men of Coke insisted. With close to a billion servings sold every day, they believed that the company had only just begun to make its mark in the world. Two billion servings were just around the corner.

They made these kinds of promises publicly, and they programmed their company to fulfill them. They had kept those promises again and again over the previous thirteen years, posting spectacular gains in sales and in earnings, beating not just the competition but most of the rest of industrial America, as well. Ivester's movie was really just another reminder, in case anyone needed reminding, not to underestimate Coke.

So complete was their obsession that these men were tormented by the way Coca-Cola remained a distant also-ran to other beverages in many parts of the globe. It was not just a matter of vanquishing Pepsi-Cola; it was also about beating back drinks like coffee, tea, milk, and water. In fly-blown, malnourished parts of Asia and Africa, people still – inexplicably, if you asked Ivester – preferred tea or juice to Coca-Cola. In France, people might buy three kinds of bottled water in their supermarkets – and, incredibly, pass up the red cans of Coca-Cola. If Coke could capture those markets, persuading consumers to drink cola instead, then the brand would grow even more. That was what Ivester and Goizueta wanted. That was what their planning was all about.

They wanted Coca-Cola everywhere. In refrigerated cases in convenience stores, out on the street in barrels packed with ice, in vending machines in school hallways, in the basements and pantries of people's houses, and on tap at restaurants, ball parks, movie theaters, hotels, cruise ships, and all the other places where people spend their time. When a person drove into a gas station, they wanted him to think *Coke* first. When somebody stood in a movie line and had to choose something to drink during the 7:15 show, they wanted it to be Coke. They wanted Coke to be available every time somebody felt a stab of thirst. And, whenever possible, they wanted it to be the only beverage on the shelf.

To the two men who held the top jobs at Coke in 1994, this was not some eccentric, highly personal approach to commerce. It was the cornerstone of their business plan. They told people like Warren Buffett about it, and he applauded them, despite the risks.

'In given countries at given times there will be hiccups,' Buffett would say. 'But that doesn't take your eye off where you want to be ten or fifteen years from now, which is to have everybody drink nothing but Coke.' They had made their promises to people like him. They were going to make them come true.

Year by year, Ivester and Goizueta invested a lot in the outcome. For the more Coke people consumed, the more money would flow into the Coca-Cola Company, which produced the concentrate – a dark, sticky, undrinkable ooze – that became the soda. More money meant greater profits, which would lift the stock price, making all the people who had invested in it – the grannies in Atlanta; the great capitalists in New York, Los Angeles, and Omaha; and, not least, the grand executives of Coke, their accounts bulging with stock options, restricted stock, and ordinary stock – wealthier with every day that went by.

To Ivester, careful planning was critical to making sure that happened. He saw potential in microscopic terms. He started with his employees, all 29,000 of them around the world. It was the duty and the obligation of every person associated with Coca-Cola, he asserted, to remember the Coca-Cola Company's mission and to do everything within his or her power to turn possibility into fact. He stocked the public areas in Coke's headquarters with monitors that displayed the stock price from the moment the market opened. He became notorious for walking around foreign markets, demanding to know why some tiny Chinese grocery store didn't have Coke on the shelves, or peering into the trash cans on the banks of the Nile to find out what people were drinking – how much Coke, and how much of everything else. He could be standing under a cloudless sky in the middle of a shantytown in South Africa, where desperately poor people nestled beside garbage heaps crawling with flies and vermin, and he would see, in addition to the problems, another great place to sell Coca-Cola. Reaching into the trunk of his limousine, he would produce a case of Coke and press it upon a local merchant, insisting that if the man could make a living selling ice cream or peanuts or dried squid or whatever he already had in his cart, he could do better with Coke.

By the time Ivester became Coke's president, the company was producing the concentrate for many other kinds of beverages –

grape drink, orange juice, canned coffee, green tea – but to Ivester and Goizueta, center stage belonged to Coca-Cola. Part of the attitude was historic; this was, after all, the soft drink that had given rise to the company in the first place. Much of it was financial: The margins on Coca-Cola concentrate, which cost pennies a gallon to make, were the most enormous of all. For people who thought strictly in terms of numbers, Coke was it.

Robert Woodruff, the most legendary Coca-Cola executive of all, had preached putting Coke 'within an arm's reach of desire'; Ivester took that further, endorsing concepts like 'a 360-degree landscape of Coke', where Coke ads, products, and vending machines would assert themselves everywhere a person looked, *making* you buy a Coke even if you hadn't known that's what you wanted. He exhorted everyone in the company to remember that they were personally responsible for 'increasing shareholder value', which meant always selling more and more Coca-Cola. His directive included the basic administrative level, like secretaries and security guards. It fanned upward through the great superstructure of jobs and responsibilities, tapering to the corner office where he, Ivester, expected one day to sit. In case people forgot, there were reminders everywhere: the stock price beaming from the elevator lobby, and the admonitions, mild and severe, delivered to people who dared drink a beverage made by some other company or take their jobs less than totally seriously. It was supposed to be not one drink among many, but *only* Coca-Cola.

Ivester epitomized the strict focus on Coke that he wanted to see across the ranks. He could cite the company's stock price at any given moment (he checked it constantly) and remembered when Coke first sold a million cases a year in Shanghai (1926). He leaned on Coke's customers – restaurants, vending-machine owners, airlines, supermarkets, hotels – to do more to sell Coke. He urged bottlers to take on more equipment and more accounts and to invest heavily in their businesses, again to sell more Coke. And he didn't like to take no for an answer.

He had made bottlers a critical element in his campaign, as they had been for most of Coca-Cola's history. The company made only soft-drink concentrate, sold as a dry powder or as a syrup. Both had to be transformed, with bubble-filled water and user-friendly packaging, into something that would fit into a consumer's hand and taste good going down. That was the bottlers' job. For generations, the bottlers had defined how they would get that done, and they prospered according to how well they performed.

But Ivester had come up with a better idea. He relaxed a little thinking about it, resting his left arm along the edge of the car door as northern Georgia unfolded past the window.

Sitting beside him in the passenger seat was a man named Jimmy Wardlaw. Wardlaw had once worked for an independent bottler, but now he was part of Coca-Cola Enterprises in Atlanta, a giant substitute for the independent bottlers that had been conceived, created, and spun off at the suggestion of Ivester. Wardlaw was the kind of bottler Ivester liked. Too many of the other bottlers out there were the kind Coke executives thought the Coca-Cola Company would be better off without.

Chapter Two

Partnership

FOR NEARLY A CENTURY, bottlers had been the indispensable partners of the Coca-Cola Company. They got dirt under their fingernails and wore down the heels on their shoes. They printed big rings of sweat inside their hatbands and strained muscles in their backs. It was all part of the process of delivering Coke to all kinds of people everywhere.

They bought syrup, added fizzy water, poured the mixture into bottles, and carried them out into the world – first on wagons, then small trucks, then eighteen-wheelers. They served high-stepping hotels and rural grocery stores. They dealt with merchant visionaries on both coasts, tramped their way over mountain ranges, and crisscrossed a countryside quilted with fields. They were indiscriminate about where they brought Coca-Cola. They made sure it was put before both consumers who had few delights in their lives and those who had plenty.

They introduced Coca-Cola to people like Bonnie Sinkfield, who one hot July morning in 1945 asked her grandmother to bring her some kind of drink from the store. The war that had preoccupied everyone around ten-year-old Bonnie for half her lifetime was nearly over, and as she played in the shadowy cool of their house on Orange Street in Atlanta's Mechanicsville section, she felt unaccustomedly happy. She could tell from the conversations among the grown-ups that clouds were lifting, that peace was at hand. Then her grandmother called to her from downstairs. For a treat, she had brought Bonnie a bottle of Coca-Cola.

In the kitchen, the child watched while her grandmother pulled the cap from the heavy glass bottle and handed it to her. She drank a sip, and then another, and then she drank the rest down as fast as she could. Fifty-seven years later, she still recalled the taste of that Coke on that summer day. She marveled at the sweetness. It made her burp at the end. From then on, wherever she was, in a corner store or in a restaurant or on a plane, she always asked for Coca-Cola.

It was a relatively simple thing, the act of delivering such an experience, and it helped guarantee Coca-Cola's dominance all over the country. Bottlers also provided a reality check, time and again keeping Coke from becoming something too proud for the people. And yet, by the time Doug Ivester set off for Rome, Coke's bottlers had been regarded for more than eighty years by Coca-Cola executives as a strange hybrid of helpmeet and adversary, a source of endless fireworks on good days and searing hostility on bad ones. The union of Coke and Coca-Cola bottlers was a marriage, for better or for worse, and, like most marriages, it had its highs and lows. Coke knew what power was and loved it. So did the bottlers.

By the time Ivester came along, things had deteriorated rather remarkably. Years of pressure on the bottlers from Coke, and years of the bottlers fighting back, had created chronic animosity that flowed in both directions. Before long, changes in the business landscape would put even more strain on the relationship.

In the late 1970s, the land was flowing with sweet carbonated soft drinks – Coke, Pepsi, 7Up, Royal Crown, Nehi, Canada Dry – and across the industry relationships between the makers of concentrate and their bottlers were often tenuous or worse. Soft-drink company executives referred to the bottlers as DFBs, short for 'dumb fucking bottlers', and the bottlers publicly ridiculed the concentrate companies over almost every move they made, from new television commercials to the promotion of different bottle sizes. The concentrate companies fumed over inefficiencies, and the bottlers raged over policies dictated to them from above.

But the Coca-Cola Company and its bottlers had a couple of things in common: their infatuation with the soft drink and their desire to keep the whole project – which had made them all exceedingly rich – rolling. For years, for the better part of a century, those passions held them together.

When Ivester arrived at Coke in 1979, there were about 500

bottlers distributing Coca-Cola, Sprite, and Tab across the nation, down from 1,200 fifty years earlier. Some bottlers had sold out to their neighbors, and a few were bought out by the Coca-Cola Company. Those remaining included people like Dick Montag, whose German grandfather started the family business in a corner of the Pacific Northwest in 1904 after coming up empty-handed in the Klondike gold rush; and Frank Barron, whose grandfather decided in 1901 that Coke would sell at least as well as the eggs and butter he stocked in his grocery store in Rome, Georgia. There was also Jack Lupton, whose grandfather shelled out his own money to help build a factory for the two men who got permission from the Coca-Cola Company to put Coke in bottles. Lupton's holdings spread like a spilled drink through Texas and Florida, and on to the West and Midwest to make him the biggest Coke bottler of all. Whether large or small, bottlers tended to be fiercely committed to Coca-Cola, because they thought of it as family.

They were all grown men, hardworking for the most part, their palms callused and their faces lined from the long hours involved in the business. And still they could grow misty-eyed at the mention of Coke, because it reminded them of their daddy and his daddy and all the good things they had grown up with – holidays and new cars, love and fishing trips and a first television set and feeling important – and that connected back to Coca-Cola. Bottling Coke was a century-long home movie for people like William Schmidt, whose loyalty to the company stretched back three generations: His grandfather, Frederick, got the franchise for Louisville, Kentucky, in 1901, and his family made it work no matter what. When Frederick's son Luke, who had inherited a small part of the company that bottled Coke in nearby Elizabethtown, died suddenly in 1941, Luke's wife, Irene, took charge and ran things for the next fourteen years, building Elizabethtown into a powerhouse that supplied Cokes to the soldiers stationed at Fort Knox during World War II. She won an award at the end of the war, a tiny gold Coke bottle decorated with diamonds, for doing such a commendable job. It was another bottler who gave it to her.

Most of the bottlers, wherever they were, worked hard to make sure they got everything they wanted out of their franchises. They made plenty of money – 'Have you ever seen a Coke bottler that wasn't rich?' Coke's chief executive would say, circa 1990 – but they lived for the prestige as well. People knew your name if you were the local Coke bottler. And your territory was exclusive. If someone living within a fifty-mile radius wanted to buy a bottle of Coke, he or she had to come to you. Therein lay the power, as far as both the market and the Coca-Cola Company were concerned. For no matter how inept a bottler might be, no one else could sell Coca-Cola in his territory – not even the Coca-Cola Company. The system protected some weak bottlers, but far more often it turned an entrepreneurial spark into a flame. Whatever business prospects lay within your area belonged to you, along with the profits you made. Under the original contracts, the price for your most fundamental raw material – the Coca-Cola syrup – was fixed. While other costs might fluctuate, being a Coca-Cola bottler was like getting a license to print money, as one banker put it. The bottlers, each and all of them, were Coca-Cola kings. But they would tell you then and tell you now: The money wasn't everything.

Bottling was never planned, organized, or even officially sanctioned by the Coca-Cola Company in the beginning. The very first bottler got into the business on a whim. In those days, the early 1890s, such spontaneity was possible.

First, though, came Coke by the glass. Asa Candler purchased the secret formula from its inventor, John Pemberton, in 1888 and began an intense campaign to sell Coke to every soda fountain he could. People came in, ordered a glass of Coca-Cola, and then watched the pharmacist mix an ounce of syrup with five and a half ounces of carbonated water. Then they drank it on the premises. They could drink it fast or they could drink it slow, but they had to drink it inside an establishment like the Penn Drug Company in Sidney, Iowa, or the original source, Jacobs' Pharmacy in downtown Atlanta. Often they dressed up to have a Coca-Cola, sweeping into pharmacies wearing their Sunday best.

First in Atlanta and then across the South, Candler made it his business to be sure every drugstore with a soda fountain of any size was offering Coke by name. There were plenty of competing syrups that tasted similar, and pharmacists often preferred to mix up their own, so his job was not easy. One pharmacist railed against 'the octopus that is fastening itself on the soda fountain trade', warning his fellow soda sellers against what he called 'patent drinks' like Coca-Cola. 'Do not display them more than is necessary,' he said. 'It does not require any great expenditure of gray matter to concoct these drinks . . . and it is easier and much more profitable to concoct your own specialty than to push somebody's else.'

But Candler persisted. Drugstores were perfect locations in which to promote a drink he had embellished with health claims; he advertised Coke as both a 'brain tonic' that could cure headaches and exhaustion and a 'nerve tonic' that could calm the most jangled nineteenth-century sensibilities. Pretty soon Candler, whose first name comes from the Hebrew word for physician, had made Coke into a nineteenth-century megabrand. In 1889, the Coca-Cola Company sold 2,171 gallons of its syrup to fountains. Just five years later, sales topped 64,000 gallons.

Merely covering the sugar-craving South with Coke was not enough for Candler. By 1895, he would tell his shareholders that 'Coca-Cola is now sold and drunk in every state and territory in the United States.' It was true, the result of his own winning formula: a combination of easy promises, free samples, and a willingness to partner with anyone he thought seemed like a decent business prospect.

One of the people he drafted to help him in his quest was a man named Joseph Biedenharn, a mannerly Mississippian who owned a candy company in Vicksburg. The city, besieged by Union troops for months, had been the site of a critical defeat for the Confederacy that turned the tide of the Civil War. At the time that Biedenharn got into the Coca-Cola business, Vicksburg's surrender on the Fourth of July in 1863 remained a painful memory for his clientele. During the siege the city had slowly run out of everything from calico for dresses to eggs for omelettes as the Yankees cut off the railroads and prevented the steamboats from coming into port. And finally the people had fled, burrowing into the cliffs along the riverfront, tending to the sick by lantern light while waiting for the cannon fire to subside.

At Asa Candler's urging, Biedenharn became a Coca-Cola syrup dealer in 1890, accepting five gallons of syrup that, at that time, came in wooden barrels. His role was to supply all of the fountains in the area around Vicksburg, and it kept him busy.

The local fountain in 1890s America was a social center both rococo and egalitarian, where drinks were served from glasses set in silver-plated holders by a pharmacist who wore a white jacket and a black bow tie on even the steamiest summer days. Ingesting something in such a setting implied that there were health benefits to be had by doing so, and fountains also provided a kind of refuge where people could drink 'soft' beverages and engage with one another without reproach. They were open to men, women, and children, who teemed around their marble counters and settled for hours in their curlicued iron chairs. Other industries developed to supply the syrups, ice cream, and carbon dioxide a soda fountain required, as well as the increasingly elaborate trappings of the business: long, polished onyx counters; silver spoons and strainers; huge displays of fruit and flowers evoking luxury as well as health.

Soda fountains became a national habit around 1815, evolving over the next seventy-five years from bland countertops stocked with jugs of plain soda water to elaborate installations in which dozens of spigots blossomed from marble- and mahogany-paneled walls. They were always democratic. An illustration published in 1872 showed customers of various ages gathered around a model of a simple, house-shaped fountain set on a drugstore counter. At the Paris Universal Exposition five years earlier, a soda fountain set up by an American company drew crowds and envy and impressed French journalists with not just the drinks but also the mass participation. 'As many as 4,000 glasses have been sold in one day,' a newspaper reported at the time, 'much to the satisfaction of the parties in charge.'

By 1876, when a Massachusetts entrepreneur named James Tufts paid a reported $50,000 to exhibit his soda fountain at the Centennial Exposition in Philadelphia, simplicity had given way to grandeur. The exposition was a much-anticipated extravaganza, where the displays ranged from a tranquil Japanese farmhouse to an enormous Roman goddess carved from butter. It was billed as the celebration of America's first one hundred years, but it doubled as a unifying event for a nation still mending the damage done by the Civil War. The soda fountain it showcased was a sight to behold.

Tufts, already a renowned soda-fountain builder in his home state, delivered himself to the fairgrounds with more than a hundred packing crates containing the elements of the most elaborate liquid-refreshment device the world had ever seen. Fully assembled, the soda fountain rose thirty feet into the air, its columns and pediments trimmed with silver-plated knobs and statuary and everything accented with potted palms. Tufts had to build a separate structure to house his Arctic Soda Water Apparatus, as he called it, and he spared no expense, illuminating it with a showy chandelier and topping it with a stylish mansard roof.

Impeccably dressed waiters prepared fountain drinks, flavored with everything from strawberries to mead, for the thirsty fair-goers who came to have a look. The expense paid off for its owner when thousands of people returned home after the centennial and began demanding state-of-the-art soda fountains in their towns, too. 'It was successful,' Tufts would later boast, 'beyond all expectation.'

But nearly twenty years after Tufts put on his display, Biedenharn discovered a flaw in the approach. He realized that the soda fountains of Vicksburg couldn't accommodate everyone in the area who might like to drink Coca-Cola and thought there must be a better way. 'The thought struck one day – why not bottle it for our country trade?' he recalled at one point. 'Even in the cities, the fountains were limited in number and scattered here and there.'

It was a sweltering summer morning in 1894 as he sat in his office, gazing at the barrels of Coca-Cola syrup he was storing there. The Mississippi unfolded like a wide brown ribbon beyond his door, pouring humidity into the heavy air. He looked over at the secondhand bottling machine he had ordered from a manufacturer in St. Louis a few years back, which he was using to bottle a little lemon soda and sarsaparilla for customers. A few minutes later he was bottling Coca-Cola.

He poured the soda into stubby-necked Hutchinson bottles, which came with rubber stoppers attached to a wire contraption that was yanked up into the bottle's neck to seal the contents. If a person wanted to open a Hutchinson bottle, he or she would jam the stopper down with the flat of the hand or maybe something sturdier. When the stopper fell back into the soda, it produced a hollow bang as the gas behind it was released. That sound became known as the drink's 'pop', and around the country the term 'soda pop' came to mean a sweet, fizzy soft drink in a bottle.

Biedenharn hadn't asked for permission to put Coke into bottles, but no one had said he couldn't, either. He sent a crateful to Candler in Atlanta, packing his fait accompli upside down, the bottles held steady by wooden planks into which Biedenharn had drilled holes that exactly fit the necks. Candler wrote back that they were fine, and Biedenharn carried on, supplying bottles of Coke to parched farmers who stopped by, to boats plying the river, to curious customers who knew perfectly well what a Coca-Cola served at the soda fountain tasted like but wanted to see how it tasted out of a bottle.

In Valdosta, Georgia, not far from the Florida border, a man named Eugene Roberts Barber started putting Coke in bottles around 1897, according to a deposition he gave sixty years later during a dispute between Coke and another bottler. It was a modest operation, sharing real estate with a completely unrelated business. 'There was a tailor shop in front of it,' Barber said of his bottling plant. 'They would tote the goods through the tailor shop to get to the door. We bought a little two-wheel truck to roll our cases on, and it got objectionable to the man, because we come off a wet floor and marked the floor.'

But the United States was a vast and thirsty country, its wilderness only half conquered and its cities still forming. It would take a third man, and the Spanish-American War, to come up with a plan that brought bottles of Coke to the rest of the nation.

In 1898, after hundreds died in the sinking of the USS *Maine* in Havana Harbor, an outraged Congress declared war on Spain and called for volunteers. One of the thousands who rushed to the cause was Benjamin Franklin Thomas, a Chattanooga lawyer who had moved restlessly through a series of occupations, always searching for the pot of gold that would set him up for life.

Named for the eighteenth-century inventor and patriot, who was no relation, Thomas had worked in a hosiery mill, a rock quarry, and a bank. He was in his mid-thirties, married, and in need of a steady income. Law was interesting, but he also invested in a paving company, hoping to cash in on the building boom that he felt sure would come to Chattanooga someday. When the war was declared, he saw it as another opportunity – both to serve his country and to figure out where his life was headed.

Friends remembered him as someone who was forever searching for a single move that would make him millions. His definition of a sure success was 'something inexpensive that appealed strongly to the general public' and that, furthermore, 'could be used up quickly and then repurchased'. Rocks, stockings, real estate, legal advice – these were all useful, but they had failed to measure up in the way he needed them to. He had to find something else.

In April 1898, Thomas shipped out to the Cuban city of Manzanilla, where he worked as an aide to an Army assistant quartermaster. His assignment was relatively dull as a military campaign, since most of the battles were fought at sea, but Thomas saw for the first time palm trees fluttering like eyelashes in the gentle breezes and tropical waters that turned every shade of blue and green as they traveled out to the horizon. He saw Cubans everywhere strolling through the streets with bottles of a carbonated pineapple drink in their hands. It was the bottled drinks that he kept coming back to. Why couldn't he take a drink that was popular and well known and sell it, in a bottle, back home?

It was not such an original thought; bottled mineral water, lemonade, and other flavored beverages had been for sale in the States for more than fifty years. But Thomas knew that Coca-Cola did not come in bottles, at least not where he lived. Like many a southerner, he had tried it and fallen in love with the flavor – not to mention the kick from the caffeine and the coca. And he couldn't get Coca-Cola anywhere but the soda fountain. When he ordered it at the counter he had to drink it right away or the bubbles lost their energy and the beverage became dull. Wouldn't it be more convenient, he thought, if it came in bottles, so all that carbonation could be kept inside?

Within weeks the war was over, for Thomas and for everyone else. America had prevailed, broadening its reach with new territories, some of them oceans away from North America. A new hero, Theodore Roosevelt, had been created after a well-publicized charge up Cuba's San Juan Hill. But Thomas was more concerned with his idea than with geopolitics. Once he returned to Chattanooga, he dragooned a friend, a Mississippi-born fellow lawyer named Joseph Brown Whitehead, into going with him to Atlanta to ask the legendary Asa Candler for permission to bottle Coke.

On a July morning in 1899, they took the train to Atlanta, for what at that time was a journey of five hours or more. They traveled accompanied by a third man, Sam Erwin, an acquaintance from Chattanooga and also a cousin of Candler's. Erwin had already decided he wanted nothing to do with their plan and deposited himself in a chair outside Candler's office after making the introductions.

Erwin's decision seemed like the right call. Inside, Thomas and Whitehead got a reception that was flatter than a glass of soda left out overnight.

To begin with, Candler didn't have a high opinion of their hometown – he had been there once, he would write years later, and 'didn't think much was going on', certainly not compared with the endlessly striving Atlanta – and thought even less of the bottling idea. By himself, he had cultivated a nation of Coca-Cola drinkers; as the supplicants sat before him, Coke was in the process of selling 214,008 gallons of syrup that year, topping the record set twelve months earlier. With every gallon producing close to four hundred Coca-Colas, Candler was pouring his trademark beverage down the throats of Americans 7 million times a month. He had already made Coca-Cola a household name.

Fountains had accomplished all this, and fountains had been good to him. Bottling, he told Thomas and Whitehead, would be too expensive. Cost was the reason he hadn't gotten the company involved in it. And he didn't want other people doing it, because having folks fooling around with bottling machinery who didn't know what they were doing might harm his Coca-Cola brand, the brand he had spent the last decade building up and that was now making so much money for him coast to coast.

Candler was still the principal owner and reverent curator of Coca-Cola. Arriving in Atlanta in 1873 with seven quarters in his pocket, he had tramped up and down the dusty streets looking for work and finally gotten himself a spot helping out in a drugstore. He had always wanted to be a doctor but settled for druggist, and by 1877 he owned a store called Hallman & Candler in the fast-growing city, where he and his partner sold wholesale and retail remedies – patent medicines, mainly, that were then the most profitable industry in Atlanta.

In 1888 he bought a one-third interest in the Coca-Cola formula, largely because its creator was a friendly rival who had become ill and wanted to retire. Within a few months, Candler, who had found that the drink helped ease his recurrent headaches, took full control of the formula, adding it to a small string of other products that he owned, like BBB, officially registered as Botanic Blood Balm, and Delectalave, a liquid toothpaste. Candler financed his efforts by selling shares of Coca-Cola in 1892 to some of his friends, though he kept a majority stake in the family.

From the beginning, secrecy was the cornerstone upon which all things Coca-Cola revolved. Candler's son, Charles Howard Candler, remembered his father and a longtime assistant, Frank Robinson, being the only people who were trusted to mix the formula. 'Later, I was initiated into the secrets of the product which have passed down by word of mouth only to the most trusted employees since that time,' the son wrote. When Asa Candler moved the burgeoning syrup business into a new building in 1898, he designed and built a laboratory that was shielded by 'fireproof partitions and furnished with a sheet-iron safe door with a combination lock', his son remembered. 'As late as 1903, the preparation of the formula was done only by my father and Mr. Robinson. They alone had the combination to the door, and except for a Negro helper, no one was permitted in this laboratory room.'

By 1890, Candler had cleared his shelves of everything that was not Coca-Cola and was energetically persuading every drugstore he'd heard of to carry the syrup. His marketing prowess was legendary from the start: He instituted a system of 'tickets', or coupons, that entitled the bearer to one free Coca-Cola. Starting in 1888 or so, pharmacists were mailed tickets by the hundreds, and when they served those free Cokes, Candler promised, they would be reimbursed by Atlanta.

Coke salesmen also stood on street corners, handing out the tickets. The program was immensely popular; people liked free samples, and when Candler abruptly cut them off in 1905, fearing he had sent out too many tickets, the hue and cry was so great that he brought the program back, bigger than ever, the following year. It ended for good in 1931, but in the 1950s the occasional ticket would still turn up in the company's mailroom, used only recently by someone who had held on to it for a long time.

The tickets also appeared in early Coca-Cola ads, one of which shows an elegantly dressed woman sipping a Coke served in a glass set in a dainty silver holder with a handle. The ticket, its message clearly visible, lies on the table in front of her. Candler supplied drugstores with porcelain urns on which *Coca-Cola* was painted in its distinctive Spencerian script (legend holds that Frank Robinson wrote the name out with a pen, and the company never bothered to change it), and with decorations for a soda fountain's plate-glass windows that reminded people to try a Coca-Cola. Later there would be Coca-Cola glasses, and Tiffany-style glass lampshades, and napkins and place mats and clocks and thermometers, children's toys, pencils, and cups, all bearing the name of the drink. Coca-Cola published sheet music, affixing its brand to such classics as 'Nearer, My God, to Thee', as well as to calendars, playing cards, ink blotters, and ashtrays.

Cheerfulness was the name of the game; a Coke was a happy thing, something to be enjoyed for a few minutes before getting back to work with a strangely light feeling in your head, which perhaps had been hurting before you had your Coke but now definitely was not hurting anymore. *What's in that stuff?* people asked each other.

Early on, Candler preached the importance of avoiding 'imitators', at a time when every pharmacist and his brother had come up with a syrup that approximated Coca-Cola. Some of them marketed their syrups under names like Dixie-Cola, Afri-Kola, Ko-Kola, and even Bicy-Cola, apparently inspired by the two-wheeler. Publications like *The National Druggist* circulated recipes, and its 'Pick-Me-Up or Nerve Bracer' sounded a lot like Candler's product: a concoction of valerian, cardamom, coriander, cinnamon, orris, coca, green tea, and alcohol. For fountain use, the author advised, 'Make a thick syrup with 350 parts of sugar and just sufficient water to fully dissolve it.'

Candler wanted people to ask for his syrup by name, and he had done his utmost to make sure they knew that name. Pharmacists had to pay for Coca-Cola syrup; he charged a premium, they soon found out, based on the name he was building up around the country. Many of them were annoyed by this, knowing full well the actual cost of the ingredients in Coke. On the other hand, backed by Candler's relentless marketing, they also got to tell people that it was, as Coke executives would say for decades, the real thing. In the nineteenth century, with no other national cola brand out there, Coca-Cola developed a certain desirability that mushroomed over time. Later the company would zealously pursue competitors who used names that sounded too much like Coca-Cola, hauling them into court to make sure its own trademark reigned supreme.

So Thomas and Whitehead, confronting Candler in his office, faced an uphill battle. There was no need for Candler to believe that he had not already succeeded in bringing Coca-Cola to Americans everywhere. There was no incentive for him to take them on as partners. But they convinced him in their best southern-lawyer style that they would make Coca-Cola better – better known and better loved – with every bottle they sold. They would not harm the brand; they would *improve* the brand. And ultimately Candler relented.

Clearly believing that they would be bankrupt before long, he issued them perpetual contracts that also set the price of syrup in perpetuity, at a dollar a gallon. They got the rights to the whole country, forever, except New England, where Coca-Cola had an arrangement with syrup brokers that the company did not want to jeopardize, and Mississippi, where Joseph Biedenharn was still bottling Coke. Texas, a separate country in so many ways, was also left out of the original agreement. With the stroke of a pen, Candler let go of what must have seemed to him a harmless sparrow of an idea. It lingered in his office for a moment, cocked its head, and then flew off through the open window. It would return as a giant bird of prey, screeching and smashing its head against the glass, an entity most horrible to the Coca-Cola

Company because it was beyond the company's control. 'A perpetual contract,' Don Keough, Coke's longtime president, would say, 'is like a marriage you can't get a divorce from.'

Candler seems to have been magnanimous about advertising the bottled product, reflecting either a genuine interest in the partnership or his certainty that it would need all the help it could get. In 1902, ads appeared in Atlanta publications for two kinds of Coca-Cola: one in bottles, the other at fountains, both priced at a nickel apiece. He provided coupons to people like Biedenharn to help persuade people to try a bottle of Coke. The early bottles of Coca-Cola had to carry diamond-shaped paper labels bearing his name in capital letters along one side. The bottles could be any shape or color, and they were, but they had to have that label.

Thomas and Whitehead opened their first factory in 1899 in Chattanooga. Before Thanksgiving, their ads started to appear in one of the local newspapers: 'Drink a bottle of Coca-Cola, five cents at all stands, grocers, and saloons.' While the bottled soda sold briskly, they quickly discovered that equipping factories, hiring people, and delivering the goods were expensive and time-consuming – more so than they had counted on. They were finding out that Candler was right: Bottling was difficult and costly. No wonder the Coca-Cola Company hadn't wanted to get involved with it. They needed a better idea, and quick.

Soon they had one. They would sell franchises to other ambitious businessmen, monitoring them and acting as brokers, by reselling the syrup they bought from the Coca-Cola Company at a slight markup. They would make money on the franchise sales, either in cash or by taking an ownership stake. And they would make money on the syrup sales. Either way, they were going to be fine. And they, the two stocky lawyers whose good idea had hurled them into the manufacturing business, would not have the sticky brown stuff all over their shoes and hands.

They attracted people, and they were good people for the most part: hardworking, independent-minded, sure of themselves. They got F. S. Barron from Rome, and they got Frederick Schmidt from Louisville. They pulled in Columbus Roberts of Opelika, Alabama; James Haley of Macon, Georgia; and his brother William Banks Haley of Albany, Georgia. In Chattanooga, they hooked

James Johnston, a farm-born entrepreneur who had become president of a bank in Idaho by the time he was twenty-one years old. Often these men were a generation removed from farming, with experience as cotton brokers, store owners, or real-estate developers. Some were already bottling something else, like Deep Rock Ginger Ale, before they took on Coca-Cola, too. Whitehead and Thomas won converts in the South almost everywhere they went. Before long they expanded north and west, as well, assembling a national patchwork of Coca-Cola franchises.

Everyone learned as they went along. The early bottlers used horses or mules to pull wagons full of bottled Coke and borrowed money to build brand-new bottling factories. They invested in wooden crates (the Never-Bust model sold by the Emery Box Company was a popular choice) and glass bottles and, of course, those paper labels. They paid the Coca-Cola Company for barrels of its gooey syrup, which Coke delivered to their doors. Other companies provided them with carbon dioxide, the key to making the syrup into Coca-Cola. One of the largest was the Liquid Carbonic Company, out of Chicago, which would ship containers of gas by railroad to the bottlers, saving them from having to generate carbon dioxide through chemical reaction.

By 1905, Whitehead and Thomas had Coke bottlers from coast to coast. There was one just about anywhere a person looked, from Sapulpa, Oklahoma, to South Bend, Indiana, and in cities like Los Angeles and Milwaukee. Whitehead and Thomas had done it. They were selling Coca-Cola in bottles and succeeding beyond their wildest dreams.

They caught the nation in peacetime, as consumer culture was flourishing and the act of drinking or eating something that had been made outside the home was increasingly acceptable. Almost like evangelists distributing a basic tract, they offered a product that was easy to ingest and made it available to the widest possible range of people. No more would soda fountains, with their marble counters and their Main Street hours, be the sole dispensers of Coca-Cola. Poor people and country people, travelers and loners, black sharecroppers and Irish immigrants and Italian stonecutters and policemen and bored teenage boys in overalls and Navajo tribal leaders – anyone in America, really, who had a nickel to spend, could try a Coca-Cola now.

'How long was it after you started bottling Coca-Cola before it took the lead over these other soft drinks that had been bottled before Coca-Cola?' a lawyer once asked Eugene Barber, the pioneer Valdosta bottler.

'Well, it was a mighty short time,' he replied.

The partnership that brought bottled Coke to the nation soon needed refining. By 1900, Whitehead and Thomas couldn't agree on contract terms for the new bottlers they were busy creating. Amicably, they divided the country along a modified Mason-Dixon line, with Thomas taking Chattanooga, plus fifteen states north and west, and Whitehead holding on to much of the South, including a new plant that had just opened in Atlanta. Whitehead's company would be called Dixie Coca-Cola Bottling Company, and Thomas's would be known as Coca-Cola Bottling Company. John Lupton, another Chattanoogan who helped bankroll the Atlanta plant, would stick with Whitehead, who gave his bottlers perpetual contracts. Thomas would continue to offer his bottlers two-year contracts, renewable as long as things worked out. In the Thomas territory, bottlers sold Coke in brown glass bottles, while in Whitehead's areas the bottles were clear or green.

The bottlers the two men selected were energetic, and they did all kinds of things to make the most of their franchises. They sent free cases of Coca-Cola to stores, just to get them to try it. They met passenger trains at the station, pushed their bottles of Coke aboard, and got someone farther up the line to collect the empties and send them back. In the beginning, some of these new customers had never tried a Coca-Cola. Bottlers yanked a bottle or two from a case of fruit-flavored sodas, replaced the empty holes with Coke, and got themselves a piece of the market that way. A. B. Freeman, who won the franchise for New Orleans, puttered back and forth through the bayous in a motorboat, the *Josephine,* to sell bottles of Coke to Louisianans living in watery isolation. Behind him followed smaller boats filled with assistants, who idled just long enough beside the ancient trees to nail up signs that said COCA-COLA.

A fraternity formed around the bottlers' activities, partly because of their shared interests and partly because the Coca-Cola Company made sure they attended company-sponsored production clinics and 'cooler schools', where Coke executives tried to make sure they all understood the latest techniques and equipment. Such gatherings led to friendships, marriages, sometimes buyouts. The bottlers formed Coca-Cola clubs in their respective cities and towns. They became well known, for selling Coke and for providing other services. When World War II arrived, one bottler put out his own literature to help prepare his customers for civil defense, covering everything from what to do in an air raid to the possible presence of foreign spies.

In peacetime and in war, the bottlers appeared to get along with the Coca-Cola Company. Their identities were distinct, to be sure. Coke made its money comfortably up front, from syrup sales, while the bottlers had to squeeze out their profits farther along the chain. Coke enjoyed a kind of corporate eminence centered in Atlanta; the bottler was a local guy, whose manufacturing plant usually sat near the center of town. Coke believed in mass marketing from the start; the bottlers specialized in the personal touch. By the 1920s, schoolchildren were trooping through Coke plants on tours, watching the familiar glass containers looping along the conveyor belts and filling with sweet brown soda, and they grew up to feel a connection with the Coca-Cola that they saw was made right nearby, to a chorus of clinking, hissing, and clanking that often meant jobs for one or more of their kin as well. If there were no jobs left, there would always be generosity cascading in some form: new uniforms for the football team, a scoreboard for the baseball diamond, a fund drive for the Baptists. 'There was a saying: "Your friendly neighbor, the Coca-Cola bottler",' recalled Jan Schmidt, who discovered the world of Coke bottling when she married William Schmidt, the third generation of his family to bottle Coca-Cola in Elizabethtown, Kentucky. 'It was really true.' The bottlers would be called 'as indigenous to the American scene as the post office or the fire department,' becoming fixtures that towns couldn't remember how they had done without.

Bottlers took the money they made and sowed it back into the business. They bought new equipment to make soda. They bought bigger fleets of wagons, and then trucks, to deliver it. They paid the salaries of thousands of mechanics, accountants, and deliverymen. In doing so they anchored hundreds of local economies, creating jobs not just in their plants but in every industry that expanded along with theirs. They gave away money, too, to the local schools and to Kiwanis clubs. The bottlers were so closely affiliated with the towns where they were based, and generally so well off as a result of selling Coke, that they usually expected to be asked to give things, to do things, to help run things.

Bottlers also spent money on projects that had nothing to do with Coca-Cola. They might own beef cattle or plant pecan groves. Many of them bought part of an airline or acquired real estate as another way of making their fortunes grow. This did not always sit well with the Coca-Cola Company, where executives believed that Coke was the most important calling in the world and that anything that competed with it was to be avoided. Every penny of a bottler's profits ought to be plowed right back into selling Coke, the company said, objecting vocally, sometimes aggressively, when this was not the case.

The split between the two operations continued over time. The Coca-Cola Company would always be a place of neat desks, gold watches, and three-piece suits, hushed and carpeted, cool and controlled and removed from the fray. 'We don't sell *Coca-Cola,*' a Coke executive might say with weary patience. 'Our business is the *concentrate.*' A bottling plant, meanwhile, was all about the Coca-Cola, the kind consumers would recognize. It was a messy, less predictable, accident-prone operation. Workers in a bottling plant dressed in coveralls or blue work shirts and kept cotton stuffed in their ears against the racket as they moved themselves and their handiwork across a floor made slippery by spilled soda. Everybody called and whistled and swore out loud in a bottling plant. The floor was crowded with barrels of chemicals and stacks of bottles, and the factory was one big vulnerability on display, from the breakable bottles to the fragile machinery that often halted in midstream, requiring a team of experts to figure out what had gone wrong and get it going again.

The investment required for a bottling plant was enormous. It was what had put Candler off the idea originally and what shocked

Thomas and Whitehead into coming up with their subcontracting strategy after less than a year. Bottlers had to spend thousands on real estate, then thousands more on buildings and machinery. Early bottling machines were powered by foot pedals, which were gradually replaced by electric motors. The bigger your operation, the more machines you needed, and they required not only the initial investment but steady, skilled, costly maintenance as well. You had to buy bottles, too, which broke on a regular basis and just as often were not returned by the people who drank the soda inside them. You had to have vehicles to take the heavy bottles of Coke around to customers, and you had to pay salaries for employees, too. Experts analyzing the difference between the capital investment made by bottlers compared with the Coca-Cola Company's investment in its syrup production came up with a ratio of twenty to one.

Bottlers guarded their wealth carefully and tried to run tight ships. James Johnston once dictated a letter to a sub-franchisee who wanted to buy some trucks to help him in his business. *Mr. Johnston believes trucks are very expensive, and dangerous, and will never replace mules,* the letter declared. *And if you need a good mule, we will lend you one.*

It was a lot of work, the bottling business, and that could not be denied. It wasn't for everyone. Ads in *The Coca-Cola Bottler,* the industry journal, periodically sought to unload a franchise or a plant, or to hire more help. 'Don't bother us unless you are a hustler,' read a 1919 ad seeking a foreman for a factory in Toledo, Ohio.

The bottlers also had a solid sense of their own importance. 'Certain onlookers who have watched the growth of Coca-Cola from their more-or-less comfortable seats in the bleachers choose to refer to the success as "romance",' huffed an editorial in a bottler publication, twenty years into the Coke-bottling business. 'To those who have seen the growth from another side – the inside of a pair of overalls, for instance – "romance" does not seem to fit. . . . The success of any industry is due to the brain and brawn that keeps everlastingly at it until it makes good.'

Either way, between them the two branches of the Coca-Cola business had produced a roaring success by the time the twentieth century was just a few years old. With bottles of Coke parading into baseball games, lining the iceboxes of general stores, and making their way out into the perspiring reaches of working-class America, being delivered to people who had neither the time nor the inclination to relax indoors at a soda fountain, bottling doubled and tripled Coke's syrup sales, expanding faster than Candler ever could have on his own. By 1909, Thomas and Whitehead had sold franchises to nearly four hundred people, who were busily selling Coca-Cola in portable form all over the country, and they would more than triple that number by the time they were done. The Coca-Cola Company's syrup sales ballooned from 214,008 gallons in 1898, the last year Coke was served only at fountains, to 3,486,626 in 1909. By 1928, more Coke would be sold in bottles than at fountains.

The Coca-Cola Company was making a lot of money from the concentrate, as were the bottlers from the finished product. There seemed to be plenty of profits to go around. Asa Candler built himself a palace at 1040 Ponce de Léon Avenue in the Druid Hills neighborhood of Atlanta, where he owned most of the land. His house included a central courtyard paved with marble and embellished with a rushing fountain, all of it shielded from the elements by a vaulted ceiling made of pale green glass. In the house's many rooms were beautiful rugs, elegant furniture, a pipe organ, and 'innumerable silver loving cups', *The Atlanta Journal* reported not long after the Candlers moved in, along with a huge assortment of Louis XV furniture upholstered in satin brocade. Candler had by then become not just one of the wealthiest men in Atlanta but one of the wealthiest men in the nation. He invested his money in real estate and other interests while he touted Coca-Cola coast to coast and worked to defend it against critics ranging from the beer industry (jealous of the market share) to the federal government (opposed to the caffeine). He put up the Candler Building on Forty-second Street in New York City, and another Candler Building in the center of downtown Atlanta. Then he put up Candler buildings in half a dozen other cities as well. He gave generously to Emory College in Atlanta, later Emory University, where his brother Warren became the president. He also contributed mightily to Candler College in Havana, a Methodist-run school where, the Candlers hoped, young Cubans would learn to be more like Americans.

Bottlers lived well, too. When a bottler in Oklahoma named Virgil Browne built a house for himself in the 1930s, he installed a set of massive iron gates at the end of the driveway to give his home the tone he was looking for. The gates had originally belonged to Napoléon III. And the place in Oklahoma was only one of his houses: His other holdings included a sugar plantation in Louisiana and a mountain retreat in Colorado. During the Depression, while farmers were going bankrupt and fired workers were selling apples to make ends meet, Browne formed the Oklahoma City Yacht Club and invested in a 110-foot boat. He would christen a subsequent addition to his fleet by cracking a bottle of Coca-Cola over the bow.

Enormous empires flourished because of the money streaming from Coca-Cola bottling franchises. Bernard Biedenharn, one of Joseph Biedenharn's nephews, got the Monroe, Louisiana, territory and quickly became a force to be reckoned with. He invested in Delta Airlines when it was a crop-dusting operation and, once the airline took passengers, the planes regularly called at Monroe while ignoring other cities of similar size. At the dinner table, B.W., as he was known, would shout 'Delta!' to tell the maid on the other side of the door when he and his guests wanted to be served. It was his shorthand for the airline's slogan at the time, which was: 'We're ready when you are.'

Over time, the bottlers became as important as the leaders of the Coca-Cola Company within the social hierarchy they occupied. Their tastes climbed from the blue-collar to the gilt-edged. When the Atlanta Coca-Cola Bottling Company held a dinner to mark its fiftieth anniversary in 1950, the banquet at the Piedmont Driving Club, Atlanta's top-drawer country club, began with crabmeat prepared in the French manner and culminated with baked Alaska. The bottlers had arrived.

Thomas and Whitehead became the wealthiest bottlers of all, though both died young. Thomas, known to his friends as 'Rare Ben,' helped develop Lookout Mountain, Tennessee, still the home of many Coca-Cola families, and amassed an impressive collection of rare books and manuscripts. He and his wife, Anne, endowed churches, hospitals, and libraries with trust funds and gifts. When Anne Thomas died in 1938, the Chattanooga paper described her as one of the richest women in the city, and the Coca-Cola Company sent an enormous cross of flowers to the funeral. Joseph Whitehead's widow, Lettie Whitehead Evans, served for years on Coke's board of directors. When she died, in 1953, a private train marked COCA-COLA SPECIAL transported her coffin from one end of Virginia to the other.

John Lupton, meanwhile, established Lupton City, Tennessee, where he built homes for hundreds of workers at his textile plants as well as a school, a post office, a church, a movie theater, and a swimming pool. For himself he had Lyndhurst, a 34,000-square-foot estate that didn't skimp on creature comforts: It had ten bedrooms, twelve bathrooms, a ballroom, a gymnasium, indoor and outdoor pools, and its own bowling alley.

Americans clearly had a taste for Coca-Cola, and the bottlers made sure it was available to them. By 1915, thirsty people could buy a Coca-Cola in almost any public place, and beyond that they could bring it home and store it in their pantries to enjoy later. Less than twenty years after it got started, Coke in bottles had turned out to be a very good idea.

Despite the wealth the two elements of the Coke system had in common, the dissimilarities between them persisted. On the good days, they created a natural tension and a system of checks and balances, in which notions coming out of Atlanta could be tempered by the bottlers' field experience, and good ideas that the bottlers came up with could be applied beyond some little corner of Oregon or Arkansas, for the benefit of all. On the bad days, hostility raged between the bottlers and the company. Some Coke executives were better than others at working out such situations. Coke's influence was most successful when an idea out of Atlanta was presented as an appealing choice, not a directive.

One winning directive was the introduction of a standard bottle. With so many bottles being produced in different corners of the country, Candler believed that the company needed a distinctive one that would reinforce the promise he liked to make: that a Coca-Cola would have the same taste and quality wherever it was purchased.

So he put out the word that the Coca-Cola Company would pay for a new bottle design. Ideas cascaded into the headquarters in

Atlanta, and the one Candler chose was designed by Earl Dean, a man who would recall feeling 'bilious and sick' as he sketched at the breakfast table one hot summer morning for his employer, the Root Glass Company of Terre Haute, Indiana.

Shaped like an hourglass, nearly as thick as a brick at the base, the design was patented in 1915 and approved by Coke in 1916. Three years later, every Coke bottler was using the new bottle, which sported fat ribs down its sides that had been inspired by the cocoa bean. The designer, who wanted the bottle to reflect its contents, had looked up 'cola nut' in the encyclopedia and failed to find anything. A librarian did point out a nearby illustration of the cocoa bean, which Dean apparently felt was close enough. Before long the Coca-Cola Company took over production of the bottles from Root, and millions of them began circulating all over the country and the planet, becoming the botanically incorrect symbol of Coca-Cola.

The bottle became far more than a container. Candler had said at the outset that he wanted the Coke bottle to be instantly recognizable from top to bottom, so that if a fragment was uncovered at some date in the future, everyone would know at a glance what it was. It was a stunning requirement, for a consumer product, but he got what he wanted. The bottle also entered the lexicon: The term 'Coke-bottle glasses' came to mean a pair of lenses that were extraordinarily thick, like the bottle's base. With its image showing up on signs and storefronts all over the country, very often larger than life, people who had once referred to something as 'hourglass-shaped' started saying 'Coke-bottle-shaped' instead. At a banquet in 1949 at the Waldorf-Astoria in New York, a bottling executive contended that what had begun as a mere vessel had achieved a cultural pinnacle. It was itself a thing of value, amplifying the liquid inside beyond the normal status of a soft drink, and reflecting not just Coke but the nation. 'In the mind of millions beyond the seas,' he observed, 'the famous bottle – like the bathtub, the automobile, and the refrigerator – is now a symbol of America and the rich, abundant life of its people.'

But before long, over the rustling murmur that was the sound of money being counted in Atlanta, there came a sour note.

★

With the bottlers prospering, some executives inside Coke came to believe that Candler, their fearless leader, had squandered an opportunity to generate even more money for the company. Every penny that the bottlers made, after sifting out their costs for syrup, payroll, insurance, and everything else the business required, they got to keep. That was the definition of their independence. And instead of profiting only through selling syrup to them, Coke might have been gathering all that cash on the sales of Coke in bottles, too. The charitable view held that Candler had financed Coke's enormous expansion through the bottlers, without any cost to Coke. The angrier view inside the company was that he had given it all away.

With every passing year this yoke grew more leaden and the impact of what came to be denounced as 'the Candler error' more distressing. By the end of 1915, Candler was gone from the company; he had quit to run for mayor of Atlanta, a race he won handily. He left behind a company that considered its bottling system sprawling, diffuse, and unruly – not to mention a terrible mistake.

At that time there were about twelve hundred Coca-Cola bottlers, each with a specific territory, personality, and assorted business challenges. Moving an idea from the drawing board in Atlanta out into the field controlled by these hundreds of bottlers was a hugely time-consuming undertaking that often foundered against uncooperative people. They didn't like being told what to do, and they preferred to read their local markets and follow them – instead of simply accepting orders from Atlanta. Most of the first-generation bottlers were seasoned executives, with immense skill when it came to making money from their particular markets and bossy tendencies when it came to dealing with the Coca-Cola Company. They kept their franchises in the family, passing them down from father to son with all the gravity that such a large responsibility and investment commanded. Bottlers on their deathbeds were said to summon their heirs for a single piece of advice: 'Son, whatever you do, don't let 'em mess with the contract.'

Because heredity is no guarantee of success, eventually some bottlers were not very good. Those were the ones who gave Coke executives sleepless nights. A weak bottler was like an engraved invitation to Pepsi and other rivals to seize more market share, and Coke lived to be number one. But there was not much Coke could do. The franchises stayed in the same families indefinitely, unless someone decided to sell. Syrup prices stayed fixed. As time passed, little changed. The bottler network became like an old photograph in which the quality might have faded but the composition remained the same.

Generations of Coke executives looked at the arrangement and thought there had to be a better way. In 1919, just before the country became hooked on bootleg gin and the Coke bottle displaced the soda fountain as the best-known dispenser of Coca-Cola, the Candlers sold the company to a group of bankers. The new management of the Coca-Cola Company decided to do away with the contracts that Asa Candler had signed with Coke's bottlers.

The $25 million sale of Coke took place a year after the armistice ending World War I was signed. During the war, the bottlers had permitted Coke to temporarily raise concentrate prices, then fixed at ninety-two cents a gallon under the contracts, because of sugar shortages. They agreed to a five-cent price hike, fully expecting to return to the old order once peace was at hand.

But in the new year, Coke's new owners boldly announced changes to the contracts. When the bottlers complained, they fired them. A flurry of litigation followed, with the bottlers claiming they would be 'annihilated and destroyed'. The settlement that got the system rolling again – Coke could raise syrup prices, but only if the price of sugar rose by a certain amount, and then only up to a $1.72 ceiling set by a federal judge – bred deep mistrust among the bottlers toward the Coca-Cola Company, and vice versa. No one was happy with the arrangement: It was not good enough from Coke's point of view, and the bottlers thought it gave Coke a new and unfair advantage, a reward for acting in bad faith. The ill will flowed through the Coca-Cola system, and Coke became determined to unchain itself from the bottling system once and for all.

That was in 1921. Sixty-five years later, Doug Ivester, the man on the road to Rome, became a Coca-Cola demigod by finishing the job.

In 1986, when there were still more than three hundred independent bottlers selling Coke across the country, the thirty-nine-year-old Ivester thought up a way to sweep all the messy business of bottling to one side, allow the Coca-Cola Company to control far more of it without worrying about the costs involved, and pump up Coke's income in three different ways. It was a brilliant plan. Magical, almost. And he was sure it would work.

Ivester's life had been all about hard work, and making money, from the time he was a little boy. Beyond digging odd-shaped holes in the backyard or tossing a ball around with his friends, he was, from the age of eight, raising chickens, cutting other people's lawns, and bagging groceries at the local Kroger supermarket. He worked for pay, and not just the change people had in their pockets. They had to meet his standards – they had to pay him what he thought was the right amount for his work. Those who failed to live up to his expectations couldn't get their grass mowed by little Doug Ivester. Even as a child, he had tough requirements for the rest of the world.

Ivester grew up in a tiny Georgia town where not many people had more money than they could spend. He was hugely fond of his mother, Ada Mae, whose plans for him included training him to become an organist for the local Baptist church, and his father, who was known as Buck. And he saw how hard they worked.

The Ivesters were not well off, and neither were their neighbors in New Holland, a hamlet that collapses into Gainesville, the much larger town next door. Doug's father was a shift supervisor at the Milliken textile plant in town. Mill work was hard, with tough colleagues to contend with, and Buck was an exacting boss. He didn't shower praise on his son, either, though the boy was an appealing little fellow with a head of blond hair that would darken as he got older. Instead, he surrounded him with his own expectations and fanned the dreams they came to share: dreams of fast cars and seeing the world and a college education for Doug – things his parents had never had.

The Ivesters lived on Mill Street, a short road that runs perpendicular to the mill and ends just ahead of the chain-link fence that surrounds it. Mill Street is lined with white-painted houses with narrow front porches that spill over with plants. Mill workers still live in those houses, a five-minute walk from the door of the factory where they spin cotton into yarn, day in and day out.

Ivester watched his father put in long hours and take out the mill's idea of compensation in return. With the thousands of hours spent indoors, the dust and racket that were never-ending, and all of it made more hellish by the heat in summertime, came thin rewards. Most people in New Holland lived close to the bone, postponing purchases like new cars and dishwashers, saving twine in the kitchen drawer. Life had rolled many of them a gutter ball when it came to money for extras, and something like a Coca-Cola amounted to a treat for their children.

Television came into Doug Ivester's life when he was eight years old and brought him pictures of another world. One day in 1955, there was a special broadcast of the opening ceremonies for Disneyland. Watching the antics in grainy black and white, seeing the figures dressed as Mickey and Minnie Mouse and the rides and other attractions crammed with happy, carefree children and their folks, Ivester was stricken by a single gloomy thought: *I'll never get to go there*.

But he didn't brood over his misfortune. He didn't ask his mother and father to figure out a way to take him. Instead he developed a concept he would later make his signature theme at the Coca-Cola Company, and indeed throughout his entire life. It was something he called 'mind-set'. It was a term a lot of other people used to mean a host of different things, but to him it connoted a powerful force, one that eliminated the doubt and the risk and made sure something he wanted was going to happen. As an adult, he would define it in this way: 'It's not a question of *if* we're going to get there. It's a matter of when.'

It was in the parking lot of the Kroger one afternoon that the teenage Ivester's path took another important turn. He was crossing the pavement, arms loaded with brown bags, when he spied something that stopped him in his tracks. It was a gleaming yellow Pontiac GTO, flashy and sporty, the mechanical mani-festation of devil-may-care – the epitome of everything the cars in his neighborhood were not. Here was a car worth having. Ivester had to find out whom it belonged to.

When he finally tracked down the owner, he asked the man what he did for a living. 'I'm a CPA,' the man told him. Right there, on the radiant asphalt beneath the blazing Georgia sun, Ivester made his vow. He knew now what he would do with the rest of his life. *He would be an accountant.*

It was the early sixties, and many teenage boys, exposed to *Sputnik* and space missions, were obsessed with becoming astronauts. Some had fallen for the Beatles and pleaded for guitar lessons so they could start rock and roll careers of their own. But Ivester chose his fate more calculatingly. Here was something he wanted, and now he knew how to get it. *If I can drive a car like that being an accountant,* he said to himself, *then I'll be an accountant.*

He graduated from high school in 1965, where he was cited for personality and praised for his skill in math. At the end of that summer, he enrolled at the University of Georgia, some forty miles away in Athens. He was the first person in his family to go to college.

He had been selected by a premier school, strong in every academic field and set like a temple along the gentle hills an hour and a world away from his hometown. The university, racially integrated four years before Ivester arrived, is home to the Georgia Bulldogs, perennial powers in football and basketball and the source of fun college times for many an undergraduate. But Ivester appears to have all but ignored that kind of frivolity. He focused his four years at the university's Terry College of Business around a single purpose. 'I was there for only one reason: to learn enough to get a good job when I got out of school,' he said later. There would be no wild Doug Ivester stories to tell at reunions in the future. He already had a steady girlfriend back home, a beauty named Victoria Kay Grindle, whom he had met when they were seated next to each other in the third grade. He returned home every weekend to work at Kroger, hoarding his pay to help offset his tuition. He followed his own careful plan.

He graduated in 1969, at a time when students on other campuses were lodging violent protests against the Vietnam War. Degree in hand, he immediately got a job with Ernst & Ernst, the accounting firm that later became Ernst & Young, and began a series of assignments as an auditor. Some of them were painfully dull, even by accountants' standards – audits of nursing homes on behalf of Medicaid, and examinations of farm machinery, conducted out in the rain and the mud, to make sure the serial numbers matched those on an insurance claim – but eventually he won a promotion, which put him on the team handling the Coca-Cola account not long after he arrived at Ernst.

And it was in going over the books for the company's annual audit that he impressed the people at Coca-Cola. He had some interesting, unusual suggestions here and there. He seemed to really like the soft-drink business. He had grown up in Coke's shadow, after all, a child of the Georgia hills. Maybe there was a gleam in his eye when he talked about Coke. At any rate, they liked what they saw. He was hired away from Ernst in 1979, joining Coke as an assistant controller. It would be the start of a swift rise to the top.

Accountants concentrate on a company's numbers. For them, a business is reflected in its profits, losses, liabilities, and receivables. Upon joining the Coca-Cola Company, Ivester would say later, he looked forward to seeing the world. And at the company, he was quick to make changes, like instituting a share repurchase program, proposing a new bottle size, and lowering the dividend payout ratio so that more money could be reinvested in the business.

He seemed to love the Coca-Cola Company and all it stood for. At the same time, he viewed it from the angle most commonly used by accountants: heavy on data and facts, light on such intangibles as emotions. As a manager, he would listen in silence as people discussed a business problem they were facing. They talked; he listened. And then, with no discussion apart from a question or two he might ask, he would tell them what they should do. Early on, this became the distinguishing characteristic of his style. Some colleagues called him 'the adding machine'. His reflexive shyness in social settings, which made small talk difficult for him, would become his single greatest liability as he rose through a succession of top jobs. Still, people who became friendly with him would declare that behind the wall of ice stood a friendly, compassionate, fundamentally decent man.

He kept to his principles. He was cautious by nature. In the 1970s, a group of Ernst colleagues organized an annual trip to Las

Vegas, and Doug and Kay Ivester were invited along. There, as in most things, Ivester was conservative. He liked craps but diligently kept his losses, and wins, to a minimum, sticking to the ten-dollar tables. He liked control, and he liked predictability. Gambling in Vegas got him away from all that, briefly, but he put just a toe in the water, never exposing himself more than he had to. In romance, too, he took no chances. He had eloped with Kay immediately after college.

Meanwhile, from his earliest moments at the company, he saw Coke's business as a numbers game – one he could win. Bottlers, for example, represented a set of numbers that cried out for him to manage them better. Why did a soft-drink company need hundreds of bottlers to turn out enormous quantities of an identical product? Why not streamline everything – and save money – by pushing more of the bottlers together to make larger ones? Why didn't the Coca-Cola Company, owner of this universally known, nonpareil brand, have more power in the relationship? What was a modern company doing with a system that was nearly a hundred years old?

Outsiders saw the issues, too. Peter Drucker, the management expert, once told a group of senior Coke executives that they had a great product but no distribution. A shocked silence filled the room. 'What was he talking about?' They had all those bottlers, yammering and arguing every step of the way, and they'd had them for almost a hundred years. 'You don't have any distribution', Drucker said, 'because you don't *control* your distribution.'

Ivester saw enormous potential in the sheer quantity of Coke that the company was already selling. What if you got every single person in a particular country to drink just one more Coke apiece every day – what would that do to sales? What if you were to harness holidays like Easter and Ramadan, and convince all the people who celebrated them that those were occasions that went better with Coke? What if you made sure that Coca-Cola was the only product available in certain places, by offering the owners of those places incentives that made money for them, too? Then what?

If you could do that and control your bottlers, then it was logical that the world really would belong to Coke.

Such was Ivester's thinking as he drove to Rome. He had risen quickly through the ranks at Coke, becoming chief financial officer in 1985 and president less than ten years after that. He had launched a new bottle, made of plastic, that looked like the famous one but held not six or twelve ounces of Coke but *twenty*. It was one more way to 'drive volume', as he put it, or sell that much more Coca-Cola concentrate to the bottlers. He had bonded with his boss, Roberto Goizueta, who was hailed by all on Wall Street. Ivester's promotion to president and chief operating officer in 1994 put him at the chairman's elbow, in the office formerly occupied by Don Keough, a man regaled everywhere as the heart of the Coca-Cola Company.

Every Coke executive tried his own tack when it came to bringing the bottlers into line. Some of them decided to be charming; Keough had perfected that approach. In Keough's world, it was love that drove the Coca-Cola Company to greater and greater heights, love of the product emanating from all the thousands of people involved in its care and cultivation. When it was his turn, Ivester dispensed with the small talk. Discussing his plans to streamline the system before an audience of bottlers one afternoon, he held up a Coke can and then proceeded to crush it and rip it in half with his hands. The bottlers, already nervous about their prospects, were stunned. They took it as a warning to stay out of his way.

As president, Ivester considered his new job a 'relatively simple' proposition. It boiled down to a single mission. 'All I have to do is create value, value for *our* share owners, value for *our* bottling partners, and value for *our* customers,' he declared at one point. Then, opening a small window into his mind, he added: 'That's what I think about almost twenty-four hours a day, seven days a week.'

In all of his assignments, he had set a tone of endlessly rising expectations – something his superiors at Coke liked a lot. In the same speech in which he described his job, a speech he titled 'Be Different . . . or Be Damned', he also declared that whatever the growth in the soft-drink market, he wanted it all – for Coke. He was blunt. He was direct. He essentially said in public what most soft-drink executives said behind closed doors. He compared his own company to a wolf among sheep and concluded his remarks with a recording of real wolves howling. 'That's just a group of friendly competitors over at the Coca-Cola Company,' he told the audience, his voice ringing out against the eerie sound track, 'having a good time.'

He had been at Coke only a short while when he caught the attention of Goizueta and Keough. To the two of them, Ivester represented a godsend, a man who understood how to handle the complicated worlds of public finance for Coke's benefit, who could conceive of and carry out a plan that took unneeded expenses off its books, who could dazzle Wall Street's skeptics and make them bow before Coke. He was also an aggressive worker, a man undistracted by children and not lured by golf or fishing, who spent so many hours at his desk that Goizueta called him a workaholic. Goizueta was not known for putting in long days at the office, and the surface of his desk was usually clear of everything, save a glass of Coca-Cola if it was a certain hour. He kept only an occasional piece of paper around, and most of what he needed to know he carried around with him inside his head.

Ivester clearly offered something Goizueta wanted, and he quickly became part of Goizueta's inner circle. By 1985, that circle included Keough; Sergio Zyman, the company's head of marketing; and Robert Keller, the general counsel. All of them were busy designing a future for Coke that would make it a financial wonder, a fount of profits that would draw admiration and envy and make them all spectacularly rich.

Early on, Ivester had a big fan in Keough, who had become Coke's president shortly after Ivester was hired from Ernst. Keough and Goizueta used to schedule a meeting once a year in the apartment suite just beyond the chairman's office, where they could eat and drink and talk uninterrupted. Sometimes they would spend the whole night there. They did this during the week between Christmas and New Year's, when life is relatively quiet in the soft-drink world. They would review their employees, talking about the year just past and deciding which executives had the brightest prospects. Ivester was always at the top of Keough's list – 'If I should get hit by a bus,' Keough told Goizueta.

In the age of junk-bond kings and billion-dollar leveraged

buyouts, the men of Coca-Cola crafted a way to sell Wall Street on Coke not as a blue chip but as a growth stock, the most attractive kind. They masterminded an image campaign for the company as an invincible force. They drew up the spin-off of Coke-owned bottlers that became Coca-Cola Enterprises, Ivester's prototype for bottling that he would extend to the rest of the world. It was no longer a matter of marketing the soda, as Candler and his successors had done for so long. Now they were marketing the Coca-Cola Company.

For a long time they were wildly successful. Then the group broke up. Zyman left in 1987; Keller retired in 1992. Keough was gone the following year. Then there were just two, Goizueta and Ivester. And they continued to push Coke to astonishing heights, dazzling everyone with their financial results and their rapid, successful march across new markets.

The two men could not have been more dissimilar on the surface – Goizueta was the sleek, cosmopolitan, Cuban-born chemical engineer, while Ivester was the pale, stern-looking side-kick, a country person who often seemed singularly uncomfortable in public. Goizueta was equated with Coke's success, like an old and familiar coin. Ivester lurked in the background. Goizueta was used to the back-slapping and Scotch-sipping required of someone in his position; Ivester practically shrank from that kind of physical contact. He didn't like to drink. He just liked to work.

Ivester was exceptionally smart, and beyond that he knew how to spot, as he would say, an opportunity. He had examined the numbers, and he knew he could make the world into a bigger customer for Coca-Cola. He would make that clear in his video about Rome, Georgia, which provided a perfect metaphor for Coke's plans: As Rome had gone, so the whole world would go.

Here were the two key points about Rome: The city consumed Coca-Cola at a higher rate than any other place on earth, and Rome was no longer controlled by an independent bottler. Frank Barron, its genial, hardworking third-generation bottler, had sold the eighty-five-year-old business to Coke in 1986, and Coke had quickly transferred it to Coca-Cola Enterprises, the megabottler that by the time of Ivester's road trip handled more than two thirds of all the Coke sold in the United States.

The sprawling Coca-Cola Enterprises was Ivester's catalyst for the future, a willing partner for the Coca-Cola Company's ambitious plans and a consolidator that would gobble up other bottlers, weaving an ultimately seamless whole from the fragmented landscape that he had inherited. He wanted a modern replacement for the old system, one in which the Coca-Cola Company called the shots – all the shots. And he foresaw that the Coca-Cola Enterprises model could be duplicated all over the world. Germany had dozens of little bottlers. So did Japan, and Brazil, and countries all over the planet. In all of these markets he would put together a string of revamped bottlers, better equipped and motivated to push the Coke agenda forward.

The fact that Jimmy Wardlaw was along on the trip illustrated how Coke and its largest bottler planned to work things out together. There they were, going in the same direction, with the Coca-Cola Company in the driver's seat. And they had only just begun, in Ivester's opinion. In 1994, Coca-Cola Enterprises was large, but it was poised to get a whole lot larger. Ivester's vision called for it to buy up many more bottling territories in the next few years, to concentrate even more power in one place.

An hour out of Atlanta they came to Rome, a Coca-Cola Company nirvana where people consume Coke as if there were nothing else to drink. In 1999, every man, woman, and child drank an average of 916 eight-ounce bottles apiece over the course of the year. That means 114.5 gallons of Coke for each of the 36,000 people in Rome, enough to fill swimming pools again and again, enough to make any Coke executive's heart beat faster.

Romans pronounce the soft drink's name in three syllables, not four – to them it is 'Co-Cola', as it is known across much of the South – and they drink it at more than twice the rate of the rest of America, almost ten times more often than people in Europe, and more than thirty times as often as people in Africa. The amount they drink just keeps rising, according to the Coca-Cola Company. Every year, Rome leads the world in per-capita consumption of Coke. It's not from tourists passing through, either; these are sales to workers in the lumber mills and to local families hooked on the taste. At the chamber of commerce, it's the only thing they keep on hand. 'There are people who drink Pepsi here, but Co-Cola is number one,' said Terri Corbett, who works there. 'I know people who drink it morning, noon, and night.'

The city is a modest, self-contained kind of place, despite the grandeur its name suggests. While it became the gold standard for Coca-Cola sales, its history of selling Coke is mirrored a thousand times across America.

In 1901, when Coke in bottles arrived in Rome, the country was obsessed with many things, and not the least of these was convenience. The shortcut, the time-saver, the easier way – these were concepts that Americans loved. Anyone who came up with a way to do something faster was sure to prosper. That was what Thomas and Whitehead had realized: If they could make drinking Coca-Cola easier and more convenient for people, they would have a winner.

But before long there was more to it. People didn't just drink Coca-Cola. They also collected old Coke bottles and hung up company-issued thermometers, consulted Coke calendars decorated with pretty opera and vaudeville stars, used Coke key chains when they unlocked their doors, and served snacks on Coke trays. They played checkers marked with the Coca-Cola logo or made their own from pried-off Coca-Cola bottle caps, wore Coca-Cola sweatshirts and Coca-Cola earrings, baked Coca-Cola cakes and covered them with Coca-Cola frosting. Norman Rockwell painted Coca-Cola into tranquil scenes of American life, and Haddon Sundblom, an artist commissioned by Coke, publicly bonded the soda to the image of Santa Claus.

As time went on and Coke appeared everywhere, people began to feel that it was a part of them and that they were a part of it. They associated Coke with treats, with special occasions, with moments that were valuable in one way or another. As it grew older and they did, too, they associated it with their childhoods, with memories of family outings or specific relatives they loved. They saved the napkins from restaurants where someone had ordered them a Coca-Cola. It was hard to explain, really. They did not have the same romance with other products of similar age and greater substance, like light bulbs or ketchup or shredded wheat. People bought Coke-bottle ornaments to hang on their Christmas trees, but no one decorated anything with squares of shredded wheat.

Rome was one of those places where Coke really took hold, and until 1986 its bottler dated from the Thomas and Whitehead era. Frank Barron, a pink-cheeked, blue-eyed former Navy officer aboard the USS *Ebersole,* shared bottling duties with his cousins. Their grandfather F. S. Barron ran a grocery store in town, but when he got one of the original franchises from Joseph Whitehead in 1901, he set to work building Coke into a local power. F. S. Barron's whole family worked at the Coke plant, and his son, known as Mr. Willie, took over after the old man died. The Barrons rose at five-thirty in the morning to get over to the plant and get the Coke out into the market before shoppers descended on the stores. They made plenty of money on Coke, but they also bottled NuGrape and other flavors – something Coke didn't approve of, calling the Barrons 'the rainbow bottler', when everything was supposed to be about Coca-Cola. It was one of the many points on which the company and the Rome bottler disagreed.

'We'd say, "We don't care how loyal a Coke drinker is, every so often they're going to want an orange drink,"' Frank Barron said. 'Our view was, getting the liquid down people's throats was our business.'

When people in Rome yearn for a drink, they turn to Coca-Cola, in large part because the Barrons had always been thorough – or dogged, or downright obnoxious – about making sure it was available just about everywhere. The family was active in all kinds of civic organizations, too. Everyone knew them – and knew they were the Coca-Cola bottlers. But the Barrons tend to downplay how hard they worked.

'This industry was a dad-gum accident,' Frank Barron said, his hands hardened from years of hoisting crates of Coca-Cola on and off delivery trucks. 'Nobody could possibly have predicted this business would do what it did.' Stories of Romans drinking nine or ten Cokes a day, starting first thing in the morning, surprise no one who lives in Rome.

The Barrons disagreed regularly with the Coca-Cola Company about what to sell and how to sell it. In the end, Frank and his cousins usually did exactly what they wanted to do and waited for Coke to try and stop them. The Barrons put Coke in the schools, in the mills, in the stores, and in the ball fields. The vending machines were full of Coke; so were the coolers and the ice barrels at the gas stations. Any innovation that came along, in the form of a six-pack or a refrigerator case, the Barrons ordered it and filled it right up with Coke. Working around the clock, from their trucks filled with cases of Coke and from the boards of agencies and civic associations where they made sure to get a seat, they convinced their friends and neighbors and churches and community groups that Coke was it – not Pepsi. They backed this up with abundant generosity, paying for uniforms for the baseball team, footing the bill for the football scoreboard, or contributing mightily for the new building some group or school said it needed. All of it was important to them, and all of it was possible because the profits on selling Coca-Cola – once a bottler took care of fixed costs, like payroll and the concentrate he had to buy from the Coca-Cola Company – were enormous, as long as the volume was high. Because they understood this, bottlers labored endlessly to make sure they sold Coca-Cola everywhere they could.

You could buy a Pepsi in the city of Rome, Georgia, if you really tried, down at the supermarket; but as far as the eye could see, it was all about Coca-Cola. Most bottlers were kings in their own towns; Frank Barron, like his father and his grandfather before him, became the emperor of Rome. Some people still address him as Marcus Aurelius when they encounter him in town.

To Doug Ivester, how Rome happened was of less concern than the fact that it *had* happened, and should happen more often. With Rome out there posting ever-higher consumption levels, Ivester looked at his map of the world and thought, Why not expect the same of people in Russia, in China, in India, in the Philippines, where they drank only a few Cokes a year, on average, per person? What about France, Germany, Italy, Australia, Indonesia, where people drank more than that, not to mention Burkina Faso and Belarus?

He was driven by a need. Coke's fortunes depended on selling as much of its concentrate as possible. The company, pirouetting for investors, set ambitious growth targets for itself year after year. To meet them, there had to be an endlessly expanding market for soft drinks, one that would require huge amounts of concentrate. Ivester and Goizueta were promising 6 to 8 percent volume growth, even 10 percent, on nearly a billion drinks a day. A billion drinks a day added up to 365 billion drinks a year. A 7 percent increase would mean another 25.6 billion drinks in 1995, and another 200 million gallons of concentrate in the year ahead on top of the nearly 3 billion already being made. It was stunning to think of the world drinking that much soda. But that was the world of Coke.

Bottlers had often gotten in the way of such plans by refusing to cooperate or arguing long and hard that something couldn't be done. But by 1994 many of them had been persuaded to sign a revised contract that for the first time meant frequent price increases for syrup. It was a radical departure from the past, and it made the bottling business much more profitable for Coke.

As Coke seeded change with that new contract, the rest of the world was inflicting its own damage on the bottlers. The notion that all a bottler needed was diligence – getting up early in the morning, befriending the store owners, never letting the shelves empty out, insisting that people drink Coke, not 7Up or Pepsi, the way the Barrons locked up their own market – grossly understated the business of selling Coca-Cola by the early 1980s. Retailers were being bought up into larger and larger corporations, which meant the manager of the local grocery store was no longer the one who ordered the soft drinks for his shelves. Prices and orders were being negotiated at the home office, wherever it was, not out by the truck. Coke saw what was happening but was powerless to stop it. The customers were getting larger and more demanding. It was awkward to negotiate a national contract with Wal-Mart, for example, and then have one or two bottlers refuse to go along with the plan. Then there was price to consider: To keep costs attractively low, bottlers needed to be efficient. Efficiency came from savings, and the best means of getting those was to merge bottlers together.

All over the country, bigger meant better. The mom-and-pop

stores were vanishing as Main Streets gave way to shopping malls
rising on the outer fringes of cities and towns. Barbershops,
newsstands, and other small businesses that used to be stops on a
local bottler's sales route found it easier to buy a case or two of soda
down at the Kroger than to deal directly with a bottler. So much
was being shaped by the interstate, with its bland networks of
highly efficient pavement carrying travelers around cities and
towns, not through them. So much was boiling down to numbers.

The bottlers felt the pressure swelling up against their business,
like carbonation taken a step too far. The answer was to add
franchises if they could. Bigger was cheaper in the long run and
more attractive to customers – Kroger, Wal-Mart – who were
rapidly expanding as well. But adding territory wasn't always
possible, certainly not without the blessing of the Coca-Cola
Company. Coke had its own ideas about which bottlers would be
allowed to grow.

More and more, individual bottlers thought about selling. In
1986, a significant handful went to Atlanta to let Coke know that
they were ready to get out. Frank Barron and his cousin Alfred Lee
were among them, and so was Jack Lupton, grandson and
namesake of Joseph Whitehead's partner, whose early stake had
grown into the JTL Corporation, the largest Coke bottler in the
country.

That was the year Doug Ivester came up with his plan to remake
the bottling system, to take back what Candler had so blithely
given away.

The plan was known as 'the 49 percent solution'. It called for
Coke to spend $3 billion to buy the bottlers that were for sale.
Then Coke would reconfigure them as a revolutionary kind of
bottler, in which Coke would be the largest single stakeholder,
wielding power that would ensure the bottler followed Coke's
plans. Coke executives would populate the board of directors,
which would be another good thing for Coke. Part and parcel of
the new bottler was a new contract, in which at any time there
could be price increases for concentrate. With a 49 percent stake,
Coke would have unprecedented influence over the bottler,
without actually owning it or having to account for it as if it owned
it.

The whole concept was about as removed from the old system as it could possibly be. None of the old-time independent bottlers would have agreed to such an arrangement. But the franchises that became Coca-Cola Enterprises were not independent bottlers anymore; their independence had been swapped for piles of cash, and now that Coke owned them, it could do with them what was best for Coke.

At last, Coke would control a hefty segment of the bottling business. Coke would boost its earnings through syrup sales and profit sharing from its 49 percent stake. And Coke would be a cleaned-up, modern, more efficient company – so much more attractive to investors. This was a total victory for Coke.

It had been Ivester's idea. With it, he changed life inside the Coca-Cola Company. Now he could step on the accelerator, driving the rest of the Coca-Cola system toward that place called Rome.

Chapter Three

Time to Spare

A S DOUG IVESTER SPED along the highway in 1994, with Coke at an apogee, Don Keough sat cocooned in a plush, paneled office in New York. A year had gone by since he stepped down as president of the Coca-Cola Company, forced by age to leave the Coke tower and the business that had been his pride and passion for three decades, nearly half his life.

He had not gone especially quietly. He gave up his job, which he had enjoyed for more than a dozen years, and he resigned from the board, as his retirement required. But he had also worked out a contract, courtesy of Coke's chairman, Roberto Goizueta, that kept him on as a consultant to Coke for the next five years. He could count on attending board meetings until 1998, keeping at least a finger on the tiller. He might have been forsaking his title, but he was not planning to leave the world of Coca-Cola.

On his final afternoon, the sixty-six-year-old Keough headed not for the parking lot but for a spot on the lawn just beyond the lobby's reception area. Keough remained outside the glass walls there for close to four hours, saying good-bye to people from all levels of the company who waited patiently in line under the blazing sun for their chance to see him one last time. A lot of them wore green-and-white campaign-style buttons with Keough's name on them, along with the words WE SALUTE A COCA-COLA CLASSIC.

Keough talked to them, laughed with them, shook their hands until his arm was numb. One executive estimated that three thousand people, or half the population of the Coke tower, got up from their desks to have a last bit of contact with Keough before he disappeared. Goizueta, his boss and a man he considered to be his friend, was not among them. Neither was Doug Ivester, who was poised to take over Keough's old job. They had celebrated his retirement at other functions held earlier. And, unofficially, they felt it was time for him to go.

For years, Keough had been called the heart of the Coca-Cola Company, and it was a role he self-consciously played to the hilt. Gregarious, silver-tongued, a man of multiple interests who stood ready to do almost anything if he thought it would help Coke's prospects somewhere in the world, Keough insisted that the soft-drink business was a joyful way to make a living. 'He was a cheerleader for the company and the employees,' said George Marlin, who spent twenty years selling Coke. 'You felt he had a fire in his belly for Coca-Cola. He bled Coca-Cola red.'

He loved hosting parties, and if those parties helped ultimately to sell more Coke, then that was a good thing, too. Under his leadership, the Coca-Cola Company would hold some of the biggest corporate bashes the nation had ever seen, spending millions of dollars to entertain thousands of people for days at a stretch. He had a keen appreciation of the distance covered by a graceful gesture, and knew just how effective a free dinner or a round of drinks could be when dealing with an adversary or a skeptic. He loved Coke and clearly thought everyone else should, too. 'You know, we don't sell funeral vaults,' he'd say. 'We sell a happy thing.'

His following at Coke was huge and affectionate. He seemed genuinely to appreciate the people he worked with, kissing them on the cheek, patting them on the back, asking after their mothers or their children, remembering minor details about those children, such as where they were going to college. He knew how to bond and forged for himself a following at the company composed of people who cared about him because they felt he cared about them. Outside the Coke tower on that April afternoon, these were the people who came, by the hundreds, to see him off.

His regard for the Coca-Cola Company could correctly be called passionate. While maintaining that a bottle of Coke was ultimately just a small part of life, he always saw the company that produced it as a wonderful place, magical even, owner and curator of the world's greatest brand. He loved it. Everything he believed about the Coca-Cola Company involved the heart.

When Keough spoke about a bottler's responsibility or the importance of people in the equation that made and sold Coke, everyone listened. He was a commanding speaker, inspiring to those who spent their days heaving cases off assembly lines and pestering store owners to take more Coca-Cola. Keough understood them, they thought, and of all the multimillionaires overseeing the selling of Coca-Cola in the 1980s and 1990s, he was the one they related to best.

Still, it was not just the bottlers who were drawn to him. Anyone who was remotely interested in the things he was interested in – Notre Dame football results, Irish history, the delights of a particular European hotel, the price of Coca-Cola stock – loved talking to him. 'He can make you feel like you are the most important person in the room,' people often said of Keough.

Born in the republic's sesquicentennial year, he exuded an all-American style, the kind that prompts descriptions like 'corn-fed' and 'home-grown'. He was tall, thick-set, and white-haired by his late fifties, with eyes the color of the turf meeting the sea. He claimed that one of his ancestors was the last man standing at Little Big Horn, and he still carried himself like the football player he once was. And if you attended a party and he was there, too, chances were he'd come and find you and introduce himself. He was boundless in his enthusiasm, enveloping in his friendliness. He could talk for hours at a time. People remembered his name.

His childhood coincided with the Depression, and his father, Leo, delivered newspapers for a time to support his family. Born in Iowa, Keough spent his earliest years on a farm. Even though he moved to Sioux City shortly after he turned two, he would refer to himself forever as a farm boy. It was a great ice-breaker, and he knew it. It helped make him as quintessentially American as Coke. And it had once been true.

He spotted his first bottle of Coca-Cola when he was a child, but he came to work at Coke without planning it. He had enlisted in the Navy before the end of World War II and enrolled at Creighton University when he got out. After a series of jobs that took him from the world of radio to the far less glamorous food industry, he cruised into Coca-Cola when Coke bought the coffee company he was working for in 1963. The takeover cost him his hard-won status in one headquarters, but gave him a far bigger opportunity at Coke, where he burrowed in deep and reaped rewards beyond anything anyone could have imagined back on the farm.

It was his verbal skills that took him to the upper reaches of Coke, along with his ability to convince people that he was on their side. *Don is especially gifted as a public speaker,* his mentor, Charles Duncan, Jr., wrote in a letter to Bob Woodruff, the seemingly permanent leader of Coca-Cola, ahead of Keough's interview with Woodruff for the job of running Coke's coffee-and-juice division. What Keough did in his professional life was not just business to him, Duncan added: *Don probably has more personal friends in the ownership and general management of retail grocers than does any other executive in our company.*

Once across Coca-Cola's doorstep, Keough became known as the most mesmerizing of spokesmen for everything the company did. An audience of one or more brought out the natural performer in him, and his style was as folksy as a country preacher's. He verbally rummaged through a seemingly bottomless sack of one-liners, made frequent eye contact with the people in the front row, and reinforced a sense of intimacy with them by engaging in a continuous refinement of his personal appearance right before their eyes. During one speech, delivered in 1974 to a group of Coke field-sales executives gathered in Atlanta, Keough adjusted his socks, removed his eyeglasses, cleaned them on his suit coat, put them on again, took out a cigarette, rubbed the back of his neck, smoothed his hair, and lit the cigarette, all in the space of about twenty minutes of talk. He told the group about a job he had once had, selling slaughtered turkeys over the telephone while a railroad car loaded with them hurtled east. His duty was to find buyers for those turkeys, which had grown less appealing by the minute, by the time the train reached each of its successive stops. He loved a challenge, he told everybody with a chuckle, and those dead birds were a challenge.

He was fond of promoting loyalty – the kind that required a certain amount of blind faith. He once told an audience about discovering the imperfections of his wife, Mickie, over the course

of their long marriage – which began when he was twenty-three –
and loving her anyway, which was one of his favorite metaphors
for the way a person should regard the Coca-Cola Company.
Maybe everything about it wasn't perfect, but the big picture was,
Keough insisted. He was married to Mickie, and to the Coca-Cola
Company, and not planning to part anytime soon from either of
them. His audience remained rapt throughout the presentation.
They appeared to love it.

With the gift of gab and a sharp sense of how to manage his own
career, he rose to the position of president of Coke, and he worked
in tandem with Roberto Goizueta for twelve critical years, trying
to fix what one or both of them believed was wrong with the
company. With Ivester and others, they created a new company in
the process. One of their main goals was to replace the bottler
system with something that they could control, and another was to
paint a promising financial picture of the company that would
bring investors running. In both respects, they succeeded beyond
their wildest dreams.

It was amazing that they could work so well together. The two
men at the top of Coke in 1981, the year Goizueta was named
chairman and chief executive, were stylistic opposites. Both would
have preferred to be solo acts, but both had to learn to get along
with each other, flaws and all. 'Their relationship was such that I
don't think you fully understood it unless you were a fly on the
wall with them,' said Donald McHenry, a longtime Coke director.
'We know what it appeared to be.'

Goizueta tended to observe bankers' hours. His office was kept
as cold as a meat locker, the way he liked it. Employees
complained, through chattering teeth, but Goizueta, listening to
them through the smoke rising from the cigarettes he puffed
fanatically, didn't change a thing.

People never mentioned the temperature in Keough's office
because Keough did not spend a lot of time there. He ricocheted
from breakfast to lunch, through the cocktail hour and into dinner,
always out searching for opportunities to make Coke's case, at
home and around the world. You might disagree with Keough, in
a permanent, insoluble kind of way, but it could be a pleasure
having him try to persuade you to come around to his point of

view. Everyone seemed to love him. 'Don Keough was the best thing that the Coca-Cola Company ever had,' said Roger Enrico, who battled him as the head of Pepsi-Cola. 'I accused him one time of having three doubles. He was everywhere, all the time.'

Coke people perhaps saw in Keough a father figure; he so often mentioned his wife and their road trips in a car packed with half a dozen restless kids. He could also play the role of another kind of father: the tough-talking disciplinarian. Marking Coke's one hundredth anniversary in 1986, Keough told a huge assembly of bottlers from all over the world that their responsibility was to reinvest in their Coke businesses – not in real estate or airlines or racetracks or any of the other distractions that he felt had led some of them astray. Without skipping a beat, his tone switched from cheery to dark. 'In my lower left-hand drawer, God's truth, I have a list of names,' he said. 'A list that makes up the graveyard of Coca-Cola bottlers who went this route.' Though he spoke from the other side of the table, he knew what was best for them. And he wasn't shy about telling them.

While he was intensely popular at Coke, people also feared what they called 'the Irish Wind', their nickname for Keough's temper. Executives hardened by years abroad in the most inhospitable environments could be intimidated by one of his rages. 'His way of arguing pinned it to the personal,' said a former senior executive who worked with him for years. 'He seemed to be attacking me, in the words and attitudes he presented in a dispute. And yet the dispute didn't involve me.' Everyone who shared his orbit, including Doug Ivester, experienced the Wind at some point.

When Keough said good-bye to Coke on that April afternoon in 1993, he told everyone that he did so under his own steam. Indeed, he was more than a year past the usual retirement age for a Coke executive, even a beloved one. It was he who told Goizueta that he wanted to leave, he would say, and he insisted that Goizueta had asked him to stay on. But once Keough did leave Coke – 'Mother Coke', as many people called it – it was as if he had left much of his heart behind.

Leaving Coke had always been unappealing to him. He had given an interview to an Omaha, Nebraska, newspaper in 1982 in which he showed off his new business card. 'It says Donald R.

Keough, president of the Coca-Cola Company,' he noted then. 'Now, in the last analysis, the only thing that is really mine is the Donald R. Keough. I'm a temporary president. I'm a temporary resident of this fancy office.'

Even then, he seemed to be concerned about what life would be like when he was no longer at Coke. 'I hope that when I have to tear this card up, when I carry one that just says Donald R. Keough, that I will be enough of a total person that I will still be considered worthwhile,' he continued. Then he peered at the reporter, his head tipped a little to one side. 'I think about that,' he said, 'a lot.'

Gone from Coke, Don Keough was far from idle. He joined Allen & Company, Inc., the private investment bank headed by Herbert Allen, a Coke director who had come aboard as part of the purchase of Columbia Pictures in 1982, which he then helped Coke sell to Sony seven years later at a huge markup. Allen installed Keough as the company's chairman, a role that gave him plenty of opportunities to schmooze with clients, advise on deals, fly around the country to various events, and generally fill up his days, now that he was not at Coke. He still hobnobbed with friends like Anthony O'Reilly, the chairman of H. J. Heinz, with whom he shared passions for Irish culture and American corporate life, and Barry Diller, the entertainment mogul, whose picture, in which he wore a sign around his neck that said WILL WORK FOR FOOD, adorned one wall outside Keough's new office. He still had positions on several corporate boards, among them McDonald's, where he made decisions that affected thousands of people. He had some American paintings hung in his office, including a Guy Wiggins cityscape showing Federal Hall, built on the spot where George Washington took the presidential oath of office in 1789, amid falling snow. He had just about everything an executive might want.

But the Allen job was not the same as being second-in-command at the world's biggest soft-drink maker. Keough had relished every minute that he spent at Coke; it had been a hell of a ride, even though he had not been happy about winding up number two there, instead of number one. Now he no longer had the company jet, and, far worse for him, he no longer had the company. There was only one Coca-Cola, and he missed being there. He missed the legions of people who addressed him respectfully by name, as 'Mr. Keough', back in Atlanta. And he missed the diplomats and other globe-trotters who invited him for lunch or dinner, wherever he happened to be that day. And he no doubt missed the sense of dominion, and of largesse, that he had had in his old job. He called routinely to find out what was going on. He said people back there called him a fair amount, too.

A year after he departed, there was little magic left for Keough. He had been banished to the sidelines by age and circumstance, and now he was forced to watch while his onetime partner, Roberto Goizueta, lavished his attention on a new president, Doug Ivester; he also had to listen while the accolades for Coke poured in. Back in 1986, Keough had been fond of warning others in the Coca-Cola system, particularly the bottlers, about the dangers of becoming irrelevant. And now he, the architect and enabler of so much that had made Coke great, had to sit and bear witness to other people's relevance.

The thought of Ivester could send a grimace across his wide Irish face. Keough had been one of Ivester's biggest cheerleaders in the 1980s, over a decade in which the two of them, plus Goizueta, left a broad collective imprint on Coke. Ivester was the money man, the one who understood the accounting rules and limitations better than anyone and could come up with creative, workable solutions to sticky financial problems and, yes, a few strategic ones, too.

Keough and Goizueta admired Ivester enormously, especially when he found them all a way out of the bottling dilemma. For in 1986, when so many bottlers were on the block, the Coke executives initially had not been aggressive about dealing with the changes confronting them, even though they had pushed hard to re-create the bottling system. In fact, they were on the brink of panic, deeply afraid of losing control of the whole show.

That year was the high-water mark of the eighties, and it would be another year before the bottom fell out of the spiraling stock market, a market built on inflated expectations and a lot of highly leveraged missions. That year, the names Henry Kravis, Boone

Pickens, Carl Icahn, and those of other corporate raiders sent shudders of fear through executives all over the country. Not long before, practically no one had ever heard of a leveraged buyout. Now they were happening all over, to old-line companies that had once seemed secure, even hallowed. You could pick up the newspaper every morning and read about another one, sometimes two or three happening at once. Companies that actually made something – cookies, panty hose, glue, soft drinks – had everything to lose if an investor squirreled away a little stock and all of a sudden decided to make a run at acquiring their business. Plenty of executives got swept up in the wave, sometimes willingly. It was only after the ink dried on the documents that the reality set in, that the companies could be chopped into parts and sold off bit by bit, leaving nothing behind but disembodied brands and the poignant memory of the way things used to be. Cracker Jack and Oreo, both peers of Coca-Cola when it came to age and image, were captured in this way. No brand was safe.

This was the spectre that haunted Keough and Goizueta. They tossed in their beds at night, worrying about what to do if a Kravis got hold of one of their big bottlers. They wanted the bottler system broken up, but their plan was to put it back together again their way.

Soon their fears became real. Kravis's buyout firm took over the Beatrice companies, a conglomerate of food makers. One of the Beatrice properties was BCI, the Coca-Cola bottler for Los Angeles. Keough and Goizueta knew that anyone who wanted to press the cash out of a bottler could do so easily, laying off people, cutting costs in other ways, and demanding help from the Coca-Cola Company. There was no way that Coke could let one of its bottlers weaken, since Pepsi and other competitors were always hovering nearby, and the company would have to do whatever it took to keep its business – in other words, pay and pay and pay to keep the bottler going.

Kravis put BCI up for sale right away. At least he wasn't going to be the owner for long; but now the question was, who would take his place? The price for BCI was $1 billion.

At the same time, Jack Lupton, grandson and namesake of the man who had bankrolled the Chattanooga lawyers setting up the bottling network at the beginning of the century, announced that he, too, wanted out. Lupton was legendary, just like his granddaddy. He cut an enormous profile across the Coca-Cola landscape, with his houses in Tennessee and Florida and his role as a megabottler who had locked horns with Coke for years. He had spent nearly twenty-five years on the Coca-Cola Company's board of directors and knew everyone in the company. He owned bottling franchises in Texas and Florida and all over the Midwest. In 1986, his company, JTL, bottled about 10 percent of all the Coca-Cola sold in the United States, more than any other bottler.

That spring, Lupton had failed to show up, citing 'unexpected circumstances', at the huge centennial bash that Coke had organized for itself in Atlanta. He was indeed too ill to attend. But he sent a birthday present to Coke management: a crystal ball commissioned from Steuben, on behalf of all the bottlers.

A bottler friend from Birmingham, Alabama, named Crawford Johnson presented it to Goizueta onstage before twelve thousand bottlers, Coke brass, and their guests. Lupton's crystal ball was mounted on a marble base, etched with clasping hands evoking the partnership between the bottlers and Coke. Circling it were birds in flight: ducks, perhaps, or golden geese. They were purposeful and noble-looking creatures, as fragile as the ball itself.

Now it was clear where the biggest one of them was headed. Lupton wanted out, and he named his price: $1.4 billion.

Next came Frank Barron and his cousin Alfred, who drove down to Atlanta one morning and asked to see Keough.

Keough's secretary ushered them into the office, then left, closing the door behind her. Keough, seated behind his big desk with the light glaring through the window behind him, knew why they were there. And even though the Barrons wanted only about $80 million for their family business – chicken feed, compared with Lupton – Keough had had enough of these kinds of visits.

'Damn it, Frank,' he said, snapping a yellow pencil in two with his large freckled hands. 'This wasn't supposed to happen.'

But the Barrons, like Jack Lupton and Henry Kravis, had made up their minds. Now the question of what happened to their bottling properties, after all the years of chipping away at their power, was Coke's problem. Suddenly, after Coke had been trying so hard and so long to get rid of the bottlers, some of them were leaving and the company didn't know what to do. The erosion was supposed to take place bit by bit. All of a sudden, a very expensive avalanche was headed their way.

It was Doug Ivester, barely a year into his job as chief financial officer and not yet forty years old, who quickly thought of a way to keep everything in the Coke family without creating financial burden for the Coca-Cola Company.

At that moment, Ivester was still emerging from the enormous chrysalis that was Coke, still striving to make a name for himself inside the company he had joined seven years earlier. He had already accomplished a few impressive things, including organizing an internal audit shortly after he arrived that highlighted where and how the company could strengthen itself financially. He represented the emphasis on financial management at the Coca-Cola Company that Goizueta had endorsed immediately after becoming chief executive in 1981. He and Goizueta were already close.

Ivester won praise for other accomplishments, like his handling of Columbia Pictures, purchased in 1982 by Coke as one means of improving its earnings. He bundled the studio's receivables and sold them on the open market, generating fresh cash for Coca-Cola, and he had thought up plenty of other cost-saving measures after that. But this would be the biggest problem he would solve for senior management, and the move that would cement his position as a Coca-Cola rising star. No longer would he be simply one of the accountants, part of the back office and not listed on the marquee. He would elevate Coke and its regard for others in his profession, derisively called bean counters, in a single move.

Without a doubt, Ivester's idea was ingenious. It called for Coke to buy the bottlers that were for sale. Then, out of those random, far-flung pieces, a new company would be created – Ivester named it Coca-Cola Enterprises – a huge Coke bottler, with an important difference. Coca-Cola would own a tad less than half of that new bottler, making it the single largest shareholder and giving it the right to name several directors to the board. It would control the bottler without having to consolidate its finances with the bottler. At the same time, the new contract governing syrup prices would guarantee that Coke could raise those prices as it saw fit. It was perfectly legal, and it amounted to the best of all possible worlds.

Everything that had been lost in the nineteenth century, when Asa Candler signed away the rights to bottle Coca-Cola to the first people who asked and gave up the chance to control what turned out to be a major part of the business, would now be returned to the Coca-Cola Company. History would be not just corrected but improved upon. And people like Ivester – the CPAs and MBAs – would ascend, displacing the 'operations people', or those who actually mixed it up outside the Coke tower with customers and bottlers and consumers. It was the beginning of a transformation from one kind of management to another that would ripple across everything that everyone at Coke did. It was the beginning of the end of power for people like Keough.

Ivester saw the reformulated bottler as a way to 'drive volume' – a Coke-ism for increasing sales of the concentrate that bottlers transformed into Coca-Cola. Besides having their people in the boardroom and at the helm of the new company, he and other Coke executives would not have to spend so much of their time discussing plans with the bottlers; here, instead of several independent voices to deal with, there would be just one, responsible for nearly a third of the Coke sold and drunk in the United States.

What Coke wanted, this new bottler would do. The new bottler would save money itself, because it would be more efficient in many ways than the several littler ones that it replaced. Meanwhile, the Coca-Cola Company would rake in almost half the bottler's profits, the benefit of holding such a large stake.

Ivester's plan amounted to the shattering of Coke's historic relationship with its bottlers, replacing it with one that was much more advantageous to the Coca-Cola Company. A more muscular, more responsive bottling partner would now help Coke attain all of its objectives – primarily the selling of Coca-Cola concentrate and the continuous increasing of the share price. Coke would finally share in the profits from the sale of the bottles and cans, which had for decades been a reward for the bottlers alone.

It was a stupendous plan, almost too good to be true. But there it was, typed up by Ivester's secretary as a neatly organized memo that anyone could read. Keough and Goizueta were ecstatic. There was one more feature, a little icing on the already abundantly generous cake: This bottler would be publicly traded. It would be underwritten by all the investors who bought shares in it, and its shares, if all went according to plan, would grow in value as its fortunes progressed. Not only had Ivester swept the financial drag of bottling off Coke's books; he had created a way to get other people to help pay for his 49 percent solution.

The bottlers by then were far fewer in number, thanks to various sustained efforts by Coke management over the years. Though the Coca-Cola marketing trinity – Delicious, Refreshing, Sold Everywhere – relied on them, the Coca-Cola Company had concluded that the fewer bottlers there were, the simpler bottling would be to manage. Keough had been working toward that end, along with a group of other Coke executives, for quite some time. In 1979, as president of Coca-Cola Americas, a territory that reached from Saskatchewan to Cape Horn, he presided over an enormous fiesta in San Francisco. It was organized officially by Brian Dyson, then running Coca-Cola USA, to boost morale as Pepsi fanned its notorious Pepsi Challenge, the taste test that publicly humiliated Coke every time a blindfolded person, sipping from unmarked paper cups, pronounced Pepsi the better-tasting cola. The Pepsi Challenge exposed Coca-Cola's deepest fear, of someday losing its title as the nation's top-selling cola. And as the 1970s wore on, Pepsi picked up market share while Coke remained stagnant.

To shore up everyone who felt battered by the enemy's campaign, Coke arranged for San Francisco to be all but corralled for Coke so that the bottlers and assorted other guests could enjoy themselves. The store windows at Gump's featured mannequins wearing Coca-Cola gear, and a replica of the city was built along one of the wharves for the Coke people to tour through. Everyone was put up, at Coke's expense, in the best hotels, and restaurants as well as bars were theirs for the asking. No demand was too great from a member of the Coca-Cola family.

For that is the way Keough framed it: They were all family. And in a speech that week, he cemented his position as a man of the bottlers. 'Keough was coming to the forefront,' recalled George Marlin, who had joined Coke a few months earlier as a regional sales representative. 'And he gave one of the finest business speeches I have ever heard. I had had three tours in Vietnam and I had played football, and I didn't consider myself a wimpy guy. But I was just about in tears listening to this guy.'

Keough's theme was the importance of banding together to sell the world's greatest soft drink, and he drove that home by citing example after example of Coke's wondrous performance over the years. But a year earlier, the company had come up with a revised contract for the bottlers to sign. Known as the Amended Bottling Agreement, the contract allowed Coke to raise concentrate prices at will. It was all presented as a perfectly reasonable proposition. By increasing profits for the Coca-Cola Company, Keough and others maintained, and therefore making more money available for marketing and advertising, the bottlers would benefit. That was the selling point of the amended contract. Come on, he'd say. We need the money to fight Pepsi. We've got to come together.

With the way the country had been divided up by Ben Thomas and Joseph Whitehead back in 1900, there was variety in how bottling contracts were written. A few bottlers still did not have perpetual contracts; that was the legacy of Thomas, who wanted to move more cautiously than his former partner. Dick Montag, a bottler in Bellingham, Washington, inherited a bottling franchise from his father and grandfather that had to be renewed every year. He struck a deal with Coke: He would sign the amended contract if he could have his contract rewritten in perpetuity. 'It was a factor that they offered,' said Montag, who agreed to the new syrup-pricing terms and remained in the business for another nineteen years.

Many other bottlers signed as well, some wooed effectively by Keough, some afraid of ending up on Coke management's bad side if they didn't. But others refused, contending that this was just the latest example of Coke's decades-long effort to undermine them. Coke's president at that time, Lucien Smith, worked to convince them that this was not the case. 'The bottlers trusted Luke,' recalled Emmet Bondurant II, an Atlanta lawyer who wound up bringing several lawsuits against Coke on behalf of bottlers. And suddenly, in 1980, Smith, a man some would call 'the last gentleman' of the Coca-Cola Company, was gone.

The official word was that he had retired. 'He was there one day and gone the next,' Bondurant said.

But he left a legacy. Smith's line, repeated again and again around the country, had been that with Pepsi ascending, Coke and its bottlers needed to make 'common cause' against the enemy. 'This is a partnership and we're on your side,' Bondurant recalled the company saying. 'The bottlers believed it.'

When Smith vanished, Keough, by then a vice chairman, took his place as chief engineer for the company's bottler strategy. He stroked and cajoled and used practically every reason to get bottlers to take on Coke's new contract. Aboard a company plane one day, according to one story, he buttonholed a bottler from one of the midwestern states with a typical pitch. He had offered the man a lift home, and once aloft, the bottler quickly realized that there was no such thing as a free ride. 'Tomorrow is my wife's birthday,' Keough told him, 'and it sure would be a nice present for her if I could tell her that you had agreed to sign the new contract.' The bottler hemmed and hawed and all but ran from the plane once it touched down.

The late 1970s marked a critical moment for the bottlers. There had been relative peace between them and the Coca-Cola Company until the end of World War II. With the syrup price permitted to rise only if the market price of sugar went up, Coke enjoyed a windfall for most of the years between 1921 and 1945. Sugar fell lower than the seven-cents-a-pound floor established in the settlement with the bottlers, but the price of concentrate was never reduced to reflect that. It didn't have to be, under the terms of the contract. It could be adjusted only upward, and only if the price of sugar on the open market rose accordingly. 'It was a long period in which the contract was favorable to Coke,' Emmet Bondurant said, 'and the bottlers were lulled into a position of trusting the Coca-Cola Company.'

Coke was still bent on removing as many of the restrictions on its profits as it could. In 1934, it began a campaign to buy up the parent bottlers, the large central brokers of syrup that Whitehead and Thomas set up at the turn of the century. The brokers purchased syrup from Coke, then resold it at a slight markup to the local franchise bottlers. This was another source of profit that the Coca-Cola Company didn't want someone else to have.

Coke spent millions of dollars and took more than forty years to acquire the parent bottlers it targeted, purchasing the last one, the Thomas company, for $35 million in 1975. But owning them turned out to be more of a moral victory than a financial one, for the independent bottlers still enjoyed their power. Coke was now selling them the syrup directly, but the prices were still fixed.

After World War II, sugar prices began to rise. Time and again, Coke executives would bemoan the fact that more than half the business had to be conducted under these fixed-price contracts. In 1954, someone at Coke got an idea, and the company unveiled an ultramodern substitute for the thick syrup sold to fountain businesses. It was known as premix, and it was a prepared Coca-Cola, one that did not need to be diluted with soda water. It came in a large container that could be installed at the fountain or the lunch counter, and for a country obsessed with doing things swiftly and efficiently in the cold-war years, it seemed to be a perfect fit. Besides, with its arrival, the Coca-Cola Company declared that it was not syrup — it really wasn't, though it had been made from syrup — and therefore it was a new animal, not covered by the contracts with the bottlers. The company could have bottlers take it around to restaurants and other places that in the past had been part of the fountain business, Coke reasoned.

Premix was one part of the solution. And some bottlers embraced it. On June 23, 1954, the bottler in Hamlet, North Carolina, became the first to sign the contract Coke offered for premix. Every bottler got a contract, but not all of them wanted to sign it.

By the 1970s, generational changes — as well as the fact that some bottling families, acknowledging their difficulties, had brought in professional managers to run their companies — meant that a different cast was in place at many bottlers. The faces had changed at Coke, too. The momentum for an overhaul of the bottling situation had never been greater as Keough made his stirring speech in San Francisco.

The company had already put together a plan to divide the

country into several large megabottling territories. Certain bottlers were being singled out to become much larger, by being permitted to buy other franchises as they came up for sale. And the bottlers decided to sell after Keough and others told them things like: Times are changing. Make sure you and your family get a good price. Bigger is going to be better. 'It was unreal,' said Richard Larson, who spent sixteen years as a bottling executive in Minneapolis and elsewhere. 'All these little family bottlers that had been kings of the world were now getting all this pressure from Coke to sell out.'

A few of the bottlers understood Coke's motivation. 'The idea was that the Coca-Cola Company had to have the ability to determine its own fate,' said Frank Barron, 'and it couldn't do that as long as the bottlers were there.'

Meanwhile, Coke decided that certain bottlers were going to be around for good, and they were handpicked by Coke executives. One of them was Summerfield Johnston, whose Johnston Coca-Cola Bottling, based in Chattanooga, was one of the original Coke-sanctioned independent bottlers. He and a few others would be not just permitted but encouraged to take on more territory as it became available, through natural means (like families deciding they just didn't want to bottle Coke anymore) and through Coke-initiated pressure. They had demonstrated loyalty to Coke in various ways, and Coke was going to help them.

If they couldn't pay for an acquisition outright, Coke encouraged them to take on debt and backed them on the enormous loans they took out. Heavy borrowing by one bottler to buy another would become a pattern that Coke actively supported, first at home, in a small way, and then around the world as the stakes grew larger. It was a major departure for the bottlers, who had historically managed their money closely and had resisted leveraging what they had. 'We kind of rolled over and played dead,' Summerfield Johnston recalled.

The bottlers Coke anointed parted from tradition in other ways. Every bottler that added territory had to sign a revised bottling agreement, which promised Coke regular and unlimited increases in the price of concentrate that had been denied for so many years. That was what Coke executives really wanted: complete control over the price they charged for syrup, influenced not by words in an antiquated contract but by what they needed to do in order to make their company's profits soar.

The new contract was known as the MBA, which stood for 'master bottling agreement'. To bottlers who wanted to grow or survive, it seemed like an offer they couldn't refuse. They took out their gold fountain pens and signed. 'It was traumatic,' Johnston said. 'Coke's viewpoint was that they couldn't do the advertising without the flow of funds. And I suppose that was right.'

The pressure on bottlers to come around to that way of thinking was enormous and unrelenting, and not always polite. 'There were some cases where the bottler was told, "We don't want you in the business anymore if you don't do it our way,"' a former Coke executive recalled. At the company's disposal were hundreds of millions of dollars in marketing support, the underpinning of a bottler's ability to offer a 'special' against his competitors, or to persuade a new account to take Coca-Cola because he would personally install a new refrigerator case. A bottler cut loose from that largesse would find himself in trouble as a result, even if everything else about his business was fine. Pepsi bottlers had all kinds of marketing support, and Coke bottlers had learned long ago that they couldn't live without it themselves. By 1980, the soft-drink field had narrowed considerably, with more than three fourths of the market in the United States held by Coke and Pepsi. The also-rans were just that, barely in the considerations of executives at the two giants.

Coke executives understood the power of marketing funds, which became an ever-larger proportion of Coke's corporate budget as time went on, and quickly realized they could be used to drive Coke's agenda. The professional managers hired to run family bottling businesses as the entrepreneurial spirit thinned in some bottling bloodlines presented another means for Coke to reorder the world its way. 'To make a manager look good, and to persuade him to sign the amended contract, Big Coke would provide a dollar a gallon in extra marketing support,' Bondurant said. That support fattened a bottler's profits, leading to rewards for the manager. While such spending could be costly in the short term, 'Big Coke had a long horizon.'

The various pressures reduced the bottlers' ranks by about 50 percent between 1978 and 1985. During those years there was also another important development, which came not from Atlanta but from Washington. For some time, off and on, the Federal Trade Commission had been investigating the exclusive franchise system under which the bottlers of Coke, Pepsi, and every other soft drink in the United States operated. Were the franchises legal? Did the system promote competition, or was it ultimately harmful to consumers?

In 1971 the FTC had sued Coke, Pepsi, and nine other soft-drink concentrate makers, claiming that the exclusive agreements were not conducive to fair pricing. By 1978 the case was languishing on appeal. But for the Coca-Cola bottlers, as well as bottlers of other drinks, it created an enormous cloud over the future. If exclusivity was upheld, it would enhance the value of a Coca-Cola bottling franchise. If it was not, that would probably destroy the world of Coke.

Despite all their contentiousness toward Coke, the bottlers remained like family to one another. They got to know one another at picnics and conventions. They had professional associations, trade journals like *The Coca-Cola Bottler,* and annual get-togethers where they were taught new bottling and sales techniques. And they were bound by common tradition, by being Coca-Cola bottlers who not only poured soda into the marketplace, but also handed out souvenirs to remember Coca-Cola by. One of the most popular was a wooden ruler, printed with this advice: 'Do unto others as you would have them do unto you.'

As a child, Bill Schmidt used to jump onto the conveyor belt that carried cases of empty soda bottles in from the trucks so they could be washed by the machine in his father's bottling plant in Elizabethtown, Kentucky. Workers outside would see a case of bottles, followed by another case of bottles, and then a case with a jubilant two-year-old boy inside, waving to them as the conveyor belt swept him along. Sometimes they'd settle him into a corner with a crate and a hammer and a handful of nails and just let him pound to his heart's content. When he was sixteen, Schmidt began working in the plant.

'Our two sons knew that if they ever had any trouble on the road, anywhere, they were to get in touch with the local Coca-Cola bottler,' said Jan Schmidt, elegant and California-born, who had never set foot inside a bottling plant until she met Bill. 'One night our phone rang, and it was the police. They said a man driving through town had had a heart attack, and they called us because he was a Coca-Cola bottler.' The Schmidts made sure the man, who was from Ohio, was getting the medical care he needed. Then workers at their plant checked on him every day while he was in the hospital.

The idea that the market value, as well as the business rules, of all these family enterprises could be wiped out by government decree frightened the bottlers. The Schmidts and their friends referred to the possibility as 'if the walls come down': the walls that separated one bottler from another and allowed them each to independently flourish without fear of one another. If the walls vanished, then being a Coca-Cola bottler would be meaningless. Someone bigger and better organized could invade your territory, sell to all your customers, and destroy your business.

Rather than waiting for the ruling from the FTC, a group of congressmen, encouraged by Coke and Pepsi, took matters into their own hands. In 1979, a matching pair of legislative proposals was introduced into the House and the Senate. Both urged unusual protection for the soft-drink industry from the antitrust rules that governed nearly every other sector, arguing that exclusive franchises made sense from a number of perspectives. First of all, the bills contended, many bottlers were mom-and-pop businesses, kept in their families for generations and struggling, as it were, to make a living. At the moment that the bill was written, bottlers all over the country were among the wealthiest people anywhere. Though they may have worked hard, they also made a lot of money, and the implication that they in any way resembled the usual definition of a struggling small-business owner was a strained one.

Then there was the environmental argument. The United States in the late 1970s was a country worried about global warming, about wasteful packaging, about using up precious resources unnecessarily. The authors of the legislation tapped into that worry, maintaining that though most bottlers used glass returnable bottles, if exclusive franchises were taken away it would be that much harder for a bottler to recover all of his returnables. Anything that supported the use of returnable bottles also helped conserve energy. In fact, the industry was rapidly moving to substitute glass bottles – always dangerous, because of their fragility, and always costly, precisely because of the need to track them down and collect them in the field – with plastic.

Inside the administration of President Jimmy Carter – whose unlikely campaign in 1976 for the White House had had the strong support of Coke's president at the time, Paul Austin – the legislation, known as the Soft Drink Interbrand Competition Act, caused plenty of anguish. Members of Congress, urged on by local bottlers as well as by the Coca-Cola Company, said they would support it, by and large. But 'the bottlers bill is special interest legislation,' wrote Ky Ewing, the Justice Department's antitrust expert. 'This would be the first time since 1922 that Congress has authorized an antitrust exemption for conduct that is not part of a federal program and not specifically regulated by a government agency. The soft-drink industry has presented no evidence sufficient to demonstrate that it should be singled out for a special exemption not granted other industries operating through franchised distributors.'

Soon it was 1980, an election year, and Carter faced opposition within his own party from Senator Edward Kennedy. There was also John Anderson, a congressman who was running as an independent. And then there was the governor of California, Ronald Reagan, who campaigned hard as a friend of business. 'The bill provides a rare opportunity for the president to demonstrate his beliefs in a manner that is likely to regain support in areas of recent losses and defections to Kennedy and Anderson,' a Carter adviser, Bob Malson, told one of his peers in a memo. At the same time, it was 'particularly troublesome because it brings into conflict the pro-competition and pro-consumer policies of this administration, on one hand, and the overwhelming Congressional votes, on the other.'

Carter faced a nearly impossible situation. The bill had undeniable support – there were, after all, still hundreds of local bottlers in business – and the political quagmire didn't help. Coke, Pepsi, and their competitors in the soft-drink industry did their part, investing in hundreds of drinks, lunches, gifts, and other forms of influence to support the bill as the vote neared. The vote in the House was 377 to 34, and the Senate passed it 89 to 3.

Carter declined to veto it, asserting, after obtaining some language changes, that it did not hinder competition. The new law reinforced the system, ending the FTC's challenges to the franchise practice and making it abundantly clear that the competitive practices involved in owning a Coca-Cola franchise were practically inalienable rights under the Soft Drink Interbrand Competition Act. While Coke had argued on behalf of the mom-and-pop nature of the soft-drink bottling business during the deliberations, after the bill became law the company's plan to eliminate as many of those bottlers as possible picked up speed.

'The preoccupation of the company in the late 1970s was to preserve the system, not to promote the product,' Keough recalled. Once victory was in hand, the priorities could shift.

Because the bottlers did not compete with one another, Coke theoretically could sell syrup at one price in one franchise territory and at a lower or higher point somewhere else without attracting the attention of federal antitrust enforcers. As sole dispenser of that syrup, Coke could do what it liked without fear of government interference. Some feared that Coke-owned bottlers, or Coke-approved bottlers, might benefit at the expense of other bottlers that Coke wanted to see shut down.

The company stepped up its campaign to get every bottler to agree to that amended contract. Some acquiesced, just to have peace; others promised to sign in exchange for more franchises. The families that wanted out of the business, for reasons ranging from internal strife to the desire to do something else, put their franchises up for sale. Coke oversaw the transfers, signing off on the deals that met with its approval.

Out of the upheaval, Coke crafted Coca-Cola Enterprises. The bottling company went public in November 1986, although the price, at $16.50 a share, fell far short of the twenty-seven dollars Goizueta had wanted. Even at that discount, the project generated an enormous windfall for Coke. At the end of the first day of trading, Coca-Cola Enterprises had spouted a total of $1.18 billion in cash, despite doubts and questions surrounding the new company.

Not one analyst completely understood the relationship between Coca-Cola Enterprises and Coke, and more than one didn't like the concept. They questioned it, to the annoyance of Goizueta, and some felt the company's responses were arrogant. 'There was a sense of them saying, "We're the Coca-Cola Company, and you either believe us or you don't,"' one analyst recalled. But when the time arrived, the stock did sell, with Goizueta and Keough laughing and applauding with delight.

They had rolled the $3 billion debt from the purchase of those bottlers right off the Coca-Cola Company's books, depositing it onto the balance sheet of the new company instead. Coke was relatively debt-free by comparison, and with suddenly no interest to pay after having bought up all those bottlers, its earnings got an extra lift. Meanwhile, thanks to the new contract terms, it was selling more syrup and making more money on every gallon than it ever had before. Bells went off in the canyons of Wall Street, faintly at first, as investors noticed what was happening at the Coca-Cola Company. Then they grew louder.

Coke's new bottler, despite its mountain of debt, began to get some respect as well. 'At the end of its first year, Coca-Cola Enterprises, the biggest soft-drink bottler in the country, has made good on its grandiose plans and won grudging acceptance on Wall Street,' *The Atlanta Journal-Constitution* reported late in 1987, noting that cash flow had risen 19 percent for the first three quarters of the year. 'The company's performance,' the paper continued, 'is what Chief Executive Officer Brian G. Dyson likes to refer to as "the proof of the vision".'

By then, analysts and investors had fallen head over heels for the Coca-Cola Company. With virtually no debt, and more control over its bottling than it had had at any time in the past, Coke had that much more money to share among investors. Even currency fluctuations, the longtime bête noire of the company, mattered less now. Earnings were generous, and happy shareholders talked about them. Their friends surged in to buy themselves some shares, too. Coke's stock took off, rising and splitting, rising and splitting again.

People all over the country, but especially right around Atlanta, where thousands owned shares of Coke that in many cases dated back to the 1920s, were suddenly rich. And the spiral, helped along by the new Coca-Cola system, continued.

The more Coke earned, the more excited investors got. The excitement extended to Omaha, where Warren Buffett, the leader of Berkshire Hathaway, saw what was happening and quietly sank millions of dollars into Coke stock until Berkshire was the company's single largest shareholder. Coke also attracted the managers of scores of mutual funds, who were in charge of handling money for investors large and small. The excitement was everywhere.

All this figured prominently in the plan to remake Coke, a plan that Roberto Goizueta had in mind as he took over as the company's CEO in early 1981. He found himself leading a company that was afflicted. More than two years with all six men holding the same title, that of vice chairman, had stalled some things about the business, as everyone waited to see who would be chosen. All of them wanted to snare the top job, the grand prize, the chance to run Coke.

Keough, to his great surprise, had finished second in that contest. He had done all the things he thought he was supposed to do, and more. He had cultivated Bob Woodruff, Coke's longtime chairman, the way a person had to if he was going to get ahead. Woodruff liked to mark his senior executives' birthdays with a delivery of red roses – sometimes one, sometimes three, sometimes dozens. Most of the time they were Tropicanas, which were Woodruff's favorite. Keough got the flowers, just as Goizueta did, and Claus Halle, another contender, and Ian Wilson, yet another. Keough made a point of responding with thank-you notes year after year, which Woodruff squirreled away into a file. 'I'm a very lucky fifty-one-year-old,' the rising star mused in 1977, after receiving a few stems from Woodruff.

Keough wanted very, very badly to be the next chairman of the Coca-Cola Company. He was inching toward the prize, and felt confident that he would get it. He'd traveled all over the world for the company, worked with the bottlers as no one else had, and developed strong relationships, even friendships, with all kinds of people on behalf of the Coca-Cola Company. He was heard, more than once, declaring that he would be taking over the reins from Paul Austin.

Keough had always believed in personal politics, and he knew they could play to his advantage. When he was in the third grade he had begun serving as an altar boy in Sioux City, working the 6:30 A.M. Mass held every Sunday at the bishop's residence. He continued right through high school. The same bishop intervened to get him a spot in the Creighton University freshman class in 1945, the year returning servicemen flooded enrollments at colleges all over the country. Keough got through Creighton, then interned at an Omaha radio station, where he befriended a then-obscure announcer named Johnny Carson. Carson's sidekick on *The Tonight Show* years later, Ed McMahon, looked almost exactly like Don Keough.

On the air, Keough called plays for the Nebraska Cornhuskers football team, and he learned how to take the offensive on his own behalf. In 1971 he began shipping baskets of lemons from the Minute Maid Company in Houston, where he had become president, to Woodruff's office in Atlanta. *The Boss appreciates your thoughtfulness,* Woodruff's longtime assistant, Joseph Jones, wrote on a sheet of onionskin, *and sends you his very best wishes.*

When Woodruff alerted Keough that a friend of his flying somewhere on Eastern Airlines had asked for a Coke and had been told there was only Pepsi at 35,000 feet, Keough launched a thorough investigation into the matter and submitted a thick report. And when Keough traveled to Ichauway, Woodruff's favorite hunting and proving ground in southern Georgia, he produced an encomium for the place and its owner that went well beyond the typical thank-you note. *I'm a very lucky man, Mr. Woodruff, for a great many reasons,* the letter, in Keough's sprawling cursive, concluded. *One very special reason, which will always be special, is that I have been privileged to know you – and therefore to know all of the best of human character.*

His luck would change in 1980, when Roberto Goizueta was picked to become the president of Coke, en route to taking over as chairman and chief executive the next year. Before Goizueta was chosen, there had been a flurry of letters to Woodruff on Keough's behalf. It was clear who had urged the writers to stick their necks out. *I would like to suggest that your fine Company, even with its diversified interests, needs the strong leadership of a dynamic American salesman,* Bob Wilkinson, a Huntsville, Alabama, resident who had acquired a bottling franchise in the 1950s, informed Woodruff.

Such appeals made no difference. No one knew precisely what prompted Woodruff to pick Goizueta and not Keough. Perhaps it was Goizueta's habit of popping in on Woodruff when their offices were next door to each other in Coke's old headquarters. Some tell a story about Woodruff's not liking the toilet in his private bathroom in the new building, which Goizueta, then the head of the technical department, addressed by ordering in a team of engineers who figured out a way to make the porcelain throne more acceptable. Others say Goizueta's patrician bearing was irresistible to Woodruff, who enjoyed spending time with U.S. presidents, and other celebrities. In any case, Woodruff clearly preferred him, and that was that.

Keough demonstrated that he knew when to fold. With his fate decided, he pledged allegiance to Goizueta, telling Woodruff that he was looking forward to what he called 'the decade of the 1980s', when he would be 'working under the banner of Roberto Goizueta'.

And as he went out the door more than twelve years later, having helped create a Coca-Cola Company that was as much a financial operation as a maker of soft-drink syrup, Keough had extracted one favor from Goizueta: Keough would continue to attend the board meetings, because of that five-year contract Goizueta gave him that made him a consultant to the board. He could keep an eye on things. He could keep an eye on that Doug Ivester.

He was far from sold on the idea that Ivester should run Coke one day, though by 1993 Ivester was poised to take over as president. Yes, the man was brilliant as a tactician and had played a major part in changing the company's fortunes. Still, sometimes, when Ivester was asked by Keough to bring him up-to-date on some project he had been working on, Ivester would come into the president's office and, almost offhandedly, mention that there were a couple of other things he wanted Keough to know about. When they were through, and Ivester had vanished again, Keough often found himself wondering: *What if I hadn't asked him to stop by? When would he have let me know about those two or three other things?* Keough did a lot of talking. Ivester did hardly any.

When Keough left Coke, to become chairman, at last, of Allen & Company (where there had been no chairman for more than twenty years), he persuaded Goizueta not to name anyone to the president's job just yet. Keough would tell people that he wanted his boss and friend to take plenty of time to make up his mind. If it had been up to Keough, he would have picked John Hunter, an angular Australian and a longtime protégé of his. Hunter seemed the obvious choice for Keough. Once, at a meeting in Japan, Keough even introduced him to a large gathering of Coke employees as the next president of the Coca-Cola Company.

Another favorite of Keough's was Peter Sealey, the creator of the 'Always' advertising campaign that was revolutionary for Coke in so many ways. Sealey had gone to Hollywood for Coke, running Columbia Pictures for the company during the years that Coke owned it. Sealey liked Hollywood so much that he grew a beard, like many of the moguls, and decided to stay. Coke wanted him back in Atlanta and said so. But he refused to budge.

It was Keough who had wooed him back in the fall of 1990, urging Sealey to revitalize Coke's advertising. Sealey had delivered, too, with a plan that gathered in Michael Ovitz, the Creative Artists agent, and assigned twenty-six commercials to a variety of film directors, box-office luminaries like Rob Reiner. They all worked around a single concept and came up with images like the computer-animated polar bears that would be a perennial favorite with viewers for years to come. The campaign was a success, and Sealey was a hero – for a while.

He understood the romantic underpinnings of Coke's place in the American scene. He had bonded the best of Hollywood to the Coke bottle, and the results had exceeded even Keough's wildest dreams. Coca-Cola got a new lift in the public consciousness. But Sealey was at odds with Ivester, who asked Sergio Zyman, the former Coke marketing chief, to help him develop an alternative advertising campaign. The two men met in Ivester's garage for a long series of Saturday-morning sessions, which Ivester would later describe as tutorials to bring him up to speed on marketing.

A few months after the unveiling of 'Always', and despite all the applause, Sealey was summoned to Ivester's office. It was near the end of 1993. 'Things just haven't worked out,' Ivester told him. Sealey, bereft of allies now that Keough was gone, had no choice but to go.

In the end, Ivester moved up into Keough's old job. John Hunter took early retirement. And from his office on Manhattan's Fifth Avenue, with its view of the University Club across the street and the bells of St. Thomas tolling down the way, Keough, bruised by that final power struggle, watched and waited. He kept an office in Atlanta, too, in a modern high-rise a few miles north of the Coke tower. He hoped for the best at Coke, and he had much invested in such an outcome: about 90 percent of his net worth, some 5 million of shares of Coca-Cola stock.

Though he was gone from the Coke tower, he was hardly unplugged from his old world. Bottlers and customers and shareholders still called him, from places like Chile and Italy and small towns in America. If they wanted his opinion, he was always happy to give it. When necessary, he would make a call to someone senior at Coke, to try to get whatever it was taken care of for whoever it was who had called him. He would pass along concerns – his own, and those he said came from other people.

He was also in close touch with two key directors on the Coke board. One of them was Herbert Allen, of course, who worked out of an office just down the hall. In Allen, he had a true admirer. 'He's the only businessman I've ever met, besides maybe Jack Welch, who could run for president and *be* president,' Allen would say. The other director was Warren Buffett, Coke's single largest shareholder, with some 200 million shares owned through Berkshire Hathaway.

Still, these days Don Keough's phone didn't ring quite as often. He had many more hours to devote to lunch, to his grandchildren, to interests like hunting and philanthropy and the activities of other publicly traded companies. He occupied a smaller space now. He had a lot more time for a lot of things, now that he was no longer the president of Coke.

Chapter Four

This Little Cuban Fellow

IN 1994, DESKTOP COMPUTERS were not yet wired to receive all the information foaming out of the New York Stock Exchange. So the Coca-Cola Company had one of its many conference rooms set aside for a very important purpose. The room, down the hall from the top executives' offices on the twenty-fifth floor of the Coke tower, held a machine capable of tracking moment-by-moment changes in trading volume, index performances, and specific share prices. A squat-looking little thing, it sat on a table all by itself, powered up nearly all the time.

During the day, at any given hour, people passing by that conference room might see a dark-haired man standing before the table. His back would be to the open door, his hands stuck inside the pockets of his suit jacket. Even from behind, everyone knew who he was: the chairman and chief executive of the Coca-Cola Company. And they knew what he was doing. He was watching the market move. Unaware of the employees passing down the hall behind him, undisturbed by conversations wafting in from other rooms, he was oblivious to everything but the green light coming from the screen.

Every time Roberto Crispulo Goizueta stopped to think about it, he had to remember. It was thanks to him that the world was crazy for Coke.

Normally, Goizueta did not preen. He was an intense man who took nearly everything he did seriously. He urged integrity and symbolized consistency. His schedule, when he was in town, was so precise and unchanging that people said they could set their watches by him. He stepped into his office every morning by seven forty-five, and stepped out again at four-thirty, regardless of what was happening in the world – the world of Coke, or the other one. But even he couldn't help noticing, not when his picture kept showing up on the cover of *Fortune* and his company was named the country's most admired, that he was special. When he went to an industry function and people treated him more like a pontiff than a chief executive, he noticed, too. When he stepped up to the podium to address a group of Wall Street analysts and the questions came at him politely and every single person nodded quietly as he spoke, then raced for the phones, he must have thought about it. It was really a remarkable thing.

He was the hero at the center of a company that, day by day and year by year, dazzled everyone. He had formed it, shaped it, taken the bones of the old Coca-Cola Company and turned them into something no one ever dreamed Coke could become: a hot stock, at the age of one hundred–plus, a sexy growth company with unlimited prospects despite its having peddled the same product for generations. Early on, Goizueta had styled himself as a master undaunted by history, unperturbed by the passage of time. He knew what he wanted to do with Coke, and he did it.

He made his mark by breaking down traditional ways of doing business, challenging people to justify what they did all day and then ordering them to do it differently. When he was made supreme leader of the Coca-Cola Company in 1981, he brought with him a notion that the company needed to change, and that he was the one – the soft-spoken renegade in pinstripes – who would make it into something better.

Goizueta was in many ways a different kind of leader from all the others who preceded him at Coke. He was the first non-southerner to lead the company. He had been born in Cuba, hundreds of nautical miles from the nearest peach tree, and he had never been directly responsible for persuading anyone to buy a Coca-Cola. He was a technical expert whose Coke life began as overseer of a bottling plant. His training was as a chemical engineer, and his job was to deal with the drab mechanics of transforming an ingredient list into a recognizable flavor. He was about the furthest thing possible from a salesman charming his way across the landscape. He told the occasional joke, but mostly 'he was a serious Cuban,' as Herbert Allen put it.

To the American bottlers, he was 'Row-burr-toe', a name pronounced in three exaggerated syllables, a person whose manner and background were completely foreign, even comical at times. To the rank and file at Coke, he was 'Mr. Goizueta', a name they at first had trouble pronouncing (it is 'Goy-SWEAT-uh', though it got butchered into 'Go-zeetah', 'Gazettah', and worse) and a character they had trouble trying to comprehend. But the choice of him to be Coke's supreme leader was a signal to the world that Coke was a global company, not just an American one, and from the start he made himself appear an unflappable, aloof individual with conservative political and personal views. Modest, sometimes, too. 'I don't know what this little Cuban fellow is doing here,' he once told a room packed with Coke bottlers, in the accented English that remained with him all his life, 'but anyway, I'm enjoying it.'

He concealed much beneath the surface.

Change had tattooed his own life so thoroughly and irretrievably that few people at Coke – many of whom lived a stone's throw from where they had been born and brought up – could begin to understand it. In 1960, when he was not yet thirty years old, he had discovered what it meant to have his heart crack into pieces, and then to have to proceed with a life that was a hollow substitute for what he had had before.

His experience made it that much easier for him to orchestrate massive change, to take risks in business that others might consider daunting. 'How much more could I lose than I have already lost?' he would say when contemplating a business move. This fate of his had come about because of who he was, and because of Coke, and because of the point on the planet where those two elements intersected at a particular moment in time.

He was born in Havana on a windy mid-November day in 1931. He was the third generation of his father's family to breathe the rum-splashed, gardenia-scented air of Cuba. The love of liberty that his forebears carried with them from the Basque region that is neither Spain nor France had been turned into something else by the time he came along. His people had arrived in Cuba yearning for freedom. Then they rose to the top of the social ladder and made it their business to stay there.

The Goizuetas and the Canteras, his mother's family, developed copious fortunes through a variety of enterprises, and Goizueta's boyhood was a catalog of privilege. He grew up in El Vedado, a neighborhood built where an ancient forest once stood. The homes were lavish and the children well fed, and El Vedado was also the spot where many Americans had settled after the Spanish-American War in 1898. The area begins at the eastern bank of the Rio Almendares, where a small colonial fortress, El Castillo de la Chorrera, marks the way to the sea and laps the coastline overlooking the Straits of Florida until it runs into Old Havana. Along the waterfront, as the young Roberto was growing up, were the hotels and nightclubs and restaurants that helped give the Cuban capital the allure of a tropical Las Vegas. Gangsters like Al Capone and Lucky Luciano are said to have followed the money, the booze, and the women to El Vedado, creating an empire of temptation that matched the one they built in the desert.

The Goizuetas lived in an ersatz Moorish castle that Crispulo Goizueta, an architect and real-estate developer, put up after the arrival of Roberto, his firstborn. When the elder Goizueta decided to follow the style of the finer homes in Havana and install a double-height stained-glass window over the sweeping staircase in his new house, he had to choose an image for the glass. He did not choose saints or a biblical theme, though the Goizuetas were churchgoing Roman Catholics. Nor did he ask an artist to come up with something abstract. Instead he settled on the image of Don Quixote, windmill in the background, sword at the ready – a traditional Spanish symbol for a traditional Cuban family, one that traced its lineage directly to the Old Country. That was the image that Roberto and his sisters, Olivia and Vivien, studied day in and day out as they scaled the stairs to their rooms and descended them again. What they saw was a two-dimensional Don Quixote, standing all alone there in the light seeping through the panes. No one else from the legend appeared.

Schooled by Jesuits at Belen Academy, Havana's premier private school for boys, Roberto Goizueta was dimly aware of another student a few years ahead of him, an heir to a sugar fortune who

had a reputation as a great baseball player. It was not until some
time after Goizueta had finished Belen, as well as a postgraduate
year at Cheshire Academy in Connecticut and four years at Yale,
that the other student, Fidel Castro, started to make a reputation
for himself in the Cuba they both considered home.

After graduating from Yale with a degree in chemical
engineering in 1953, Goizueta returned to Havana to marry his
childhood sweetheart. The wedding was a major social event in the
early days of that summer, and afterward Goizueta slipped easily
back into the life he had always known. He went to work for his
father, an arrangement that everyone agreed, in an unhurried sort
of way, would be temporary. He felt the warm sun on his face,
picked up games of tennis at the club with old friends, smoked his
cigarettes, and cut a familiar figure along the boulevards of his
neighborhood. It was what he had expected to do all along, during
the five-year absence that getting a first-class education had
required. He was back in Cuba, back in the place he loved, and this
was where he would make his living, raise his family, and grow old
and wrinkled like the fishermen perching on the seawall that held
back the restless waves.

He lived in a place known as the Queen of the Antilles, famed
for its beauty and long a destination for the disenchanted. 'No
pencil can give an adequate picture of Havana as one enters its
harbor,' wrote Eliza McHatton Ripley, a Georgia woman who fled
the ravages of the Civil War for Cuba in the 1870s. 'It is the
loveliest gem of the ocean. To us, who had so long dealt with the
rough realities of life, it was as a bit of fairy-land, where everybody
was happy, sailing, driving and gliding about, for very lack of
work-day occupation.'

Havana in the 1950s was every inch a paradise for Cubans who
had made their fortunes in tobacco, sugar, pineapples, and real
estate. They wandered from their palazzos along the waterfront to
their business appointments or lunch dates, stopping for tiny cups
of thick Cuban coffee or bottles of sugary-sweet Coca-Cola with
their friends. Everybody in this circle, *todo el mundo,* had boats and
big cars and a fine education, the better to manage their fortunes
with. As teenagers they traveled abroad for school; as adults they
were expected to follow the example set by their parents,

participating in a society both elegant and indolent, part fact and part desire. In summer the women wore pearls and ate ice cream at El Carmelo, a popular gathering place, and in winter, which barely occurred, they put on lavish furs and ordered hot chocolate there, too. The men played golf and tennis with one another and entertained guests on their boats and at their seaside retreats. They behaved like sturdy, conservative custodians of the status quo, appearing in the right places with their wives on their arms. At the same time they had their flings, too. It was their island, and it was a wonderful life for everyone who had money.

Families like Goizueta's got everything they wanted in Cuba. They controlled every industry on the island and pocketed enormous proportions of the wealth. But they comprised a tiny proportion of the whole. The vast majority of Cubans traced their ancestors to Africa, the source of the slaves who worked the sugarcane plantations that brought so much wealth to their owners and made Cuba the largest producer of sugar in the world. The gap between rich and poor usually involved skin color, and there was unhappiness on a massive scale among many of the poor. Some of them, while working as maids or drivers or merchant sailors or garbagemen, cursed their lot and gave to a cause that promised to correct this imbalance. The cause was led by Castro, at times an exile in the United States, at other times a guerrilla warrior hiding in the leafy mountains of Cuba, waiting for his moment.

Most of Castro's sympathizers worked for people who were all but oblivious to his existence. They lived their lives; the servants and the blue-collar workers lived theirs. This was the way it had always been.

Goizueta and his wife, Olguita, were expecting their first child in the summer of 1954, when Goizueta, who had been working for his father, decided to find himself a real job. Cigarette in hand, he was perusing the want ads in the local newspaper when he spotted one that sought an English-speaking chemical engineer. 'A recent graduate', the ad specified in Spanish.

He would say later that he had no idea what company it was when he applied for what was obviously an entry-level post. He was granted an interview by mail, and, still clueless as to the specific company, he drove to the address he had been given for the interview. When he arrived, he saw the wooden COCA-COLA lettering on the outside of the building and realized where he was going. Of course he was well acquainted with Coke; everybody was. Coke was the kind of company, he must have thought, where he would be sure to have a good, prosperous, contented future.

Coke at that time had been doing business in Cuba for close to half a century. Coke looked to Cuba for much of the sugar that was such a critical ingredient in Coca-Cola syrup, and Cuba had also played an unwitting role in the creation of the Coca-Cola bottling system. Cuba held special significance for Asa Candler, the man who put Coca-Cola on the map, on a completely different front. One of his ten siblings, Warren Akin Candler, became a Methodist bishop in 1898 and was instructed to begin a mission in Cuba following the war's end. At the same time, Asa Candler was searching for new markets in which to sell Coca-Cola. The brothers set their sights on Cuba simultaneously, and both met with disappointing results. Bishop Candler complained about the Cubans' 'dullness', while Candler's deputy in Cuba wailed about how 'the average Cuban doesn't know and doesn't care what he is drinking, and the words "hygienic", "pure materials", and "cleanliness" have no meaning to him.' On an upbeat note, the same man also asserted that, 'once he learns that there is a difference, that Coca-Cola has more to it than wetness or sweetness, we have secured a steady customer and an advocate of the drink.'

Bishop Candler started a college in Havana, and its biggest benefactor was his brother Asa. This was the legacy they left in Cuba, along with Warren Candler's winning a few converts to Methodism, and Asa Candler's selling millions of servings of Coca-Cola. Both of them viewed education as an intrinsic part of capturing souls, whether for ideology or for soft drinks. What they wanted was for the world to grow to imitate the United States – for better or for worse, for business and for salvation. Education, courtesy of the Methodists, was supposed to accomplish this. 'Our universities, if they are richly endowed and adequately equipped, will serve this end more effectually than all the consuls and commercial agents in the world,' Warren Candler once declared. 'In this matter our commercial interests and our religious duty coincide.'

Coke continued to sell its drinks in Cuba, with results that rose and fell like swells after a storm. In 1919, Cuba was going great, according to a report in the bottlers' magazine that year. 'He has never seen Cuba so prosperous,' the magazine announced, quoting H. F. Bray, a manager at one of the plants there, 'nor with a better outlook for every kind of industry on the island.' In the thin years, Cuba was dismissed with a murmur, by the same publication, as one more place where Coke was doing business.

Goizueta knew little about the history woven between Cuba and Coke; in his world, when someone in Cuba mentioned Coke it was usually to give an order to the waiter. His interview at the Havana bottling plant went well and he started work on the Fourth of July. For the next five years he was a quality-control specialist whose job was all about the tedious but essential technical details of making Coke fit for consumption: the ingredients, the coloring, the results after it was bottled and distributed. He worked for the Coca-Cola Company, making sure the bottling plant did everything right. He occupied himself with problems like rusty marks on bottle exteriors, coming up with solutions he derived from his chemistry studies. Eventually his responsibilities widened to all five of the country's Coca-Cola factories.

During the years that Goizueta was establishing himself as a Coke executive, Castro's influence was growing, too. Fighting the forces of President Fulgencio Batista, Castro's troops assembled a string of victories that led them into Havana by January 1, 1959. Their bearded leader declared himself the leader of all Cuba. And as his vision of a socialist utopia gave way to dictatorship, many of his new subjects found his exercise of power appalling.

For Cubans like the Goizuetas, Castro's regime began harshly. Martial law was declared, monitored by *barbudos,* the rough-edged and heavily armed fighters who made up Castro's guerrilla brigades. Houses in the better neighborhoods were ransacked, their frightened owners standing mutely by, and safe-deposit boxes were confiscated, all in the name of patriotism. Wealthy men were stopped on the street and sometimes taken prisoner for days at a time, all under orders from the new government. Most of the time they came home again; now and then they did not. Many people decided to leave Cuba, starting with the wealthy. Owners of sugar refineries and textile mills vanished, then resurfaced in Mexico or Miami and other safe havens. Their families followed them, always saying they were 'going on vacation'. Huge and beautiful palazzos stood empty along the streets, seeming to hold their breath while they waited for their owners, who had said they'd be back before long. As with countless upheavals in the past, nearly everybody believed this one would last only a short while.

At the Coke plant in Havana, Goizueta continued to arrive for work every day as if nothing had changed, as impeccably dressed and clean-shaven as always. But the new reality caught up with him. Soldiers stopped him and emptied out his briefcase one night, apparently to make sure he was not hiding any important company information from the government. Another time, he was ordered to alter the formula for Coca-Cola, something a Coke man would do only at bayonet point. He had to use burnt sugar instead of caramel color to give the finished product its characteristic dark brown shade, since sugar was an indigenous, and therefore patriotic, element and the caramel color was not. Goizueta did as he was told, and when the officials tasted the soda that resulted they recoiled and left Coke alone to follow its usual recipe.

A little more than a year after Castro rose to power, Goizueta and his family concluded that they could no longer stay in Cuba. A visit to Atlanta apparently sealed the decision; intelligence reports gathered by the Coca-Cola Company indicated that sooner rather than later, anyone with anything to lose should get out of the country. The company feared that its factories could be nationalized by Castro, and in any case, with hostility growing between the American government and the Cuban leader, an American company was an obvious target for retaliation.

Leaving Cuba was the bitterest pill for Goizueta, by then a father of three, who weighed his heritage on one hand and his family's safety on the other. The difficulty in getting to the hospital the day the third baby was born may have helped him decide that it was time to go. He sent the children, Robby, Olga, and Jaime, on their own to Miami in the spring of 1960, where Olguita's parents had already fled, and once he had wrapped up one last company project – making sure a soda called Sprite would launch as planned – he and Olguita packed their bags, too.

They left inconspicuously. Cubans were still permitted to travel; but to discourage permanent flight, no one was allowed to take more than a few dollars with them on any plane bound for points outside the country. There was no wiring cash abroad, no transferring assets beyond Cuban shores. Everything – the elegant drawing rooms, the gardens overflowing with red and yellow blossoms, the light on the sea in the afternoon – had to stay where it was, moored forever to the island under Castro's control.

The Goizuetas had a little money with them when they turned away from their country. They had suitcases, too, filled with only enough clothes to support their claim that they would return in a couple of weeks. They abandoned everything else they owned: their house, their cars, their books, their bank accounts, the children's toys, the stained-glass portrait of Don Quixote. It was a farewell to what they had been. Roberto Goizueta, his wife, and his children would have to start over, in the United States, from scratch. Though in the beginning he, like many upper-class exiles, probably believed that he would be back before long, he would never see his beloved country again.

He became one of the thousands who left Cuba, but for whom Cuba would never leave their thoughts. The new Cuba, the one ruled by Castro, was just a temporary inconvenience. The old Cuba would surface in their dreams, causing them to smile as they slumbered, and disappear again with the morning light. It remained tantalizingly close, just ninety miles from Miami, but impossible to reach. On some days, when they felt the ache and the longing for Cuba especially sharply, exiles comforted themselves with the thought that before long, Castro would be finished. A man like that couldn't hold on; the United States, champion of democracy, could not stomach a Communist regime so close to home.

Goizueta covered his anguish with work. He had always had the ability to focus completely on a task, whether it was studying for exams in college or engaging his friends in debate. And now, living in Miami with three small children and a wife who felt at least as displaced as he did, he threw himself into the Coca-Cola Company once more.

Coke had a job waiting for him in which he would supervise technical operations across the Caribbean as part of the Latin

American division. The job paid $18,000 a year, a decent salary in the early sixties, even for a family of five. But the whole experience of having to live on a salary – in Havana, his way had been paid by his family – and the concept of making his income cover his expenses were strange and unfamiliar ones. For a while they lived crowded into a one-bedroom apartment, the best they could find, and waited for things to get better. Other former executives washed cars or served meals for a living, scraping by in a country that, despite the palm fronds and the tropical waters and the sky stirred by thunder all summer long, was definitely not their own.

The Goizuetas also had to rebuild their social lives, which was not so hard in Miami. They soon had a network of old and new friends within the Cuban community that became known as Little Havana. The influx colorized Eighth Street, or Calle Ocho, with all the memories of Cuba that the new residents could muster. It became a place where you could find a band that knew the tunes you had been accustomed to hearing back home, and order a plate of *ropa vieja* with sides of black beans and fried green plantains that weren't bad. There were dominoes, and there were often good cigars. You might even be able to forget, for a moment, that unaccustomed sense of being an outsider, the stares of other Miamians when you spoke in Spanish or the looks they gave you when they took in your darkness, whether it was in the eyes or the hair or the skin. They said rude things, too, referring to 'Cuban time', which implied that Cubans arrived later and did things more slowly than everybody else. Cuban children might find seats in the schools, but their Cuban parents were not welcome in the country clubs.

The truth was that strolling down Eighth Street in Miami hardly compared with being a prince of the real Havana. Like many exiles, Goizueta sometimes seemed to be simply waiting for the day when he would be able to resume his old life. He kept the clothes that he had brought with him in the suitcases he and Olguita took to the airport on their last day – clothes that had been washed and ironed and cared for by people who used to work for him, clothes that stood out in his new home, where other exiles purchased fresh wardrobes in local stores and tried hard to fit in. *Two years,* many of them told themselves when they left. *Two years, and we'll be back.*

Some filed claims on the property they had left behind – claims they planned to pursue once the Castro regime ended. They were sure it would end; they just had to wait a little while.

As time passed, it became clear to many of them that they could not return to the Cuba they had known and loved. Goizueta's parents and his sisters got out of Cuba, heading to Mexico the same year he and Olguita fled. Even the Jesuits who ran his old school picked up and left, relocating Belen Academy in Miami. Castro turned Crispulo Goizueta's house into a school, leaving the window with the quixotic knight intact but rededicating the place to his own purposes. Appearances were deceiving; neighborhoods might seem the same from the outside, but the life going on inside the grand mansions of Goizueta's youth had been completely transformed.

Goizueta kept most of his feelings hidden. With his long ovoid face, the kind of face that turns up in portraits of Spanish noblemen and curates, and his wonderful grooming and his quiet manner, hardly anyone he met in Miami would have guessed the turmoil churning just behind his eyes. 'Olguita would often ask if they could go back,' recalls one former colleague. 'And he would say he never wanted to go back, because the Cuba that he knew no longer existed.' He believed that he had been through the worst experience of his life.

Meanwhile, he did his job and did it well. Within four years he was called to Atlanta and moved the family there, into a small four-bedroom house that he would live in for the rest of his life. He would study the company's management structure and win himself promotions through a series of changes in the way Coca-Cola had always done things. He saw no reason to stick with the past, with Coca-Cola tradition, if it wasn't working as well as it possibly could. He could be ruthless about change. He knew all about change now. And he had little sympathy for people who didn't want to go along with his plans. Altering a business model or fine-tuning a procedure was small-time compared with what he had endured.

He transferred to Atlanta at the behest of Paul Austin, a rugged, redheaded Georgia native with a pair of Harvard degrees who had become Coke's president in 1962. Austin led Coke with drama and

flair. For years before he arrived, Coke had enjoyed its reputation
as purveyor of the country's best-known soft drink, but to Austin
many of its executives had displayed a tendency to be content with
all the brand already stood for – and did not try to improve upon
that. Despite owning the bestselling soft drink in the world, Coke's
stock had been a plodder, generating a solid return but doing
nothing spectacular. Austin wanted to change that, and he wanted
Goizueta's help.

With no special training in how to motivate an organization,
Goizueta took on the task, reconfiguring various aspects of the
company, from the way salaries were determined to the way
research and development were conducted. He cut through
tradition, dictating that old habits must be improved or jettisoned
so that Coke's business could be stronger. He and Austin became
close and, more important, he saw how the vast corporate
superstructure of the company worked. He saw how he could
make it better.

His rise was steady and sure. He even learned the formula for
making Coca-Cola, something that remained a highly classified
nugget of company information, as it had been in Candler's era. He
gained a toehold in the technical department, the true home of the
brand, by taking a job as executive assistant to Cliff Shillinglaw,
who at the time was the man entrusted with gathering, from
various places around the globe, obscure raw materials, like cassia
leaves, that were essential ingredients in the Coke formula.
Executive assistants at Coke shadowed their bosses, working as
their right-hand men and also, when necessary, standing in for
them. When Shillinglaw, globe-trotting to collect the ingredients,
suffered a massive heart attack in his London hotel room in 1974,
Goizueta found an opportunity. Coordinating the care of
Shillinglaw from afar and calming the concerns of Coke's revered
but aging chairman, Robert Woodruff, at home, he distinguished
himself as an even-keeled executive, the kind the Coca-Cola
Company preferred. He coordinated the safe transport of the cassia
leaves and other materials Shillinglaw had in his possession when
he fell ill. Goizueta got them to Atlanta – inside someone else's hat.
It was after this that he was told the secret formula, in a rite carried
out at the Atlanta headquarters with all the solemnity and pomp

one might expect. With that knowledge came a promotion, to senior vice president of the technical division. It made Goizueta a prince in waiting, someone destined for the top of the Coke pyramid.

Along the way, he and his family suffered another devastating blow. This time it was the death of their fourth child and youngest son, Carlos, born four years after they arrived in the United States. The little boy was given a diagnosis of leukemia in 1968 at the age of four, and in 1970, just before Christmas and only a few weeks after Goizueta quietly told colleagues that his son was ill, little Carlos was gone. He was buried in an Atlanta cemetery, and his loss took another piece of his father's heart.

But there was work waiting for Goizueta when he emerged from the brief period of mourning that he allowed himself, and he was soon in full swing again, moving his way up the Coke ladder. His non-American background held immense appeal for someone like Paul Austin, who had always considered the company to be an international one. Goizueta's sense of duty, too, combined with the formality he maintained at the office (he made a point of rarely being seen in shirtsleeves), helped turn him into a Coca-Cola superstar.

By 1980, the time had come for a changing of the guard at the very top of the company, the first such moment since Goizueta arrived in Atlanta. And he was in the running.

It would not be an easy glide at all. Austin, for reasons he kept to himself, had named six people, including Goizueta, to the same post – vice chairman – by 1979. That year, as the moment approached for Austin to retire (he was about to turn sixty-five), the jockeying among those six vice chairmen grew sharper and more intense. Goizueta thought he had a good shot, a legitimate claim to running the company; so did Don Keough, and Ian Wilson, Ira Herbert and the others, all for distinctly different reasons. The company shook from within as the six battled for power. They blocked one another's plans and stymied movement within the company. One former accountant with Ernst & Ernst, Coke's auditor, remembered that it became difficult to get anyone to sign off on anything, so sustained and distracting was the competition among the forces each of the vice chairmen controlled. Austin was said to have watched it all unfold with a detached glee. Everyone paid careful homage to Woodruff, in the process, too.

It was Goizueta who finally took control of what he considered to be the greatest company in the world. Early in 1981, he moved into his new office, which opened onto a broad circular staircase that connected the top three floors of the Coke tower. As he stood along the railing on the twenty-fifth floor, pondering all that lay before him, Coke itself stood on the cusp of enormous internal change. Not only were there new processes in place that he had helped design, gradually but insistently altering the old way of doing things, and not only did Goizueta have ideas he was anxious to put to work – there was also the prospect of a future without Woodruff, the legendary Coke leader known for good reason as 'The Boss', who had wielded power officially and unofficially for the past fifty-eight years. Woodruff had been responsible for anointing Goizueta, after Austin had chosen another vice chairman, Ian Wilson. But it was probably his last stand. Goizueta knew that Woodruff would not be a force within Coke much longer.

For so long, longer than Goizueta's entire life, Robert Winship Woodruff had controlled nearly everything about the Coca-Cola Company. He was ninety-one when Goizueta became chairman and chief executive, and he certainly knew who Goizueta was: There was no chance that anyone could have worked his way to the top of the company without Woodruff's stamp of approval. He lived and breathed Coke; he *was* Coke.

Stocky, usually unsmiling, he had gained power in the company by virtue of patrimony, like a nobleman, but he had worked hard for the better part of a century to keep it. He would be a taskmaster and a tough act to follow for all who came after him. His power was, as everyone readily admitted, absolute. Other men might be president or chairman, but this man was the one everyone called 'The Boss' and he was treated that way, too.

Woodruff's father, Ernest, had been the leader of the consortium of bankers that paid $25 million to take over the Coca-Cola Company from Asa Candler a few months after the end of World War I. By 1923, with multiple problems weighing down the business, the elder Woodruff asked his son, an executive at the

White Motor Company in Cleveland, Ohio, to come to Atlanta and help him out. Woodruff was dutiful, and though there was little affection between him and his father, he did what was asked of him. He got the title of president, and control of the company for the next sixty-two years.

When he arrived, the company was sputtering, despite owning the best-known soft drink in the land. Sales of Coca-Cola had been flat the year before, even after management introduced innovations like a cardboard carton that held six bottles and was supposed to encourage people to buy more and take it home. A recent slogan, 'Thirst Knows No Season', was intended to drive more sales during the historically slow winter months but had not worked well. The battle with the bottlers had hurt morale, and at the same time, an ill-timed plan by one Coke executive to beat them at their own game by cornering the sugar market collapsed, costing Coke hundreds of thousands of dollars when sugar prices fell instead of rising, as the company had expected, and Coca-Cola prices stayed higher than competitors'. Sales of Coca-Cola had actually been declining since 1920, after the company was sold, the bottlers dismissed, and the rifts between the company and its essential partners exposed.

But Woodruff saw possibilities before him. He transformed Coke into a global power over the next two decades with a pair of sweeping, brilliant, and risky strokes.

His first bold move was to set up something in 1927 that he called the Foreign Department, perhaps inspired by the State Department. Based in Atlanta, the Foreign Department, later renamed the Coca-Cola Export Corporation, oversaw sales and marketing of Coke in every country outside the United States, except Canada and Cuba. It became a powerful entity in its own right, one through which many of the top executives at Coke would pass on their way to becoming stars. They were forceful, colorful, and flamboyant characters, almost to a man, and over the next thirty years they would use all sorts of connections, postures, and tactics to arrange for Coke to be sold in more than 150 countries. They would distinguish Coke as the most well-known American product, sold everywhere from the cafés of Buenos Aires to the tributaries of the Nile. The company would be gathering three quarters of its income overseas by the time Goizueta ascended – a situation that made some people within Coca-Cola nervous but that had also made them all very rich. Cities like Shanghai were selling a million cases a year by the mid-1920s. Countries like Germany, with a people raised on milk and weaned on beer, developed a definite taste for Coca-Cola around the same time. On the heels of World War I, Coke salesmen poured into France with their bottles, concentrating in the beginning on Paris, where they offered it from stands along the streets and in the Eiffel Tower. Price, apparently, was no object. 'What the h— is a franc, compared to a bottle of Coke?' one American soldier exclaimed, within earshot of a Coke man who happily quoted him back at headquarters.

Woodruff layered his own wide-ranging, equal-opportunity philosophy onto the company, which was: Wherever there was a perceived demand, and wherever Coke management could line up a bottler or distributor to help it with the details, such as packaging and delivering the drinks, that's where Coca-Cola would be sold. He urged everyone at the company to think that way. Isolationists, he said, need not apply. Countries like Turkey, Cameroon, and Australia all qualified as customers of the Coca-Cola Company. Soon would come Iceland, Argentina, and Spain, then China, Ireland, the Philippines, Indonesia, and more – he wanted it sold in as many countries as the planet held, by whatever name they wanted to be known. As trade barriers and ideological hurdles came down, one of the first American presences on the scene would be the Coca-Cola Company, always smiling, always cheerful, always ready with that familiar bottle.

Bob Woodruff made his other pivotal decision after the United States, shocked into action by the Japanese attack on Pearl Harbor, entered World War II. His hand covering his heart, Woodruff declared that he would 'see that every man in uniform gets a bottle of Coca-Cola for five cents wherever he is and whatever it costs'.

It was a grand patriotic gesture, and like much that happened at Coke, it had more than one purpose. It sold a lot of Coca-Cola to soldiers, sailors, and airmen abroad, many of whom were frightened and homesick and considered a Coke the closest they could get to home. Soldiers training or awaiting assignments overseas were also covered by the pledge, so Coke flowed into the barracks at places like Fort Knox. Woodruff portrayed Coca-Cola as a 'morale food' that was essential to get American servicemen through the war, and it was a concept that worked out well for his company, particularly when his friend General Dwight Eisenhower climbed on board. In 1943, Eisenhower's staff was cabling Atlanta and asking for Coke bottling plants – not just one or two but ten at a time. 'Ship without displacing other military cargo,' read the telegram asking for equipment and enough Coke syrup to supply the tent cities of North Africa.

It was a brilliant tactic. Ten billion bottles of Coke were sold to the troops from 1941 to 1945. Coke made money from those sales, marketed itself abroad on the backs of soldiers and traded on its role in the war effort to get more sugar out of the U.S. government. Though rationing should have restricted the company's access to that key ingredient, the concentrate flowed unvexed to the bottlers. In Elizabethtown, Kentucky, not far from Fort Knox, William Schmidt's mother, Irene, got all she needed. Syrup arrived in a massive railroad car and parked on a siding until the plant workers could unload it. As the war went on, more and more of those cars arrived. In 1941, the Elizabethtown plant produced about 100,000 cases of Coke. By 1944, it was producing 750,000. An entire generation of fighting men and women became loyal forever to Coca-Cola.

Meanwhile, not all of the Coke the company trucked, shipped, and sent by rail to various battle zones ended up in the hands of American soldiers. There always seemed to be enough left over to hand around to the local men, women, and children near every battlefield, and to supply the cafés and restaurants where the soldiers on furlough liked to go. So people in those countries drank it themselves. And whether they really liked it or came to associate it with the American power that had saved them, they became enchanted by this liquid that combined the dark with the light. While Coke had been for sale in many places before the war, the Woodruff plan galvanized the association of Coke with American vigor, sparkle, and strength. A popular story inside Coke described a German refugee – or a French one, or an Italian – who, upon arriving in New York, gazed in wonder at an American bottle of Coca-Cola and marveled, 'You have Coke in your country, too.'

Woodruff befriended some bottlers, like the Biedenharns, and generally kept contentiousness to a minimum. He would be Coke's president, chairman, or executive chairman for thirty-two years, officially stepping aside just before Eisenhower replaced Truman in the White House. But in retirement he was perhaps even more powerful than before, controlling the board's crucial finance committee and making sure that no important decisions were made without him.

He had a soldier's bearing, the legacy of the years he spent at the Georgia Military Academy. He had never finished college, but he was intuitive when it came to business, both in money matters and in the fine art of anticipating the machinations inside his own company. He was not a lighthearted man; most people who met him immediately noticed that his mouth was usually set in a grim straight line. He sold sweet and fizzy soft drinks for a living, but nearly everything else about him had a tone of seriousness, as if to make up for the frivolity of what he did all day.

He broke up his solemn expression by sucking on a pipe or chomping a big cigar from time to time. He counted ballplayers, department-store magnates, Bible-toting evangelists, and debauched Hollywood movie stars among his friends. Billy Graham came to his house to pray, and Ty Cobb to hunt. He knew presidents in both parties and had access to all of them. When the telephone on Lyndon Johnson's desk rang one April day to tell him that the Reverend Martin Luther King, Jr., had been assassinated, Woodruff happened to be sitting on a couch in the Oval Office.

From his rah-rah writeups of the company in the annual reports, which could bend the truth (in the 1924 report, Coke claimed that 'it was not until the development of Coca-Cola that a demand for soda fountains was created') to his fondness for turning a shotgun full of number-eight pellets on the wild birds that chirped and rustled in the tall grass on his retreat in a far southwestern corner of his home state, Bob Woodruff defined Coke for all the years that he led it.

He and his wife, Nell, a onetime nurse whom he adored, had no children, and by official accounts he poured his patriarchal instincts into Coke instead. 'The Coca-Cola Company was his baby,' noted a biography published in 1982, three years before he died, and no doubt written under his close supervision. 'While he had not been present at its birth or even through its toddler years, he had adopted it as a weakling, unsteady on its feet, and had fathered and mothered it into a giant.'

Woodruff didn't seem much interested in leaving this child in anyone else's hands. While he formally retired in 1955, his first act was to move into an office larger than the one he had had before. He was still a director and chaired the critically important finance committee at the company – meaning no senior executive could be chosen, or make any major strategic move, without winning his approval first.

'Woodruff remained The Boss in performance and spirit,' his biographer observed. 'He continued to operate as before.' His office still held the enormous wooden desk that he had used before retirement, and he still had his secretary decorate it every morning with a single red rose in a small vase. To his left on that desk sat his Bible, with his full name embossed on its blue leather cover. To his right was the paper calendar he used, showing one day at a time. He kept memorabilia all over the place, from a toy Coke truck to a silver award from the sixty-seventh annual Thomas P. Hinman Dental Meeting, and everywhere there were pictures: of Nell, of his mother, of Eisenhower, of his hunting dogs, and of Coke executives past and present. He loved those dogs so much that whenever one died he would make sure the animal got a proper burial, complete with a marble headstone that read something like, PREACHER DICK, FAITHFUL TO THE END.

In 1963, when he had been in retirement for eight years, the company held a party to mark the fortieth anniversary of what it called his 'connection with the Coca-Cola Company'. If observing just how long he had been a presence at Coke was intended as a nudge to the old man, it failed. Woodruff would be around for another two decades, strolling in and out of his roomy quarters, meeting with all the important people in Atlanta – most of whom owed at least a part of their success to all the progress he had made with Coke – and nearly everyone who was important to the Coca-Cola Company.

As international as Coke had become under Woodruff's guidance, it was still very much rooted in Atlanta. Within Atlanta as Coke's star rose, people began to boast of their links to the company, however tangential. Bankers, lawyers, real-estate developers, and plenty of others traced some connection to Coke. If you didn't work there, maybe you were a shareholder, or related to someone who was. As the company blossomed, so did Atlanta.

For decades Atlanta had struggled with its image as a striving Southern metropolis – something that brought it contempt both from the older industrialized cities of the North and from the more genteel and historic cities of the South. In Charleston and Savannah, Atlanta was considered a comical upstart, not much more than a train depot even in the 1940s and 1950s. Those other cities shared a lineage with presidents and other important figures, their pre–Civil War history shimmering like an old mirror and their identities secure. Atlanta had none of that, and it also had to bear the shame of having hosted Sherman's troops during the latter part of the war. While it had no choice in the matter and was burned to the ground, Atlanta still got plenty of blame for what happened to the South in the end.

In peacetime, Atlanta tried on different identities, from patent-medicine capital of the nation to 'Gate City' of the 'New South', which just brought more scorn. In 1895 the editor of *The Atlanta Constitution* came up with a map that showed that anyone who wanted to go anywhere between two points in the hemisphere 'must pass through Atlanta'. Eighty years later, the claim had been made somewhat more reliable by the construction of the South's biggest airport, through which hundreds of flights a day did pass. People in other southern states liked to say that whether a person was going to heaven or hell at the end of his life, he'd have to change planes in Atlanta.

Being acknowledged as important seems to have been a need, bordering on obsession, for the Atlanta city fathers. One editor noted in 1919 that the success of the Coca-Cola Company, then thirty-three years old, amounted to a 'demonstration that Georgia can float and handle big enterprises'.

During the 1920s local politicians tried drawing new business to Atlanta by proclaiming it the capital of the New South, a place where racial attitudes were more moderate than in other parts of the region and where companies could grow and flourish, their executives housed in manicured neighborhoods and their customers served by an increasingly large and sophisticated airport. By the early sixties, the message had been compressed, and by the 1970s Atlanta's boosters spoke optimistically of becoming 'the world's next great city'.

As the civil rights movement swelled, white Atlanta named itself 'the city too busy to hate'. But many people – black and white – did not consider that a terribly accurate portrayal. The subsequent revelation in a national study that living conditions were as bad for blacks in Atlanta as in some of the more dilapidated cities up North meant among other things that Atlanta would be forced to keep on searching for its identity.

All the while, Coke offered hope. The more Coke grew, and the more global and successful it became, the greater were Atlanta's chances of transforming itself into a powerful place. Everything Woodruff did to elevate Coke's image in the world raised Atlanta's image and inflated his prowess within Atlanta. He was admired everywhere for all he had done for the city that was Coke's home base. He was generous, donating money to hospitals, the arts, and causes of all kinds, becoming the biggest benefactor of his generation. By the late 1990s, his foundation had assets of $2.5 billion and gave away hundreds of millions to support education, medical research, and the arts across the South. Like Asa Candler, he channeled Coca-Cola stock into the endowment of Emory University, with gifts that were worth $1 billion by the mid-1990s, and encouraged others to do the same. J. Bulow Campbell, a Coke director, started a foundation of his own in 1940 with $6 million, which increased to $750 million by the time the century was out.

Coke and the other great institutions of the city became intertwined. The 1969 edition of the Emory yearbook had a Coke bottle on the cover and the publication's name written in Coke-style script. A longtime mayor of Atlanta, William Hartsfield, took to christening new aircraft with a bottle of Coca-Cola. Even after Woodruff vanished from the scene, the ties between his company and the rest of Atlanta remained as tight as ever. When the city was chosen to host the Olympic Games in 1996, it was in no small part because of the role the Coca-Cola Company played in framing

Atlanta as a global player as well as lobbying hard behind the scenes to secure what would be a prime-time marketing opportunity for Coca-Cola. Officials of the Greece Olympic committee, who sought to be the 1996 hosts because those Games marked the centennial of the modern Olympics, fumed that Coke, with its connections and its promises, had 'stolen' the event from them. Coke executives just smiled and took their turns in the torch relay.

As chairman, Woodruff stamped Coke with his own relentless desires. He liked innovation – new brands were introduced, and new wings of the company, during his reign – and he liked knowing that Coca-Cola was the top-selling soft drink in the country. But it was never enough, he told himself and others all the time. Never enough.

He initiated billboard advertisements, spending millions of dollars to color the landscape red with Coca-Cola images on signboards, on rural land, along highways, and on the sides of barns and the brick walls of general stores. As the automobile became a permanent fixture, he advocated ways of selling soft drinks to motorists – from ice barrels in gas stations along the highways and even the minor roads. He made sure the Coca-Cola Export Corporation continued the patterns he set at home all over the world. What was true in America could be true everywhere, he contended, borrowing heavily from the nation's values to promote his beliefs. 'Life, liberty, and the pursuit of thirst,' a 1926 ad declared, 'just naturally bring people together every day at the 400,000 places where Coca-Cola is served.'

He did not have easy victories every time. In the 1920s, prohibitionists went after Coke, claiming that although it contained no alcohol, it could be just as debilitating as liquor. 'The Women's Christian Temperance Union of Arkansas City announces that it will devote the year 1929 to stamping out the Coca-Cola habit,' a Kansas newspaper reported, reprinting the group's position statement, which decried 'the Hydra-headed menace of Coca-Cola to our Puritan civilization'. There were also periodic concerns about the caffeine and cocaine content to address, and lingering effects of movies like D. W. Griffith's *For His Son*, a 1912 production that attacked a drink called Dopokoke by showing the rapid deterioration of a man who was addicted to it.

Woodruff marketed through such concerns, trying to make Coke into a friendly corporate citizen at a time when the concept was relatively new. To carry out his plan for supplying Coke to the American troops, he ordered bottling plants built near the battlefields to make everything that much more convenient. Domestic bottlers also supplied camps and bases. At five cents a bottle, the Coke system's gross proceeds from that operation came to $500 million. The patriotism was no doubt real, but so was a sharp sense of the bottom line. Besides, there was marketing value to be exploited back home. A 1942 ad, captioned 'Howdy, friend,' showed a soldier in his khaki uniform crossing a desert where a single, lonely signpost held a Coca-Cola logo.

The Boss kept a sign on his desk declaring that a man could do anything and go anywhere he wanted in life, 'if he doesn't mind who gets the credit'. Even so, he continued to make all the major decisions at Coke until well past his ninetieth birthday. That may be why the corner office seemed to have a revolving door once he left it. He chose A. A. Acklin to succeed him in 1939 as Coke's president, but reassumed the post when Acklin fell ill six years later. Then William Hobbs was tapped as president in 1946, resigning in 1952 to make way for a man named H. B. Nicholson. Just three years later, Nicholson too was gone, replaced by William Robinson, who lasted only three years himself before Lee Talley was named to the job. Talley got four years at the helm before being replaced by Paul Austin in 1962. Austin lasted nearly twenty years, though his power did not extend to choosing his successor. When Roberto Goizueta, not exactly a household name around the company, was picked to rise to the top, everyone knew who'd had a hand in it, though the old man was by then ninety-one years old. One midlevel Coke executive, upon hearing that Roberto Goizueta would be the company's new leader, observed that he knew next to nothing about him. But he was sure of one thing: 'He must be a good friend of Woodruff's.'

Currying favor with Woodruff had long been part of Goizueta's strategy. Someone, probably Austin, clued him in early that he would go nowhere without The Boss's nod, and so Goizueta embarked on a campaign to ingratiate himself with Woodruff. He began sending letters, notes, gifts of all kinds at least as early as 1974.

Once someone brought him a Cuban cigar, known as a Romeo and Julieta No. 3. Cuban cigars were legendary – rolled on the ample thighs of Cuban women, so they said – and since Castro, they had been difficult to obtain. But off this precious object went – to Woodruff. *I hope you will enjoy it,* Goizueta wrote in a note accompanying his gift. *It is supposed to be fresh.*

He was not asked to make the requisite pilgrimages to Ichauway, Woodruff's beloved country estate in south Georgia, until fairly late in the game. The name, pronounced 'itch-away', came from a Native American word meaning 'the place where deer sleep'. It was the place where Bob Woodruff felt most at home, and anyone who did not make the grade on one of his Ichauway weekends, which generally consisted of hunting and drinking and playing card games like gin rummy around the clock, stood little chance of remaining in Woodruff's good graces. Don Keough, invited down in 1977, sent a thank-you note that may have reflected that more honestly than most. *In a very real sense,* Keough wrote, *after a person has experienced Ichauway, he will never again be the same.*

It was a place suspended in time, a vanished moment caught in amber. Spanish moss hung like woolly shawls from the arms of sturdy oaks, and the customs and traditions of the rural South a century earlier, like hunting and keeping a kitchen garden and making syrup from your own cane crop, were alive and well. Nearly all of the employees, from the kitchen to the fields, were African Americans. Gopher tortoises roamed the property, along with wild turkeys and quail. Alligators could turn up in the lakes. Hundreds of pancake-flat acres were sown with corn, soybeans, okra, and peanuts, to be harvested and sold. Woodruff even collected disaster relief from the government when his property suffered through one of the area's periodic droughts. Some of the land was kept wild, covered with low brush and tall grass that provided hiding places for hunters' prey. And the live oaks that were everywhere at Ichauway kept their gray-green leaves winter and summer, never giving up, never changing.

Woodruff joined dozens of exclusive clubs and organizations – the Adventure Society, the Atlanta Athletic Club, the Homosassa Fishing Club, the Rose Tree Fox Hunting Club, the Piedmont Driving Club, and Augusta National Golf Club were among them

– but it was at Ichauway that he felt he really belonged. It was his real home, and he even transplanted bits of it – like the combination floor-lamp-and-gunrack he took to his office at Coke – to places where he was required to be instead. Framed photographs of happy days at Ichauway, showing him at the reins of a horse-drawn carriage or standing with guests in the underbrush, holding the day's feathery kill by the feet, surrounded him at work and at his several homes. He loved to talk about his dogs, his horses, and everything else about Ichauway. It was more than a place on a map; it occupied a large place in his mind.

He often invited people to spend the weekend. They could be politicians, baseball stars, Coke directors, ventriloquists. *Usually our guests are companionable,* Woodruff wrote to Eisenhower, by way of getting him to visit the same weekend Edgar Bergen was expected, *and in the evening, there is bridge, gin rummy, and poker.* Others remembered it as a place where 'people were forced to be informal'. How they responded to the challenge told much about who they were.

After he was named president in 1980, Goizueta got his first invitation to Ichauway. He showed up wearing a silk ascot underneath his shirt and did not know how to shoot at all, which could have been a problem at a place where a person was often sized up according to the number of birds he bagged. There was steak on the table when everyone came in from the hunt, followed up with performances of good Christian hymns by groups of workers who materialized from the kitchen or the kennels whenever The Boss, as he was known there, too, requested them. People who disappointed Woodruff on any level having to do with Ichauway often did not hear from him again. A case in point was Richard Nixon, who after losing to Kennedy in the presidential election tried to get himself hired into Coke's legal department. A few years earlier, after visiting Ichauway, he had thanked Woodruff with a note in which he erroneously referred to the homemade treacle that Woodruff served him as sorghum. It was actually cane syrup, as Woodruff stiffly pointed out in a letter back to the former vice president. Between that and his demonstrated inability to hit anything with a shotgun, Nixon was dismissed.

While the other guests fanned out across the property in search of wildfowl, Goizueta had to spend an afternoon in Woodruff's version of a marksman's clinic, trying to blast shot into Coke cans lined up on a fence. He managed to escape critical failure. By 1980 he stood in sharp contrast to Paul Austin, who had been stellar for a long time but whose final years at the helm had been rocked by a variety of issues, from failing health to his interest in turning Coke into a diversified conglomerate.

Woodruff clearly liked Goizueta. He had begun saving all of his correspondence to him in 1974. Before long, Goizueta's notes filled two folders, entwining his own life with the older man's through observations both businesslike and curiously personal. *I'm bathing in the largest bathtub I have ever seen,* Goizueta wrote to Woodruff from a conference he attended in England in 1978.

Goizueta appears to have gone out of his way to make himself a kind of disciple to Woodruff, whose beloved Nell had died in 1968. Goizueta kept up a steady stream of communiqués with Woodruff even after he had been made chairman and CEO, more often than not including his itinerary, sometimes attached to the manifest for one of the Coke aircraft. He telexed Woodruff from distant parts of the globe to tell him about his travels and to say how well some product – diet Coke, for example – was doing in a far-off city. He passed on all kinds of big-ticket compliments. In 1983 he sent along an article noting that Coke had been named one of the five best-managed companies in *Dun's Business Month*.

Goizueta knew the Coca-Cola formula, but he also impressed Woodruff with his ideological purity – an inviolate, unfettered dedication to the Coca-Cola brand. In July 1979, Woodruff celebrated Goizueta's twenty-fifth anniversary at Coke with a giant bouquet of red roses. There was more to come.

Once he was Coke's leader, Goizueta had to figure out how to distinguish himself at the company. What would be his legacy at a place where legacy counted for a lot? Most of the major, memorable accomplishments already belonged to someone else. Woodruff built Coke into an international brand. Sprite, Fresca, and other sodas had been introduced under Lee Talley and Paul

Austin, along with a host of packaging changes and mergers with companies like Minute Maid. Now he, Roberto Goizueta, whose name most of his employees could not pronounce (some of them did not bother trying, and just referred to him as 'Ricardo', after the Cuban bandleader who played Lucille Ball's husband in the *I Love Lucy* television series), had to figure out a way to leave a mark of his own.

It was a daunting task, and Goizueta would have a couple of false starts before he finally figured out what to do. Initially, as he took over at Coke, the prevailing view was that Austin had moved too much of the company to the international arena and had been oddly intent on diversifying away from the product for which it was so well known. Goizueta listened and nodded. One of the loudest voices in the debate belonged to John Collings, the company's chief financial officer. Collings favored getting away from this overseas focus – the dollar was strong, and earnings that came from outside the country were getting crushed as a result – and concentrating on U.S. businesses instead. He pitched a plan to Goizueta that called for 50 percent of Coke's earnings to come from domestic operations, instead of the 25 percent that was then the case. One of Goizueta's first moves was to buy Columbia Pictures, then a promising movie studio and thought to signal a Coke move into the entertainment industry. The choice was between getting into the pharmaceutical business or the entertainment business, and Goizueta picked the movies.

From that point on, the Coca-Cola Company ceased to be all about the selling of Coca-Cola and its other soft drinks. That was the old company, the one built and controlled by Woodruff. Under Goizueta, Coke would be about selling Coke but also about redesigning the financial aspects of the business. Instead of merely making money off sales of soda, Coke would make money in myriad other ways, from trimming expenses to reconfiguring its systems to making acquisitions that would pour more money into its treasury.

Goizueta wanted to dazzle investors with growth, not just deliver a certain conservative percentage rise in value every year. 'If you're running what you consider to be a growth company and it's giving you a one percent return, and someone can get a five to ten percent return on bonds,' Don Keough once noted, 'well, that's a dangerous reality.'

Goizueta decided Coke would pay $750 million to take over Columbia Pictures, its name taken from the poetic symbol for America. Bob Woodruff, attending a board meeting, made the motion to approve the purchase. With the deal, completed in 1982, came a shower of glitter, and out of it stepped Herbert Allen, who figured as both a banker, through Allen & Company, Inc., and a key player, since he was chairman of Columbia. Allen, then just forty-two years old, won a seat on the Coke board as part of the sale; he instantly made more than $500 million on his own $1.5 million stake and took a leading role in Coke's strategic decisions from that moment on. 'I learned more from being on the board of Coke, from watching Goizueta and Keough,' Allen said. 'The personal experience of being around them was enormously rewarding. And it was financially enormously rewarding as well.'

He kept out of the spotlight himself, despite making his living from the attention-craving worlds of media and entertainment. He enjoyed mixing and remixing the various players in his world, and his annual summertime investment conference in Sun Valley, Idaho, was the crucible for unexpected unions like the buyout of Capital Cities by Walt Disney. Allen's company, spun off in the midsixties from a firm founded by his father and his uncle, made its money by acting as investor, underwriter, or broker, as the situation warranted. Working there, amid the paneled conference rooms and the fine art on the walls, was like being part of 'a very special, secret society', according to bankers. Schmoozing was essential for them, the means by which deals began, developed, and were sewn up. Meanwhile, Allen, a wiry, athletic man, liked to be up before sunrise. He became legendary for leaving parties in time to get to sleep by 9:30 P.M., even if the parties were being held in his own house. 'He's less likely to be around for the due diligence,' Frank Biondi, a former chief executive of Viacom, once said. 'He's going to be in bed.'

Columbia Pictures was Coke's attempt to branch out and aggrandize itself through other industries, but it was Columbia, and the surreal world that it represented, that absorbed key parts of

Coke. Executives who lunched in the twelfth-floor dining room chattered endlessly about the box-office take of this or that movie, instead of discussing the consumption of Coke in Australia or Argentina. Goizueta and others would slip away to screenings of pictures like *Ghostbusters* and *Ishtar,* and take their seats at the Academy Awards, decked out in black tie, where they appeared distinctly not Hollywood, though anxious to spend as much time inside the velvet ropes as possible. Don Keough loved attending the Academy Awards, and frequently Roberto Goizueta was by his side. With the deal came a building, too – the Columbia headquarters at 711 Fifth Avenue. Soon it would be renamed the Coca-Cola Building, and it would house a variety of tenants, among them Herbert Allen's company, where Keough would eventually alight.

Various employees from Atlanta were assigned to duty at Columbia, and many of them enjoyed the work tremendously, whether in New York or out on the West Coast. But there was always a vague note of disapproval from the home office, as if, in enjoying working at Columbia, they had somehow demonstrated a lack of fidelity to Coke. For Coke continued to be the principal focus of the company. Columbia's purpose was to provide a wellspring of cash to help even out Coke's numbers. It did not go so well from an artistic standpoint. 'We had flop after flop,' recalled Donald McHenry, the Coke director who also served on Columbia's board. 'We were lucky the Japanese came along and paid a ridiculous amount of money to buy it.'

Although the relationship with Hollywood would officially end in 1989, when Goizueta approved the sale of Columbia to Sony for $3.4 billion, Coke's dealings would be permanently influenced by the world Columbia represented. Allen would remain a director of Coke, on the all-important finance committee, and his firm would serve as an investment banker to the soft-drink maker year after year, collecting millions of dollars in fees for deals large and small. To Allen, Coke's decades of selling its brown soda to the world amounted to a life in show business anyway. In the future, as in the past, the lines between hope and reality, fiction and fact, would be blurred again and again. 'Marketing is a nicer word,' he said. 'It's show business.'

*

Shortly after the deal was made, John Collings suffered a heart attack while riding in his company limousine through the streets of New York one night. He died a short time later.

Sam Ayoub, a longtime Coca-Cola man, took Collings's spot as chief financial officer. But Ayoub's tenure would be curtailed by age; he was only three years away from turning sixty-five, Coke's mandatory retirement point. When he stepped down in 1985, it opened the door for his deputy, Doug Ivester, to become the man in charge of Coke's financial operations. The CFO's role had always been important at Coke, but it became even more so under Goizueta's plan.

With Collings's death, a fresh theory dominated Coke's business discussions: that the future of soft-drink sales lay not in the well-developed U.S. market but in the scores of developing countries where Coke was already being sold, where consumption levels fell far below those at home. Gearing up the company to increase the frequency with which people in the Philippines or Nigeria drank Coca-Cola – something that Coke people referred to as 'per-caps', short for per capita consumption – became a primary goal of Goizueta's. He vowed to do everything possible to capture that growth, from building bottling plants to hiring the best workers to coming up with the most persuasive advertising that would drive people to drink more Coke. He fully appreciated what was happening in Rome, Georgia, and he wanted the rest of the world to follow suit. There was also one big difference between the United States and the rest of the world: The bottling contracts abroad were controlled by Coke; the syrup price could rise at will, and the contracts were for distinct and shorter terms.

Goizueta had presented his plan at a board meeting in March 1981, barely a month after he had moved into his new office, declaring that 'there are no sacred cows'. that everything about the company was up for grabs – even the famous formula on which all their fortunes were based. He wanted now to increase Coke's volume sales. He wanted per-caps to rise. Indefinitely.

He had pulled his old adversary Don Keough into the ring with him, and now they formed an interesting though unusual team. Goizueta was the taciturn scientist who knew the precise combination of flavors, extracts, and sweeteners to make Coke. Keough, meanwhile, was the dulcet messenger who could explain to everyone else in the company what their leader was thinking and what he expected. At the beginning, Goizueta called managers in from around the world and essentially jettisoned the five-year plans they had been working on to present to him. It would be a three-year plan from now on, he instructed them, and it had better be good. The encounter soon became known, in the kind of ethnic pejorative that Goizueta seemed to inspire often in his early days, as 'the Spanish Inquisition'.

After a few efforts like that one, Goizueta seemed to realize that he could rely on Keough to deliver unpalatable news to people, and it would be taken a lot more willingly. Keough, as American as the day was long, could not be accused of being Spanish or Cuban or otherwise not in tune with the Coke way. Besides, people could pronounce his name. So Goizueta passed the baton of communicating with the company to Coke's new president in 1981, giving Keough fresh power over part of the chairman's role. He remembered what Woodruff often said: There was no limit to where a man could go if he didn't mind who got the credit.

There was one place Keough would not get the credit, though. Goizueta made sure he himself was the one who controlled every bit of information flowing from Coke headquarters out into the public realm, especially to Wall Street. He developed a specialty in speaking to analysts, wooing them, caressing them, slapping them around when they didn't do what he wanted. The Coke juggernaut, once it got rolling, endowed him with extraordinary powers. His critics got punished: with notes to them, and notes to their supervisors, written in Goizueta's wordy but forceful style. He didn't call anyone stupid, necessarily, in these notes. He did call into question their ability to question *him,* the chairman and chief executive of the Coca-Cola Company. He had learned a few things about power, and he would use them for Coke's benefit.

He also set out to improve on Coca-Cola itself.

In 1982 he gave the green light to launch diet Coke, a low-calorie version made not with sugar but with artificial sweetener. It immediately found a foothold among weight-conscious Americans, even though Coke already had a diet cola, Tab, that had been sold for decades. The introduction of diet Coke was not just about promoting another diet cola for consumers. In its own way, some believed, it was also about punching another hole in the bottlers' contracts.

Goizueta had already decided to substitute much cheaper, high-fructose corn syrup for the sugar in regular Coke's formula in the United States. Both diet Coke and the corn-syrup version of Coca-Cola, coming within a year of each other, neatly skirted the bottler contracts, since neither concentrate used sugar. Concentrate for diet Coke should not be governed by the prices for syrup set in those contracts, Coke executives held, and concentrate for regular Coke, similarly, was also unhitched from the pricing guidelines that dated from 1920. Getting around the complicated sugar market was one advantage, and promoting a new product was also high on Coke's priority list. Anyone who wanted to sell diet Coke would have to sign a separate contract – on Coke's terms.

A group of bottlers begged to differ and sued the company over the changes, setting off a legal battle that would drag on for a decade. They were led by William Schmidt from Elizabethtown, Kentucky, who had refused – politely, of course – to sign the 1978 amended contract that Keough and Luke Smith championed, the one that allowed Coke to raise syrup prices at will.

Schmidt's life was tied up in bottling Coca-Cola. His grandfather obtained the franchise for Louisville in 1901, and the Schmidts sold Coca-Cola briskly in Elizabethtown all spring and summer. They spent their winters in St. Petersburg, Florida, where the weather meant more demand for Coke.

Bill Schmidt became a full-time bottler in 1955. The following year, Coke introduced its first variation on its traditional six-and-a-half-ounce glass bottle: the King Size, which was meant to better compete with Pepsi's twelve-ounce bottle, around which Pepsi had built an annoying jingle – 'Twice as much for a nickel, too' – and made inroads among cola drinkers that Coke executives found even more annoying.

Schmidt had been a team player all along, just as his mother and father and grandfather had. They knew their markets like the backs of their hands and believed in Coca-Cola – not just in the beverage but in the company that owned the brand. 'We always had a great feeling of love, if you want to call it that, for the business,' Schmidt said.

But in 1982 he gathered a band of sixty independent bottlers who wanted Coke to rethink its dealings with them over the changes in the Coca-Cola formula. They first asked for meetings with Luke Smith, the much-beloved president of Coke at the time, who oversaw the bottlers. Smith listened to the bottlers' grievances, Schmidt recalled. The bottlers listened to Coke's argument, too. 'No one got excited or excitable,' he said. 'We agreed to disagree.'

The next stop was the lawyer's office. Not many attorneys wanted to pick a fight with the Coca-Cola Company. Eventually someone suggested Emmet Bondurant II, a respected Atlanta lawyer who, another Coca-Cola bottler told Schmidt, 'would not be afraid to battle Coke in their hometown.'

Bondurant had grown up drinking Coca-Cola in Athens, Georgia. He had fond memories of the local bottler, who took children on tours of his factory and gave out Coca-Cola pencils at the end. Bondurant examined Schmidt's situation and thought he detected an intriguing tale of hubris and greed flowing from the company that owned the brand. He saw a wrong and decided he would right it. He would be at it for years to come.

For Schmidt, taking a position opposite the company that had meant so much to his family was extremely difficult. Part of him was sympathetic to Coke; part of him knew that if Coke got its way, the bottlers would be finished.

'The company felt they needed price relief,' he said. He was willing to grant that, as long as there was some kind of formula to keep Coke from running away with the opportunity. The company offered to spend more on advertising and marketing in exchange for the revised contract. But in 1977 the advertising budget was cut back dramatically; almost anything would have been an improvement. Schmidt worried that if Coke didn't have some sort of price ceiling in place for syrup, as there had been for so long, the bottlers would be at a complete disadvantage and the whole system would break down.

He became the unofficial leader of the loyal opposition after he wrote a letter describing his feelings about Coke's proposal to a couple of friends in the bottling business who asked for his opinion. They asked permission to send copies of that letter to other bottlers. It was mailed all over the country, by them and by others. 'Before we knew it, Bill was a pamphleteer,' his wife, Jan, said.

He formed the Coca-Cola Bottlers USA, a kind of counterweight to the Coca-Cola Bottlers Association, where Schmidt had been on the board of governors for many years. He had come to feel that the official bottlers' association was too intent on granting the Coca-Cola Company's every wish. Members of the new group sent in contributions for the legal fees, and they began a long and arduous process: confronting the Coca-Cola Company with the reality of its bottlers' needs and, some believed, the reality of the whole relationship.

Goizueta paid scant attention to their complaints and pushed his plans along. Until the court ruled otherwise, Coke would contain corn syrup and diet Coke would be considered a separate brand, bound by a different contract. Whoever didn't sign the diet Coke contract would lose out. Keough would consider the bottlers' lawsuit a kind of quixotic effort, a sideshow to everything else that was going on inside the company.

Goizueta had other projects to preoccupy him and everyone around him. By 1984, he was absorbed in the planning of a highly significant birthday party for Coca-Cola. The very first Coke had been poured in 1886, and the one hundredth anniversary of that event loomed. What better moment, Goizueta must have thought, to draw attention to his plans for the company than the occasion of its centennial? He set about planning a party of epic proportions, one that would cost Coke $30 million, at the time more than any other party given by any company in America's history. It would be not just a tribute to the past but a huge and public wakeup call for everyone – inside Coke, outside Coke – about the future that he intended to orchestrate for the company.

He was planning a second act for what was already a colorful history. Coke's creator, John Pemberton, arrived in Atlanta four years after Lincoln's assassination. He had served as a cavalryman in the war on the Confederate side. After bearing witness to the horrors of combat, he then found himself immersed in the agony that was Reconstruction. As bad as it was, it provided him with a ready audience for his postwar career.

He formulated medicines and other products that promised relief for the aching hearts and weary bodies all around him. He addressed anxious southern whites and newly liberated blacks and people who had been in Atlanta for generations, as well as carpetbaggers come to afflict them. Someone in need of a hair-straightening ointment or a remedy for a cough that refused to go away might have purchased one of Pemberton's products. He engaged in a highly competitive business; by 1890, the census showed that Atlanta drew proportionally more of its manufacturing income from patent medicines than any other city in the nation. Someone with a successful formula could count on a quick line of imitators, which drove Pemberton to keep searching for something that would be all his own.

He had a product that he called French Wine Coca, a syrup that contained cola flavor and coca extract and could be turned into a drink. But since it also contained alcohol, it was not for everyone. He removed the alcohol one day, added a blast of carbonated water from one of the jugs that every self-respecting pharmacist kept on hand, and called the result Coca-Cola.

From the start, he regarded it as a medicine and sold it as a 'tonic', good for brain and body. That part was easy, for people had long believed that what they drank from a soda fountain was good for them. This one was supposed to cure headaches and relieve fatigue. For a long time, people had been hearing that, too.

When the first Coca-Cola was served, soda water had been dispensed for seventy years by American pharmacists with claims that it could reverse all kinds of illnesses, from shingles and liver disease to simple malaise. The belief flowed from Europe, where for centuries people flocked to the Grotto del Cano near Naples and other springs of naturally occurring bubble-filled water. They were fascinated with the idea of carbonated water – drinking it, bathing in it, and attempting unsuccessfully for decades to duplicate it. The 'fixed air' present in carbonation – the little bubbles themselves – represented healing. They could not imagine how the bubbles got there. It had to be magic, or something crafted by the angels.

In the seventeenth and eighteenth centuries, scientists demystified much of the natural world but continued to be stumped by carbonated water. With all its beneficial properties, a process to transform ordinary water into the sparkling kind would mean more good for mankind – healthier people and healthier societies. As it happened, a scientist and philosopher concerned with maximizing human potential figured out the way to do it. It would mean little to him, in the long run, but it would change the world.

The scientist was Joseph Priestley, a scholar of the Enlightenment whose achievements ranged from breakthroughs in chemistry to social change. Born in 1733, by the time he was thirty years old Priestley was already a well-known minister, scientist, and exponent of provocative theories on government reform. He would be credited with the discovery of oxygen, and he would study electricity, inspired by Benjamin Franklin. But to the general public, his biggest breakthrough came in 1767, the year he developed a way to transform flat, unremarkable liquid into a beverage dancing with bubbles.

He had observed, he would write, that grain fermenting in huge vats at a brewery near his house gave off a gaseous stench. He poured water back and forth in containers he held over the vats, and some of the gas was captured as bubbles in the water. Now he knew where the bubbles came from; he just had to refine the process.

He gathered up a pile of equipment that he found around his home in Leeds, England, including a laundry basin and a couple of empty bottles. He mixed sulfuric acid and crushed chalk in one bottle, then pumped the resulting gas into another bottle, which he had filled with water and suspended upside down in the basin, also brimming with water. The gas made the bottle of water bloom with thousands of tiny bubbles, to Priestley's great delight. He stopped it up with a cork, lifted it from the basin, and observed how the effervescence lingered. He pulled out the cork and took a sip. He knew that he had done it.

Ever generous, Priestley illustrated and published the procedure in 1772. The scientific community was stunned. England's Royal Society awarded him its highest honor, the Copley Medal, a

French scientist published a similar procedure in France, and before long man-made carbonated water was being offered for sale to eager customers all over Europe.

Priestley believed his invention could prevent scurvy, the bane of every sailor at the time, if carried on the lengthy voyages of the English explorers. He thought degenerative disease was the result of too little 'fixed air' in the human body, and he was sure that carbonated water could prevent the hideous decay, reaching from teeth to bones to brain, that scurvy brought. *If this discovery (though it doth not deserve that name) be of any use to my countrymen, and to mankind at large,* Priestley wrote to the Earl of Sandwich in 1772, *I shall have my reward.* He supplied a version of his carbonated-water apparatus to Captain James Cook to use during his second trip to the Pacific. Cook returned after several years with not a single hand lost to disease, but it was credited to all the stops he had made, taking on fresh fruit and vegetables every time – not to Priestley's invention. Cook had unwittingly saved his men from scurvy. It would be decades before scientists discovered the link between vitamin C deficiency and the disease.

Plenty of others, though, took Priestley's ideas and put them to work. One of the commercial pioneers in selling carbonated water was Jacob Schweppe, whose company, Schweppe's, would evolve into a sometime Coca-Cola ally after it became Cadbury Schweppes. Bottled carbonated water became the rage, flavored with mixtures of minerals named for the great natural spas. People flocked to these artificial sources as they had once flocked to natural wells, believing that they could be cured of maladies major and minor.

After publishing his process for carbonating water, Priestley had nothing to do with it. He concentrated on what he felt was his true calling, as a political philosopher and peaceful religious reformer who found the policies of the Church of England and the British monarchy incompatible with the rights of man. For his thinking, he was hounded from his homeland by the increasingly nervous George III. In 1791, a mob tore through the streets of Birmingham, England, setting fire to a church where he often preached and then to his house. His books, manuscripts, scientific gadgets, and other treasures were reduced to smoldering ash. A devastated Priestley wrote an open letter to the people of Birmingham, informing them that 'this has been done to one who never did, or imagined, you any harm'.

He left Birmingham for London, where he continued to feel ostracized by 'some persons in power'. Finally, in 1794, he sailed for America, settling in Northumberland, Pennsylvania, not far from Philadelphia. He already counted Benjamin Franklin and Thomas Jefferson among his confidants. He would seek a new life in a new country, one that promised liberty for all.

As he stood on the deck of the ship carrying him west and watched the English shoreline disappear into the sea, the basic rights he advocated had been taken up in France. He would arrive in his adopted land a celebrity, his absence mourned in poetry and pamphlets by sympathizers back home. In America, he would write, he felt for the first time that he had found his place. He did not expect or want everyone to agree with him but asked for tolerance, to have the freedom to pursue his own definition of a meaningful life. The path would be rocky at first; John Adams offered at one point to deport him for his 'French sympathies' under the Alien and Sedition Acts. But other patriots rose to the defense of Priestley, who would remain in America until his death in 1804.

His political ideas nurtured modern democracy, and his discovery of what would come to be called soda, soda pop, tonic, and finally soft drinks had a major impact on industry and commerce in the United States. By 1820, carbonated water was sold in most pharmacies, and by 1866 soda water, whether plain or flavored, had been declared 'an innocent beverage' by the city of New York. The notion of healthfulness never went away, even as pharmacists outdid themselves to offer both luxury and innovation.

In the late nineteenth century, the drinks themselves began to take on all manner of titles, from ciders and crèmes to punches and hot consommés. Some were based on homely fruits; others ventured further, adding spices, extracts, and this and that from the pharmacist's shelf to the mix. Flavored drinks on a soda fountain's menu could include greengage plum, zoysia, and plain lemonade. They were given names like Golden Sceptre, True New Yorker, and Bimbo Flipp. Even in small towns, the local soda fountain became a place of exhibition, sometimes taken to extremes. A Texas pharmacist's handbook, published in 1902, recommended taking a hundred-pound block of ice and setting it on the counter, with a pan to catch the drips as it melted in the searing southwestern heat. Once positioned, the ice should be carved full of cavities, the book instructed, and those cavities alternately stuffed with fresh pineapples, oranges, flowers, and bowls of homemade fruit-flavored syrup, with fresh flowers and leaves garnishing the finished chilly creation. Labor-intensive, yes, but worth the effort, the author insisted. It was a sure way to attract attention, especially from female customers.

Drinks reflected the times, too. There were cold drinks for heat-exposed climes and hot ones, like clam bouillon, for places where the chilly winter came and stayed. Drinks were medicinal, or said to be, and also just plain refreshing. A blob of ice cream dropped into flavored carbonated water became an ice-cream soda, celebrated in its own right. When cars emerged as more than just a passing fad, pharmacists came up with drinks to capture their essence. One called the Auto Smash consisted of shaved ice in a tall glass, covered with a blood-colored syrup made from strawberries and grapes.

Despite the effort required for activities like cooking fruit into syrup and creating tropical fantasies out of icebergs, soda fountains were highly profitable. Their appeal was wide, and their markups substantial. *The Modern Guide for Soda Dispensers,* published in Chicago in 1897, included a page from author Wesley Bonham's ledger showing that expenses for syrup, ice cream, carbon dioxide, and ice in a typical week totaled $42.81, while revenue came in at $114.75.

Pemberton and Coke's successive owners insisted that Coca-Cola had medicinal properties, and the formula's trace amounts of coca, extracted from the plant used for cocaine – then believed to be a harmless analgesic – enhanced that image. Cocaine, morphine, and opium were frequent companions of the infirm during the 1880s, dulling their pain, amplifying their good moods. Family doctors dispensed them readily, and there was no stigma involved in consuming them. Cocaine, in fact, had been introduced to Europe and the United States as a danger-free tonic and analgesic by climbers who conquered the Andes with the help of the stimulant. Their suppliers were friendly mountain peasants who had grown up knowing all about the powers of the coca plant.

But coca was not the only powerful ingredient in Coke. The sugar provided a lift, too, as did the caffeine, which came from the kola extract derived from cola nuts. The other ingredients included oil of cinnamon, oil of coriander, citrus oils, vanilla, water, and lime juice. All of these were essential for taste and balance, although when Asa Candler, marketing the product as always, urged a Georgia physician in 1890 to buy the drink, the coca and the caffeine were his major selling points.

The medical properties of the Coca Plant and the extract of the celebrated African Cola Nut make it a medical preparation of great value, Candler wrote, *which the best physicians unhesitatingly endorse and recommend for mental and physical exhaustion, headache, tired feeling, mental depression, etc.*

Candler himself became a believer after discovering that a glass of Coca-Cola erased the migraine headaches he suffered. They began after he fell out of a horse-drawn wagon as a little boy and had always been thought incurable. One of the iron-edged wooden wheels crunched over his head, leaving him unconscious for several days and distorting his eyesight for the rest of his life. But here was something that really helped with the pain. *You know how I suffer with headaches,* he wrote to his brother Warren in April 1888. *Well, some days ago a friend suggested that I try Coco Cola. I did and was relieved. Some days later I again tried it and was again relieved.*

It was not long after his first glass of Coke that Candler bought the company. By then he had learned to correctly spell its name, and he made sure that name was known by everyone. When the government insisted that he pay a tax on proprietary medicines, imposed as an emergency funding measure during the Spanish-American War, Candler went to great lengths to have Coca-Cola declared a food. He won, but during the trial a witness confirmed that the formula contained trace amounts of cocaine.

Candler had never shied away from the fact that the formula contained cocaine. Even his letterhead, circa 1894, trumpeted Coke as 'containing the tonic properties of the wonderful COCA PLANT, and the famous COLA NUT'. But by the end of the nineteenth century, with America vehemently opposed to narcotics, Candler was in a tight spot. He removed the cocaine's analgesic properties from the formula and advertised all over the country that he had done so. Though the drink would be referred to as 'dope', throughout the South especially, for decades to come, Coke executives would deny from that moment on that it had ever contained cocaine as an ingredient.

In 1986 that product, and all the excitement about it, was going to be one hundred years old. *One hundred years old*. And the party, Roberto Goizueta concluded, should be a premier marketing event – as opulent as possible, embracing everything about the Coca-Cola Company as it had been and signaling as much as he could about what it was going to become. It should celebrate Coke in a way that would take people's breath away.

The bash took place during four days in early May. The entertainment, thanks to Columbia Pictures, included Kool & the Gang, Vanna White, and Merv Griffin. There were also artifacts of the past, such as a replica of Jacobs', the drugstore where Coca-Cola was first sold, and an appearance by a pint-size 18-wheel delivery truck, owned by a bottler that Coke had helped get into the business, inside the auditorium where thousands of Coke friends and admirers had gathered. There was a parade on the last day through the heart of Atlanta that included dozens of 'Coke floats', one of them an enormous birthday cake on wheels – 'Just like the one in *Animal House*,' said Joe Wilkinson, a Coke executive who attended – and old-fashioned Coke trucks. Bill Schmidt was at the wheel of his family's 1932 Ford van, his wife by his side. One group of marchers dressed as enormous Coke cans. Most of the cans survived the entire route, although one deflated along the way.

Streets were closed off and large public forums commandeered to accommodate the party. The company flew in more than twelve thousand customers, bottlers, and analysts to take part in the festivities. All Atlanta watched in wonder as one Coca-Cola moment after another unfolded in their town. 'It was very much a pure, vintage Coca-Cola marketing event,' said one executive who was there. As a grand finale, Coke organized a worldwide domino tumble, hosted by Dick Cavett, in which nearly 700,000 dominoes were carefully arranged on six continents and then toppled, each one touching off the next until finally they all lay flat. The destruction was broadcast live on television.

On the evening of May 9, as partygoers chattered about all the wonderful things that had taken place in honor of Coke's birthday, the company held a black-tie dinner for thousands of bottlers and their guests in the cavernous Georgia World Congress Center, a stone's throw from the Coke headquarters at the corner of North Avenue and Luckie Street. The huge cake appeared, trundled from the wings with its candles glowing. A woman dressed in silver – a goddess, or an angel – was lowered from the ceiling inside a tube of light as she held a three-foot-high bottle of Coke above her head. *This is getting sacrilegious,* thought George Marlin, who had spent the last eight years as a Coke marketing manager in the Pacific Northwest. He was right next to Keough, who turned around, grinning, as the woman neared the ground. Keough spotted Marlin and gave him a thumbs-up.

Keough and Goizueta each had their own moments onstage that night, looking out at the festive crowd as they delivered messages meant to inspire everyone to go out and give everything they had to the Coca-Cola Company for the next one hundred years. Behind them shone a message in lights, one favored by Woodruff: THE WORLD BELONGS TO THE DISCONTENTED.

The always voluble Keough bounded onto the stage, waving and smiling, pointing a finger at people he recognized and emoting like a cross between Billy Graham and P. T. Barnum. 'Has there ever been a bigger industrial birthday party?' he asked the audience. And then he answered his own question, perhaps mindful of the multimillion-dollar price tag. 'Never!'

He delivered a speech that celebrated the contribution of the bottlers to the Coca-Cola family but also rang with warnings: of the risks of not taking risks, and the risks of taking too many that were not centered around the selling of more and more Coke. He singled out a bottler from southern Argentina who had made the trip to Atlanta for the birthday party, and cited a poem by William

Blake, 'The Marriage of Heaven and Hell', by way of summing up Coke's relationship with its bottlers.

'In a world full of tension and conflict and suspicion,' Keough said, 'isn't it special to be here today, in an atmosphere of simple affection?' He asked everyone to stand, and to reach out, and to touch. He instructed his guests to take one another by the hand. Shifting uncomfortably on their feet at first, they did as they were told.

'We love each other,' he declared. 'We've been through war, we've been through hurricanes, we've been through every kind of tragedy and trial, and we're standing here holding hands.'

Amid the hand-holding, some of the bottlers were thinking as they stood there that they had better sell their businesses and get out. The process of eroding their power had begun decades earlier, but it was accelerating under Keough and Goizueta. Their number was dwindling, and the opportunity to sell Coke in bottles, an opportunity they considered their birthright, was disappearing before their eyes.

More than three years before the big party, Goizueta had served notice that times had changed. On December 27, 1982, John Lupton II, the grandson and namesake of the Chattanooga investor who early on realized that bottling Coca-Cola might be worth a person's while, had resigned from the Coca-Cola board.

Other Coke bottlers, as well as their widows, had served as Coke directors over the years. But in 1982 Jack Lupton was the only one left. He had been a Coke director since 1956. He had been a director or an adviser to many other bottlers as well. He exuded the history of the independent bottling system, starting with his name. And after he left the board that winter day, no bottler would have a voice in any decision made at the top of Coke.

Keough had the last word as the Coke family marked the one hundredth birthday of the soft drink that had brought them together. Roberto Goizueta, who was wearing a dinner jacket lined with satin the color of a Coca-Cola can, had spoken ahead of him. The red lining flashed with each step he took as he crossed the stage to the podium. He paused before beginning his remarks and looked out across the vast array of Coca-Cola faces – flushed, happy faces, sitting atop ziggurats of money made possible because of the past and all jubilantly anticipating the future. Then he delivered a Coke benediction, one that he said he had heard many times from The Boss, Bob Woodruff himself.

'May all your luck,' said the chairman and CEO of the Coca-Cola Company, 'may *all* your luck be good luck.'

Chapter Five

New Coke

OF COURSE, GOIZUETA KNEW what bad luck was. He had had some in his life. And he had created some of Coke's.

A little more than a year before the big centennial bash, he had unveiled, with enormous fanfare and pomp and promise, something christened – after many, many focus groups, high-level meetings, formal discussions, and random conversations – New Coke.

He revealed the plan to some of the bottlers at a meeting at the Woodruff Center, Atlanta's premier performing-arts center. He showed it to other bottlers at a lunch at '21' in New York. Some of them thought it was going to be the greatest thing in the world. Others were not so sure. But as the delivery system for Coca-Cola, they had no choice but to go along with Goizueta.

Many of the bottlers were assembled hastily and made to swear to secrecy. In early spring Bill Schmidt got a call to go to Pittsburgh for 'an extremely urgent meeting', he recalled. 'Don't tell anyone where you're going,' he was ordered. 'Not even your wife.'

That was when he was let in on the plan, though Schmidt had trouble absorbing some of the stuff he was told at that meeting. Changing Coca-Cola in any way amounted to heresy, most of the bottlers believed. It had never happened before, and why was it necessary? Just because of Pepsi? 'I was kind of amazed and shocked by the whole thing,' said Schmidt.

A few weeks later, he and Jan went together to another gathering in Atlanta at the Woodruff Center. There was going to be a new Coca-Cola, they were told. Then came a break, an intermission in this strange show. The bottlers and their families spilled out into the lobby, buzzing about what they had heard. Some of them already had doubts; others were trying to keep an open mind. So far it was merely an idea; no one knew what it would taste like.

Women neatly dressed in red sweaters and carrying silver trays came toward them. On each tray were four or five glasses of a brown sparkling soft drink, this New Coke that was going to set the world on fire. 'Well, of course it had been poured even before the people left the auditorium, so it was warm and it had been sitting there,' Jan Schmidt recalled. 'I was talking with my friend Ann Hauck and I had never, ever heard her say anything stronger than "Golly", or maybe "Goll-leee". We took our sips and our eyes met over these glasses and she said, "Goddamn! This'll *never* sell!"'

Sweeter and less fizzy than Coca-Cola, New Coke was to be the company's salvation, arriving just in time, in the ninety-ninth year of Coca-Cola, to shield cola drinkers from the spreading influence of Pepsi. As the company's architect of change, Goizueta felt confident that he could improve upon the formula. As a man who had survived acute personal upheaval, he saw nothing intrinsically sacred about a soft-drink recipe. The Coca-Cola formula had been assigned its importance by the men who ran the company, the ones who decided the marketing messages and told people what they should believe. Now he was the one running the company. So he took the formula into his own hands, and changed it.

What many people did not fully grasp in the early days of the project was that there would not be both New Coke and old Coke for sale. There would be no pluralism at the Coca-Cola Company, in other words; no accommodation of varying tastes and preferences in the cola department. It was going to be New Coke or no Coke.

'The best just got better,' Goizueta declared at a news conference in New York on April 23, 1985, pulling back the curtain so that all the world could see this creation. He gave the fifty states New Coke and pledged that this was the Coca-Cola of the future, soon to be available across the planet – replacing Pemberton's recipe, pushing aside all the previous decades and the relationship people had constructed with Coca-Cola. He had ordered the preparation of an enormous advertising campaign, starring luminaries like Bill Cosby, who stood on a set filled with Greek and Roman antiquities while he said, 'You like Coke the way it is? Me, too. Like this one better.'

Goizueta had thought about this for a long time. He may have believed he had no choice. The extremes to which Coke drinkers went for their beloved soft drink were well known, documented in newspapers and entrenched as part of the lore around the product. The die-hard Coke fans included Kay Phelan, a woman from East Cobb, Georgia, whose love for Coca-Cola ran so deep that her husband-to-be once lined up forty-eight cases of it along her driveway, each tied with a ribbon bow. 'Merry Christmas, honey,' he told her when she opened the front door. The neighbors, watching from behind their kitchen curtains, thought it was a hoot.

It was a good move, one that got Mr. Phelan what he wanted. 'She's constantly sipping a Coke,' Mr. Phelan would report, after they were married. 'She keeps one by the bed.' Every so often, as a labor of love, he'd clean her Oldsmobile − removing at least a dozen empty Coke bottles each time. He called it 'de-Coking' her car. Fortunately, he was fond of Coke, too.

Besides the actual drinking of Coca-Cola, there were the artifacts − the old Coke bottles, the bits of ephemera, like old paper signs and even the press kits that sold for vast amounts at flea markets, the toy Coke trucks and the vintage trays and the old calendars and the wall clocks − that people sought out and collected as if they were precious gems. Societies formed around collecting Coke memorabilia, and writers published entire books filled with examples, together with price lists that played to an enormous audience. In the late 1980s, Coke would realize the potential of this particular bandwagon and jump on it, copyrighting the use of its logo on T-shirts and other products and developing a licensing program worth hundreds of millions of dollars to the company. That was the new stuff, and it was extremely popular. Meanwhile, the old stuff just kept climbing in value.

People were oddly but abundantly enthusiastic about decking themselves − and their babies, their dogs, their Christmas trees − in Coke paraphernalia. Coke fans created miniature villages, featuring tiny Coke trucks and little stores with Coke signs painted on them, on their coffee tables. They kept old Coke bottles, even the ordinary ones. They talked about the time they had a Coke with a boyfriend, or the Coca-Colas their grandparents kept stacked on the back porch in all kinds of weather. And beyond ingesting Coca-Cola as a beverage, they had figured out other ways to weave it into cuisine and culture. The sugar-heavy diet of the typical southerner, with its sweetened tea and pecan pralines and sweet-potato pie and pitchers of syrup on dinner tables to be poured over ham and biscuits if someone desired, all made the region a prime target for a soft drink like Coca-Cola. Those consumers made it more than just a soft drink; it became an ingredient in the foods and habits they formed, wrapping itself into their culture like a powerful enzyme. You were a Coke drinker, and that was that; people rarely switched.

The most basic Coke-inspired food was the farmer's lunch, or goober cocktail – a package of salted peanuts funneled into a bottle of Coca-Cola, creating a concoction that could be guzzled and chewed all at the same time. There were barbecue sauces for chicken, ham, and ribs that required the contents of a bottle of Coke. Coca-Cola cakes became popular at church suppers and picnics across the South sometime in the 1920s. They were chocolate cakes, their texture made lighter and their sweetness intensified with two cups of Coke. They were iced with a mixture of cocoa, powdered sugar, and more Coca-Cola. There was something called Coq au Coke, which involved two chickens, a stick of butter, a splash of pineapple juice and half a cup of Coca-Cola. And through the 1990s, the *Atlanta Journal-Constitution* published the steps for making dishes like congealed Coca-Cola cranberry salad (you needed a bottle of Coke, a package of gelatin, and some canned cranberry sauce to get started) in a weekly feature called Recipe Swap. Other soft drinks tried for the same level of culinary infiltration but were less persuasive. The makers of Dr Pepper and 7Up published a cookbook of their own that recommended, among other things, poaching fish fillets in a bath of simmering 7Up.

What continued to be remarkable about the public's love affair with Coca-Cola was that it had a life of its own. As the company was spending millions to remind them to drink a Coke – the advertising budget rose from $100,000 in 1901 to $10 million by 1941, and was closing in on $2 billion by the end of the 1990s – people were making a place for it in their daily routines. They played games based on Coke in the small towns scattered across the South, where the wonder surrounding Coca-Cola was fed as much by the paucity of other enterprise as by the product itself.

An office, a gas station, or a general store with a vending machine would become the setting for a game called Far Away. Bottlers put their hometowns – Big Spring, Texas; Kalamazoo, Michigan; Hays, Kansas – on the bottoms of returnable Coke bottles, and under the rules of the game the person who put change into the vending machine and retrieved a bottle that had traveled the farthest from its origins was the winner. (The prize was a free Coke, courtesy of the other players, on the next round.) The first coin-operated vending machines were installed in 1935, setting the stage for games of Far Away, which soon had multiple variations, influenced by the creativity of the players.

And before long, there was the integration of Coca-Cola and another great object of the nation's affection: the car. Some people poured Coke onto their windshields to clean them in the rain, insisting that nothing cut through the greasy film of stuff that built up on the glass like good old Coca-Cola. Others used it to clean the interior, scrubbing at stains on the dashboard with a rag dipped in Coca-Cola. The animal kingdom, too, joined the Coca-Cola faithful. Dogs, horses, canaries, elephants, and honeybees were all witnessed drinking Coke.

All that passion and lore that was so well documented involved the old Coke. As wonderful and traditional as that might have been, it was old now, under pressure and no longer good enough. Goizueta planned the rewriting of the secret Coca-Cola recipe as a way of getting the product to transcend what it already was. As big as Coke was, it could be bigger, better, and even more enthusiastically hailed, he thought. Changing the formula would constitute a dramatic flourish on all the other changes he'd made in the Coca-Cola Company, succinctly defining the new entity he had spent so much time creating, and inspiring awe and envy in all of Coke's competitors. He intended New Coke to be revolutionary, ultimately the most spectacular of all the changes at so many other levels that he had organized and carried out since arriving in Atlanta.

Most of all, it would firmly establish him in the pantheon of Coke's leaders. He would be seen as a keener visionary than Woodruff, more instinctively successful than Candler. He had already served warning on the entire Coke family four years earlier, when he intoned that 'there are no sacred cows'.

Now he wanted to serve notice to the rest of the world that he was a genuine Coca-Cola hero, carrying the name and the product forward to greater glory, boldly taking the necessary steps to win the cola wars for Coke. This would be his most important moment.

But somehow, in a way that Goizueta would spin and gloss over and deny until his dying day, it did not go according to plan.

The predictions of the bottlers' wives, sipping New Coke in the lobby of the Woodruff Center, turned out to be correct. New Coke became the biggest marketing flop in modern history, a textbook example of how not to succeed in the consumer-products business. For years afterward, flawed or failing products all over the world would be held up to ridicule that, as a means of gauging just how disastrous they were, compared them to New Coke.

Long before New Coke, Coca-Cola was a product of great mystery. Over the years, hundreds of thousands of people, after drinking a Coke or observing someone who was a true Coke drinker, had asked themselves, *What is* in *that stuff?* And for just as many years, the Coca-Cola Company had refused to say. The formula lay locked in a bank vault, management insisted. No one at the company, except two or three people at a time, knew what exactly went into Coke. It hadn't changed since the turn of the century, they would say, and it still required a long list of ingredients. But beyond that, everything was a secret. Even the location of the vault was never disclosed, although many people concluded that it must be somewhere inside the dank reaches of SunTrust, the big Atlanta bank that controlled millions of shares of Coke stock on behalf of the foundations named for Candler and Woodruff and Whitehead and Thomas that nurtured the educational and cultural and medical institutions of the South.

After a certain point, when technology had caught up to rhetoric, the secret formula was little more than a marketing gag. Schoolchildren could approximate Coca-Cola in science class, using the right combination of known elements. But the continuing insistence that there was something special, *something secret,* about the drink helped create an allure around it, a veil of intrigue that served the product well. Chemists and others would at least partially decode the mystery, listing ingredients for publication. But even if you managed to make it at home, it still wasn't Coca-Cola. It might be delicious and refreshing. But it would not be the one sold everywhere.

The 1920 litigation between the bottlers and the company over concentrate prices revealed that every gallon of syrup contained 5.32 pounds of cane sugar. And like all sodas, Coca-Cola contained carbonated water – energized with thousands of tiny bubbles of carbon dioxide, the same vapor that is released in every human exhalation, the 'hot air' of long-winded speeches and the 'wild gas' that intrigued seventeenth-century scientists curious about where naturally sparkling springs got their effervescence. Too much carbon dioxide can kill a person trapped in a space with insufficient oxygen. Collecting under the earth, carbon dioxide can spew forth in an eruption, as a geyser or a volcano. Poorly controlled, it can be a lethal substance, and people in the soft-drink business know that.

Without it, a drink like Coke would have been dull and unappetizing; with it, Coca-Cola truly became greater than the sum of its parts. 'In a still drink where no gas at all is used, in order to make a palatable beverage it is necessary to use almost twice as much sugar as that used in a highly charged soda water,' wrote the authors of a 1924 guide to making soft drinks. Carbonation lifted a drink, made it taste better, cut down on costs. Every soda has measurements, known as Brix and volume, that represent the sugariness of the concentrate and the amount of carbonation. Getting them properly coordinated is considered essential if a soda is to taste good.

Goizueta's decision to tinker with the taste and the carbonation was bold, to say the least. The aura surrounding the formula, that it was fully understood by only a chosen few and that it provided the lifeblood of the company, undoubtedly had discouraged other Coke executives in the past. The formula always had its guardians, like Candler, with his little locked room in Atlanta. There was also the idea that if it wasn't broken, why fix it? Coke sold so well for most of its first century that not many people would have thought there was anything wrong with it.

But those people didn't have the Pepsi Challenge to contend with.

Goizueta thought he had done all the correct calculations and knelt before the right thrones before committing his most dramatic act on the road to changing Coca-Cola. With the development of New Coke nearly complete, he paid a visit to Woodruff, ninety-five years old and living in semi-seclusion at Ichauway. Woodruff, ailing, had stepped back almost completely from Coke's operations after Goizueta became chairman and CEO. He occasionally made his way into the office in Atlanta, getting a warm reception from everyone he saw, but within a year or two most of his days were spent far from the Coke tower. Still, Goizueta knew that to have Woodruff's blessing would be critical to the success of any project he might try. And while Woodruff might have bristled at anyone else's suggestion that the Coke formula needed modification, Goizueta had market share data to back up his position. Sometime in early 1985, with New Coke already a reality and just waiting to be unveiled, Goizueta went to Ichauway and, with the old oaks sighing in the background, told The Boss his plans.

He had plenty of evidence to illustrate his worry that Pepsi might soon outsell Coke. For years, Pepsi-Cola ads had been built around a theme: 'Let Your Taste Decide'. The campaign was known as the Pepsi Challenge, and it involved a simple but humiliating procedure, humiliating if you were connected to Coke. Participants – people taken off the street, usually – were filmed as they sipped from unmarked paper cups of Coke and Pepsi. Invariably, in the ads that got air-time, they would announce that they liked the cup of Pepsi best, even if they had already identified themselves as dyed-in-the-wool Coke drinkers. The documentation ran as television commercials, and they were everywhere unhappy Coke management looked. Even more maddening was the fact that sales data backed them up. When it came to cola, Pepsi's market share had climbed from the mid-1970s to 1984. It stood at 17.8 percent in 1985, compared with Coke's 22 percent. And Coke's share had not increased in years. The growth in the admittedly mature cola market had all gone to Pepsi. What if Pepsi's momentum continued? What if, one day in the foreseeable future, Pepsi deposed Coke as the alpha brand of cola?

It was the kind of situation no self-respecting Coke executive could ignore. The shame of losing the number one position to Pepsi, the upstart that had been needling the Coca-Cola Company since 1898, when a North Carolina druggist came up with the formula in an irritating echo of the Coke story, would be too much to bear. They had to do something. They had meeting after meeting where they collectively wrung their hands. What was going on? What was Pepsi's advantage? How could they get their own momentum back?

The feud between Coke and Pepsi, twelve years younger as a brand, had been going on sporadically since the early part of the century. But it had reached a serious pitch in the 1930s, when Pepsi, perennially on the brink of bankruptcy, was casting around in desperation for a way out of its troubles. A used-bottle dealer suggested to company management that it would be less costly to use old beer bottles than to buy new ones for Pepsi-Cola. And so Pepsi bottlers began running twelve-ounce bottles through their machinery, putting out a product that was twice as generous as Coke's. Coca-Cola came in six-and-a-half-ounce bottles then, and they sold for a nickel. Pepsi's bottle was a lot bigger, but Coke was much bigger in terms of market share. No one at Coke was too worried about this latest scheme of Pepsi's.

At first, Pepsi tried charging ten cents apiece for twelve ounces of its cola, reasoning that at twice the size, people should be willing to pay more. Nothing happened. Sales stayed where they were, becalmed.

Then someone at Pepsi thought of pricing the more generous serving at the same level as Coke, and Pepsi-Cola flew from store shelves. People wanted it, and they didn't want to pay so much for it. Maybe they liked Coke, but Pepsi was half the price, and they were both pretty much the same – both brown, both caffeinated, both sweet. Pepsi's volume rocketed upward, and suddenly, all based on price, Coke had a serious competitor on its hands.

Those were the origins of the cola wars, which would turn into one of the longest-running marketing blitzes in the country's history and a swirling eddy in the river of pop culture. The competition between the two soft-drink makers was brutal in its relentlessness and bizarre in its dimensions. Coke and Pepsi spared no expense in belittling each other, using any means possible. They spent billions of dollars on ads, on promotions, on giveaways like beach balls, T-shirts, and, as the stakes grew, computers, cars, and million-dollar signing bonuses. And as they spent, they may not have done all that much to each other's market share, but both of them gained a little ground in the public's imagination. People took an interest in the battle between the two and often felt compelled to commit themselves to one or the other. Yet their allegiance was ultimately an empty thing, undermined by a detachment they also had when it came to professional sports championships or presidential elections. The real beneficiaries were the advertising agencies, which took in billions while trying to come up with campaigns to assist one company or the other.

Within Coke, and at Pepsi, the battling was taken extremely seriously. A victory for Coke would be dissected endlessly behind closed doors at the highest levels of Pepsi, and a victory for Pepsi meant disaster inside Coke. Neither of them wanted to give up even a fraction of a market share point to the other. It was too awful, too humiliating.

All kinds of effort was expended on both sides to gain an advantage. George Marlin, the field sales manager for Coke, was staying in a hotel in Coeur d'Alene, Idaho, one night when he heard a burst of applause and thought he caught the word 'Pepsi' from behind the closed doors of a banquet room. Investigating a little, he learned that it was a big meeting being held for Pepsi salesmen and bottlers about how the Pepsi Challenge would be run in Seattle and other parts of the Northwest. Marlin persuaded a hotel waiter to lend him his jacket and tray. He cruised into the meeting, passing out ice-cold Pepsis from his borrowed tray, and absorbed every detail of the upcoming campaign. He even took a few notes on a scallop-edged paper napkin. As the meeting ended, Marlin stayed for the applause, then ran for the nearest telephone, where he relayed everything he had heard to his boss. 'I've got bad news, and I've got good news,' he gasped into the phone. 'The bad news is, the Pepsi Challenge is starting in the morning. The good news is, I know everything they're going to do.'

People who did not work for either company found themselves bowing to the traditions of the conflict. Analysts were careful not to wear a red tie to a Pepsi meeting or a blue tie to a rendezvous with someone from Coke. At the Ritz-Carlton in downtown Atlanta, a Coca-Cola meeting in 1998 prompted the confiscation of all the bags of Lay's potato chips and Rold Gold pretzels from the minibars in the hotel rooms. Both snacks were made by PepsiCo, and someone at Coke had phoned the hotel, reminding them of that. One guest watched in amusement as a hotel worker made his way down the carpeted corridors of the Ritz, removing the snacks one by one.

Jennifer Solomon, a beverage analyst for Josephthal & Co. at the time, walked into Coke's headquarters in Atlanta one afternoon in 1994 for an appointment. She was carrying a plastic bag from an industry conference she had attended earlier in the day. The bag, handed out to everyone at the conference, had the logo of Royal Crown cola, which perennially finished a distant third to Coke, printed on one side. As she crossed the Coca-Cola threshold, Solomon was confronted by a receptionist. The woman asked her, politely but firmly, to put the bag in the coatroom for the duration of her visit. 'They said it would upset people,' she recalled.

Sure enough, it was a war. Goizueta knew he had to do something about the Pepsi Challenge. Too many market-share surveys showed Pepsi creeping up on Coke. He commissioned a top-secret plan, led by Sergio Zyman, Coke's marketing expert, and a small cluster of trusted top executives that included Don Keough and Doug Ivester. They planned a counteroffensive, a project that would be known by a series of code names, all chosen to maintain secrecy and throw off spies. One of the early names was Project Kansas, selected by Zyman because it evoked a favorite description of Coca-Cola penned by a revered Kansas newspaper editor in 1938. Interviewed and photographed by *Life* magazine on his seventieth birthday while drinking a Coke, the editor, William Allen White, had inspired a senior Coke executive, Ralph Hayes, to send him a thank-you note. *Thanks for the free advertising,* Hayes told White after seeing the picture.

Writing back to Hayes, White endeared himself further. Coca-Cola, he insisted effusively, was *a sublimated essence of all that America stands for, a decent thing honestly made, conscientiously improved with the years.* Hayes hung on to the letter for the rest of his life, and White's summing up of the company's flagship product and raison d'être went into a Coke file marked FAVORITE THINGS. From time to time it would be reprinted, cited, brought up whenever the company wanted a reminder of just what it meant to people. Everyone at Coke learned the phrase, sooner or later.

That final notion of White's letter – 'improved with the years' – was the wedge Goizueta relied on to convince longtime Coke executives that altering the formula was not sacrilege but a part of their tradition. Hadn't Asa Candler, once cocaine became scandalous, changed the original himself? Over the years, other adjustments had been made here and there, for ingredients that were suddenly hard to obtain or otherwise rendered obsolete. Goizueta's plan would merely be the latest in a long line of alterations, all designed to make the product better. It would be a new, improved Coke – like so much in America, the result of exhaustive research into what the consumer wanted.

The consumer appeared to want Pepsi. All those blind taste tests, all the groups that Zyman and others had interviewed, pointed to the same conclusion: People preferred the sweeter, slightly less sharp taste of Pepsi to that of Coke. No one at Coke was going to get them to change their minds. There was only one thing to do.

When Goizueta visited Woodruff, stooped and fading down at the plantation, life had changed there, too. The hum of activity that Woodruff used to generate, with all his visitors and his shooting parties, had stopped. Now there was an air of sadness over the place, slow and thick like a lump in the throat. Woodruff the man was in his last months. Goizueta would not repeat any details of their conversation, but he indicated later that he had gotten the go-ahead from Woodruff. Not everyone was convinced. 'I do not believe that this idea was signed off on by Bob Woodruff,' Bill Schmidt said.

It hardly mattered, in the end. By the time New Coke was formally announced, Woodruff was gone. He died in his bed at Emory University Hospital in Atlanta on March 7, 1985, with one of his servants from Ichauway holding his white and wrinkled hand. All of the power he had once enjoyed inside the Coca-Cola Company vanished that day, too. Goizueta could do as he pleased.

Six weeks later, at a glamorous news conference staged at the Vivian Beaumont Theater in New York, Coke shocked the world. Goizueta, Keough, and Brian Dyson, the gangly Argentinean who was president of Coca-Cola USA, got up together and declared that there was now a new formula for Coke. What the world knew as Coke would be replaced by this revised version, this thing known as New Coke. The 'old Coke' would be a thing of the past.

Reporters in the audience were silent. Then they began to pepper the executives, who stood there like proud parents, with questions.

What was different about New Coke, they asked? Goizueta called the revision 'smoother, rounder, yet bolder', and 'a more harmonious flavor'. How hard had it been to decide to change the old recipe? Goizueta grinned. The decision, he said, was 'one of the easiest we have ever made'. Would the whole plan work? Goizueta was ready for that one, too. Thousands of consumers, offered a taste of the new formula, said that they preferred it to the old one, he said. In Coke's own blind taste tests, people preferred the taste of New Coke to old Coke by a ratio of 55 to 45, he said. The old recipe, by the way, would continue to lie in its bank vault in Atlanta as it had for decades, locked away as always but never to be used again. Going forward, there would be only New Coke.

In an interview a day later, Goizueta would go out of his way to express his regret that The Boss could not witness the great leap forward that New Coke represented. 'The saddest part is that Mr. Woodruff is not around to participate and to celebrate in the introduction of New Coke,' he told a reporter. 'Mr. Woodruff would have been among the most enthusiastic supporters of the change, because he always believed in giving the consumer what he wants.'

Within the Coke system, most of the people who tried this nouveau formulation had reactions far different from the ones Goizueta described. Richard Larson, an executive with Coca-Cola Midwest Bottling in Minneapolis, remembers the day an important-looking package arrived from Atlanta a few days before the April announcement to the world. Inside the package was a videotape showing Brian Dyson waxing ecstatic about the drink. He promised it would be a big deal, the agent of change they had all been waiting for to wake up the cola market and get Coke's sales moving. It was going to replace the old formula surely and spectacularly, starting soon. The video was accompanied by several bottles of New Coke for the executives to try.

They poured it out a little nervously, and sipped in unison, in the privacy of their boardroom. Then came the reaction.

'There were about three minutes of silence, and then someone said, "Oh my God, it tastes just like Pepsi,"' Larson said. 'Everyone in the room knew it was just a disaster in the making.'

At least they knew about it ahead of time. Several bottlers did not and got their first clues from reading newspaper reports about the company's plans that leaked out a few days ahead of the official launch. George Marlin, driving around the Pacific Northwest with his boss, heard it on the radio. Some people who heard about it from friends thought it was a joke, or a Pepsi prank. When they called in to Atlanta, they found out that it was true.

In Atlanta, Coke employees were briefed en masse at the beautiful old Fox Theatre a mile or so downtown from the Coke tower. Larry Jones, a benefits coordinator in the human resources department, started work on April 1. A few days later, he happened to be looking out of the window in his office and noticed a long line of buses snaking along the pavement in front of the building. 'What are those buses for?' he asked someone. Before the day was out, he and hundreds of other Coke employees were sitting in the plush seats of the theater, listening to Goizueta and Don Keough describing the virtues of New Coke. *New Coke?* Jones thought. *What was the matter with the old Coke?*

Other employees felt the same way. 'I was aghast,' said one former executive. 'You didn't mess with the formula.'

At PepsiCo headquarters in Purchase, New York, word of the rejiggered Coca-Cola had been circulating for days before the official announcement. Don Kendall, the chairman of PepsiCo, had heard about it while traveling in Japan and called Roger Enrico, Pepsi's president, in disbelief. 'These guys are nuts,' Kendall told Enrico. But Enrico began to fret. *Maybe this thing is magic,* he thought. *Maybe it could be something that puts us in a corner.*

Early in May, a Pepsi executive flew down to Atlanta to get a six-pack from a grocery store that stocked the new flavor and rushed back to Purchase with it the same day. Inside the Pepsi executive suite, dozens of paper cups were filled with New Coke. Everyone waited expectantly as the senior executives lifted their cups to their lips.

It tasted flat, to Enrico and everyone else sitting in Kendall's office. They were surprised. No one said anything.

They sipped again. And then they began to smile. 'God knows how they did it, but they had blown it,' Enrico recalled. 'It just didn't taste good. It was not like the old Coke. It wasn't a good Pepsi, either. It was like painting by numbers, built from consumer research. It wasn't any good.'

Then Enrico, who had been planning a reaction for days, ordered up a series of taunting newspaper ads, declaring a holiday because Pepsi had won the cola wars. With New Coke, the Coca-Cola Company had conceded that people preferred Pepsi, Enrico crowed. Chemists on the Pepsi payroll deconstructed New Coke, determining that it had less of the flavored oils that the old formula contained, as well as less vanilla. Their conclusion: The new formula would save Coke about $50 million a year because it cut back on some of the most costly ingredients. It was a day that Roger Enrico, Don Kendall, and the others at Pepsi could not have imagined. Coke had turned its back on the very thing that made it great. They were jubilant.

But Pepsi's reaction was nothing compared with the public's. Across the country, Coke drinkers rose up in righteous indignation, demanding their old soft drink back. One man in Seattle formed an association of the irate, the Old Coke Drinkers of America. Columnists, cartoonists, and comedians weighed in, from Russell Baker and Art Buchwald to David Letterman on NBC. 'Coke's decided to make their formula sweeter,' Letterman said. 'They're going to mix it with Pepsi.' Not to be outdone, Johnny Carson suggested that the idea was like something that Ronald Reagan's travel aides, under fire at the time for planning a visit to a Nazi cemetery during a presidential trip to Germany, might think up. 'Next they'll change Twinkies,' Carson moaned, 'and put in a spinach filling.'

Letters and phone calls poured into Coke headquarters, where some reaction had been anticipated, but nothing on the scale of what actually took place. *Dear Sir,* one communiqué began. *Changing Coke is like God making the grass purple or putting toes on our ears or teeth on our knees.*

Bottlers got an earful, too. They were the local faces on Coca-Cola, after all, and now people called them up, screaming into the telephone day and night. 'You ruined our Coke!' they would cry. One bottler decided to escape from it all by taking a cruise. When the ship docked, the customs officer checking passports asked what he did for a living. When he replied that he was a Coca-Cola bottler, she became enraged. 'What did you do to my Coca-Cola?' she shouted. The bottler slunk away, but not before glancing at all the people he had met on the ship and considered his new friends. 'They were all looking at me,' he recalled, 'like I was a Communist.'

But the bottlers had to support it. They had no choice. 'They gritted their teeth, shut their eyes, and charged ahead,' said Emmet Bondurant. 'And they just got creamed.'

Other people closely tied to Coke felt the backlash, too. 'I went out to see the coach of the University of Arkansas football team,' said Asa Candler VI, an Atlanta businessman and great-great-great-grandson of the Coke empire's founder. 'And he said to me, "I've had Coke all my life. I can't stand this New Coke. I might have to change to Pepsi."'

Inside the company, Goizueta insisted that all consumers needed was a little time to get used to the change. 'We kept saying that as time goes on, they will forget about old Coke,' one marketing executive said later.

That did not happen. *Dear Chief Dodo,* another letter began. *What ignoramus has decided to change the flavor of Coke?* Even Crispulo Goizueta called his son from Mexico to complain. New Coke wasn't for sale there, not yet, but the elder Goizueta could not believe the fuss that had been kicked up in the States.

Within a few weeks, the mood of the Coke directors had shifted from relaxed to alarmed. The possibility of reviving the old formula came up at directors' meetings, but Goizueta insisted that the country just needed more exposure to New Coke. They had to get used to it, he said. Just give it a few more weeks.

May came and went. Consumers hoarded old Coke. Kay Phelan ordered her husband to buy it wherever he could, and Bob, intent on pleasing her, drove as far as Tennessee in hot pursuit. In June, Don Keough bragged to reporters that New Coke was going great. The company announced that its shipment of Coca-Cola concentrate to bottlers rose 8 percent in May, the month after New Coke went on the market. Keough called it 'the largest increase on a monthly basis in my memory', and added, 'The strategy we set forth with the new taste of Coke is being received beyond our expectations at this point. We never doubted its success, and this data confirms it.'

He did, however, acknowledge something else. The company had received about forty thousand letters and calls about the flavor change, he said. But, with typical breeziness, he assured reporters that that was all going to go away.

'When you consider that a hundred and ten million people have tried it,' Keough said, 'those complaints become relatively insignificant.' Coke's stock, meanwhile, was shooting up, reaching a ten-year high as he spoke. The effect Goizueta desired above all was taking hold.

Still, the letters kept coming in to headquarters in Atlanta. The tone of some of them was not just angry but mournful, as if the writers were coming to terms with the death of an old friend. *The sorrow is knowing not only won't I ever enjoy the Real Coke again,* one man wrote, *but my children and grandchildren won't either. I guess my children will just have to take my word for it.* An elderly woman wrote in, noting that it had been twenty years since she last ordered a Coke. But she was nonetheless indignant. *You have taken away my childhood,* she told the company.

The bottlers were hearing even more complaints than Atlanta was. And with their livelihoods on the line, they began to detest New Coke. The bottlers were up in arms, 'even those who had been singing the company line on the amended contracts and everything else', Emmet Bondurant said.

A little more than two months after the introduction, a group of them traveled to Atlanta to meet with top executives at Coke. One of the bottlers was Frank Barron, of Rome, Georgia. Another was Crawford Johnson, the third-generation bottler from Birmingham,

Alabama. They banded together with a group of their fellow bottlers and laid down the law to Coke. They demanded that the company bring back the old formula. Around the same time, Bill Schmidt, who was still an officer of the Coca-Cola Bottlers Association, held a special meeting for twenty of his members. 'Some of them were saying they couldn't play golf anymore' because of angry confrontations in the locker room, he recalled. 'And some of their employees didn't want to wear their uniforms home anymore.' No one was forgetting about the old Coke. Things were getting uglier by the day.

The bottlers confronted Atlanta. If you insist on having this New Coke, they said, at least let us sell the old one, too. We're losing money on this.

Keough and Goizueta demurred. We have to see this through, they said. It's only been a little while. People will get over themselves.

Meanwhile, the switchboards at Coke continued to light up with angry calls from longtime Coke drinkers. Gay Mullins, founder of the Seattle-based Old Coke Drinkers of America, remained a hot subject for the nightly news. More letters poured into the Coke mailroom. Pepsi, instead of being brought to its knees by Goizueta's strategy, kept running clever ads that exploited the similarities between New Coke and Pepsi, turning them into humiliating differences between the two companies.

By the end of June, Goizueta and Keough had grown more concerned about the fate of New Coke. And when the group of bottlers asked for a meeting with them in early July, the two men at the top of the company started to realize how deep and persistent the objections to the product were. It wasn't only about the taste. It was about heartbreak. It was about the loss of a product that people considered almost a part of them, the gratuitous banishing of something that held meaning for them. Goizueta hadn't weighed that factor in all his calculations and assessments, and apparently neither had Keough, Dyson, Zyman, or anyone else who had helped bring New Coke to life.

On July 10, 1985, just seventy-eight days after the unveiling of New Coke, Goizueta abruptly put out the word that old Coke would be coming back, this time as Coca-Cola Classic. News anchors interrupted the afternoon soap operas to spread the word: The Coca-Cola Company had backed down. Consumers had won.

'It was like a Frank Capra script,' one senior Coca-Cola executive recalled. 'Big company tries something that people reject. Big company admits it.'

A former executive thought the whole experience brought home the real truth of Coke, not just in 1985 but throughout its history. 'We did not know what we were selling,' he said. 'We are not selling a soft drink. We are selling a little tiny piece of people's lives.'

A day later Goizueta stood before another news conference and put his own spin on the event, saying that New Coke would continue to be sold, just as before, but that bottlers would have both formulas at their disposal, to sell as they liked. In no way had the new recipe been rejected; it was simply recognized now that people wanted the old one, too. He was right to have introduced New Coke; he was now going to make everyone happy by bringing back old Coke, too. He had not made a mistake. He was just going to be more inclusive from now on.

'Today we have two messages to deliver to the American consumer,' Goizueta said. 'First, to those of you who are drinking Coca-Cola with its great new taste, our thanks and gratitude. You are enjoying the best-tasting Coca-Cola we have ever made.' Then he added, 'But there is a second group of consumers to whom we want to speak today, and our message to this group is simple: We have heard you.'

By the end, more than 400,000 calls and letters had poured into Coca-Cola headquarters, railing at the company for taking away old Coke and begging to have it back. To the men running Coke, that turned out to be a significant number. And within a year, sales of Coca-Cola Classic, as it was now known, outstripped sales of New Coke by ten to one. Not many people sympathized with the Coca-Cola Company's grand effort to change the formula. The Atlanta paper's Recipe Swap pointedly specified 'the old kind' whenever it called for Coca-Cola.

Fifteen years later, there were still one or two bottlers in the United States who ordered New Coke concentrate from Atlanta.

They insisted they had some customers who liked it, so they had to have it. But others believed that the bottlers just wanted to prolong the memory of the Coca-Cola Company's biggest fiasco a little while longer. Or maybe they realized that, with all the other changes being forced on the system, this was the last big moment they would share with the Coca-Cola Company.

'That entire event was such a strange phenomenon,' observed Frank Barron many years later. 'No one was happier than me when it was all over with.'

Chapter Six

Everything According to Plan

GOIZUETA STOOD IN THE sticky ruins of New Coke and declared victory. People had stood up for Coca-Cola in an unprecedented way, he said. It was a vote of confidence in the product, a declaration of loyalty and love. In the annual report for that year, he would refer to the event as 'the further development of mega-brand Coca-Cola', and praise the company's management team for responding in a way that was 'testament to our ability to listen to, and our willingness to meet, consumer demand for choice in the soft-drink marketplace'.

Elsewhere people thought, *Thank God for the bottlers*. They were the ones who had intervened. Had it not been for the pressure from the independent businessmen in Rome, Georgia, Birmingham, Alabama, and other points on the map – the people who were closest to the consumers of Coca-Cola – Goizueta and Keough and everyone else at the Coca-Cola Company might have pressed on indefinitely with Project Kansas. Forty thousand angry calls and letters hadn't convinced them by early June that the whole notion was doomed. Without the bottlers, the whole Coke empire might have come crashing down.

To some, the outcome of New Coke was a stroke of fortune for Goizueta and everyone else involved in creating the brand. 'New Coke was a disaster in every respect that turned out, through no fault of the company's, to have reignited consumer loyalty to the Coke brand, as in Classic Coke,' said Emmet Bondurant. 'That was serendipitous, inadvertent, unplanned good luck.'

But Goizueta would never admit that, and would never concede that his attempt to alter the world's best-known brand had failed. Years after the debacle, he would be as upbeat about New Coke as if it had not yet appeared on the market. He held a mass meeting at headquarters in 1995, marking the tenth anniversary of the altered formula, which by then had mostly vanished from the marketplace except in a few stubborn pockets of the country, where it was called Coke II. At the meeting, he insisted that the critics and journalists had been wrong. The whole project, said Goizueta, with the memory of it still strong, had been a stunning success.

He spoke on an April day when all of Atlanta seemed in flower, and the Coca-Cola Company was performing as never before. Everyone invited to the tenth-anniversary meeting plucked a Coca-Cola Classic from the big ice-filled bowls set up outside the auditorium before settling into their seats.

There was just the barest mention of New Coke, and it was not by name. 'We did change the formula and we did make you chief financial officer,' Goizueta said, addressing Doug Ivester. 'And both of those events remind me how much some people like to second-guess everything the Coca-Cola Company does.'

Sergio Zyman listened intently. He had departed in 1987, in the wake of New Coke, sheerly by coincidence, the Coke front office insisted. Even Zyman himself would say that he left 'because I love marketing, and I wanted to do some things that the company wasn't prepared to do at that time'. Others saw him as the fall guy, along with Brian Dyson, who was dispatched in 1986 to run Coca-Cola Enterprises, the big new bottler that Ivester created, for five years before he eventually retired. Away from Coke, Zyman started his own consulting firm, a job that Ivester would describe as involving lots of hours spent 'sitting by his pool and talking on the telephone'. He was gone from the Coke tower for six long years. When he returned, it was at Ivester's request. Keough was gone by the time the tenth anniversary rolled around. He would tell people, much later, that he had been on vacation when the decision to bring out New Coke was made.

Now it was Zyman, the once and future marketing king, that Goizueta and Ivester turned to for help in explaining the legacy of New Coke to the employees assembled in Atlanta.

With his slight frame, hunched shoulders, and perpetually furrowed brow, Zyman looked like a nervous jockey who knows his horse could come in last. He spoke quickly, and he didn't like to be interrupted, especially if it was with a question. In meetings, he had a reputation for being domineering, earning nicknames like 'the Aya-cola'. He believed in stripping marketing down to a single idea, then sending it out across the organization, back and forth like a weaver's shuttle until everything about Coke buzzed with the same message. It was known as the 'buildout of marketing', and it had to permeate every level of the company. 'It changed the way they looked at people,' said Lauren Bryant, an assistant vice president of marketing who had been at Coke for two years when Zyman returned. 'Before, if they brought someone in, it was all about that person's beverage experience. But Sergio said, "We have enough beverage people. We need people with marketing experience."' The old Coke marketing, while highly effective, was nothing like what Zyman brought in. 'It was like turning up the dial fifty times in the time that I was there,' she said.

He hungered for excellence, and to get it he pitted advertising agencies against one another, declaring that Coke's hefty account would be scattered among ten or twelve of them at a time. He was known to leap on top of conference tables and to trample the cushions on a couch by way of making his point. Meetings hosted by Zyman were like cartoons that might have been amusing had there been no other actual human beings attending them. He would sometimes point out the flaws and cracks in his subordinates' presentations – to the extent that some of them, since they were actual human beings, went away devastated. 'He has obviously got a brilliant marketing mind, but he didn't always treat people very well,' Bryant said. 'He was always looking for that opportunity to pull the rug out from under you, and challenge you, in a way that was as public as possible.'

Such reactions to his style just brought shrugs from Zyman, who had convinced himself long ago that he was right about everything having to do with his job. He had gotten results, no matter how that happened. And now, having returned to a company where image was everything and marketing was about to define everything, he had no reason to question himself.

He had been invited back to Coke as chief marketing officer in 1993, and now he had to put the corporate spin on New Coke once again. He could speak the forked language of marketing better than almost anybody at the Coca-Cola Company, and he was expert in delivering a little something to everyone, just enough to keep them hopeful.

To him, New Coke was an inevitability, as he said, and a risk that the Coca-Cola Company absolutely had to take. 'While it may have seemed like a dangerous thing to change the formula of Coca-Cola, the reality was that doing nothing was far, far more dangerous,' Zyman declared. So the project had been the right course of action.

But after the brouhaha brought on by changing the formula, Coke learned another lesson, he added. 'People want Coca-Cola to be its same enduring, relevant self,' he declared, 'not a shallow chameleon that routinely sells out its own fundamental nature just to mirror the trend of the moment.' That the two ideas contradicted each other seemed not to worry him in the least. The drink had to be different, and yet it had to stay the same. 'Coca-Cola,' said Zyman, the chief marketing officer, 'must be Coca-Cola, always.'

Roberto Goizueta wanted all that behind him. With New Coke lingering like a permanent stain on his reputation – books came out about the fiasco a year after it ended, and the company continued to be an object of ridicule long after the product ceased being news – Goizueta worked hard to make the episode go away. New Coke had been a disaster, though he would never admit it publicly, and he had to be sure that something else became linked forever with his name.

He also had to contend with fallout from his plan to disengage Coke from its longtime bottling system. While dozens of bottlers had agreed to the amended contracts that allowed the Coca-Cola Company to raise the price of syrup regularly, others remained opposed to the plan and had sued the company in federal court. With the introduction of diet Coke, the lawsuit widened to oppose Coke's unilaterally imposed restrictions on bottlers' access to that formula as well.

In 1986, the bottlers' complaints were nearing trial. The number of bottlers involved in the lawsuits had shrunk considerably, from eighty to about twenty, but still the action was going forward. Bill Schmidt remained at the forefront, the leader of the loyal opposition. In the meantime, New Coke had complicated matters for the Coca-Cola Company.

However, Goizueta had other plans that were unfolding. New Coke had been merely one element of his design for the company, in which he staked careers and reputations not on how well people did in the field, selling Coke and managing the bottlers, but on how much they helped deliver on his promises to the financial community. Rejiggering the relationship with the bottlers to make bottling more profitable for the Coca-Cola Company was another part of that. But there was much more.

His strategy, he would explain in 1988, was 'designed around a single objective: increasing shareholder value over time'. He had developed techniques to make sure that happened, and something like New Coke would not stop him.

Coke's image on Wall Street had not been especially good when Goizueta became chairman and CEO. The company was well regarded, a blue chip because of its history and its large number of investors but not especially exciting to anyone. You could invest your money in Coke and not be disappointed; it paid a dividend year after year, and over time an investment could be counted on to grow in value. A single share of Coke purchased in 1919, the year that Candler sold the company to the bankers' group headed by Ernest Woodruff, had grown to 192 shares through stock splits by the time Goizueta ascended, sixty-two years later. The compounded annual return, however, hovered in the low single digits. Problems like currency devaluation plagued the earnings, since three quarters of Coke's sales came from overseas. A dip in the yen or in the British pound could knock a hole in even the best-planned quarter. And for too long, in Goizueta's opinion, growth had been dictated by the bottlers and the markets: What seemed reasonably attainable was what the company ended up selling. No one had pushed the envelope for years.

But the 1980s would be different, Goizueta promised. 'What we wanted to do,' said one longtime colleague, 'was to be clearly the number-one beverage company in the world and to maximize that growth – not to be satisfied with the growth that just came naturally.' Coke was number one in many markets, including the United States, but what Goizueta and his colleagues wanted was for it to be emphatically, unequivocally, and fearsomely number one. And even before he scheduled the ostentatious spectacle to mark Coke's centennial, Goizueta was building an elaborate program to woo and please shareholders that was unprecedented in the history of the Coca-Cola Company.

It began at the top. He created a role for himself as the oracle, the one who could speak to analysts and investors and have them listen. If Don Keough was the beating heart of Coca-Cola, then Goizueta was the coolly controlling superego. For eight years after New Coke, Keough would be the one who dealt with all sorts of people in the chain that created sales of the soft drink – the bottlers, the supermarket executives, the mandarins of McDonald's and Burger King. Goizueta would master the art of selling the Coca-Cola Company itself to those who molded public opinion about what made a wise investment, what constituted a growth stock. Ivester would help both of them, finding ways to crank additional profitability out of every aspect of making and selling Coca-Cola. They would make sure their company was no longer subject to bottlers or currencies or regulators. They would figure out routes around all those things, because this was Coca-Cola and they were the ones in charge.

Their timing was impeccable. The stock market, by the mid-1980s, was no longer a foggy province open only to the expert few. Workers at all levels were investing their money, confident of bigger payouts than they could expect from traditional savings and retirement accounts, and Wall Street was a suddenly populist place. Meanwhile, newspapers were filled with articles detailing takeovers and buyouts of companies that had thought they could maintain their circa-1970 status quo. Words like 'greenmailing' and 'insider trading' were becoming familiar to many Americans. Everyone, from sanitation workers to chief executive officers, wanted to maximize the returns on their money. And like health care, which was by then being managed in a corporate environment, retirement funds and family savings had to be managed, too, and not left to quietly build up in some corner until the day a person hit sixty-five.

An information industry burst forth to spread and share information about the business world. If you were a broker, you had to confront a suddenly more aware clientele, and at cocktail parties people talked about their stocks and their rates of return the way they had once talked about pennant races and vacation plans. CEOs who posted superb results lost their facelessness and became celebrities, their photographs featured on the covers of magazines and their names dropped on talk shows. It was a startling shift, for them and for the public.

Goizueta examined the situation and realized that he had an unusual opportunity. If he could control all of the information that flowed out to the public about the Coca-Cola Company, then he would have the advantage. If Wall Street looked to him for guidance on the company's fortunes, as he was busily redesigning the company, it left the ultimate authority in his hands. Such control would not be easy to establish. He would have to create an expectation, and then meet or exceed it. Then he would have to do it again, to build a track record and earn trust from the skeptics. He would have to be the sole source of information about the Coca-Cola Company. But he was sure he could pull it off.

'Roberto would always say that he could not delegate the reputation of the company to anyone but the CEO,' said one former Coke executive. It was a responsibility that he took on seriously and thoroughly.

Like so many others at Coke, he was proud of what he was doing at the company and perhaps a little spellbound by it, too. Coke was Coke, and it was strange and powerful, so much more than the sum of its parts. He was its king, but all of Coke's mystique, all of its strength, belonged to some larger entity that overshadowed even him. 'When you are working for Coca-Cola, you circulate around the whole of planet Coca-Cola,' said a former senior executive. 'You are a moon that is attached to that planet. You stare down at it all the time. You are fascinated to be in that orbit. It is wonderful to be in that orbit. It is a brand that essentially does no one any harm. It is clean and wholesome and you feel good about it.'

Goizueta was also joining in a Coca-Cola tradition that was at least as important as the soft drink itself: the art of marketing concepts – expectations, definitions of success – to an unsuspecting and not terribly discerning public. 'Life is pretty much a selling job,' Robert Woodruff had declared, time and again. 'Whether we succeed or fail is largely a matter of how well we motivate the human beings with whom we deal to buy us and that which we have to offer.'

Goizueta was ready to start motivating someone, and his target of choice was the dozens of Wall Street analysts who covered Coca-Cola stock. They were an unaggressive bunch, for the most part. For most of their careers, getting information out of the company had been like wringing water from a stone. And anyway, Coke was unsexy. It was not exactly a growth stock, and in the eighties growth was what people cared about.

Coke's reputation on Wall Street was prickly. Earlier Coke presidents and chairmen had literally refused to talk to anyone who wasn't directly involved in the company's banking needs. Information came in droplets, and analysts waited thirstily for whatever the company felt like sharing.

Suddenly, there was Goizueta, in his beautifully tailored suits and his pomade-slicked hair, with his aristocratic bearing and his staccato, authoritarian pronouncements about growth and earnings targets. He looked like someone they could trust; he looked a lot like them. He met all the targets he laid before them. The relationship between Wall Street and Coke, suddenly, was different.

Whether by desire or under orders, the new Coke chairman knew from the outset that lifting the share price would be his priority. It became his motif and his mantra. *I am a bit disappointed,* he wrote to Woodruff in November of 1982, *because I wanted to celebrate my fifty-first birthday with our stock being traded at 51.* The stock was then about fifty dollars a share. *Obviously, I fell short of the mark,* Goizueta continued, *but if I did, it was not because I didn't try.*

Keeping a tight rein on the analysts, who had the power to make or break Coke's reputation, was an essential part of accomplishing that. To the analysts, Goizueta's self-appointed role was a mixed blessing. They were used to dealing only with the investor-relations experts at Coke, who generally were people who knew them and knew the kind of information they needed. Now, while they had direct access to the leader of this hugely admired company, they ceded power to Goizueta. He dispensed the information he thought they needed, as he wanted it to appear.

Conference calls were nonexistent at Coke, though most companies scheduled them at least once a year to discuss earnings. At Coke, under Goizueta, analysts would have to call in with questions and the company would return their calls, one by one. The favorite analysts were called back first; the others might have to wait until the late afternoon. 'You always had this situation of, when do they call you back?' said Jennifer Solomon, the longtime Salomon Smith Barney beverage analyst. 'I did not get the eight-thirty A.M. call. And Allan Kaplan – they would never call him back.' Allan Kaplan had once run afoul of Goizueta, and the Coke chairman decided to make a lesson out of him.

Goizueta was practically alone among the nation's CEOs in deciding to deal directly with analysts himself. He believed that it gave him, and his company, greater control over the information flowing to investors, and in many ways he was right. In deciding what he would say and to whom, he could come across as more of a sphinx than an oracle. In explaining how Coke's profit goals could be achieved despite lower gross profits in a particular quarter, he might revert to a needlessly detailed discussion of an incident in the past that he insisted had influenced the same kind of thing that was happening at that moment. *Over the next few years, you will see the net revenue line and the gross profit margin be impacted positively or negatively depending on whether we are acquiring or disposing of bottling operations,* he wrote to one analyst in late 1996. Pointing out that this analyst had only recently begun covering the company and therefore could be forgiven for not understanding everything about the way Coke worked, he declared that the situation was not unlike the early and mid–1980s, when, *as we were changing concentrate supply points to tax advantaged locations, cost of goods were going up, thus impacting negatively gross profit, which in turn impacted negatively operating income, but then, these negative impacts were more than made up by lower tax rates and the strong positive impact on the net earnings line.* Such communiqués about Coke's business plan were common in the days when Goizueta ran the show. Did he deliberately mean to confuse, or did the company have to keep all those balls in the air to keep the business strong? The analyst hung on to that letter for a long time. Like all of Goizueta's correspondence, it was signed *Sincerely, Roberto.*

Goizueta also came to understand that his pronouncements could be timed to maximize returns on the stock price. He began issuing announcements of the company's volume estimates – the growth each quarter in terms of the amount of soda it was selling – ahead of the earnings reports themselves, which were due a few weeks later.

It was a calculated move. 'We discovered we could get two bumps out of the stock price, instead of just one,' said one executive who worked closely with Goizueta. The stock would rise on the volume estimates announcement, and rise even more when the earnings came out. It was practically the same information, but served up twice, like a meal divided into two parts and presented both times with fanfare. The ultimate effect was always greater than the sum of the parts.

Goizueta quickly came to love being the authority on Coke's stock. Few people outside the company were equipped with either the knowledge or the chutzpah to challenge him. This meant that he controlled the game.

Early in his regime, Fidel Castro patched ideological diatribes into private telephone lines. People living in Havana in 1960 learned to expect to hear a woman's voice shrieking, 'Fatherland or death!' instead of the dial tone when they picked up the receiver. Castro knew that what people heard, if they heard it often enough, could eventually color their minds.

At Coke, Goizueta's continuous refrain – of growing shareholder value, of building a better company, broken down into minutiae of the company's dealings if somebody really wanted to know – brought about similar results. What he promised was legitimized by the rising stock price and the matching surge in profits. It became hard to separate which drove which. From 1982, the profits began to accelerate. From then on the stock price was on a continuous upward climb, too. Meanwhile, if anyone wanted to understand how it worked, they had to ask *him*. Those were the conditions that Goizueta created for Coke.

Soon no one in the financial community – the people charged with generating hefty returns for the investors created in the great democratization of the stock market – wanted to be left out of the Coke miracle. The money managers all wanted to be popular in this highly popular movement. So Goizueta became increasingly powerful as time went by. Pouchy-faced and professorial by the late 1980s, he liked to dictate his information from a podium at investor meetings. He was not a casual man. He didn't take a lot of questions, but if he got one he didn't like his dark eyebrows would move a little closer together and his mouth would purse as if he had just tasted something that contained too much salt. He always answered, but he did not necessarily answer the question.

It was not just Wall Street that discovered this. Inside the company, the same attitude prevailed. 'You could ask a very pointed question, and the answer you got back had nothing to do with your question,' said a former executive who spent ten years at the company, six of them with Goizueta. 'If the question is "Did you eat Cheerios this morning?" the answer will come back: "Breakfast is one of the most important meals of the day."'

While he appeared jolly and relaxed around the office, he could be nasty if crossed. Analysts who disagreed with him about the company's prospects often got curt notes in reply. Some of them thought it was odd that someone in such an exalted position, at such a well-known company, had the time to dissect their reports and issue prompt and personal responses the way Goizueta did.

When it came to Allan Kaplan, Merrill Lynch's longtime analyst covering Coke, the responses were extremely personal. Kaplan believed that too much of Coke's earnings were coming from the strength of the yen. About 5 percent of Coke sales took place in Japan, but about 25 percent of the profits emanated from there, where Georgia coffee, Coca-Cola, and other company brands were all priced far higher than anywhere else in the world, as was the concentrate bottlers needed to make them. He wrote of his suspicions in a note to investors, which made its way to Goizueta's desk, too.

Kaplan's mistake, as far as Goizueta was concerned, was going public with his doubts about the sustainability of Coke's earnings, based on the business in Japan. Goizueta responded with angry letters, not only to Kaplan but also to his bosses at Merrill Lynch.

'That hurt our relationship, to put it euphemistically,' Kaplan said of his own candor. 'They excluded me from meetings. They used to have these meetings once a month in New York for all the analysts, and I was banned for more than a year.'

His company did not punish him, but his treatment at the hands of Goizueta shocked the other analysts and discouraged them from publishing or saying anything critical about Coke.

'In all the time I have covered beverage and tobacco companies, I have never seen anyone act like that,' said Emanuel Goldman, who followed Coke for PaineWebber, Merrill Lynch, and ING Barings over the years and became the éminence grise among Coca-Cola analysts after Kaplan retired in 1998. 'This is *the chairman of Coke,* phoning the top people at Merrill. And Allan was respected in the field,' Goldman said. 'What they were doing was trying to head off the issue at the pass. It meant that it was a really touchy situation.' On Wall Street, word went out: Don't mess with Goizueta.

And almost no one did. 'He ruled with an iron fist, inside a velvet glove,' Kaplan said. 'If you were his friend, he was a good friend. If he didn't like you – he was mean.'

Barely a month after the centennial party for Coca-Cola in 1986, Goizueta made another move designed to spark interest in his company's growth by announcing a three-for-one stock split. It was the first such split since January 22, 1960, a time when Goizueta was still going home to his house in Havana every night. The stock had split two-for-one three more times since then: in 1965, in mid-1968, and in 1977. Stock splits were doled out conservatively and guarded carefully by Bob Woodruff, like everything else about the company.

But Goizueta, the man who liked to watch the stock monitor, was different. Drawing attention to the enhanced value of the stock, which by the late spring of 1986 was topping one hundred dollars a share, was essential to building loyalty to his company – for people on the inside and on the outside. The stock was his currency, with which he would reward his executives and carbonate the value of his company before the eyes of the world.

In early June he won approval from the board to make the amount of stock held by old ladies in Decatur, management-level employees in the Coke tower, and big foundations in Atlanta triple magically. Coming on the heels of the grand Coca-Cola centennial, in a year when the stock market kept climbing for all sorts of other reasons, this plan achieved the desired result. Goizueta benefited, too; his personal holdings of thousands of Coca-Cola shares were suddenly, at least on paper, three times their former size. Everyone inside the company, every single shareholder all over the world, felt the impact of Goizueta's move.

He didn't do it in a casual way. He had Coke issue a glossy 'Special Progress Report', describing the stock split and explaining the rationale behind it. 'Splitting the stock three for one will bring the stock's absolute price back to the level of five years ago when our current management team was assembled,' the report said. 'This presents us with a challenge we relish: to bring the stock price again up to $100.' The report also dwelled on the success of the centennial party the month before, quoting at one point from a speech Brian Dyson gave. 'We are not here to commemorate our history,' Dyson had told his audience. 'We are here to celebrate the next *three hundred trillion servings* of Coca-Cola.'

For Goizueta, June 1986 was a month of undiluted triumph. Coca-Cola was one hundred years old, and drawing fresh attention from market makers. The company had a plan that would replace the old independent bottling system with a creation that was more responsive to Coca-Cola executives. Meanwhile, he had pushed the share price up past the magical hundred-dollar mark after just five years at the helm. The applause rang in his ears. He liked the sound of it.

Less than four years later, on May 1, 1990, he persuaded the board to split the stock again, this time two-for-one. A few months after the first stock split, Coca-Cola Enterprises had been spun off, and by 1990 Coke's books had been free for years of the $3 billion debt accumulated as a result of buying the bottlers on the block back then. Coke's syrup sales kept going up, much of that because of its hefty sales to Coca-Cola Enterprises, and profits swelled, again because of the changes to the bottling system that Coca-Cola Enterprises represented. Coke now looked like a can't-miss stock. Investors came running.

Some of them were small, and some of them were very, very

large. By the time of Goizueta's second stock split, Warren Buffett, a longtime Coke drinker who had made money as a child buying six-packs for 25 cents and reselling the bottles to his friends for a nickel apiece, had quietly amassed more than a million shares of Coke. It was the kind of company he always sought out, he would eventually explain to the world. It had a well-known brand and it alone controlled that brand. It seemed to have the potential to keep on growing, which justified his requirements for a 'value investment'. Buffett owned 8 percent of Coke, more than anyone else, more than all the trusts in Atlanta, even, that had been set up by Coke legends like Woodruff. Though he would refuse on principle to split Berkshire's stock, he was drawn to the Coca-Cola Company that Goizueta had created.

In 1989 Buffett was made a director of Coke, and he joined the finance committee, since the days of Woodruff the most powerful arm of the Coke board. He and Herbert Allen and James Williams, chairman of SunTrust Banks, which controlled thousands of shares of Coke stock, comprised the committee, which made the most important decisions about the company's direction.

Goizueta assembled the rest of his board of directors with care. Lupton, the last bottler, left before Christmas in 1982, and Goizueta did not name another bottler then or later to take his place. Meanwhile, he was constructing anchor bottlers whose directors always included senior executives from Coke: the chairman, the president, or the chief financial officer. It was explained as part of the process of 'alignment', or the developing of a mutual strategy for Coke and its principal bottlers. No one on Wall Street seemed to care that at the board level, the alignment occurred only in one direction.

By the late 1980s, the analysts asked few questions of any kind, for everything about Coke and its bottlers was going swimmingly. Goizueta brought home the results, year after year after year. Did he say midteens earnings growth? There it was: 15 percent, 17 percent, 19 percent. 'They had this incredible, consistent profit machine,' Jennifer Solomon said. 'It was mind-blowing when you think about how consistent it was.'

Others whom Goizueta put on the Coke board included Charles Duncan, Jr., whose protégé was Don Keough, going all the way back to the years when Keough worked for Duncan Foods in Houston, which Coke's Minute Maid division purchased. Duncan was a private investor in 1981, the year he joined the board, and chaired the audit committee in the early 1990s. Goizueta also invited Peter Ueberroth to become a director in 1986, when Ueberroth was midway through his term as commissioner of Major League Baseball.

Later he brought in James Laney, the president of Emory University, a school built on acreage that came from Asa Candler. In 1985, Goizueta also tapped Paul Oreffice, chairman of the Dow Chemical Company, who became one of Coke's most widely respected outside directors. James Robinson, an American Express chief executive for many years, had joined the board in 1975.

Though women had served as directors in the past, there were none on the board when Goizueta arrived, and there would be none for ten more years. In 1991, Susan King, the president of the Steuben division of Corning Glass Works, became a director – the first woman in decades. Two years later, there would be another woman, Cathleen Black, the president of Hearst Magazines and a former publisher of *USA Today*. The first African American director had been chosen by Woodruff in 1974; the second arrived in 1981 and would be the only nonwhite to have a say in Coke's affairs at the board level for the next twenty-plus years.

The director was Donald McHenry, who had been the U.S. ambassador to the United Nations during the Carter administration. McHenry, a longtime diplomat who grew up in a Pepsi-drinking household, left government in 1981 for a teaching post in international affairs at Georgetown University. He also started a consulting firm called the IRC Group, where he was president and where Coke arranged a perennial contract for advice on its transactions in Africa. The contract was worth an estimated $185,000 a year to IRC, though McHenry would eventually seek to end it.

'Don't be surprised if it looks like a geriatric ward,' Goizueta told McHenry before his first board meeting. The board was filled with Woodruff cronies – his lawyer, his doctor, his younger brother – as well as the nonagenarian Woodruff himself. 'It was not a model of corporate governance,' McHenry observed.

McHenry's selection coincided with circumstances that were extraordinarily painful to a company like Coke. In July 1981, barely six months into the creation of the Coca-Cola Company that Goizueta envisioned, Don Keough had run afoul of the Reverend Jesse Jackson. Through a civil rights organization known as the Rainbow/PUSH Coalition, Jackson had been urging Coke for months to improve relations with blacks and other minorities. A program was all but in place in which Coke would buy more supplies from minority-owned companies and in other ways spread its wealth more generously to people who were not widely represented in the Coca-Cola business. One of the aspects of Coke that Jackson wanted to change was the overwhelmingly white ownership of bottling companies and distributorships; out of an estimated four thousand such companies, only two were owned by blacks. As a gesture of solidarity, Jackson invited Keough to address his group's annual convention in Chicago. The convention took place in July. Keough, however, sent William Allison, a black executive in charge of Coke's community affairs program who had been Coke's first black board member before stepping down to join the Carter administration.

The substitution enraged Jackson, and he called for a boycott of Coca-Cola by blacks everywhere. Allison, Jackson said later, was 'a messenger with no authority', and his arrival in Chicago, in Keough's place, meant that Coke was 'pulling back' in its commitment to the program for minorities. As the boycott began on July 11, at the peak of the year for anyone in the soft-drink business, Coke began negotiations with Jackson in earnest, and in secret.

By early August, the company announced that it had reached a final agreement on the changes it would make to improve its dealings with minorities. A total of thirty-two blacks would be named distributors or wholesalers; bottling franchises on the block would be referred to a pool of prospective black investors; Coke would commit the advertising for one of its brands to a minority-owned ad agency; and a black person would be named to the board. After that, Donald McHenry, who was already waiting in the wings, became a Coke director, following a news conference in which Keough stood surrounded by African American ministers and made jokes about his place in such exalted company.

To say that the Coke board was in thrall to Goizueta from his earliest days would be imprecise. In the beginning, like any newcomer, he had to sell the directors on his plans, whether it was buying Columbia Pictures or investing in a ne'er-do-well bottler overseas that Goizueta believed could do more with Coke's help. Everything inside the boardroom was cool, polite, dispassionate. There were only even-tempered exchanges. Goizueta seemed to have had the board's trust from the start, and when the company wobbled, people like Herbert Allen and Jimmy Williams stood firmly behind him. There was Don Keough, in another corner, and eventually the great Warren Buffett. Perhaps it was the result of his smooth presentations; perhaps it was because they were confident that nothing too terrible could happen to this wonderful brand. And then again, despite a public humiliation like New Coke, there was that marvelous consistency of the earnings, year after year, combined with the steady rise of the share price that began not long after Goizueta took over and lent the man a gilded image.

At the same time, Goizueta worked the board like a mayoral candidate presented with a roomful of babies to kiss. He never forgot a birthday; Donald McHenry, traveling to the Far East one October, stepped off the Coke plane during a stopover in Hawaii to find a full-scale party waiting for him. If Goizueta saw a necktie he admired, he'd send one to each of his directors. 'You knew his staff was helping him,' McHenry said, 'but staff doesn't come up with these things on their own.'

Goizueta became so close to his board that even during discussions of his own compensation, he never left the room. There was a famously enormous bonus given to Goizueta for his performance in 1991, a million shares of restricted stock. It was, at the time, the largest bonus ever awarded to the chief executive of an American company.

In 1992, exactly two years to the day after the 1990 stock split, the board authorized another split. Buffett, as a result, owned 4 million shares of Coke. The Coke machine was nearing a state of perfection. The U.S. economy seemed to be shaking off the 1990 recession, and all over the world, demand for American products – clothes, shoes, health and beauty items, food – was escalating. One of the most popular products was Coca-Cola, and investors clamored to share in the wealth that such popularity spawned. They were enchanted by the stock splits and the consistent earnings growth reported in every quarter, which all added up to a good investment, and now there were new consumers to sell to, on top of that. Goizueta trumpeted the opportunities abroad, adding to the excitement by declaring that Coke had only begun to penetrate those emerging markets.

'People used to ask Goizueta, why are you spending so much money internationally?' recalled a former Coke executive. 'And he would paraphrase the bank robber Willie Sutton. He'd say, "Ninety-five percent of the world's population lives outside the United States. And as people go from poverty to middle-income and free market economies around the world come into play, we're going to be there. We'll establish a beachhead and they will go from monthly drinkers to weekly drinkers and daily drinkers."'

This was the notion he presented to the board, and the directors signed off on his plans to open factories, hire workers, set up partnerships, and increase the marketing budget. He was getting results, too, and he showed them off like a proud parent. To so many of the people in these emerging markets, a Coca-Cola was a little draft of America and a step toward an improved kind of existence, wherever they happened to live. In 1950, *Time* magazine had put Coca-Cola on its cover, with an illustration of the planet sipping a bottle of Coke through a straw and the headline 'World and Friend'. On six of the seven continents, Coke was a popular and usually market-leading soft drink. Montagnards in the hill country of Vietnam craved it. Angolans deprived of other comforts during their civil war had it. Inuits living north of the Arctic Circle paid several dollars a can for it. The profitability of this was something Goizueta understood extremely well.

At one speech, before trustees of the J. Bulow Campbell Foundation in Atlanta, he outlined his vision of a world of Coke. Goizueta explained that some 70 percent of the company's earnings came from sales overseas, 'and he viewed that as sort of the tip of the iceberg,' recalled John Stephenson, the foundation's executive director. 'What the company was doing was building infrastructure with trucks and bottling companies, arrangements with whatever bureaucracies were required to feed this inevitable pipeline that he predicted would occur as markets developed larger middle classes, particularly in Asia.' And, Goizueta said, this was not about Coke versus Pepsi. Instead, it was 'Coke versus people who don't drink Coke yet'. It was a spectacular vision, and one that was easy to believe in. He dispatched Keough to East Germany to scout out opportunities there. Keough bought up what seemed like every soft-drink bottling factory in the country. Coke was poised to dominate a unified Germany, thanks to such foresight and planning.

Goizueta also set up partnerships between his company and local distributors, which were sometimes breweries, sometimes arms of the local government. That local touch – familiar faces using their contacts to sell a new product – helped Coke transcend its foreignness, where necessary, and appeal to consumers on a level that was closer to home. It was the lingering lesson of the old United States bottling system, the one that Goizueta had worked so hard to unravel: A soft drink produced by someone you knew and liked was inevitably more appealing than something shipped in from far away.

'It was part of the wonderful scheme in some of these countries that local companies were making it,' recalled one former executive. 'And they were able to market it as a symbol of America but also as a symbol of a better way of life.' Like the bathtub, or the car, Coca-Cola bottles were rolling across developing countries everywhere, freighted with a message of wealth and promise, bringing caffeine and carbonation into cultures where basic groceries, medicine, and shelter were hard to come by. 'People in remote corners of the world, who don't know their own capital cities, know the name Coca-Cola,' Ike Herbert, a Coke executive vice president, had boasted in the 1980s.

It was easier to buy a Coke than to build a hospital or a free society, and Coca-Cola seemed to be welcome everywhere. The share price rose and rose. Americans were pouring their money into mutual funds and disdaining the low interest rates on savings accounts, and fund managers were anxious to show impressive returns. They saw what was happening at Coke, and decided that it was madness not to have a piece of the action. 'It was seen as a growth stock,' recalled Skip Carpenter, a beverage analyst with

Donaldson, Lufkin & Jenrette, who began covering the Coca-Cola Company in the early 1990s, in time for Coke's adventures in emerging markets. 'It was the Cisco of that time. If you weren't owning Coke, you were losing. If you were a portfolio manager and you held it, you were afraid to sell.'

Coke's volume targets – the amount by which the company said it would increase sales, measured in cases of finished soft drinks – were always the same, projected at 7 to 8 percent a year. Goizueta and his team hit the target every year without fail, starting in 1987 and continuing through most of the 1990s. That helped maintain the momentum. Coke seemed incapable of anything but sustained, impressive growth.

In fact, it seemed to have no issues other than the currency-related kind that would dog any global company. The reports of Coke's successes coming out of the company were never refuted, and the Coke image proceeded to balloon. It outpaced other beverage stocks, and then other consumer-products stocks. It appeared golden, untouchable, beyond the reach of gravity. 'Coke just seemed so clean, so worry-free,' as Jennifer Solomon put it. 'It was borne out by the consistency of the results, and simplicity of the business. They sold cola concentrate, and that was it.'

Even when market conditions changed in the United States with the introduction of generic soft drinks at supermarkets and discount chains in 1993 and the company had to cut prices to compete with them, Coke continued to meet its earnings targets – always 15 to 20 percent. Even in years when volume slipped, as it did during the Atlanta Olympics in 1996, Coke's profits met or exceeded what Goizueta had promised. The seesaw always seemed to balance neatly in the end, and investors were never disappointed.

There were those who wondered how the Coca-Cola Company did it, time after time. The company leaped at the chance to answer those kinds of questions, with elaborate descriptions of its programs to bring refreshment to people all over the world, or of its global bottler network, then being formed piece by piece by Ivester and a team of experts he assembled. A strong bottling partner in every market meant that the company could coordinate its goals with those of the bottler's, benefiting both of them, Goizueta said. Coca-Cola Enterprises was the model, and by 1999 there would be ten more similarly large-scale bottlers positioned around the world, which the company referred to as its 'anchor bottlers'. The complete details of the relationship between Coke and these bottlers would not be made public by either side. But it was clear that they were essential partners in the gold-plated kingdom that Goizueta was creating.

Goizueta also maintained that the bottlers he had created since 1986 contributed to Coke's bottom line in significant ways. 'He'd say, "Coke derives profitability from the syrup business, from bottlers they owned outright, from the equity income stream, and from cash gains on buying and selling bottlers,"' said Andrew Conway, who interned at Coke while in business school in 1990 and 1991 and went on to become a leading beverage analyst, bullish on Coke through most of the 1990s. But Conway did hesitate at the notion that Coke's earnings were sustained by the buying and selling of bottlers, figuring that such enterprise was finite. He would tell Goizueta that 95 percent of what a Coke shareholder took home on dividend day came from the sale of syrup – not from the transfer of a bottling franchise from one place to another.

Conway was careful, though. He kept his disagreement polite and low-profile. Goizueta felt he had won the debate, and Conway, well aware of what happened to analysts the Coke chairman disliked, let him think so.

In fact, syrup would always be the single largest source of income, but Coke had figured out several ways to make the bottlers it created help generate cash for the Coca-Cola Company's books. First there was the sale of bottlers that Coke bought from their original owners, which were held for a period of time and then resold. The prices for those franchises were largely set by the Coca-Cola Company, which could afford to wait for the ideal buyer. Coke had to approve any transaction involving a bottling franchise it owned, so it controlled the buying and selling, beyond having a voice in the price.

There was also the issuing of new stock by the anchor bottlers that fed Coke's profits. In 1996, the year the Olympics failed to turn into an enormous selling opportunity for the company, Coke was able to collect $130 million in what it termed a 'noncash pretax gain' from a transaction that proceeded as follows: Coke's publicly traded Australian anchor bottler, Coca-Cola Amatil, issued 46 million new shares that brought in $522 million for the bottler. When those shares were sold to the public, Amatil became a bigger company and Coke's stake, originally 39 percent, dropped to 36 percent. Coke's share of the cash – 39 percent, because that was the size of its stake before the new stock went on sale – was added to the Coke balance sheet, with $47 million in deferred taxes on the gain, according to that year's annual report. A similar deal the same year brought in another $283 million from the merger of three German bottlers with the Coke-created German anchor bottler known as CCEAG. These transactions were the kind of thing that, given Coke's huge stakes in its anchor bottlers all over the world and its willingness to dilute those positions in favor of cash, could go on forever. The largest bottlers were like factories printing money, it seemed, for the company that had created them.

By the time the 1996 annual report was published Goizueta would be able to declare that the Coca-Cola Company had established for itself a uniquely wonderful, supreme position from which to guide its own fate. His revolution had taken hold. He had the minds and the wallets of the people who mattered most to him in America – the people who bought shares of Coca-Cola stock. He felt comfortable quoting Goethe, whose philosophy of bold change he admired. 'Boldness has genius, power, and magic in it,' he told his senior managers at a meeting in 1996. 'Begin it now.'

By 1997, he had perched for years atop an enormous wave. In the late 1980s and early 1990s, new markets were opening all the time for Coca-Cola. There was China, inaugurated in 1978 but only truly activated in the 1980s as restrictions on capital investment by foreigners lightened and comrades were permitted to exhibit individual consumer behavior, rather than collective, all-for-one movements in one direction or another. Coke partnered with a Hong Kong entrepreneur who already had strong ties to the Chinese government and began opening bottling plants and distribution centers in dozens of cities. As in so many countries, Coke at first was sold only in spots frequented by foreigners and the few Chinese with hard currency to spend, in places like hotels and bars and discotheques. But gradually, starting in the mid-1980s, the field widened to include mom-and-pop stores, the kind set up on university campuses and along the teeming side streets of cities like Shanghai and Beijing. If you were a student at the Shanghai Normal College in the western part of the city at that time, you could buy, along with the salty pickled fruit sitting in huge containers near the cash register of the campus store and the Chinese-made pencils and the Great Wall–brand nougat candies, a bottle of Coca-Cola: Ke-ko Ke-le. It was often warm, and it was more expensive than local sodas. But it was American, and it was well known, and people wanted it.

As other markets presented additional opportunities, Goizueta made sure Coke was ready for them, rushing in with a soft-drink maker's heavy artillery – bottling plants, trucks, American executives to dictate strategy – at once. Russia had eluded Coke for years. So when the door did swing wide, Goizueta lunged at the opportunity.

In 1989, the company had finally cleared away all the obstacles – political and competitive – to selling its soft drinks in Russia. In the early sixties, Russia had been entirely Pepsi's, thanks to a little help from Richard Nixon. Rebuffed by the Coke management when he sought a senior position at the company during that era, Nixon had transmogrified into Coke's archenemy. Pepsi management, led by Donald Kendall, moved quickly to befriend him, and by the time Nixon became president in January 1969, he had Pepsi high on his priority list. The company began selling Pepsi in Russia a year later, and Coke, despite valiant attempts to compete, would be kept out. When Coke did win permission to make Coca-Cola the official soft drink of the 1980 Olympics, which were hosted in Moscow, President Carter unhinged those plans by announcing a boycott of the Games over Russia's invasion of Afghanistan. Both Coke and Pepsi had no choice but to comply with the boycott, although their products did appear here and there – a development the companies blamed on their bottlers, who, they said, already had the concentrate on hand before the boycott was announced.

China and Russia were two huge markets, but with enormous obstacles ranging from the infrastructure – the roads, the telephone systems – to the ability of the proletariat to pay for pricey American soft drinks, they were not easy ones to exploit.

In other areas, Coke had a much smoother experience. Romania welcomed the company with open arms in 1989, its government anxious to make up for lost time. The owner of the largest soft-drink company in the country wrote to Goizueta that year, aggressively proposing a partnership. *You are the No. 1 soft-drink maker in the world, and I am the No. 1 soft-drink maker in Romania, so let's do business,* the executive declared.

He got what he asked for. Not only did Coke move in with a brand-new factory and a phalanx of executives who set about ordering signs and putting up huge advertisements for Coca-Cola but Goizueta also trotted out Romania as an example of the kind of power Coke represented to a developing nation – not simply by selling it containers of brown sugar water but by boosting its prospects, creating a demand for all sorts of functions, from driving trucks to manufacturing neon signs, that made people money. The new governments in such places, meanwhile, used Coke's presence as a stamp of political approval. If Coke was investing, they must be doing something right. Coke saw benefits in the situation as well, sending a film crew to Romania to document everything the company was doing there and leading reporters on tours of Bucharest by way of explaining the company's usefulness as an international development tool. Once Coke was for sale in a drab, economically stifled place like that, so the message went, other businesses naturally would spring up, too – businesses that made neon signs, for example, or refrigerators, or parts for the trucks needed to ferry bottles of Coca-Cola around. Business meant jobs, and jobs meant income, and income would allow people to pursue their dreams, whatever they were.

It worked, to a degree. 'It was company propaganda, and clearly they were trying to put the best spin on things,' says a longtime Coke executive who left the company in 2000. 'But I saw people in developing countries who were touched by the magic of Coca-Cola.'

With genuine growth coming from countries that were being newly introduced to Coca-Cola, the volume targets got easier to meet and the stock price kept rising. A sea of brown syrup was washing over the planet, driven ahead of the magnificent vision that Goizueta had for his company. On May 1, 1996, the board approved one more stock split. People who had owned a hundred shares of Coke at the beginning of 1986 and did nothing but hang on to them now held title to 2,400 of them. For the people who held thousands or millions of Coke shares, wealth blossomed like a well-fertilized peach tree, a tree beyond their imagining, and began to change their lives.

Coke employees, faced with a choice of investing in Coke stock or something else, almost invariably chose Coke stock. By 1997, 90 percent of all the money set aside in employee paychecks for retirement investment had been channeled into Coca-Cola stock. All of these people – some of whom Goizueta knew extremely well, others he would never meet – were being bathed in the Coca-Cola Company's success.

The total value of all the public shares of the Coca-Cola Company had risen from $4 billion in 1981 to $145 billion that year. Some 25 percent of the shares were owned by people in Georgia, most of them concentrated around Atlanta. About 40 percent of the shares were held by individuals – people who bought them with their own money or inherited them through their families, who could have been Coke executives or Coke bottlers or people who were affiliated in some other way with the company. The rest belonged to pension funds, like the New York State employees retirement fund, or investors like Berkshire Hathaway, Fidelity, or Bessemer Trust. These were the huge investors whose holdings dwarfed everyone else's.

Fredric Russell was one of the midsize investors, a money manager who bought $3 million worth of Coke shares because, as he put it, 'there couldn't be any greater, more attractive company than Coca-Cola.' Everyone had heard of Coke; everyone understood what the company did, and it led the soft-drink market by almost every conceivable measure. Russell invested on behalf of a fund he managed in Tulsa, Oklahoma. He visited Coke's headquarters and met with Larry Mark, the head of investor relations, who took him out to dinner at Bones, an Atlanta steakhouse. 'At one point, he pulled out some graphics on growth,' Russell recalled, 'and it did strike me that there wasn't a heck of a lot of substance. But he had a wonderful presentation and he is a very likable guy.' Between the porterhouse, the wine, and the continuing strength of Coke's stock price, Russell said, 'it was one of my less penetrating meetings. I leaned back and thought about the wonderful position they had, and I didn't challenge myself or Mark as much as I could have.'

He was hardly alone. People everywhere had begun to take the Coke miracle for granted. Across Atlanta, ordinary people who owned Coke stock began to spend money in a way that was unprecedented on trophy houses, imported cars, and fine wines stored in their new climate-controlled cellars. Thanks to Coke, private schools had waiting lists. Suddenly there was a demand for plastic surgery, for gold-plated fixtures in bathrooms, for large boats and private aircraft and cruises to take Coca-Cola shareholders around the world.

Goizueta, meanwhile, engaged in almost nothing that would suggest that he, too, had benefited from the run-up in the stock price and the lavish pay-off that accompanied it. He was driven to work every morning in his armored company car, which was an American car, not a Mercedes or a BMW. And he was driven back again at night. He continued to live in the same modest four-bedroom house that he and Olguita had purchased, with Coke's help, when he first arrived in Atlanta in 1964. If he needed to go somewhere, he arranged to fly aboard one of the *Wind Ships,* the Coke Gulfstream jets that existed to ferry him around. He could have a Coca-Cola a mile up and watch one of the videos that the company kept in an extensive library aboard the planes. And he could light up one of his cigarettes and smoke to his heart's content. Wherever he went, he kept smoking cigarettes, one after another, the way he had since he was a teenager in Havana.

He admonished others around him that they must never sell their stock. Holding on to it implied a number of things: that the stock was going to keep on rising, that they were not in need of additional money, that they were taking the long view of all this.

Goizueta was in a unique position to ban others from selling their shares. He himself received so much restricted stock and options that even if he had parted with a substantial chunk of what he owned, he was accumulating more so rapidly, between fresh awards and stock splits, that he would have barely noticed the difference. He got barrelsful of options or restricted stock at the end of every calendar year, together with a generous salary and a cash bonus that invariably exceeded that. The pay was impressive, but the stock – thanks to all his hard work – was worth so much more.

Coke never paid wildly excessive salaries to its employees, even those at the very top. In the 1990s, executive salaries were gauged against an average derived from other consumer-products companies, and though respectable, they were never at the upper extreme. But the company was abundantly generous with stock options. It was those options that kept people going and allowed them to borrow enough to pay for a college education for their children or to buy a bigger and better house in Buckhead, the neighborhood in Atlanta where so many Coke executives lived. Senior managers received options by the hundreds of thousands, which was dutifully reported in the proxy statements every year. Someone who spent thirty years at Coke and collected stock options for fifteen or twenty of those years could easily accumulate millions of dollars' worth of them by the time retirement rolled around. The stock, after all, just kept going up and up and up. Options split when the stock split, and so the longer the miracle lasted, the better it was for everyone.

No individual at Coke had as much stock as Goizueta. By 1997, he had accumulated more than 20 million shares, then worth about sixty dollars a share. He had benefited from the splits, and he had benefited from the adulation poured on his company like water.

There were other benefits, kept out of the spotlight that Goizueta trained on his achievements at Coke. Some who examined his compensation found that Goizueta would pay next to nothing in taxes when he collected his stock and other awards. Most of his compensation, which exceeded $1 billion between 1979 and 1996, was paid in some form of stock. By 1996, he had received 11.2 million restricted shares on the condition that he not borrow against or sell them, although he could collect the dividends. The restrictions meant that he would not have to pay taxes on the stock as income until he officially possessed it, and the company even agreed to pay the federal and state taxes he would owe on 5.2 million of those shares when he took title to them upon his retirement. That tax bill was estimated at $116 million, payable in cash.

There was more for Goizueta in 1991, the tenth anniversary of his elevation to chairman and chief executive of Coke. In addition to the million-share bonus, he and Keough were going to collect more cash through a 'performance unit agreement' that promised the two of them, also upon retirement, payments for any increase in the Coke stock price over $10.3125, which was the split-adjusted share price on January 2, 1985. In other words, whenever they cashed in they would pocket an additional payment matching whatever the rise was in Coke's stock price. It added up to a whole lot of money.

Those payments were supposed to be made upon the retirement of the two executives, whenever that day came. But a note in the 1992 proxy statement mentioned that 'under the agreements with Mr. Goizueta', the board's compensation committee could pay him as much as 20 percent of what he was owed 'in each February from 1991 to 1995'.

It explained at least some of Goizueta's interest in the glowing little machine in his conference room, the electronic furnace that fired so much wealth. He had plenty to gain from the stock's performance, and he made sure that others became just as enthusiastic about taking it higher. Herbert Allen thought that while money was not meaningless to Goizueta, after a while 'it was all symbolic'.

During the time that Goizueta led Coca-Cola, the share price became the motif for everything the company did; every marketing plan, every new product, every acquisition and transaction had to be evaluated in terms of its power to add to 'shareholder value'. Share price was the doubloon he nailed to Coca-Cola's mast, a reward for everyone. Share options were handed out as payment for jobs well done, and those who didn't get them were encouraged to aspire to places in the company where they would be eligible for them. Gleaming from the stock monitors in the elevator bank, quoted at meetings between managers, cited in every company report, quarterly newsletter, and executive presentation, share price came to mean many things. Marketing drove sales and sales drove share price. Anything in the marketing budget that could not be shown to drive sales was dropped, even popular commercials and promotional programs – free glasses, free posters, free anything – that people said they liked. The company was focused on a single target, and nothing was supposed to get in the way.

Among the Coca-Cola faithful, there were still questions about the size of Goizueta's pay package in 1991. Reporters made much of it, and some experts questioned the gross tonnage of it. It was the first sustained criticism to reach the ears of Goizueta since the New Coke fiasco, and he insisted that he was surprised by it. Hadn't every other Coke shareholder benefited from his brilliant leadership over the past year, and all the years before that, too?

He used his trademark managerial style to take care of the problem. With issues large and small, he was exceptionally skilled at getting others to do what he wanted, often without their realizing it. He would have a conversation, sometimes dropping in a reference or two to his experiences in Cuba, which was code for 'You need to make a change.' Eventually he might suggest one or two things, but almost without suggesting them. 'He would call me up to his office, and we would chat about things, and I would walk out of the office and say to myself, what the hell was that all about?' a former senior executive said. 'He managed us very, very gently. We didn't know we were being managed.'

At the company's annual shareholder meeting – normally held every April in Wilmington, Delaware, in the theater of the Hotel du Pont but moved to other cities occasionally – Coke executives usually review events of the past twelve months and make rosy forecasts about the year ahead. It is usually a sedate gathering, with no controversy to speak of, and it usually takes no more than an hour. At Coke, the joke was that the directors' chauffeurs were instructed to keep the engines running because they'd all be done in just a few minutes. But in 1992, with the meeting taking place in Atlanta for a change (it was the centennial of Coke as a publicly held company), Goizueta knew there might be questions about his compensation. So he took the microphone and stood to address the crowd, his dark eyes peering soberly into the faces before him, ready to deliver the answer of all answers, the one that would put an end to this question about whether he was overpaid.

He pointed out that every single person who owned even one

share of Coca-Cola stock had seen his or her net worth rise as a direct result of the work he did all day long. Coke was growing as a company, and its markets were continuing to expand all over the world. He deserved every penny he got, he said, though not in so many words. So did they. You are all in this game, too, he seemed to say. And they knew that it was true.

The audience burst into applause four times during his remarks. They were friendly to Goizueta to begin with, and this simply laid to rest what was a small issue for most of them. The question of whether he was worth everything he was being paid was never put to him at a shareholder meeting again. No one mentioned, then or later, the 1.5 million share options Keough had received at the same time.

A year after that gathering, Don Keough retired. It was about time; he was sixty-six years old. This left Goizueta with a momentary problem: Whom would he choose to replace Don? He wanted Doug Ivester, who seemed to be the natural choice, given his place in the hierarchy and his role in the company's rise. But Keough, his fellow warrior, who said he was ready to retire but rarely let a day go by without demonstrating just how much he would miss his job, urged him not to make up his mind right away. There were a couple of good candidates, Keough told him. He wanted him to have a choice.

Goizueta knew how to manage Keough, too, also without letting Keough know too much about what was going on. Their styles were so distinct that it was not terribly difficult to let Keough be Keough and go on being Goizueta. Early in the relationship, Goizueta had urged Keough to take on certain roles that in other companies might have been considered the chairman's job. Giving the stirring keynote address at the Coke birthday party played to Keough's strength and freed up Goizueta to do other things. Now he let Keough go on his own terms, even if that included dictating how Coke should function in his absence.

Keough had a shortlist of favorites that he handed over to Goizueta. He had not included Ivester, the company's chief financial officer during an essential time in the Coca-Cola revolution, who was now executive vice president. What about Ivester, Goizueta asked Keough, his face partly obscured behind a cloud of cigarette smoke.

At Keough's urging, Goizueta had sent Ivester to London in 1989, where he ran the company's beverage business in Western Europe. Keough, to whom all the international divisions reported, insisted that Ivester needed experience in operations if he was going to continue to rise in the company. Goizueta told Ivester this was something he needed to do.

A year later, Ivester was back in Atlanta, or more precisely, he had stopped commuting across the pond. He and Kay never moved to London, where a Coke executive in charge of Europe typically lived. They hadn't seen the need to leave Atlanta, and maybe it was just as well. A few of Ivester's projects, like trying to increase consumption in France, appeared to have backfired. He sued the company's longtime bottler there, Pernod Ricard, over his belief that the French bottler was promoting its own drinks, like Orangina, more vigorously than it promoted Coca-Cola. That was simply not allowed in the world of Coke. The contract with Pernod was severed ahead of schedule, and Coke regained the franchise. Ivester would later fold France into the already enormous European and American territory controlled by Coca-Cola Enterprises. Of course, Coca-Cola Enterprises would have to pay to acquire France, and that lucrative transaction − more than a billion dollars, despite the uneven record of Coke sales there − would add to the Coca-Cola Company's bottom line that year.

Ah, Coca-Cola Enterprises. That was a success story that reflected well on Ivester, Goizueta thought. In the beginning, Coca-Cola Enterprises had been a ragged operation, with Coke executives at the helm. Brian Dyson, the former head of Coke's North American business and another Keough protégé, was blamed by some investors for the way in which the division was struggling.

But then, in 1991, there had come another master stroke. Coca-Cola Enterprises had acquired the Johnston Coca-Cola Bottling Group, which owned Coke bottling rights in places like Minnesota and Tennessee. Johnston Coca-Cola was symbolic, too; the grandfather of the current owner had been one of the very first Coke bottlers, at the turn of the century, and bringing that kind of history into the remade bottling system indicated a certain aligning of the planets in the Coca-Cola Company's favor.

The acquisition also brought a stellar manager to the anchor bottler in the person of Henry Schimberg, who had attacked his new role with unprecedented gusto and by 1993 built the bottler up into a force to be reckoned with, its stock almost as beloved as Coke stock.

By then, too, the issues raised by the independent bottlers, led by Bill Schmidt, had been largely decided in Coke's favor. The presiding judge, Murray Schwartz, had become ill and dropped off the case after the trial phase concluded in 1989. The case had to be tried again, from the beginning. When Jan Schmidt got that piece of news, she burst into tears. Fighting Coke on principle in a Delaware courtroom had already consumed close to ten years of the Schmidts' marriage, their work, and their lives.

The rulings, when they finally came, were mixed. The Elizabethtown case, the one that held that Coke illegally substituted corn syrup for sugar despite the contracts, brought the bottlers a $20 million award in damages. But the award was reversed on appeal, though the ruling was not. In the meantime, the Coca-Cola Company said it would rather replace sugar in the formula, paying the sugar companies for the ingredient, than share whatever cost savings it got from using corn syrup instead. Bottlers like Bill Schmidt weren't going to get a penny. To drive home the point, Coke cut off his marketing funds. Diet Coke was ruled to be a new product, despite what Schmidt and other bottlers had contended.

Coke was just like Russia, the Schmidts' lawyer, Emmet Bondurant, told the court at one point. 'What's theirs is theirs,' he declared, 'and what's yours is negotiable.' Bottlers who challenged Coke were like 'an independent Lithuania or Poland on their doorstep', he said later. Coke couldn't abide the dissent. Coke had to have control. 'They were determined to dominate them. If they couldn't dominate them, they would invade them.'

Coke bottlers who had signed the amended contract fared a little better. Those who hadn't had permission from the Coca-Cola Company to bottle diet Coke were now eligible to get it. Those who had signed the diet Coke contract but not the amended contract also did well by the courts. Bottlers like Schmidt, who had tried to uphold the arrangement that his father and his grandfather had lived by and felt that both Coke's handling of diet Coke and the amended contract breached that arrangement, got hammered. In 1999, Schmidt decided he should get out of the bottling business. He hired an agent to solicit bids, and the bidding was brisk. The eventual buyer was not Coca-Cola Enterprises, or Coca-Cola Consolidated (a kind of miniature Coca-Cola Enterprises based in Charlotte, North Carolina, where Coke also owned a sizable stake). Schmidt sold his family's franchise to another independent bottler, Steve Ennis, who already had a franchise in Tullahoma, Tennessee, and was a man not unlike himself.

Moving out of the Elizabethtown headquarters was not easy. Schmidt packed up his museum – a huge collection of Coke memorabilia like trays and clocks and calendars and posters that reminded him of the Coca-Cola he had grown up with – and he filed away all the court documents, letters, and other records from his challenge to the Coca-Cola Company. The museum would reopen, and Schmidt and his wife began to plan a new one designed by Frank Gehry to display all that they knew about the making and selling of Coca-Cola. But they would not bottle Coca-Cola anymore.

Some of the Coke managers were sorry to see the small family bottlers disappear. 'The larger bottler was where the muscle of the company was,' said George Marlin, who spent twenty years working with bottlers in the western part of the country, 'but the heart of the company really was with those small independent bottlers. It was my great sorrow to see that the heart was not going to be as strong as it had been. And over time, that became even truer than I thought it was going to be.'

The world now seemed to belong to bottlers like Coca-Cola Enterprises, headed by men like Henry Schimberg. Then in his late fifties, he was short and slight but had assertiveness to spare. No job was too tough for Schimberg, who had started out in the soft-drink business as a truck driver for Royal Crown cola. He loved everything that came with being in charge at Coca-Cola Enterprises, from the private jet he had at his disposal to the suites in five-star hotels that he occupied on his frequent runs to cities like Paris to check on the business, which had expanded to Western Europe by 1996.

He was a man conscious of image, starting with his own. He had a thick thatch of hair that he kept dyed dark brown well into his sixties.

He could also be bad-tempered at times and became known for tearing into subordinates who he felt had not done their jobs well. But this sort of behavior never received much attention from Atlanta. Henry Schimberg produced the market share and sales that the Coca-Cola Company liked. That was a welcome change.

In the early days of the bottler that he arrived to run, the bottler that Coke had reconfigured to suit its goals, almost nothing had gone right. Pepsi continued to score against Coke in the marketplace. The former chief executive, Brian Dyson, arrived at Coca-Cola Enterprises on the heels of the New Coke debacle, a man with almost no incentive to do well. His new assignment had the stink of exile. He had run Coke's business in North America for years – selling concentrate to the bottlers, not working with or *for* a bottler. His net worth was tied up in Coca-Cola stock – not Coca-Cola Enterprises stock. In Atlanta, though, such considerations did not cause anyone concern. In fact, it was probably best this way. As a Coke man, Dyson could be counted on to do what was best for Coke as he ran the bottler.

However, all kinds of things went wrong as time went on. Gone from this supersized bottler was deep-rooted knowledge of local markets, the kind of thing the independent bottlers had managed almost as easily as breathing. People in the big central offices of Coca-Cola Enterprises were not on a first-name basis with the mayor; they did not have the same kind of local authority. Meanwhile, the orders coming from the Coca-Cola Company, setting goals for volume growth, were not easy to achieve. They came now from Atlanta, after some negotiation, and they took into account first not what a local market could absorb but the amount of concentrate that the Coca-Cola Company wanted to sell. The bottler's stock soared the first year, but by the second year its performance was sagging. Getting the acquired bottlers to do what Atlanta decreed was not easy. As problems emerged, people both inside and outside Coke blamed Dyson, the head of that new bottler.

The sea change in Coca-Cola Enterprises came when

Schimberg arrived. He brought with him another treasure for the Coca-Cola Company: a man named Summerfield Johnston, Jr.

Johnston was at least as dedicated to persuading people to drink more Coca-Cola as Schimberg was. He was short and gray-haired, and despite appearing most of the time in business attire, he still resembled the farmer he had wanted to be. His father had pushed him to take over the family bottling business, which his grandfather had acquired as just one more promising investment at the turn of the century. Summerfield agreed to do it.

He came to enjoy the glad-handing and the salesmanship that any good bottler had to perfect. He lived well as the result of being a big Coke bottler. But as the Coke world entered its period of upheaval, one of his biggest aces was his friendship with Don Keough.

Johnston had come forward after one of the many Keough speeches that warned bottlers, in language alternately oblique and direct, that a chill wind was coming: They had better make up their minds about whether they wanted to grow or get out. Johnston put up his hand and said he'd like to become one of the bigger bottlers. This meant that when franchises came up for sale, the Coca-Cola Company would approve his acquiring them. One of the first that he bought was Midwest Coca-Cola Bottling, based in Minneapolis, in 1982. He borrowed most of the money he needed to acquire it, initiating a pattern that would be copied by all of the big anchor bottlers for years to come. And he became king of a highly leveraged empire, one that owed almost everything to the Coca-Cola Company. That was another part of the plan, as designed by Coke.

Johnston had also agreed to the 1978 amended contract, the one Bill Schmidt and his fellow bottlers opposed so strenuously. He eagerly anticipated the advertising help Coke promised once the money paid for syrup increased, but at the same time his view of the bottling business was, as he put it, that 'you live or die on the street. Advertising is like the icing on the cake.'

Johnston relied on Schimberg, and he also had a son in the business, Summerfield III, whom everyone called Skeeter. With that team in place, Brian Dyson decided to retire. He was just fifty-five years old, but he had a big cattle ranch in Argentina, a ski house in Telluride, Colorado, and other interests that were worthy of his attention. He kept a place in Atlanta, too, where, like so many Coke executives before him, he might be gone but not entirely forgotten. Some people at Coke would have a hard time forgetting his exploits, which had included shepherding the introduction of New Coke.

He was leaving a business that had answered many a prayer offered up from the executive suite of the Coca-Cola Company. Coca-Cola Enterprises was tidier than the bottling business of yore. It was big, it was centralized, and it could push all sorts of products through its meticulously organized network of trucks and salespeople. Perhaps most important for Coke, it had established, on a far larger scale than ever before, a process by which Coke made the maximum amount of money it could on syrup sales. The process was a balancing act, one that was not discussed except on demand and largely unacknowledged except at the highest levels of the concentrate company and its biggest bottler.

With the revised contracts, syrup prices could rise when Coke wanted them to. That had been Coke's goal for so long, and now Coke executives knew their power outstripped that of the bottlers. In other places around the world, where there had never been limits on concentrate price, the company charged a variety of rates. Bottlers in Japan, where a Coke sold for at least twice what it cost in the States, paid the most; bottlers in some emerging countries paid far less. But Coke controlled the pricing. Low concentrate prices could be used like a hook to persuade a reluctant partner to come aboard; then, because nothing was fixed, they could go up rapidly if the company desired.

Coke's costs in the 1980s and 1990s remained low when it came to manufacturing concentrate. Ivester had thought up a number of smart moves, such as producing the syrup in tax shelters like Ireland and France, which kept costs down. The concentrate cost just pennies a gallon to make. It was simply sugar, or much cheaper high-fructose corn syrup, combined with flavorings and packaged in the most basic of plastic containers.

The executives at Coca-Cola Enterprises were informed of Coke's growth targets at the beginning of a new year. There would be negotiations over concentrate price, with the full knowledge that it would rise by at least 2 or 3 percent that year – roughly the pace of inflation. There would be more negotiations over the amount of marketing support that Coke would provide to the bottler as a means of making sure all those bottles and cans of Coca-Cola were sold. In the end, Coke would prevail on the concentrate price, because it could, and often on the marketing support as well.

'The company evolved into a company that had a control mentality to it,' Summerfield Johnston said. He and the other bottlers put up with it. As long as their stock was rising – and it did, for many years – they felt well taken care of. They did not try to change anything. For a long time, too, his company had new franchises to streamline and new markets to handle. The growth was genuine – up to a point.

While Coke was the largest shareholder at most of its anchor bottlers, it was not the only shareholder. The others included institutions as well as individuals, and they had to be satisfied that their investments were growing in value, that the bottlers were profiting from the arrangement with Coke. Otherwise there might be trouble.

But with a little sophistication this could be smoothed out, too.

At Coca-Cola Enterprises, Coke refined an age-old practice in a way that kept everyone happy by giving the impression that the bottler was independently succeeding. Coke's prices for syrup escalated with Coke's needs. The amount of syrup the bottler purchased also reflected the company's volume-growth targets – the ones it pitched to Wall Street; but these were not necessarily the same as the bottlers' targets.

Coke collected the money from syrup sales up front, but at the same time, because of the public nature of Coca-Cola Enterprises, executives knew they could not let the bottler become unprofitable. There had to be a balance of sorts between what Coke wanted and what the bottler needed. Now that the power in the relationship had shifted and Coke had most of it, the company had to be careful not to ruin everything. The bottler's success was a reflection of Coke's success. Coke's skyrocketing profits and share price would be suspect if the Coke bottlers, particularly the largest one, did not make money, too.

So, depending on the kind of year the bottler was having, Coke could return enough money in the form of rebates to keep the bottler looking respectable. For despite the reconfiguring of the bottlers by Coke, the relationship had not really changed. Coke still sold only concentrate and collected its money, nearly all profit, ahead of the product's arrival in the marketplace. The bottlers had to make money by selling that finished product, and they did so after the costs of concentrate and other production expenses were covered.

Only if Coca-Cola Enterprises could sell all the Coca-Cola it made – all the millions and millions of sodas in bottles and cans that Coke's volume targets translated into – would the bottler make money. If there was no market for that soda, then the bottler would lose money. Unless, of course, Coke intervened.

Coke provided money in the form of marketing support, an amount that was duly summarized in the Coca-Cola annual report, though no details were ever given about when those payments were made. After 1991, Coca-Cola Enterprises executives would announce cash-operating profit targets – essentially the profits before taxes, interest, and depreciation were subtracted – and Coke's support meant that there was money to meet them if the bottler couldn't do it on its own.

The arrangement presumed that Coca-Cola Enterprises would one day stand on its own, that the marketing support would dwindle as the bottler tightened its operations and trimmed fat from the dozens of franchises it acquired. The plan was nonthreatening to Coke because Coke's profits from the sales of concentrate were enormous. As volume grew, the profits also grew. And for a long time the profits from Coke's investment in Coca-Cola Enterprises were enormous, too. The stock soared, based on the cash operating profit goals that were attained. Coke was collecting money from Coca-Cola Enterprises on three levels: from sales of concentrate, from sales of franchises it owned, and from its share of the bottler's profits in the good years.

Marketing support, whenever it was paid, could mask any problems at the local level – such as decreased demand for Coca-Cola – by creating the appearance that a bottler was selling 6 or 7 or 8 percent more than the year before and making as much money on those sales as it had promised. Syrup was sold at the beginning of the year or the quarter at a rate that implied a healthy increase in soda sales, and if the finished products didn't sell, Coke could channel money for discounts or other incentives to the bottlers. If necessary, at the end of the year, it could write one big check to cover any difference between promised cash-flow growth and reality. Asked about the practice, executives from both Coke and Coca-Cola Enterprises would say they did not know how much marketing support would be in a given year until the end of that year. Support was tied to goals set in various programs that took place across the calendar, they said, so figuring out the money flowing from Coke to the bottler ahead of the year's end was impossible.

Coke's practice of propping up bottlers in need was ancient. Before Coca-Cola Enterprises was created in 1986, marketing support had streamed from Atlanta to the bottlers as a kind of carrot-and-stick arrangement. If you wanted the family that ran the Portland, Oregon, franchise to increase sales, you gave them a promise of a rebate, say fifty cents a case, on every case they sold beyond a certain target. The money wasn't payable until the target had been met. The system gave Coke at least an illusion of control over some of its more distant bottlers, and it also gave the bottlers a reason to work harder. Both things were essential in the relationship between Coke and the independent bottlers.

But after 1986, with the biggest bottler so closely aligned with the Coca-Cola Company, there was no need for the stick. Coke was already telling the bottler what to do, and the bottler was, by definition and corporate structure, listening. The carrot still arrived as needed, and often it was just in time to keep the whole Coke system looking healthy. Sometimes it wasn't just marketing support but 'infrastructure payments' as well that added hundreds of millions to the bottler's balance sheet. When Coke urged the installation of vending machines almost everywhere, it helped pay for that effort, in addition to the marketing support. Coca-Cola Enterprises recorded the money as a reduction of its costs for that year; Coke capitalized the spending over several years.

Few outside the two companies knew how the process worked.

'If the bottlers can't take the cost of a concentrate price increase, it is rebated back to them in the form of marketing support,' said Richard Larson, who rose to the position of corporate vice president at Coca-Cola Enterprises before retiring in 1999. In some instances, a pool of cash sat in the wings, he added. 'It was never shown anywhere on Coca-Cola Enterprises' books until they actually needed it. They take what they need to make their cash operating profit.'

Coke set performance requirements, such as sales growth targets, for the bottler as a condition of receiving marketing support. But even those were largely fictitious, said a former Coke executive, because whether or not the targets were met, the money still arrived. 'They try to keep that semblance of being able to pull it back,' the executive said, 'but in practical terms, they can't pull it back.' The bottler became as reliant on Coke for the payments as it was for the syrup. The whole system, as rewritten, leaned heavily on the Coca-Cola Company.

At the bottler's, the marketing support payments were recorded as decreases in the cost of doing business. But at Coke the cost to the company was reported in the notes section of the annual report, and its effect on profits buried in the equity-income line. Few analysts thoroughly understood the financial relationship between the two companies. Little insight was provided by the company, apart from bromides about alignment and how strong bottlers made good partners for the Coca-Cola Company. For all analysts knew, Coke raised concentrate prices and its bottlers paid what they had to, and that was that. Marketing support was recognized as a necessary expense, but the way it was distributed to the bottlers remained shrouded.

The rapid gobbling up of other bottlers during the 1990s by Coca-Cola Enterprises also confused outsiders trying to determine the profitability of the big bottler. The acquisitions added huge sweeps of new territory and millions of cases worth of new volume, promising that, as it grew, the bottler would become more efficient and produce more at a lower cost per case of soda. Every new franchise that came under the control of this megabottler went under the knife. Jobs were eliminated and unproductive plants closed down. The bigger the bottler got, the more fat was supposed to be eliminated from the system as a whole, and the faster and more efficiently the identical bottles and cans of Coca-Cola – which had no local quirks, no intrinsic sense of place – could be produced.

With Goizueta's help, Wall Street came to see Coke's bottling strategy as a highly admirable, completely acceptable arrangement, despite the gaps in information. What the analysts knew was simplified, optimistic, and incomplete. 'There was a view that Coke could charge a syrup price increase, and the bottlers could absorb that through acquisitions, which lowered their costs,' said Andrew Conway. Wall Street believed for years that the bottler and the Coca-Cola Company shared equitably in the profits from their arrangement. It was assumption, not fact, and it would be more than a decade before it became clear to investors that 'this was a model where Coke took eighty percent of the profitability from the value chain, and the bottlers took twenty,' as Conway put it.

The credit markets, meanwhile, viewed Coke and its bottlers as a single entity, lending money freely to Coca-Cola Enterprises even as its debt rose out of all proportion to its revenues. By 1998, debt at the giant bottler had grown to more than $7 billion, more than half the revenues of $13 billion. Interest payments on that debt consumed all the bottler's profits that year, and then some. The capital markets, where Coca-Cola Enterprises went to borrow money, were tolerant nonetheless. At Standard & Poor's, where debt quality was assessed, executives treated Coke and its biggest bottler as a single entity. Even when the bottler's debt began to dwarf its revenues, the ability of the bottler to pay off that debt was never in doubt. The agency firmly believed that Coke would never let its biggest bottler fail. No matter what the arrangement was between them, ultimately no one who lent Coca-Cola Enterprises money would lose. Their mutual destiny would force Coke to support the bottler. In 1998, Coca-Cola Enterprises reported another banner year, at least in terms of its cash operating profit. But Coke paid a total of $1.2 billion in marketing support and infrastructure spending, without which it could not have made that number.

Through its anchor bottlers, which numbered eleven by early

1999, Coke presented to the world a unified front, strong bottlers and a strong concentrate seller moving in lockstep to carry out the goal of selling ever more Coca-Cola to a thirsty world. The less dispensed about the details, the better. And for Goizueta, who insisted that people should pay more attention to earnings than to sales or gross profits, the bottling arrangement helped burnish the image of this new company he was inventing, a company in which the control exercised by the people at the top would determine the image of the entire operation. His statements grew increasingly confident, breezy, even snide when it came to Coke's chief competitor, Pepsi-Cola. 'As they've become less relevant,' Goizueta told one reporter in 1996, 'I don't need to look at them anymore.'

As its adversaries noted, control was the central element in the formula for the new Coca-Cola Company. Goizueta had decided long ago that Coke could not afford to take the chances that it had in the past. The relationship with bottlers had to change. The relationship with customers had to change. The relationship with Pepsi had to change, too, Goizueta decreed.

After New Coke, Roger Enrico's incessant jubilation over Coke's missteps died down. By 1987, when Coke was showing every sign that it had put New Coke behind it and was focusing on steady, impressive sales and earnings growth, Enrico and other senior executives at Pepsi saw that they had their work cut out for them. The Pepsi Challenge had been shelved. PepsiCo's Frito-Lay division continued to dominate the nation's snack food aisle, but Pepsi-Cola, the company's namesake, was lagging. PepsiCo got into the restaurant business, buying up Taco Bell, Pizza Hut, and Kentucky Fried Chicken to create more outlets that would serve Pepsi soft drinks only. Then its chief executive, Wayne Calloway, a tall and courtly former basketball star for Wake Forest University, got some bad news: He had prostate cancer. He went to his board, asking to be allowed to remain on the job. The board, fond of Calloway and his strategy, said yes.

But the job had just gotten a whole lot harder. Calloway and others at PepsiCo realized that Coke was a tough player, but they did not fully comprehend all the internal changes Goizueta had put together. Beset by squabbling and power plays among the various divisions, PepsiCo even on its best days had trouble keeping up with Coke.

And as Coke sailed across the world, opening markets like China, Russia, and Eastern Europe between 1978 and 1989, Pepsi could not hope to match that success. While Pepsi had been in Russia first, Coke had gone full throttle once it got an opportunity and by the mid-1990s was outselling Pepsi, despite its rival's head start. Coke's access to China was enabled by the thaw in relations between the United States and Beijing, a thaw brought about by President Carter, who knew the men of Coke well.

For Coke there was always more territory to conquer. By 1996, the company's products commanded a huge slice of the market in almost every country on the planet. Coca-Cola was the dominant soft drink in most of Europe, and across most of Africa. It was moving in fast on China and outselling Pepsi by two to one in Russia. In Indonesia, the Philippines, and Australia, Coke had enormous leads over its next-closest competitors, whether they were big companies like Pepsi or Cadbury Schweppes or smaller local brands with large followings.

In all but a handful of countries, Pepsi was in second place or sometimes not present at all. It did well in India, Pakistan, and the Middle East, but across entire continents it finished far behind Coke in sales. In Latin America, though, there was one note-worthy exception. That was Venezuela, the nation that runs the gamut geographically from sparkling Caribbean beaches to misty Andean foothills. There is also great economic diversity: Some of the richest people in the world live in Venezuela, in haciendas in the countryside or costly villas in the cities, alongside some of the poorest, who press together cartons and other jetsam to shelter their children from the rain.

It was a perennially emerging market because of all those poor people. Thus it made a great place to sell soft drinks, particularly if there was a powerful local partner available to help put an American product front and center. For half a century, Pepsi had ruled Venezuela with the help of the Cisneros family.

Oswaldo and Gustavo Cisneros and their relatives had fingers in many pies around Venezuela, not to mention business interests in Miami and beyond. They were among the wealthiest of Venezuelans,

controlling the Embotelladora Cisneros bottling company, which
began in the 1940s as a distributor for all kinds of drinks, including a
brand called Hit, which the Cisneroses championed into a cheap
option for people who were either unwilling or unable to pay for an
American soda. Covering all their bases, they teamed up with Pepsi
to sell the American soda, too. Later they would get involved in
banking, then telecommunications. They knew all the right people,
and they had all the right skills. An American company couldn't ask
for better help than the Cisneroses were willing to provide.

For more than fifty years, they sold Pepsi-Cola across Venezuela,
from their own trucks and through vending machines that
displayed the Pepsi name and color scheme. In Venezuela, Pepsi
had an 80 percent share of the cola market, with Coke getting the
crumbs left over. People in Venezuela knew the name Pepsi and
drank Pepsi, not Coke. It had been that way for a long time, since
the days when Woodruff called the shots at Coke. No one had ever
figured out a way to change it.

In 1996, fifteen years into his reign, Goizueta had a plan to do
something about Venezuela. He enlisted Ivester to oversee the
project. No glitz, no fanfare, just get it done. Coke already
dominated so much of the world, but not this one spot on the map.
It was time to correct that, he told Ivester.

Ivester went on the offensive. The Cisneros family, which had
expressed their interest in selling to Coke, became a group he
would court assiduously, holding clandestine meetings day and
night, in places as dreary as airplane hangars and as luxurious as
Casa del Campo, a tony resort in the Dominican Republic. The
Cisneroses, their eyes on other industries, had been thinking
about selling their bottling business for some time. Enrico, shortly
after becoming PepsiCo's chief executive earlier in the year,
became puzzled when Oswaldo Cisneros didn't return his phone
calls. Enrico suspected something was up. He had people in
Venezuela who worked for Pepsi, and he sent them to ask Ozzie,
as he called him, if he was in talks with someone else. Cisneros
denied it.

The thought of selling the business had crossed the family's mind
more than once. A new generation was getting ready to take
charge, and the world was rapidly embracing technology and other

industries that hadn't existed when the Cisneros-Pepsi union began. Oswaldo Cisneros had once told Enrico that he worried about his health.

When Doug Ivester came calling, he got a warm reception. And in the middle of August, on the kind of dog-day afternoon when almost no news happens without a push or a shove from someone, Goizueta jubilantly announced a new partnership for Coke in Venezuela – starring the Cisneros family, the longtime bottlers for Pepsi.

Now Enrico knew what all the unreturned phone calls meant. He got a tersely worded letter, advising him that six Coke-owned bottling plants had been placed in trust to allow Pepsi, by Coke's estimates, to stay in business for about three weeks. Practically overnight, the Coke logo was painted over the Pepsi logo on Cisneros-owned trucks. Blue equipment was exchanged for red; vending machines were unplugged and pushed out; drivers' uniforms went into the garbage, to be replaced by new ones, with COCA-COLA over the heart.

'For decades, Venezuela has been the only dark spot on the Coca-Cola map,' Ivester declared as the deal was announced. He had made certain that it was now a black spot for Enrico and the rest of PepsiCo. Enrico, who had suffered a heart attack a few years earlier while fox-trotting across a floor with one of the Cisneros wives, now had another one, figuratively speaking. His biggest international market, indeed the only one where Pepsi sales exceeded Coke's, had just been stolen out from under him. And what about the Cisneroses? Where was the loyalty? The defection was deeply personal to him.

While the deal was originally described as a great opportunity for Cisneros, since it was a fifty-fifty joint venture with Coke instead of a mere franchise agreement, that was soon to change. Ivester had a plan for eliminating the cost to Coke of acquiring this particular bottler. Within a year, he had sold the Cisneros operation to Panamerican Beverages, Coke's anchor bottler in parts of Mexico and Brazil, for $1.1 billion.

The Cisneros upheaval caused a big stir in New York, where analysts ticked off another victory for Coke and put another question mark next to Pepsi's name on the cola wars scorecard.

Here was one of Pepsi's strongest foreign markets, yanked away overnight by Coke's strategy. What would be next? Where would it end?

Pepsi filed a lawsuit in Venezuela, calling the move a contractual violation and 'an illegal attempt by Coke to control the Venezuelan market by creating a soft-drink monopoly'. But it hardly made a difference in the investment community's opinion. The Coca-Cola Company seemed like a runaway train, rolling faster and faster toward ever-greater profits and ever-grander dominance of the soft-drink industry – not just in America but all over the world.

Goizueta smiled to himself. It was all happening according to plan. In that year's annual report, he would make special mention of Coke's newest bottling partner, rolling out the red carpet for these brothers who were now bound to him and his vision. He had even more plans to carry out in the coming year: more growth, greater earnings, additional expansion of the world of Coke that would take his competitors' breath away.

Then something else happened that he had not planned.

Chapter Seven

Something Instantly Recognizable

THAT WHICH WAS UNPLANNED descended slowly, almost imperceptibly, like a light mist that later becomes a driving rain. In the beginning, only the people who knew him best saw it at all.

Sometime near the end of 1996, the year the Olympics came to Atlanta and his most triumphant year yet as the leader of the Coca-Cola Company, Roberto Goizueta began to slow down. He had always been so robust, so ubiquitous, so confident of himself and his company. He had orchestrated wrenching changes in the Coca-Cola Company and all the entities around it, turning opportunity into victory, always with a firm hand.

He had kept the same hours and the same routines for fifteen years. He had his secrets, to be sure, but for the most part he was a public man, the chairman and chief executive of one of the most successful companies on the planet, lauded on magazine covers and cited in business schools for everything he had brought about.

Now he seemed a little distant to some of his colleagues, a little detached, and the motion of his arms and legs reminded some people of the kind they expected to see on a much older man. His smooth skin with its healthy tone looked pale, and his always erect posture began to sag. Just a little, but to anyone who looked closely, the difference was there.

Goizueta turned sixty-five in November of that year. For a long time he had had a slight palsy in his right hand, which caused the fingers to shake from time to time. But this latest development was something else; a kind of fatigue settling over the man like dust, taking the bounce out of his step and some of the light out of his eyes. His voice trembled when he spoke. He seemed, suddenly, old.

At that point, he had lived two half-lives: the first one twenty-nine years long, spent baronially in Havana. Then there was the second chapter, the life he had been forced to construct in a new country. He had spent those American years translating every word he heard from English to Spanish inside his mind, and translating his fury and loss and grief into an ambition that had achieved mightily for him and for thousands of others. He got the credit for launching an engine of wealth that was unparalleled in the American corporate world. He had taken a good but aging brand and turned it into a thrilling growth company as he built up Coke's empire and made sure that Coke was sold everywhere in the world it could possibly be. There were a handful of exceptions where Coke did not sell its soft drinks in the 1990s, places the State Department would not let any American business go. One of them was Cuba.

As he had since his youth Goizueta still smoked his cigarettes – a pack a day at least, sometimes three. He preferred Kool menthols as the chairman of Coke. His smoking habits were both a joke inside the company and a logistical concern. When aides combed a location for security purposes before a Goizueta speech or appearance of any kind, they had to make sure there were ashtrays on hand. Sometimes in the 1990s, when tobacco had become officially recognized as a lethal substance, his hosts insisted that he not smoke. This is a nonsmoking area, they would tell the aides. The aides would nod. Then they would take an ashtray and conceal it in a drawer, and make sure Goizueta knew where it was by the time he arrived for his speech or his ribbon-cutting. The Coke tower was a nonsmoking area, too, but Goizueta went up and down the halls with a cigarette in his hand, a curling cloud of blue-gray smoke trailing behind him. 'We used to say that the company's designated smoking place was wherever Roberto was,' a former executive recalled.

Smoking may have been his only outlet. He spent money on little else, and people at Coke talked about how difficult it was to get him to replace a battered suitcase or a raincoat he had owned since college. Plenty of other Coke executives lived far better, lavishly entertaining themselves and their friends, building extra wings onto their already roomy houses, investing in toys like big speedboats, which they named in honor of their favorite product – names like *The Real Thing*. But Goizueta was the paragon of understatement, careful and cautious in everything that he did. It seemed like just another part of his fondness for close control. He had it in business, and he wanted it in life. By the age of sixty-five he had achieved it in both, except for his daily inhaling of dozens of cigarettes.

Around the beginning of September 1997 he took a trip to Monte Carlo, where there was an annual bottler meeting and where he always enjoyed himself. When he came back, just after Labor Day, he kept a date for lunch that he had made with Andrew Conway, then a Morgan Stanley beverage analyst.

Conway, whose demeanor is as pleasant and sincere as a schoolboy's, was regarded by many on Wall Street as the analyst closest to the company. Conway had once worked at Coke as a summer intern, about as faceless a cog as anyone could be inside Coke's complex on North Avenue in Atlanta. But he had made some friends and was still believed to have good contacts inside the company. He was a great admirer of Goizueta and, like every other analyst covering Coke in the 1990s, he frequently issued upbeat reports about the company's prospects.

In 1997, most analysts were Coke believers. They all foresaw more years of Coke staying at the top of its game, since Pepsi's strategy appeared unlikely to interfere with the Coke juggernaut. Internationally, with the scars of the Cisneros defection still fresh, Pepsi remained weak. Domestically, its soda business was struggling. Roger Enrico had announced plans to sell off the restaurant chains. While Frito-Lay dominated the American salty-snack market, PepsiCo's other divisions seemed stalled. Enrico continually promised investors a turnaround, but he had a lot of work to do first.

As long as Goizueta remained in place, and the machine that Goizueta built remained intact, Coke could be counted on to dominate, to succeed, and to leave scorched earth in its wake. This was the kind of thing that analysts liked: It made for predictability and reliability, with no nasty surprises.

Everyone on Wall Street also realized that Goizueta would not be CEO forever. He was set to turn sixty-six in the fall of 1997. And he had prepared his successor, Doug Ivester, who had a long

list of achievements beside his name, along with the imprimatur of
Goizueta. Analysts believed Ivester was the right man for the job.
In 1997, he was just forty-nine years old, a proven winner within
the Coke system. Many considered him the most brilliant strategist
that the new Coca-Cola Company had produced. Conway, for
one, thought he had everything it took to continue the company's
amazing rate of growth. The succession, whenever it took place,
would be smooth and professional.

At the lunch with Conway, who had brought two executives
from Fidelity Investments with him, the men sat in Goizueta's
private dining room and Conway noticed that the chairman of
Coke looked very tired. Goizueta sipped occasionally from a cup
of broccoli-cheese soup and discussed the company's outlook with
little of his usual enthusiasm.

'Andrew, you'll have to excuse me,' he said at one point, in his
courtly, clipped tones. 'I'm a little fatigued.'

He reached for a cigarette, lit it, and sucked in the smoke,
holding it a while in his mouth before letting it out again. From
time to time, he coughed. Conway thought it might be the smoke.
The other men at the table coughed from time to time, too. It
definitely was the smoke.

The meal ended, and Goizueta and Conway and the Fidelity
bankers went their separate ways.

A week later came the sparely worded announcement from
Coke that its longtime chairman and chief executive was being
treated for an unspecified 'growth'. Goizueta had been to the
doctor. He had studiously avoided the doctor for decades, for
reasons that were known only to him. The most contact he had had
with them was when his little boy was so sick, more than twenty-
five years earlier. Maybe he didn't trust them after that. Maybe he
was afraid they would tell him to stop smoking.

But now, not having bounced back from his last business trip,
he finally did go, donning the pale-green smock and submitting to
an inquisition about his living habits, his diet, his stress levels, and
his allergies to medication. He took a battery of tests made with
needles and X rays. And after participating in this process, he got
some news that shocked him, his family, and the Coca-Cola
Company to the core.

Goizueta had an enormous malignant tumor on one lung. It was cancer, almost certainly the result of smoking cigarettes.

He immediately went into the Emory University hospital and began a program of chemotherapy. That was in the middle of September. The company, wary of ruffling too many feathers on Wall Street and in other places, and no doubt under orders from Goizueta himself, announced only a sketchy description of his ailment. It did not use the word 'cancer' or the word 'tumor'. It referred only to a 'growth'. Still, Atlanta buzzed with the news. There were stories that Goizueta had strolled casually into the hospital on his own two feet, and others that described him being rolled in on a gurney, unable to move. Officially, he was not supposed to be in grave danger.

Secretaries came and went from the lavish suite in which he lay, carrying papers for him to sign. Ivester stopped by every day. A fax machine was set up, and flowers arrived by the bushel. Olguita sat by the bed and read him his mail: the official correspondence, the get-well cards, everything. He wanted to keep up with all of it.

Goizueta expected to be in the hospital only a short time, to fully recover from this minor inconvenience and go on to complete the year at Coke – there was a lot of work to do, after all – and then, sometime in the future, make a decision about when he might retire. Retirement for him had been looming for a while, but he had decided that his would be similar to Bob Woodruff's. He would cede title and office to someone else, yet remain on the scene. He might not always be visible to outsiders or even acknowledged as a continuing force at Coke, but everyone, from Ivester on down, would know who was in charge.

There was even a plan he had discussed that would make him the company chairman until he reached his early seventies, while Ivester carried out the duties of the chief executive. That way, he could remain in place to supervise and consult with his successor. He could carry on some of the work he was so good at, like schmoozing with the Coke directors, while Ivester took care of the nuts and bolts. He would not be obsolete. It would work well for everyone. 'Ivester thought he needed Roberto's guidance during the transition,' said a former Coke executive who sat in on discussions about the plan. 'And, of course, Roberto thought it was a good idea, too.' Ivester had told Goizueta years before that he didn't need to be chairman and CEO. He was content to serve as Goizueta's president and would have gladly retired when Goizueta did. Now, with his leader lying in a hospital bed, Ivester repeated that pledge. 'I will live up to that promise,' he told Goizueta. 'You can have Stahl or bring back Keough, whatever you want.'

No, no, said Goizueta, according to a person close to Ivester. He wanted Doug Ivester to take charge when he was gone.

He believed in Ivester, believed that he could run the Coca-Cola Company. But he would need help. Just as Goizueta and Keough had been a team all those years, and then Goizueta and Ivester these last four years, Ivester could not do it all alone. Goizueta knew that, and Ivester probably agreed. For some time, the older man had been sitting offstage when Ivester spoke to analysts, or listening in when Ivester handled a call. He was an unseen force behind the younger man he had groomed to be his successor, trying to make Ivester more like him.

Then again, like Woodruff before him, Goizueta did not really want to leave the Coca-Cola Company. He wanted to keep working, and he wanted the status that came with the job. It was not the trappings, such as the company jet or the secretaries or the invitations to every important event all over the world. It was not about the money. He already had a lot of money. *It was the job.*

Goizueta would be in the hospital longer than he thought. In the process of eroding the tumor on his lung, the chemotherapy had laid waste his immune system. He caught a cold that became an infection. He reclined in his bed in the same suite in which the great Woodruff had taken his last breath, a private aerie at the very top of the hospital that owed great chunks of its financial underpinning to the Coca-Cola Company's largesse. Now it was Goizueta who was hooked up to a series of machines that measured everything about him and yielded the information without discretion. His kidneys, his lungs, his blood gases, his respiration — all of it was there to be analyzed, discussed, and graded by the squadrons of doctors who now filled up his days. Sometimes he gazed at the screens, whose blinking patterns must have reminded him of the machine on which he used to trace Coke's progress, hour by hour, minute by minute. Only here there were peaks and valleys instead of a continuously ascending path like the one that he had cleared for Coke. And he could not have any more cigarettes.

One day his results showed more valleys than peaks. And he was in pain, a pain that would not go away.

On a blustery October evening, as the wind rattled through the drying leaves of the pear trees along the boulevards, the knock on Goizueta's hospital suite door was not a doctor or a nurse but a priest, come to dab Goizueta's head with holy oil and give him the last rites of his church. There had been the usual bustle of medical professionals before that, prodding and looking, all of them asking him, not really listening all the time for the answer: 'How do you feel, Mr. Goizueta?'

'Fantastic,' he might reply, when he could summon the energy he needed to speak. Fantastic.

It had always been one of his favorite words.

Chapter Eight

Changing of the Guard

HIS FUNERAL WAS A STATELY affair, crammed with dignitaries from throughout the world of Coke. The Mass was celebrated in Atlanta at the Holy Spirit Church, where a room downstairs was dedicated to the memory of Carlos Goizueta, the son who had died from leukemia nearly thirty years earlier. Flowers bloomed on either side of the altar and the casket sat at the front. From the pulpit Goizueta was hailed as an icon of integrity and a paragon of accomplishment. Former President Jimmy Carter attended. Pepsi sent a delegation; Roger Enrico, traveling in Asia, could not make it. A roll call of politicians and business leaders, starting with Andrew Young, Atlanta's former mayor, filled the pews.

Everything was formal and dignified and buttoned-down, like the man who had died. After the priest gave the final blessing – 'Go in peace' – and the body of Goizueta, carried in its casket by a group that included his two sons, had started to make its way down the center aisle, the Holy Spirit organist finished the Bach fugue and then swung into a song not found in the red hymnals. It was 'I'd Like to Teach the World to Sing', a seventies peace-and-love ballad that Goizueta had co-opted for a Coca-Cola television advertisement, changing the lyrics to 'I'd like to buy the world a Coke' and creating in the process one of Coke's most effective marketing ploys. And with that last rendition of one of his favorite commercial messages, played out in a sacred space, the public life of the chairman and chief executive of the Coca-Cola Company came to an end.

Coca-Cola employees worldwide, all 29,000 of them, had learned of Goizueta's death in a voice-mail message from Doug Ivester. The message was delivered in the wee hours of October

18, 1997, not long after Goizueta had expired. In choked tones, Ivester announced that Goizueta was gone. 'All of us,' he said, 'have lost a good friend.'

Inside the company, the reaction bordered on hysterical. People behaved as if they had lost a beloved parent and protector, not merely a friend or a boss who many of them had never met or spoken to in all the years he had been running Coke. Goizueta had made them wealthy, he had given them hope, he had created a magical castle of Coke that impressed the world. He had been an often unseen but beneficent force. Now that he was gone, they were grief-stricken. Some felt like sheep without a shepherd and wondered what would become of them.

Someone thought to set up message books in the lobby of the tower, and Coke employees stood there for hours, waiting their turn to write long notes of condolence to Olguita and the children and tributes to their vanished leader. The outpouring was reminiscent of the send-off for Don Keough, four years earlier. But it lasted longer, days instead of hours, and this time their leader was dead.

Then they went back to work, moving mountains of Coca-Cola concentrate and building shareholder value just as they had for the past sixteen years when Goizueta was alive. Life had changed, but Coca-Cola hadn't.

The company lacked drama, as a rule. It was stratified into the haves and the have-nots, with the lines of demarcation clear to all. It began with the colored badges everyone was required to wear inside the building. Senior executives wore badges edged in green, while the rank and file wore red. Part-time workers wore black, and vendors, like telephone-installation crews, got yellow.

There was not a lot of mixing among the green badges and everyone else. The executive floors were at the top of the tower – floors twenty-three, twenty-four, twenty-five, and twenty-six – and except for trips to the twelfth floor, where the executive dining room was, not many of the green badges traveled outside that area. The twenty-third through the twenty-fifth floors were connected by a spiral staircase and upholstered with thick, ivory-colored carpet interrupted by carefully placed reproduction Chippendale chairs. The very top floor of the building, above the executive areas, belonged to investor relations.

The twenty-fifth floor had once housed Woodruff's office, but the suite had been removed, piece by piece, and installed on a lower floor, exactly the way it looked on the day he died in 1985. The walls held his favorite photographs, and the same country-patterned curtains he had chosen for the office were rehung on the windows. It was a shrine to Woodruff. Meanwhile, Don Keough's office was gone. So was Paul Austin's. Not everything was thought worthy of preservation.

When Goizueta died, he was among the wealthiest individuals in America. His stock options and restricted shares, which his death enabled his survivors to cash in, moved into the Roberto C. Goizueta Foundation, which he had created five years earlier. Some of his associates believed Goizueta had planned to be the next Robert Woodruff when it came to philanthropy. Like Woodruff, he may have hoped to put his own stamp on Atlanta, to see the name Goizueta all over town. Only a few weeks before he died, Emory University had named its business school after him, in a ceremony Goizueta was too ill to attend. With his death, the Goizueta Foundation took its place among the other southern charities built upon Coca-Cola stock. Goizueta died with more than $1 billion to his name; the entire gross national product of Cuba the same year was $10 billion.

By the end of October, Ivester had been approved by the board as the new chairman and CEO, in no small part because he was Goizueta's chosen one. He would be like Goizueta the Second, carrying out the plans of the sadly departed former CEO. *Fortune* hailed the succession, praising Goizueta for arranging as seamless a transition as any corporate America had seen.

When the funeral was over, a memorial service for employees had been held; Ivester was the chief speaker, recalling how Goizueta had encouraged everyone to 'paint by numbers', and a video was screened that showed Goizueta declaring that 'the true heritage of the Coca-Cola Company is not its products or its financial strength; the true heritage of the Coca-Cola Company is its character.' When the big black books had been put away and the name of Goizueta had ceased to be mentioned quite so often in the hallways of the Coke tower, then Ivester allowed himself a moment to survey what was now his.

He had moved into Goizueta's old office, and now he got up from the big wooden desk, where a Norman Rockwell painting he had asked to have installed, of a boy fishing with a Coca-Cola at his side, watched over things. Another painting, an Andy Warhol silkscreen of Teddy Roosevelt, had been hung on another wall. An opium pillow in the shape of a cat sat near the door.

He stood at the top of the stairs that spiraled up from two floors below, culminating just outside his office. And he reflected on where he had wound up, after just eighteen years at the Coca-Cola Company. He was as high as any Coke man could go.

Every single one of the 29,000 employees all over the world now reported to him. Ivester alone occupied the apex of this giant pyramid. Everyone else was linked to him by electronic mail, by voice mail, by a rapidly expanding database of sales that he had ordered set up as a means of keeping closer tabs on the company's worldwide operations back when he was president. And they were all subject to him. Every decision about strategy, brand-building, advertising, relationships with huge customers like Burger King and McDonald's – all of those decisions would now have to seek his approval. He would be the one to sign off on everything, picking apart presentations to find out how well a person really knew his or her stuff, reviewing television commercials, evaluating promotions for key spots.

In announcing his move up, the company had seen fit to highlight many of his credentials: graduate of the University of Georgia, former Ernst & Young accountant. But the real story, to Coke, began in 1979, the year he joined the Coca-Cola Company.

'A key accomplishment as chief financial officer,' Coke's press release noted, 'was his leadership of the initial public offering process that created Coca-Cola Enterprises.' Creating a financial superstructure within Coke was another triumph: 'As chief financial officer, he recruited dozens of highly skilled finance specialists around the world and gave them a wide range of job experiences,' the announcement said. 'Today, a dozen years later, many of those young finance managers have financial or operating responsibility for significant segments of the company's business around the world.' He had also created a new bottling model for the company and duplicated it around the world, transforming the relationship between Coke, maker of the syrup, and the bottlers, who brought the soft drink to consumers.

In addition, he had successfully tinkered with the ultimate symbol of Coca-Cola – the vaguely seductive hoopskirt bottle – to help Coke even more. Instead of changing the formula, he had changed the serving size. It was a very smart move. 'Under his leadership, the company introduced a twenty-ounce plastic version of its famous contour bottle,' Coke's news department exulted. 'Today, the package is a staple of Coca-Cola USA's portfolio and a major contributor to volume growth in the United States.'

On the outside, there was more power to enjoy. There was the adulation from Wall Street, for all the magical growth that had come out of Coke for the past fifteen years. That attention had been focused on Goizueta for such a long time, but now, finally, it would be Ivester's. There was the red carpet treatment in Atlanta that came the way of every Coke CEO. And there was the thrill of flying around the world to Coke's markets, large and small, where to be the Coke CEO was to be a true celebrity. It would mean audiences with kings and prime ministers, not to mention presiding at bottling-plant openings and drinking tea with Communists. Ivester had watched Goizueta doing all that for years. Now it was his turn.

Keough was gone. Goizueta was dead. He was the only one left.

Ivester believed that he was working for the greatest company on the planet, making the best-loved product in the world. And Coke's dominance was all but assured at that moment. The company was selling 1 billion drinks a day in the two hundred countries where it had a presence. Ivester's ideology, pushing per-capita consumption higher and higher, had made Coke's earnings blossom all these years by making sure its bottlers ordered more and more concentrate. There was nowhere to go but up, and up, and up. After Goizueta, he was the largest employee shareholder at the company. Pumping up the value required selling more and more Coke, and *that* would be possible only if everyone was on the same page.

Ivester still had a little boy's fascination with Coca-Cola. One of his favorite spots in Atlanta was a tourist attraction called the World of Coca-Cola. The place was a quasi-museum of ephemera and history that Goizueta had opened in 1990. The company paid the city of Atlanta to turn over a block of public space to house the exhibit, which was surmounted by a giant Coca-Cola sign. It quickly became a tourist destination. Like the Cyclorama, which depicted the Civil War history of Atlanta, and Margaret Mitchell's house, this explained a part of the city – the Coca-Cola Company – that visitors wanted to know more about.

Inside, they could shuffle past glass cases filled with old Coke ads and watch brief videos covering a selective history of the soft drink. In an exhibit called *Bottling Fantasy,* glass bottles move around an artist's interpretation of a bottling plant, filling with brown pretend soda and clinking prettily as they knock against machinery. There is a re-creation of a 1920s soda fountain, with a jukebox playing Coca-Cola-inspired marches and other tunes. There are Coke machines and Coke cans from all over the world, displaying a variety of languages and package shapes. And there is a high-tech room where different flavors of soda, all of them made by Coke, are shot from a distant dispenser into a cup. It is the global experience of an American corporation made accessible for tourists visiting Atlanta, as long as they are willing to pay the admission price. It is also a permanent shrine to the power of marketing. 'The World of Coca-Cola allows visitors to experience what life would be like were it lived inside an advertisement,' wrote one scholar, comparing it to other corporate displays. 'This is a Barnumesque blend of learning and ballyhoo . . . where reality and illusion merge, producing magic: sorcery that sells.'

The World of Coke makes no mention of the past or present ingredients in Coca-Cola. There is no mention of the clashes with bottlers, of the lawsuits filed by Coke's most intimate partners when they felt the partnership being torn out of their hands. It transmits only the story of Coke that the company wanted the world to know.

Ivester had supporters within Coke, but there were also people who had been bruised by their dealings with him and who were now waiting to see him stumble. At the same time, they had been conditioned to think about the stock price first, so their personal vendettas had to settle for second. As long as Ivester kept the stock price high, he was going to be all right.

'Ivester had very high integrity,' said a former Coca-Cola executive who had known him for years. 'And he was extremely fair. I never knew him to play any political games, although obviously he was aware in the corporate world of how to position himself.' He had a small but loyal following of people who admired him as a man of principle, not just the curator of the share price.

He was even-tempered, for the most part. No outbursts, no surprises. He contained his temper and filtered everything through a single prerogative: what would be best for the company. He didn't bother with small talk. He was businesslike. 'He never gets angry, even on the surface,' the same former Coke executive said. 'He's not a wit or a charmer. He's a very stable kind of personality.'

He would remember people's birthdays, sending a card or some other token to a small circle of associates. He supported the child of one assistant for years, paying her college tuition and providing other financial help.

Still in love with cars as an adult, he collected them, spending freely for models that he wanted. He owned a bright-red vintage Cadillac and another red car, this one a Porsche. He tooled around in them on weekends, when he wasn't working. But most of the time he could be found in his office on Saturdays and most of Sundays as well, always chipping away at the problems and issues bedeviling the Coca-Cola Company, always communicating, through a pinging e-mail sent from his computer or with a voice-mail message left in his high-pitched voice. He was fond of telling people on the other side of the world what he thought they should do to enlarge their piece of the Coca-Cola business. He didn't think they should dismiss his advice. For the most part, he ignored office politics. He had witnessed them for years, and he had had enough.

A presentation before Ivester invariably meant an interrogation, swift and sure, usually with two or three pointed questions. For him, asking penetrating questions was all part of creating a greater, more improved soft-drink business. Colleagues would remember answering some of the questions he asked, and then realizing, one or two answers into the process, that there they stood, in a pool of their own blood. 'He would probe until he found the weakness, the one thing someone didn't know, and then he'd say, "You don't know the facts,"' one former senior executive recalled. 'It would make people feel bad. And then they'd go out of his office with their tail between their legs, when actually they had done a pretty good job.'

When he had become president of Coca-Cola, he was immediately and relentlessly compared with Don Keough, a man he resembled hardly at all. His personal style, coming so closely on the heels of Keough's, left some people baffled. Colleagues, customers, and competitors frequently felt alone when it came time to have dinner or some other interaction with Ivester. They were accustomed to the blarney and the warmth of Keough, and now they had another kind of character to deal with. Some of them thought of him as 'the Iceman'. Others referred to him as 'the accountant'. Some of them seemed to hate him for not being Keough.

Unlike Keough, who had seen his role as that of worldwide ambassador for the Coca-Cola Company, in which diplomacy and charm were indispensable accessories, Ivester believed that he should be all business. Business, for him, was about being direct, about working with numbers. He and the Coca-Cola Company had work to do, syrup to sell, money to count. He was there to build shareholder value – something that was sure to benefit a lot of people.

He was a product of his era. By the early 1980s, Wall Street seemed to admire the blunt and the fearless, especially if they got results. At the same time, Ivester did not always win friends with his behavior. 'My wife and some others were at a luncheon at someone's house in Washington,' recalled one senior executive at another consumer products company, 'and a knock comes on the door. Doug Ivester walks in, doesn't even say hello to the hostess. He walks over to the table where his wife is sitting and says, "Kay, the meeting finished early. Let's go."' Others complained about his style as well. He didn't mean it, they'd say, but he sometimes left people feeling as though he didn't connect with them.

Donald McHenry, the former ambassador to the United Nations, who by 1997 had been a Coke director for sixteen years, gave Ivester an audience and a piece of advice not long after he became chairman and CEO. 'He came up to see me in Washington, and we had a long discussion about things I thought should change, things that had to do with the lifestyle,' said McHenry, a thoughtful man who taught at Georgetown University's School of Foreign Service after observing the world as a diplomat. 'Roberto *lived* Coke. Ivester was *living* Coke. I don't think that's healthy for the individual, and I don't think it's healthy for the company.' He worried that someone who lived that way would become 'monodimensional', as he put it. He wanted Ivester to listen.

But as Ivester took over from Goizueta, none of that seemed to matter much. The Coca-Cola Company hovered at its zenith. Never before had it been so thoroughly organized, so well equipped to sell soft drinks, so technologically advanced in terms of monitoring its sales and tracking its growth, and so responsive to commands from a central point, which was Atlanta. Employees, bottlers, customers – all of them listened to what the chairman of Coke had to say.

Less than two weeks after Goizueta died, Ivester was on the road again, promising the same promise Goizueta had always made: Coke was going to keep on growing. 'What I always wonder is, why not?' he said in one speech, delivered to the National Soft Drink Association's international summit in New York. 'Why can't we keep this up? Just look around! The world has more people, in more countries, with more access to communication and more desire for a quality standard of living and quality products than ever before.'

But there were people at the company who did not share the view that everything was going their way. They worried about the effect that the new man at the top would have on their collective fortunes, and they were not sure what to do about it.

The ascension of Doug Ivester had caused a shudder through certain quarters of the Coke tower, a reaction born of their understanding of his personality; they worried that it might highlight festering problems that predated his arrival and were sure to be there after he left.

There were customs that defined the inner circle of power at

Coke and they had existed for years, all part of the psychology of the company cultivated by Woodruff, Goizueta, and others. 'Meeting the president of the United States isn't designed to be as intimidating as meeting the president of Coca-Cola,' said one former executive. It made the company seem arrogant and parochial, as if nothing in the world mattered except Coca-Cola. This bothered the people who mixed most with outsiders, the ones responsible for sales and the ones who had to deal with the press, Wall Street, and other external forces. 'Two things happen,' the executive said. 'Those who can be intimidated are, and those who can't blow us off as self-important, overbearing goofballs.'

The Coke culture remained closed and secretive, in line with Coca-Cola tradition. Employees were actively discouraged from discussing their business with anyone outside the company; anyone who spoke clandestinely to a reporter, for instance, had to live with the fear of being fired. Worry abounded that the telephone lines in the Coke tower, where most of the managers worked, might be tapped and that someone on the executive floors could listen to people's conversations on a regular basis.

It was considered an act of disloyalty to consume a rival beverage, even if that rival had such a tiny slice of the market that it was virtually insignificant compared with Coke's. The name Pepsi was not to be uttered; it was referred to as 'the competitor' or 'our imitator'. Senior executives were addressed as 'Mister' even if they asked to be called by their first names, and hierarchy was craved for the structure it gave to everyday company life. It was a big company, after all: nearly thirty thousand employees, with operations in about two hundred countries. Everything could fall apart if there weren't some rules, and rules could not be bent. Someone who was not a full-time employee, no matter how well liked, could never be invited to a company birthday party or retirement bash. Such events were for Coke people only. Showing flexibility on such a front was just not the way Coke worked.

By 1997, the company was divided down the middle between what one former executive called 'Georgia old-boy types with Coke in their veins', who saw Coca-Cola as infallible, and a younger generation, more skeptical of the marketing messages because events – in politics and elsewhere – had taught them to look beneath the surface of corporate pronouncements. 'They would use language like "Let's rekindle the love affair between Coca-Cola and consumers,"' said the former executive, a member of the younger group. 'It was a kind of cultish brainwashing, and there were always several of us who would sit in meetings and say, I can't work with this.' With the rise of Goizueta and Ivester had also come a new class of hires: the financial experts, the people who came out of accounting firms and management-consulting jobs to apply their skills to soft drinks.

Historically, new hires had been few and far between in Coke's operations; people who came to work at Coke almost never left. Most of the executives worked their way up for ten or fifteen years before they were tapped to run a division. They had to score high on a long-term loyalty test, and the hurdles were often invisible. Only certain types of people seemed to flourish. Senior and mid-level executives brought in from the outside frequently stumbled, unused to doing things the Coke way. 'We used to call it tissue rejection,' said another former executive. 'Think about a family that has never dated or married or pulled anybody outside into it. It's all inbred.'

Ivester's appointment to the top job exposed the rivalry between two distinct camps that had been in formation for more than fifteen years. One could be called 'the Keough people'. These were the executives who had spent years abroad in operations, who had run divisions in the United States, and for whom selling Coca-Cola was not a collection of data but a reality they remembered carrying out. They had stood in the cold and the rain and sat for hours trying to win over customers or bottlers, and they shared a deep disdain for the financial prowess of people like Ivester. They believed that there was no way for a person to understand the Coca-Cola Company if he had not spent time 'in the field', traveling across the country and around the world, meeting with customers – whether the McDonald's brass or the owner of a mom-and-pop bodega on some third-world street corner and understanding, firsthand, the problems and the joys of selling people Coca-Cola.

Ivester, meanwhile, was the figurehead of a group that was often referred to as 'the Doug-ettes'. These were people who had a lot in common with Ivester, the ones who were sharp with numbers and knew the accounting rules backward and forward. Many of them were CPAs, recruited from places like Ernst & Young after Ivester's star began to rise at Coke. The Keough people were thought to be ideologically uncluttered when it came to Coca-Cola: They loved the brand and would do anything to protect and perpetuate it. The Doug-ettes, meanwhile, were considered more mercenary. They were the ones who looked out chiefly for the bottom line and, the thinking went, spared nothing along the way. By 1991, they appeared to have gained the upper hand, and they were pleased now that Ivester had been tapped to lead the company. The Keough people, though, smoldered.

As Ivester took over, Coca-Cola's public image had never been better. It was a star among companies, the best performer in the Standard & Poor's index, among the most widely held stocks, and the most admired. But all that success Ivester, Keough, and Goizueta had built had also fostered a swaggering attitude that some inside Coke feared would harm the company. Perhaps it was the lingering notoriety, and honesty, of Ivester's wolf speech, in which he declared that he wanted all of the soft-drink market, not just a share of it. Perhaps it was his general lack of concern for anything but advancing the business. In any case, some of his aides almost immediately made a special effort to make Ivester address this.

In early 1998, he sat for an interview with *The Wall Street Journal*'s beverage industry reporter and the conversation eventually turned to arrogance. 'Arrogance,' said Ivester, 'is the greatest enemy of the Coca-Cola Company.' It quickly became clear, as he continued talking, that he meant complacency, not arrogance. He was concerned that Coke executives, looking at the company's past success, might be content with minimal growth or no growth, and that would subvert his plans for continuous upward progress.

He addressed arrogance, though, because he had been coached by the Coke public-relations department to address the issue. Under Goizueta, the word had been coming up again and again in connection with the Coca-Cola Company. Seminal moments like the Venezuelan bottler acquisition struck some people as unusually aggressive, even for Coke, and in other countries, particularly in Western Europe, Coca-Cola had been accused of using its power

.as a leading brand to intimidate customers and competing soft-drink companies. Some of the published remarks of Roberto Goizueta, too, had led people to conclude that Coca-Cola was arrogant. But surely the new chairman and CEO could put this matter to rest, the public relations staff thought. Someone had to.

Ivester seemed to take care of it. When the interview was published on the front page of the *Journal* in early March 1998, he came across as a dedicated caretaker of the Coca-Cola share price, a southern-born extension of the beloved Roberto Goizueta, and a man eager to stamp out arrogance. It was precisely the image Wall Street and Coke's board wanted. Ivester, and everyone around him, thought the article was just great. He had the entire front page framed and hung on the wall just outside his office, where visitors could see it while they waited for their turn to meet with him.

A few people at Coke continued to worry, though. The public relations group hired Kathleen Hall Jamieson, a Georgetown University professor and media expert, early in 1998 to review Coke's publications. Jamieson went through the annual reports and the speeches that Coke executives gave and pronounced the company in great danger. 'Listen to the bait you are putting out there for lawyers and other people,' she said, reading back passages she had circled, according to people who were there. 'The language you are using to demonstrate your strength is arrogant, and it is the language of a tyrant.'

Jamieson's advice was duly noted and typed up in a report for Ivester. That was how he preferred to receive information, and what he did with it after that was his business.

For he was alone at the top. Unlike Goizueta and many of his predecessors, Ivester did not have a second-in-command and seemed to be in no rush to name one. A solitary man, an ardent competitor whose single-minded pursuit of what he wanted did not always allow for the give-and-take of typical relationships – no, he was not going to select anyone from the seething ranks below him to be his confidant and sidekick. 'I don't need a filter,' he would say when someone asked him about filling the empty president's slot. Whenever he said that, the ears of a certain former Coca-Cola president, sitting in his own office in New York, would burn.

Ivester had had a front-row seat for the relationship between Keough and Goizueta, which had plenty of tense moments. A number two usually wanted to be number one instead. He may have thought, why rush to create the same kind of environment for himself? Robert Woodruff had done just fine for all those decades, managing mostly alone. He, Ivester, was cut from the same cloth: able, dedicated, single-minded. A true Coca-Cola man. Meanwhile, the directors urged him not to pick a number two either – not until he was ready to declare that person his successor.

Ivester pondered the monolith he now controlled. All over the world, anchor bottlers that he had set up were key partners of Coca-Cola, channeling money into the company through syrup sales, franchise purchases, and profits from the huge equity stakes that Coke controlled in each of them. There was Coca-Cola Enterprises in the United States, which had grown from controlling 30 percent of the country's Coca-Cola products in the late 1980s to 70 percent by 1997. A year earlier, the bottler had set off on an acquisition binge that had gobbled up a series of franchises – in the United States, in France, in Belgium – at a cost of more than $1.3 billion. And then it had spent another $3.7 billion to buy bottling properties in the United Kingdom and Canada, as well as a sprawling Coke-owned bottler in New York.

All that had been with the approval of Ivester, who had concluded that the more territory an anchor bottler controlled, the better for that bottler and, of course, the better for the Coca-Cola Company. Every time a local bottler in Texas, say, was bought up by the anchor bottler, the rules changed. Instead of the old contract, which often had the syrup price pegged to those historic limits, the new contract would apply. Every scrap of additional turf that was absorbed by Coca-Cola Enterprises meant one less place where Coke was subject to its bottlers in terms of the syrup price. Everything that Coca-Cola Enterprises absorbed gave its claims of greater efficiency more credibility.

For Coke, the syrup sales were just one aspect of the deal. When Coke spoke, the bottler it controlled was supposed to listen. Ivester had all sorts of plans to 'drive consumption' – one of his favorite concepts – by filling holes in places that already sold Coke. If a local McDonald's sold Coke, and the local baseball stadium, then why not all of the local convenience stores, too? Coke stood ready with the plans for such things and told its biggest bottler where and how to put them in place. When the bottler was done with that project, it would be a good idea if it could start installing Coke vending machines in supermarket parking lots, and down on the docks where people went fishing, and along the highway rest stops, and all the other places that people might get thirsty. At every point along this chain, the bottler would need consultation from the Coca-Cola Company. And nearly all of this free advice meant buying more syrup from the Coca-Cola Company, which would lead to that much more silver rattling in the pockets of the shareholders.

'Size was all they cared about,' said a former executive. 'It was always, we want this to be the biggest.' Coke was hardly alone in this; all over America, companies pushed for consolidation, for efficiency, for streamlining through size.

Another innovation of Ivester's, and one that would influence many of his other plans, was the concept of the exclusive agreement. In the real-estate world, an exclusive agreement meant that only one broker could show a house. In the world of soft drinks, exclusivity meant that no other soft-drink company could have any of its products for sale in any of the property covered by the agreement. Starting in the mid-1990s, Coke busied itself obtaining exclusives at sports arenas, hotel chains, and colleges, where the contracts were known as 'pouring rights'. At football games, track meets, music concerts, and job fairs, all a college could serve was Coca-Cola or another Coke product like Sprite. In return, Coke gave the colleges things: scoreboards at first, then, as the stakes rose higher, cash signing bonuses, computers, and a percentage of sales.

The company expanded the practice to airlines, to elementary schools. Disney theme parks served only Coca-Cola; so did other sprawling corporations, like McDonald's, Wendy's, and American Airlines. There were places where exclusive agreements could not be arranged, like supermarkets, which insisted on having a variety of products out there for customers to buy. But wherever exclusivity could be had, Ivester believed in nailing it down.

It guaranteed Coke sales. If there was no Pepsi, no Royal Crown, no Snapple available at all, and there *was* Coke – well, then, that's what people would buy. When people checked into a hotel and opened their minibar, they would see only cans of Coca-Cola and Sprite alongside the M&M's and the tiny bottles of Scotch. When they flew on an airline, they would ask for a Pepsi and be told, 'We have Coke, not Pepsi.' For years, restaurant owners as large as the McDonald's Corporation and as small as Joe's Bar and Grill had had to make decisions about whether to carry both. Many did not, for reasons ranging from preference to price.

Sometimes people who asked for a Coke were given Pepsi, and vice versa – something that rankled Coca-Cola executives no end. In a landmark case, *Coca-Cola Company v. Doris,* a Coke lawyer named Julius 'Lunce' Lunsford, Jr., convinced the judge that restaurants and other places could not simply post signs advising customers which cola they served. They had to announce that they did not serve Coca-Cola products, tableside or at the lunch counter, if that was the case.

But now Coke was taking matters into its own hands, forcing that decision up another level. Consumers would not get to make the choice; business owners would make it for them. To make its case, Coke salesmen would point out that Coke had the superior market share – some 44 percent of the soft-drink market, compared with Pepsi's 31 percent. Why have both, the salesman would purr, when people obviously preferred Coke and you could make more money by selling Coke? Sometimes the argument was an order. If you want to sell Coke, the salesman would declare, not purring any longer, you have to agree to our terms. This strategy reached from restaurants to college campuses to hotel chains and convenience stores. It was another way of securing more territory for Coke – exclusively for Coke.

Yes, Ivester liked these winner-take-all deals, and so had Goizueta, and Pepsi's senior management had been frightened into following suit. The country was being carved into Pepsi-only and Coke-only enclaves. Coke employees wouldn't spend the night in a Marriott hotel because it served Pepsi only. Pepsi workers avoided Burger King because it poured Coke and not Pepsi. The battle extended beyond the two companies as well; anyone dealing with one or the other had to consider this before setting up a lunch or a meeting.

The competition had taken a new and more complicated turn. 'From about 1996, the intensity went over the edge,' recalled one senior PepsiCo executive. The Venezuelan bottling deal, the surge in exclusive contracts, the scathing comments Goizueta and Ivester made about other companies seemed calculated to drive out competitors and gain even more of the market for Coke.

The year before, at a meeting for Coke bottlers in the United States, the president of Coca-Cola USA, Jack Stahl, had promised spectacular growth, predicting that Coke's market share would hit 50 percent by the year 2000. 'We will build a moat of Coca-Cola around the market,' he vowed. The bottlers cheered. Coke seemed an unstoppable force.

By 1997, there were just over a hundred Coke bottlers. Their number hadn't been so small since the turn of the century, when Thomas and Whitehead were just getting under way. Coca-Cola Enterprises was busy swallowing up those that wanted to sell their businesses. The family-owned bottlers had the scarcity of an endangered species. In Florida, for example, the entire state was controlled by Coca-Cola Enterprises except for a tiny circle of territory centered in Tarpon Springs, where John Aide, a third-generation bottler, hung on. Every so often, an offer to buy his business would waft into his office from someone at Coca-Cola Enterprises. Just as often, Aide would say no thanks. He began preparing his children to take over from him. He knew they would do a good job.

But now there was one giant bottler, basically managed by the Coca-Cola Company, against which other bottlers and distributors sometimes had to compete. The results were not always pretty. In 1997, David Miller, the owner of a distribution company in Maryland that sold Coke by the case and also owned vending machines, was accused by Coke of illegally shipping products across franchise lines. Miller was a longtime Coca-Cola Enterprises customer. He bought cans of Coke and sold them in his store. And he told Coke he was innocent.

But the company, along with Coca-Cola Enterprises, seemed convinced that he was not. It launched a secret investigation into Miller. At one point, Miller claims Coke even tried to trap his employees into selling Coke to them, but the effort failed; no one at Miller's company had tried to do what Coke claimed was being done.

The fury began after Coca-Cola Enterprises suddenly raised Miller's wholesale prices, so that he no longer made the same profits on a Coke that he sold through a vending machine, or through his store, that he had in the past. Miller sued the company and Coca-Cola. Miller and his lawyers believed that Coke's goal might also be to force Miller out of his lucrative vending business so that it could be turned over to CCE. The matter was before the courts as Ivester took control of Coke. But it was barely on the radar; investors did not know about it, and few people outside the legal departments of Coke and Coca-Cola Enterprises had heard of it.

Coca-Cola Enterprises was believed to be a huge success. It was intrinsic to the world domination that Coke executives dreamed of. It was the model reconfigured bottler. Ivester had re-created it all over the world: in Australia, where he formed Coca-Cola Amatil; and in Mexico, where he anointed Panamerican Beverages, a longtime Coke bottler, as an anchor and gave it additional territory in Brazil, Venezuela, and other parts of the region. Coca-Cola Amatil grew so large, spanning the globe from Sydney to South Korea and on to Eastern Europe, that in late 1997 Ivester decided to break it in two. The new bottler, Coca-Cola Beverages, consisted of Amatil's European and Eastern European holdings and went public on the London Stock Exchange the following year.

Meanwhile, there were other anchors as well: Coca-Cola Nordic Beverages, a partnership with Carlsberg, the beer company; and Fraser & Neave, a Southeast Asian bottling company that controlled Coke bottling in Vietnam, Cambodia, and parts of Malaysia. In Germany, an anchor bottler called CCEAG, short for Coca-Cola Erfrischungsgetranke A.G., was put together from the forty or so smaller bottlers that had been part of the story during the eighty years that Coke had been for sale there. Japan was the toughest nut to crack – local bottlers did not want to give up any control to the Coca-Cola Company. In early 1999, Ivester would at last get what he desired: an anchor bottler in western Japan, fused from two smaller, publicly traded bottlers. In nearly every case, at least one senior Coke executive held a seat on the board of the anchor bottlers – something that further guaranteed the 'alignment' that Goizueta and Ivester found so crucial to their plans. At more than one anchor bottler, the Coca-Cola Company enjoyed a strong influence over which executives were tapped for the senior positions. Everyone had to get along, and this helped guarantee that they did.

Finally, Ivester considered the people working for him at Coke. They were known as the 'treasure chest', the stacks of middle and senior managers who had been trained at home and abroad, had embraced the Coca-Cola culture, and stood ready to take on whatever role was ordained for them. They were almost exclusively men, and many were cut from the same cloth as Ivester: white, well educated, usually with a financial background. Among his most trusted lieutenants were Jack Stahl, a former investor-relations manager and chief financial officer; Charlie Frenette, the son of a bottler from New York State who had crossed over to the Coca-Cola Company and exhibited all kinds of talent; and James Chestnut, who had followed a long Coca-Cola trail across much of Asia and the Pacific before arriving in Atlanta. There were others, like David Kennedy, a former Ernst & Young accountant who was named head of the fountain division, and Joseph Gladden, the longtime general counsel. They were leaders of the Coca-Cola Company, the senior executives with the most power, and the most promise, after Ivester.

He had cultivated many of them, and they were loyal to him and his ideas. He positioned them in key locations throughout the company. Stahl was a senior vice president and the head of Coca-Cola USA, the biggest and oldest market for Coke in the world. He would consistently rank just below Ivester in terms of pay and bonus, leading many to believe that he was on track to follow Ivester as chairman and CEO. Frenette, whose family owned the Coke franchise for the area around Tupper Lake, New York, had been in charge of Coke's fountain business for several years. Under Ivester he would be assigned abroad for the first time, sent to South Africa to run the business there. He reported to Carl Ware, the president of Coke's Africa unit, but also to Ivester himself. Kennedy replaced him at the fountain division before being tapped by Ivester to run Coca-Cola Amatil, the giant bottler head-quartered in Sydney. And Chestnut would become Ivester's chief financial officer, taking on the role that had helped pave Ivester's way to the top. Chestnut was the one who would bat away questions, on Ivester's behalf, about the impact of weak foreign currencies on Coke's profits. He would have to explain to money managers, in painstakingly selective, Coke-approved detail, how Coke made money from its intertwined relations with its bottlers and its customers.

Below these men on the corporate ladder were dozens of people, all willing to do whatever it took to sell Coca-Cola in the most modern or primitive of markets. Ivester felt lucky to be at the center of so much talent, but deep down he believed that luck had nothing to do with it. For him the business came down to one thing: Either you worked hard or you didn't. As a result, either you succeeded or you didn't. He had little patience for people who tried to convince him that selling soft drinks didn't have to be deadly serious, that you could have a little fun – a party here or there – along the way to rally the troops. Ivester was nearly all business. While he was still president, he held a meeting at which employees were encouraged to ask questions about the company's present and future. One woman raised her hand.

'We're curious,' she said, 'as to when you are going to have day care addressed on campus.' More women had been hired in the late 1980s, and many of them had young children. Plenty of other employers in Atlanta and beyond were building day-care centers for their employees, and Coke had always prided itself on being progressive. With the long hours all employees put in, scrambling to make an Atlanta day-care center's pickup deadline at five-thirty or six o'clock was next to impossible.

There was a brief silence. Ivester stared at her. And then he replied, 'There will never be a day care on this campus.' He had no children, so he did not experience the daily tug-of-war between work and home that many of his employees did. He himself often worked seven days a week at his desk. When it came to day care, he didn't see a need, so there wasn't one. That was the message many in the audience took away.

There is a good chance he didn't mean to convey any kind of

coldbloodedness, but he could be abrupt in his responses to sensitive questions like that one, and it did not always serve him well. Ivester was forthright, and he put his emotions to one side when he was at work. He expected others to be the same way. Dissent was practically unheard-of in the upper reaches of the Coke tower. It had been that way under Goizueta, too, and employees had to accept this in order to have any conversations at all with the people who worked on the twenty-fifth floor.

But Doug Ivester – at fifty years old, nearly a generation younger than Roberto Goizueta – also conveyed an infectious belief in the ultimate success and domination of the Coca-Cola Company. He had inherited that from Goizueta, along with the responsibility – the sacred responsibility – of making sure everyone around him believed in it, too. He could outline a strategy and quickly show someone how it fit into the overarching philosophy of the company: to keep growing its concentrate sales and to keep increasing that shareholder value. The market was out there; they just had to find it. He prodded his subordinates to think that way. Coke's grand success so far was just the beginning, he liked to say.

Chapter Nine

The Imitator Awakes

HUNDREDS OF MILES NORTH of Atlanta and at least twenty-five dollars per share south, Roger Enrico sat in his own corner office and stewed.

Outside, the morning sun glittered on the streams of water cascading through the fountains that dotted the manicured property in Purchase, New York, that was the PepsiCo corporate headquarters. The copper beeches still fluttered their purplish-black leaves; the maples had turned the color of flame. Strolling through Pepsi's property was a treat for anyone who appreciated art. From the parking lot, there were outdoor sculptures by Giacometti, Rodin, and Henry Moore lining the path to the front door. Once inside, walking along a corridor, one could come across a Picasso. But the art was more of a distraction than a cause, an investment rather than a lifestyle. Here the story was business, the trial by market that everything must come to. And, increasingly and urgently, the agenda was to keep Pepsi's soft-drink business from turning into a mere grease spot beneath the wheels of the relentless Coca-Cola machine.

Enrico – stocky, dark-eyed, perennially suntanned – was an angry man as he sat surrounded by works of art and contemplated reality. Coke had hounded him in the past, and he had beaten it back after the company introduced the shockingly Pepsi-like New Coke. Back then, Enrico had triumphantly declared that Coke was throwing in the towel. He even published a book about it a short time later, ghostwritten with a journalist and boldly subtitled *How Pepsi Won the Cola Wars*.

Enrico had crowed endlessly when New Coke came on the market, and he danced a jig when, humbled, Coca-Cola pulled it back to make way once again for the old Coke barely two months later. That had been his finest hour, as a man and as a businessman. That was the kind of thing he lived for but until then had only dreamed about – an enormous victory, practically served to him on a platter by the Coca-Cola Company. It was the naked admission by Coke that Coca-Cola was inferior to Pepsi. It didn't get any better than that if your name was Roger Enrico and you had spent the better part of your professional life trying to successfully compete against Coke. He had heard through the grapevine that at the Coca-Cola Company he was considered to have 'crossed the line of death'.

The New Coke episode was more than ten years old, though, and in between Enrico had left Pepsi-Cola believing that the worst was behind the cola maker. He stepped up to a senior job at PepsiCo's Frito-Lay division and managed that for the next several years. In the meantime, PepsiCo floundered, at home and abroad. The company had bought three enormous fast-food chains to add to the empire, arguing that they thus became automatic customers for Pepsi drinks. That worked for a while, until the Coke people found a way to make it backfire. They informed the owners of other restaurants that carrying Pepsi drinks amounted to aiding the competition. Why would Domino's want to help Pizza Hut? they would say. Since when did Popeye's care about aiding and abetting the profits of Kentucky Fried Chicken? Coke got a lot of new fountain accounts that way.

The Pepsi Challenge, that endlessly needling campaign that had driven Goizueta to place Coca-Cola itself on the sacrificial altar, was no more. Pepsi had pulled it from the airwaves in 1987. Then the international business of selling Pepsi-Cola, never stellar to begin with, ran into fresh trouble. Enrico became the chairman of PepsiCo in early 1996. Within a few months, the Venezuelan bottler defected, and the executive in charge of international operations quit. Coke, meanwhile, was humming along, turning in its flawless performances quarter after quarter. Enrico, profiled for once instead of the Coke guys by *Fortune* magazine, wound up on the cover, all right, just as they had said he would – only *Fortune*'s art directors saw fit to show him squashed inside a Coke bottle, next to the headline 'Bottled Up by Coke'.

The Pepsi people, their stock sagging and their image battered, looked like real losers now. It was no fun trying to run PepsiCo under conditions like these. Even the booming snack business, which produced more than half of PepsiCo's earnings, couldn't make Enrico feel better. There were no potato chip wars to speak of; Frito already owned that market. No, the battles worth winning were all about soft drinks in America, and Enrico, a former Navy man who had seen action in Vietnam, liked to win. Winning was the thing he cared about.

But he was disturbed that winning against Coke had gotten so much harder. Forget the hand-to-hand combat in places like supermarkets and the obvious disasters like the loss of the Cisneros bottling operation in Venezuela. No, Enrico suspected there was something else going on, something he couldn't see from where he sat. Maybe no one except the Coke people knew what it was. He wore a ring decorated with the Chinese character for 'luck' on the fourth finger of his left hand. He had picked it up on his travels in the Far East and, like a lot of people who had spent time in those cultures, he believed in luck, in karma, in the hand of fate. Luck had a lot to do with where he was at that moment, and luck would figure in his plans again and again.

At the same time, he wanted to turn Pepsi's culture into something a little more analytical than it had been in the past. Enrico had a hunch that something unusual might be going on inside the deep, mysterious recesses of the Coca-Cola Company. Since about 1995, he felt, Coke had gone into an excessively high gear against PepsiCo and all of its other competitors. It had begun with a variety of stunts and statements, like a comment from Jack Stahl about building a Coca-Cola moat around the competition. Stahl had gotten cheers from the Coke bottlers, who loved that kind of talk, but the language he used made Enrico uneasy. What exactly did he mean?

Then came Venezuela. In October 1996, two months after the Cisneros defection, Enrico found himself at a cocktail party in Williamsburg, Virginia, where his nemesis, Roberto Goizueta, was also on the guest list. The two of them were speakers at a leadership conference, the kind of love fest that helped make popular heroes out of formerly invisible chief executives. Enrico planned all along to greet Goizueta, and before long the Coke executive arrived.

The two of them looked at each other and barely blinked. The rest of the crowd fell silent, watching to see how the feuding kings of the soft-drink world would interact. Would they laugh, argue, politely disengage? The spectators, all nattily attired in charcoal-gray suits, weren't sure what they were about to witness. Their hands tightened around their glasses of Scotch.

It was the first time Enrico had ever seen Goizueta in person, and things seemed to go cordially enough. Enrico made the first move, introducing himself as he grasped Goizueta's right hand. Enrico began to talk about the competition between the two companies, calling it 'intense' as well as 'real'. He told Goizueta that their rivalry was good, and that consumers – the people who bought Coke and Pepsi – enjoyed it. Then he added, 'When and if it turns mean-spirited, consumers will turn on both of us.'

Goizueta looked at him, his face expressionless, and then Enrico moved on, heading for another knot of onlookers, some people that he knew. Later he would confide that he didn't think Goizueta appreciated his advice.

On another occasion, near New Delhi, Coke advance people begged for permission to paper a known Pepsi area with Coca-Cola signs because a senior Coke executive would be touring the place within a few hours. Enrico, from his desk at headquarters, gave the go-ahead. 'Fine,' he told them, 'as long as you explain to the people in those villages that you're doing this because Pepsi is number one.'

Enrico enjoyed the battles as long as he was winning at least some of the time. But in the late 1990s, as he returned to take the helm of PepsiCo from Wayne Calloway, who had been given a diagnosis of prostate cancer in 1992, he noticed a distinct hardening of Coke's attitude toward competitors, *all* competitors, and he began to wonder about some of the obstacles that were constantly throwing themselves in Pepsi's way.

The two of them, Coke and Pepsi, had always coexisted in most markets. Pepsi always came in second to Coke, except in rare spots like Cleveland, and that was the way it was. Pepsi challenged Coke, and Coke fought back. There was not much to alter that relationship; it was as if the two soda companies were brothers, one older and more serious, the other younger and brasher and more willing to upset the status quo. Some things never change, but Roger Enrico noticed that in the years that he had been away from the cola wars a number of things certainly had.

Take the food distributors, those massive companies that trucked everything from ketchup packets and paper napkins to slabs of meat and crates of eggs into the bars and restaurants and corporate cafeterias of the nation. There were dozens of them, and they all answered to the desires of their clients, large and small. They existed to fill orders, not to thwart them. But Enrico heard through the soft-drink grapevine that some Coca-Cola salesmen had obliquely threatened to cut off the distributors from their Coca-Cola supply if they so much as offered Pepsi to their clients. Not only could the companies not offer Pepsi, they weren't really even supposed to carry it, in Coke's opinion. Since when, thought a furious Enrico. This was America, wasn't it? People were entitled to a choice.

It was merely one postcard from the country that Coke was busily redesigning, where, instead of having choices, people had to commit themselves to either Coke or Pepsi. There was no longer room for both, Coke executives seemed to be decreeing. If people wanted to sell Coke, they had to agree not to sell Pepsi. This was not only true for food distributors. People who ran convenience stores were being offered that 'choice' as well. If the competition had to be included, it was to be given the most undesirable space above eye level in the aisles, the all-but-invisible lowest shelves in the refrigerated cases.

College campuses, school systems, airlines, hotel chains, and sports arenas, too, had to choose. Coke would make them a lucrative offer, with a signing bonus of, say, a million dollars, if they would agree to carry Coke and not Pepsi. No one was dumb enough to say it that way: 'and not Pepsi'. The contracts all specified that if Coke was to be the exclusive soft drink, there could be no drinks sold by any competitors. That embraced everything but the kitchen sink; tap water was still permitted. And milk, too – Coke had not come up with its own substitute for a cow. Some school districts that agreed to such contracts discovered all kinds of complications lurking in the fine print. In Colorado Springs, a contract worth up to $11 million in one school system required consumption of at least seventy thousand cases of Coke a year. What school officials didn't realize until after they signed on the dotted line was that only the Coke dispensed through vending machines – not soda delivered in bulk to events or poured at concession stands – counted toward that minimum. When students wanted to have Coke to sell at a track meet, one principal decided to stockpile cans of soda and beat Coke at its own game. 'He's very enterprising,' said John Bushey, a school official in charge of administering the Coca-Cola program. 'He sits in front of the machine, dropping quarters in, and calls the Coke distributor every other day to say we need more.'

Coke could move fast. By the mid-1990s exclusive deals were being inked all over. In Italy, Enrico fretted when he heard that supermarket chains were being made offers that, in his estimation, they couldn't refuse. A supermarket like Esselunga, if it wanted to sell Coca-Cola at all, had to agree to turn over a specified amount of its display space to the brand. Here are the terms, Coke seemed to be saying: Take them or leave them. The display space requested was often so extensive that it left little room, in the soft-drink aisle or anywhere else, for competing brands. Pepsi was just one of the brands that suffered. And Coke could do this because it was, yes, the number one brand in Italy, just as it was the number one brand in Germany and Spain and other countries in Europe. Its superior position, attained after years of work that began before World War II and only intensified with time, was its biggest and best weapon. The company could take the advantage it had constructed and turn it into an even larger advantage, hastening the elimination of everyone else.

A similar program was in place in Mexico, except that Coke, instead of leaning on store owners, was actually buying the stores out from under them. Once Coke owned a mom-and-pop store, it would dictate that it was to sell only Coca-Cola. It would order up red awnings and red-painted signs as well, just to underscore the point. Then Pepsi moved to color some of its stores blue. The bodega business was being turned into one more battle zone.

Enrico saw all this, and realized that Coke's mentality made it just about unstoppable. 'It is born of their corporate culture,' he concluded. 'They believe that they are the only legitimate cola.' They would do anything, he felt, to make that come true.

The future of Pepsi-Cola, the upstart that was ninety-nine years old as Enrico ruminated that autumn morning, was at stake. Exclusive deals like the ones Coke was bent on obtaining in as many places as it could were deadly for its competitors, large and small. But they were great for Coke. 'We are fundamentally opposed to exclusives,' Enrico would say, 'and they fundamentally love them.'

He didn't want to be known as the man who stood by and watched Pepsi-Cola go down the drain. He had to do something. And purely by chance, he soon had an opportunity.

Goizueta, the great architect and visionary of the modern Coca-Cola Company, suddenly went into the hospital. Barely a month later, he was dead. Enrico was sorrowful, to be sure. He recognized the end of an era, and he admired many of Goizueta's achievements. He was traveling when he got the news, half a world away from Atlanta, in Jakarta, and so he could not attend the funeral. He sent others from PepsiCo to stand in his place.

When he got back to Purchase, he summoned all of his senior executives for a council of war. With Goizueta gone, Enrico figured, the Coca-Cola Company might be entering a rare moment of relative weakness. He and the others knew little of Doug Ivester, other than his reputation as a hard-core financial expert. They had felt the back of his hand, in Venezuela and elsewhere. They realized he played for keeps. But now, Enrico vowed to himself, so would Pepsi.

One Wall Street analyst liked to describe Coke and Pepsi in terms of two diametrically opposed college students: Coke was the studious one, the one who was always in the library and aced his exams. Pepsi, meanwhile, was the fraternity brother who lived to socialize, studying just enough to get by and occasionally surprising himself by doing very well – often enough to make him believe that his approach worked just fine. In product development, in marketing, and in overall strategy, throughout all the years of their competitive relationship, Coke had been the diligent one and Pepsi's record had been hit-or-miss. By 1997, when Goizueta died, analysts all believed fervently in Coke, that Coke could do no wrong, while Pepsi was regarded as a joke. Their stock prices reflected this as well: Coke's was more than fifty-five dollars a share, while Pepsi's hovered in the low thirty-eight-dollar range. Coke's price-earnings multiple, another measure of the Street's love for a stock, was in the mid-forties, about twice that of Pepsi's.

But now Enrico, the warrior, decided that Pepsi's methodology was going to be different. He was going to examine the mystery of Coca-Cola, like a scientist, and figure out a logical, rational, well-timed way of combating it.

His first move was to assign a senior executive, Indra Nooyi, to immerse herself in the Coca-Cola strategy. What were the details of their plan, starting with the bottler system, continuing through the marketing and, finally, the financial statements? What were their goals? What were their Achilles' heels? Nooyi, an Indian-born, U.S.-trained economist, had been named chief financial officer only a few months earlier. She had already shown herself to be one of Pepsi's brightest lights, supporting Enrico's plan to spin off the restaurant chains as a separate, publicly traded company and backing his notion that it was time to rid Pepsi of the bottling companies it owned in favor of something more like Coca-Cola Enterprises. Both of them had studied the Coke bottling strategy and concluded that if Pepsi was to compete effectively, it had to duplicate the good parts of the system and do it soon.

Now Enrico told her to spend as much time as she needed to understand the Coca-Cola Company, whiskers to tail, and to report back to him when she was done.

Nooyi got her assignment in late 1997. But Enrico couldn't wait for her to finish. He launched another campaign, this one through the Pepsi legal department, where a lawyer named Rob Sharpe, fresh from litigating tobacco warfare at R.J. Reynolds, had been hired a few months earlier.

Sharpe was tall and thin and driven. He had helped knock down opponent after opponent in the skirmishes over the safety of cigarettes, though the larger war, with the federal government, was lost by the tobacco companies in the end. When Enrico summoned him for a strategic discussion, he was ready to take on another giant. And the giant this time was the Coca-Cola Company, the soda known and loved around the world.

There was a quick opening for Sharpe, almost before he realized it. At the very end of 1997, as his first major act as chairman and CEO, Ivester announced that Coke would buy the Orangina brand from Pernod Ricard. At a price of more than $800 million, for a brand with sales of only about a million cases a year in the United States, some people at Pepsi were perplexed by the move. Why would Coke, the biggest soft-drink company in the world, want to mess around with such a tiny brand? Coke already owned an orange soda, Fanta, which it had started in Germany during World War II, and Orangina wasn't that different from Fanta. Why the big fuss? Coke said it would feed the brand into its sprawling worldwide bottler network, growing it into proportions that would be impossible for any other soft-drink company. But why would it want to?

Sharpe figured it out, along with Bob Biggart, an international expert in the Pepsi legal department. Rumpled but intense, Biggart had been languishing in the legal department for years, begging various bosses to let him take on the Coca-Cola Company in foreign markets. Biggart had noticed for a long time that Coke was fond of throwing its weight around. He devised charts and graphs showing the growth of Coke's sales in Europe and collected newspaper clippings about Coke's expansions in bottling and brand acquisition. On the rare occasion that there was an investigation by a government agency into Coke's behavior, Biggart gathered that material, too. Over time he had built up a Coca-Cola dossier, and he had been waiting, and angling, for the right time to use it.

Pepsi's method, until Enrico came along, had been to pick up the phone and call Joe Gladden, Coke's general counsel, whenever Pepsi salesmen or bottlers complained about a Coke tactic they had noticed in the field somewhere.

Gladden was a polite and honorable fellow, and he always promised to look into whatever it was. No one doubted that he did indeed pursue it as he had promised. But nothing at Coke ever changed, and inside Pepsi the frustration swelled.

Pepsi had also been offered a chance to buy Orangina by Pernod's president, Thierry Jacquillat. Pepsi had turned it down, never dreaming that Coke would take it. It was a case of cola wars making strange bedfellows; despite Ivester's lawsuit against Pernod a few years earlier, when Pernod was the Coke bottler in France, both companies were willing to do the deal. Cash was king for Pernod, which was desperate to get out of the soft-drink business so that it could concentrate on liquor and other brands it owned. Coke's strategy, to eclipse its competitors, dictated what Coke would do.

With the Coke bid for Orangina, Biggart saw the situation in sharp relief. Buying smaller brands would allow Coke to take over those niche markets, lending even more strength and power to the Coca-Cola Company. Where Orangina had been, there would soon be only Coke. If Coke owned a brand, it alone would decide that brand's fate. The bigger Coke got, the more control it would have everywhere.

Biggart had been waiting years for this moment. He had a powerful tool at his disposal: the European definition of a monopoly. In American antitrust law, a company could grow and grow almost indefinitely, as long as there were competitors out there who had at least a slice of the market for soft drinks or electronics or clothing. If a company was found to be stifling competition, then it became subject to regulatory action.

But under the laws of the European Union, a company with a 'dominant market share', usually 50 percent or more, became governed by a stricter set of rules designed to guard against monopolistic practices. Coke had far more than the 50 percent in most of Europe, and Biggart realized that he could make a cogent argument against Coke's acquiring more soft-drink companies simply by invoking the market-dominance theory. He had documents, including one from Italy in which a Coke executive promised his boss the 'elimination' of Pepsi from the marketplace by the twenty-first century. He had comparisons of Coke's growth over the past ten years, showing a rapid climb while Pepsi and other competitors stayed about the same size.

Not because they cared at all about Orangina but because they felt they needed to make the soft-drink world safe for the Pepsi brand, Sharpe and Biggart designed a program of interference that they hoped would stop the Coca-Cola Company in its tracks. They would hire lawyers around the world, wherever Coke was marching on a target, and try to overturn Coke's plans. And they got support that they had wanted for years from Enrico. 'We can't have the legal department sitting there apart from the business departments, just pontificating,' one senior PepsiCo executive said. Instead, the Pepsi lawyers were told 'to be absolutely proactive', to do whatever they could to give Pepsi an edge everywhere. The lawyers were ready. 'We want to see if we can stop this,' they told Enrico.

Orangina marked the first test of their program. The deal, to Enrico, was almost completely without logic for Coke. Almost. 'It would only work,' he said once, 'if you got your competition eliminated and then raised prices.' Coke's desire to be the only soft drink on the market seemed to be reflected in the Orangina purchase. In a limited way, Pernod Ricard helped distribute Pepsi to some restaurants, cafés, bars, and other accounts in France. It was similar to the role Pernod Ricard had played for Coke until 1989, the year Ivester took over management of the Western Europe division and fired Pernod for not promoting Coca-Cola as Atlanta saw fit.

Now Pepsi lawyers marched into the offices of the French competition authorities and demanded an audience. When it was granted, they explained that if Coke's deal to buy Orangina went through, it would spell doom not just for the small amount of Pepsi being handled by Pernod but for all smaller soft-drink brands in the world. Coke's market dominance, they argued, was a very bad thing for its competitors. Coke could, and would, use its clout to raise prices and to intimidate customers into carrying only Coca-Cola. It was already happening in Italy, they pointed out. France was simply the next domino.

The French listened, with little reaction, and then submitted the matter for review. Nine long months elapsed, from December 1997 until late September 1998, before the decision was issued. With all the pomp one might expect from a government agency in a country where the desire to sell lemonade had been rendered elite by a guild formed under the Sun King, the French rejected the acquisition of Orangina by the Coca-Cola Company. Too much control, they determined, would be concentrated in a single soft-drink company's hands if Coke bought Orangina. Concentration, declared the committee, was not a good thing for France.

In Purchase, there were cheers of elation. In Atlanta, there was gloom, but it lifted quickly. The French had left open the possibility that Coke could revise its business plan and submit it again for review. Ivester ordered his lieutenants to do so, and on the double. He didn't want to waste time.

In other Coca-Cola corners, however, there was shock at the rejection. Since when did the mighty Coca-Cola Company stumble? Why did a government see fit to turn the Coke machine down? Had someone not done his homework, not massaged the right egos? For some people, it was a wake-up call. Others blamed the French for being even more snobbish and pigheaded than ever. Coke and France had long been like oil and water. The French turned their noses up at many things American, and there was no beverage more American than Coke. 'The only place more arrogant than the Coca-Cola Company,' one longtime Coca-Cola employee said, 'is France.'

From his office in New York, Don Keough was watching, and he shook his head. Never, he thought, had Coke failed to push through a plan like this – so small! So ultimately minor! What had Ivester overlooked?

This would never have happened, he told himself, under Roberto.

Something else had happened to Keough a few months earlier in 1998. His five-year contract as a special adviser to the Coca-Cola chairman, a kind of extralong farewell handshake from Goizueta that allowed him to remain in close contact with Coke's board of directors, had expired. It had begun in 1993 on the day he walked away from the company to begin his retirement. It had enabled him to keep a hand in, to continue conversations with the board, to attend the meetings, and to feel that he still participated in decisions that affected Coke. He had moved from the middle of the conference-room table down to one end, but he was still there – still deep in the affairs of Coke.

Five years later, as the azaleas bloomed across Atlanta, Doug Ivester had to decide whether to renew that contract. He mulled it over for as long as he needed to, and then decided no, he did not have to have Don Keough, who was approaching his seventy-second birthday, continue in that role. At the same time, Keough did not expect to have the contract renewed, since it had been a parting courtesy from Goizueta. Goizueta was dead. Ivester was in charge. And Ivester thought that finally letting go of Keough would be best for the company.

Chapter Ten

Too Busy to Discriminate

ALTHOUGH COKE UNDER GOIZUETA and Keough had hummed with productivity, spitting out cash like in someone's Vegas fantasy, deep inside there were widespread, consistent signals of unhappiness. By 1992, some employees, looking at the published reports of the salaries and copious stock options paid out to Goizueta and other top executives every year, had begun to feel that they were not getting their due. Lower-ranking workers took home pay that was nothing to brag about, and those not in management did not get any stock options at all. Coke had always made the most of its renown as a top brand, and that cachet helped it keep pay scales modest for its workers, even as its chairman's salary and bonuses became the talk of the nation.

Still, the allure of working for the biggest soft-drink maker in the land, and the world, had a certain value. People wanted to work for Coke, and they could be convinced that that might be worth a little sacrifice. It was the kind of company that took care of people, in little ways, and that was worth something to them, too. Someone with a sick relative in a far-off city might be offered a lift there in a company plane. Someone with an ill spouse might be kept on the payroll and told not to worry about coming in until everything got better.

But what began to bother some of them, around 1992, the year the company reported that Goizueta had received a million shares of restricted stock the previous year and Don Keough had taken home one and a half million stock options, wasn't just the money. Sure, they would have liked more money, but most of all they were upset about how their careers were progressing, and about their treatment on a daily basis in the workplace. They felt stuck, suppressed. They weren't going anywhere. They had different backgrounds, work histories, education levels, and roles at Coke, from managing departments to keeping watch at the front door. They were all African American, though. Race was the one thing they had in common.

They had no single leader, no one around whom they rallied. They reached their conclusions more or less on their own, in conversations over Coca-Cola, in quick tales told in the hallways, in moments together after church, in what they saw and heard over time from the very bottom of the company all the way to the top. And what they concluded began to bother them a lot.

As global as the Coca-Cola Company was, it was still, in its heart of hearts, a southern place. It craved formality as much as it craved profits, and though it could claim its place as a modern global corporation, it remained in many ways hierarchical and in the grip of certain old-fashioned customs. The senior executives worked in quarters removed from the rest of the employees and they enjoyed perks that were not available to the others. Their lives were the stuff of legend – rubbing elbows with presidents and prime ministers, jetting off in all directions to dine with Hollywood celebrities and cut deals with diplomats – while for others much of the business of Coke was tedious. They had to be addressed with an honorific, while everyone else was called by their first names.

Until Goizueta, all of Coke's top leaders had been born in Georgia, and the legendary ones, like Asa Candler and Robert Woodruff, had supported progress at the same time that they upheld tradition. The people who packaged and sold and advertised Coca-Cola were nearly always white, but the customers ran the full range of races and religions. Woodruff had been perhaps the most progressive Coke leader when it came to being mindful of the toxic effect racial unrest could have on his business and his city. He lobbied other executives in Atlanta to buy tickets to a dinner honoring Martin Luther King, Jr., after he won the Nobel Peace Prize in 1964, and he otherwise tried to keep the movement's violent clashes out of his hometown. He also named the first black to Coke's board of directors in 1974, a man named William Allison, who directed an antipoverty program in Atlanta.

Allison seemed to know how big a step that represented. *There are not adequate words to express my gratitude for the honor you have bestowed on me,* Allison wrote to Woodruff after his nomination. *I am also indebted to your kind generosity for the shares which you purchased in my name.*

At the same time, few blacks were hired into the Coca-Cola Company, and few made it past entry-level jobs during the sixty years that Woodruff was in charge. Candler, whose 'Negro helper' for his clandestine preparations of the Coca-Cola syrup must have had his trust and maybe his affection, too, did not hire blacks as brokers or salesmen in the early days of Coca-Cola, though that would change with time. In general, blacks were few and far between in the soft-drink business, at Coke and everywhere else.

Created in the aftermath of the Civil War, the Coca-Cola empire could sometimes seem locked in a world where that conflict, with all its torment past and future, never left center stage. A 1959 article in *The Coca-Cola Bottler* celebrating the original bottlers, Thomas and Whitehead and Lupton, resolutely viewed them through the prism of the war waged almost one hundred years earlier. 'While it was sheer coincidence, it is, nevertheless, interesting to note that the three men primarily responsible for the origin and early development of the business of Coca-Cola in bottles were born during the greatest man-made cataclysm the country has ever witnessed, the Civil War,' the author, Franklin Garrett, wrote as passionately as if the event had occurred the week before. 'Benjamin F. Thomas began life in 1861, as the conflict was getting under way, John T. Lupton as the struggle was approaching high tide in '62, and Joseph B. Whitehead in '64 at ebb tide for the Southern Confederacy.'

As adults, all three were actually positioned to benefit from the fact that in the postwar South, a good deal of enterprise moved off the farms and into the factories, where consumer products like stockings and steel and fabric for suits and gowns were being made. A new day had arrived in Dixie; its agrarian roots had been covered over in places with more manufacturing than ever before. Southerners hurled themselves into the work of creating a New South, a place where gentility was still prized but where life was increasingly about making money. Mark Twain, describing the Southerners he encountered during Reconstruction, called them 'brisk men' who made 'the dollar their god, how to get it their religion'. Chattanooga, the home of Whitehead and Thomas, eventually would become one of the most polluted cities in the nation, but along the way many Southerners opened factories that helped them rise to positions of wealth and power.

When Thomas returned from war in 1898, support for manufacturing in Chattanooga, a city in search of a brighter future, made it possible for him to build a plant and finance a second one within a year of becoming a Coca-Cola bottler. He and Whitehead, who was described by Garrett as taking his first breath 'less than two weeks before U. S. Grant was named commander-in-chief of the Union Armies', subcontracted bottling franchises to scores of other businessmen. And those factories, built in small towns and cities all over the country, became symbols of progress, emblems of the march toward modernity that towns like Henderson, North Carolina, could expect of themselves. They helped bypass primogeniture and other strictures of the past. All a man needed was money, his own or someone else's, and he could set himself up in business.

But the end of the Civil War was hardly the end of the country's racial struggles. Coke would be caught up in those struggles again and again.

The house of Coke that Goizueta, Keough, and Ivester built was enormous, employing 29,000 people around the world by 1997. About 6,000 of them worked in the company's headquarters in Atlanta. There, at the corner of North Avenue and Luckie Street, in a complex ringed by iron fences and dotted with flowering trees, Coke managed a tightly run empire where the executives at the top had little tolerance for error. There was the Coca-Cola way and the wrong way. The enemies were clear-cut. PepsiCo was the primary one, but others included Cadbury Schweppes, with which Coke had an on-again, off-again relationship because its bottlers distributed some of Cadbury's brands. Then there was Royal Crown, the cola maker that had once been a power but by the mid-1990s held just 2 percent of the cola market. Enemies of Coca-Cola got in the way of expanding Coke's reach. And that got in the way of boosting the share price, the ultimate reward still twinkling from the mainmast.

Even before he was named president, Ivester was making many

of the company's major decisions in tandem with Goizueta. His allies included Sergio Zyman, the colorful, controversial chief marketing officer who had left the company after the debacle of New Coke.

Zyman had returned at the invitation of Ivester, who wanted him to become chief marketing officer. It was then that marketing at Coke became a new entity, something much larger than simply promoting Coca-Cola, Sprite, or diet Coke. Zyman was not a large man, but his ideas were outsize. He maintained that competitors were out there, to be sure, but now the contest had to be one that pitted Coke against Coke, history against the present, if the company was to beat itself at its own game.

'Coke became fiercely about the brand and what the brand stood for,' remembered Lauren Bryant, who worked in the company's marketing department for nearly a decade, starting in 1990. 'It was a pretty fundamental strategic shift.' At the marketing meetings, enormous campaigns were constructed around what Coke meant, only to be ripped apart by Zyman and sent back to the drawing board. Was it love? Was it nostalgia? Was it something else? A commercial that played well with almost every consumer group, featuring the football player known as Mean Joe Greene tossing his game jersey to a little boy who brings him a Coke, was yanked off the air by Zyman. It wasn't moving the needle, he testily explained after a while. It wasn't selling more Coca-Cola. Just because consumers liked it was no reason to keep it around.

He had an unusual zeal for internal competition. Where McCann-Erickson had been Coke's lead advertising agency, he scattered assignments among a dozen agencies, urging them to compete against one another to come up with great commercials for Coke. He got more polar bear variations, and a new campaign for diet Coke. He kept the agencies on edge, always worrying that they were not performing up to par.

But despite all that, the biggest problem facing the Coca-Cola Company wasn't going away. People were not drinking cola the way they once had, not in America, anyway, and everyone at Coke knew it. Consumption had been dropping off since 1984, and those sales had been lost to juice, to water, to bottled iced tea. Zyman wasn't sure how to fix the problem. No one was.

For decades the company's moves had been determined by what Pepsi was doing: the twelve-ounce bottle, the Pepsi Challenge, the new products and promotions. In the mid-1990s, with Zyman in charge of marketing the Coca-Cola image, the company made a conscious decision to turn its back on its rivals. Under Zyman, the motto became: 'We set our own course.'

It was a time-consuming strategy, and with so much focus on managing the business, no one at the top of the company paid much attention to *any* sort of discontent, much less the issue of race. Atlanta had for years prided itself as 'the city too busy to hate', though there were those who thought that was a pretty empty reason. It had not hosted the kinds of violent confrontations between peacefully marching blacks and club-wielding whites that cities like Birmingham had. By the 1990s there was no 'race problem' in Atlanta, and certainly not at the Coca-Cola Company, white people were fond of saying. In fact, they looked at you strangely if you dared to bring it up.

But within Coke, black employees became certain that they did not have the same kinds of successes as whites. The proof rose to the top. There was only a handful of senior executives who were black, even though, by the 1980s, many African Americans were being hired by the company. They came, they lasted a couple of years, and then they left. Was there a problem, or were all of these people merely bad fits for Coke?

There was indeed a problem, many black employees believed. Outside the four walls of Coke, they were envied for their jobs at such a well-known and successful company, where the stock price was on an upward tear and top people were so amply and publicly rewarded. On the inside, they formed support groups and met in secret, exchanging stories about racially charged incidents at Coke that made them laugh and cry.

The highest-ranking African American at Coke in the 1990s was a former Atlanta city council member named Carl Ware. He had large, soft hands like catcher's gloves and a quiet but sure demeanor. Ware had been recruited in 1974 to work for Coke as a corporate affairs executive. That was an exceptionally broad term for work that essentially helped perpetuate the cheery Coca-Cola image despite the social dilemmas Coke faced at home and abroad as it tried to sell its soda. Early on, Keough would send Ware on a mission to South Africa, to help figure out how to handle the increasing pressure to pull out of a country that was one of the company's ten biggest overseas markets but whose apartheid regime was under attack by rights groups all over the globe. Racial discrimination, institutionalized in South Africa, could not be tolerated by the Coca-Cola Company, not if it expected to expand sales of Coke.

Coke did find a solution, one that was almost too good to be true. To comply with public pressure to abandon and thereby undermine the apartheid regime, the company announced with great fanfare that it was exiting South Africa. Then it opened a syrup plant and bottling operation in Swaziland, a small nation ringed on all sides by South Africa. It was virtually impossible to prevent Swaziland Coke from permeating South Africa, through borders that were porous, to say the least, and Coke continued to be sold in South Africa, though it was no longer being produced in plants whose foundations were on South African soil.

Ware's political skills and his sense of humor, which had served him well in the jagged-edged world of Atlanta politics, came in handy for a long time at Coke. He ascended the ladder, becoming a senior vice president by the mid-1990s with responsibility for all of Coke's business in Africa, which by then included South Africa again. He directed sales and marketing and business development across an entire continent that Coke, like many American consumer-products companies, had paid next to no attention to over the years. One of his mentors was Keough, who, with his innate public-relations sense and his own experience on the receiving end of a racially charged issue, saw infinite benefit for Coke in promoting a man like Carl Ware.

As he ascended the ranks, Ware could not have missed the fact that the higher he went, the fewer people like him he saw. Atlanta politics were not like that; blacks held positions of power all across city government. Black political participation was high, and no one got elected without significant support from black voters.

But the Coca-Cola Company, he found, was different. It got whiter and chillier as one ascended. He wrapped himself up in his work, which was plentiful, and carved out an identity abroad – as the powerful Coke president in charge of Africa – that he could not hope to duplicate back in the Coke tower. He was the only black person of his rank in the entire company in 1995. Not only was he alone at that moment: There had been just one black senior vice president in the entire 109-year history of the company. He was it.

Ware tried not to let that kind of thing get in his way. He bought into the vision promulgated by Goizueta and Keough and Ivester. He believed in the unlimited growth that Goizueta envisioned, and he saw how he would directly benefit from a rising share price; he himself held plenty of Coke shares and options, though he was not among the top six executives when it came to compensation. He was making a lot of money, more than he had ever dreamed possible. As long as the share price kept going up, he could make even more.

So he hit the road, traveling to places like Angola, Kenya, and Burkina Faso, trying all sorts of gimmicks – like a windup radio that could be distributed in areas without electricity – in order to sell more Coca-Cola. He persuaded the company to invest in events like the African Cup of Nations, a soccer tournament that got lots of attention all over the continent, and where, thanks to him, the Coke banners sporting the Coke logo almost outnumbered the spectators.

His job was difficult, maybe even crazy. In most of Africa, he didn't have to persuade people to drink Coke instead of Pepsi. He had to persuade people who had next to no money to spare, and whose nutritional and health issues were enormous, to take the rands or the shillings out of their pockets and spend them – not on a sandwich, not on a bottle of juice, not on a can of infant formula for the squalling baby at home, but on a *Coca-Cola*. The extreme conditions of African life for most Africans worked against that concept.

But Carl Ware did his best. When traveling in his territory, he lived the life of a VIP. He dined with Nelson Mandela. He raised his glass at the embassies and fraternized with government ministers. He checked into all the best hotels and had tables in all the best restaurants. Everyone knew his name. He was the man, the Coke man. But back in Atlanta it was hardly the same.

First of all, he was alone. That in itself could be troubling. And sometimes he got the feeling, ever so slight but persistent, that he was not being taken seriously. A big conference would be scheduled and analysts noted that all the other presidents would be there, but Carl Ware would be missing. Coke saw Africa's massive, mostly young and undereducated population as a gold mine for selling soft drinks, but the region was the smallest one of the six that Coke designated for its business around the world. It was a mere sliver of the profits, compared with the money rolling in from Asia and Western Europe. But that didn't mean it didn't count.

Ware bounced between the dual realities of his job for a long time. Then one day he took a highly unusual step. He sought permission to convene a committee. It would be a secret committee, of course, and its findings, when written up, would be stamped HIGHLY RESTRICTIVE and HIGHLY CONFIDENTIAL. It would examine the issue of race at the Coca-Cola Company, questioning whether Coke was doing a good job in hiring, promoting, and keeping African Americans like him.

It was the fall of 1995, nearing the end of one of Coke's best years ever, when he went to Doug Ivester to request funding for this research. He was careful to gift wrap it in corporate purpose; this was something that a company needed to do, he said, to make its image as modern and strong and as influential as possible. Ivester, looking up from his computer, said sure, go ahead. It had been his idea, though he had suggested that Ware think about it on his own. Then he turned back to his screen, and his calculations, and his management of that year's volume increase and earnings growth – the issues with which he occupied himself most of the time.

Ware assembled a committee of the most senior blacks working at Coke. There was Ingrid Saunders Jones, a longtime corporate affairs specialist and a vice president; Juan Johnson, another vice president; and two others, Thom Peters, an assistant vice president in Coke's treasury division, and Paul Graves, a human resources director in Ware's Africa division. He hired a consultant, J. O. Rodgers of nearby Stone Mountain, Georgia, to assist them. Over dinners and during a late-November weekend at the Palace Hotel in New York, far from the office, they discussed what it meant to be a black executive at the Coca-Cola Company 130 years after the end of the Civil War.

By the next month, Ware had a report ready for Ivester, neatly typed and organized along the topics the committee had addressed. Its pages, despite being written in detached, emotionally blank corporate language, described a professional wasteland for African Americans inside the great and global Coca-Cola Company. The company had broken no laws, but it had failed, profoundly and spectacularly, on a front that mattered immensely to Carl Ware, and Martin Luther King, and hundreds of thousands of others who had lived and died in the name of civil rights across the vast panorama of American history. While pumping the planet full of soda, Coke had created an atmosphere, consciously or unconsciously, that came across as hostile to blacks. The world of Coke, so busy producing pure and innocent moments of refreshment at the rate of nearly a billion a day, had an embarrassing, morally questionable cloud around it, anyone who read the report would have concluded.

'There is no evidence that the company, in the absence of laws requiring affirmative action, has a commitment to achieve further diversification of its workforce,' Ware's report stated in its summary. There needed to be immediate, corrective action to end what he described as 'the lack of tolerance by the organization toward those who are different'. He pointed a finger straight at the corner office, noting that 'diversification of its workforce' could not happen in the absence of 'strong leadership from the top' and a 'clearly communicated company position and policy which activates the company's commitment'.

Throughout his report, Ware seemed mindful of the disturbance he was likely to create with his conclusions. He carefully couched his proposals in the mildest language possible, often indicating that his concerns were for all groups, from the handicapped to the elderly, not just blacks at Coke. At the outset, he described his purpose as 'to further raise the bar and set a "gold standard"', implying that Coke had already done a decent job of seeking diversity in its workforce.

But in places he seemed impassioned, as only a man who had experienced the downside of the program could have been. 'The company has no clearly articulated vision of how diversification of the workforce is linked to business success,' he wrote. 'One approach may be to have Doug Ivester define the company's philosophy or approach to diversity and then champion the activation of this approach in the company's business plans, policies, and programs.'

Goizueta and Ivester, if they cared to take this on, had a big job ahead of them. Ware described an environment of overt and subtle hostility, where blacks, according to the senior people on his committee, had been stunned by their treatment at the hands of whites. 'Some African Americans are viewed inappropriately as lacking the skills and intelligence to succeed in certain areas,' he wrote. 'Diplomacy, resourcefulness, and the ability to deperson-alize prejudicial behavior were noted as common experiences among the group members. Instances were mentioned where members had been humiliated, ignored, overlooked, or un-acknowledged.'

This came from the very top of the company, from people who had made their way out of the arguably born-to-be-dissatisfied lower ranks and who were now executives, enjoying hefty salaries and perks and stock options, the currency with which Goizueta had transformed the world of Coke. And yet they were still unhappy. It may have seemed incredible to other senior executives who saw the report. What did these people want? They had already gotten all a person could hope to get out of a company. These other issues – well, maybe they were the result of paranoia, or a lively imagination, or some other problem that had nothing to do with the Coca-Cola Company.

'Even when African Americans were few in number in the organization,' Ware wrote, 'an informal network of African Americans was operating to provide sanity checks and a comparison of related experiences with the social realities of the organization.' He added, 'This allowed many of them to retain their psychological health.'

With his report, Ware supplied a list of eight areas the company needed to address. Chief among them was what he termed 'the issue of why there are so few African Americans in certain areas and levels of the business'. He called on Ivester to 'challenge the pattern the company has fallen into, of placing disproportionate African American numbers into certain areas'.

Ivester's response, after receiving the report that December, was to set up a lunch with Ware so they could discuss it. The lunch took place as planned. But the report's recommendations seemed to fall to some back burner. 1995 marked another series of successes for Coke; volume, earnings, and share price all continued to soar. Preoccupied with the business, and with the goals he and Goizueta had for the following year – the Coke-sponsored Olympics were at long last coming to Atlanta, and Goizueta himself would be marking fifteen years at the helm – Ivester was prepared to listen to Ware's recommendations, but there were other things crowding the top of his agenda. Meanwhile, the report, and all of its findings, remained a secret.

By the time Ware and Ivester sat down to discuss the state of race relations at their company, a woman named Linda Ingram had been a Coke employee for seven years. Ingram, who is black, had been working at another company in Atlanta when she applied for a job at Coke on a friend's dare; both of them thought it highly unlikely that Coke, that place where everybody wanted to work, would hire her. 'I thought, well, why not?' remembered Ingram. And sure enough, she got an interview and then an offer. In 1988 she became a Coca-Cola information analyst, putting in long hours at her desk as one of the thousands of people assigned to the Atlanta headquarters.

She floated into a place that in many ways was unusually old-fashioned for a global company. Women were prohibited from wearing pants to work; one woman, recruited from another company, arrived at the office on her first day wearing a pantsuit she had bought specifically for her new job and was sent home to change. There were also strict unofficial rules about who met with senior executives; a junior person was not supposed to set up meetings with anyone high-ranking unless his or her supervisor was also available for the meetings. 'Face time' was highly valued, and so was close supervision of everyone at all levels. Coke was stuffy, and it was stratified.

But Ingram could see past all that. She went into Coke with her eyes open, and she found that she enjoyed her work and liked her colleagues, and for all intents and purposes she was happy. The company was flourishing under Goizueta; the new design was taking hold, and everyone admired Coke. Then, in 1996, the year after Carl Ware submitted his report, everything suddenly became awful for Linda Ingram.

She was having a discussion with her supervisor, Elaine Arnold, that abruptly turned nasty. Arnold, who was white, leaned close into Ingram's face and proceeded to scold her, saying, 'This is why you people don't get anywhere.' For Ingram, the only African American in her department, the public upbraiding caused shock and shame. And she was stunned by the tenor and the tone of what she heard. 'When you have someone that is standing in your face and you can feel their breath on your face and they are making these comments,' she said, 'you all of a sudden start to ask yourself, Where am I? Am I in the fifties?'

Well versed in corporate protocol, she reported the incident to the right people at Coke, including human resources executives and the company's director of equal employment opportunity. They began an investigation, and for Ingram that was the start of a swift downward spiral. Her boss was fired, and other people in the department, who liked Arnold, blamed Ingram. Some of them ignored her; others openly refused to talk to her. She became depressed and tearful and felt isolated, adrift. Her pleas to be moved to another part of the company went unanswered. For her, the worst part was not the incident but the way Coke executives handled its aftermath. At a company where close control of every situation was a point of pride, dealing professionally with racially charged confrontations seemed to be completely beyond anyone's capability. To Ingram it seemed not an act of omission but an intentional way of avoiding an enormous issue.

'They understood what it was,' she said. 'It was just that they didn't do anything.'

She felt unable to escape the fallout from an incident that she believed had been precipitated by nothing more than the color of her skin, and as time went on, her sense of her own helplessness wore her down. Colleagues who had once been friendly avoided her. She began taking more and more sick days. Sometimes she couldn't bring herself to climb out of bed in the morning. 'Everything was like going through a maze,' she said. 'It was like a horrible, horrible dream. They had all these thousands of conversations, and they didn't do anything.'

She sought counseling from her minister, the Reverend Joseph Roberts, who presided over Ebenezer Baptist Church in Atlanta. It is the church where Martin Luther King, Jr., preached while he lived in Atlanta. It is a church where people know and care about racial justice, a place where the great tides of social change that washed across the country gained strength. Ingram just couldn't believe what had happened to her, how she had danced into the Coca-Cola Company and worked so hard and been so content for so long, and now this. It made the tears flow, hot and steady, from her eyes.

'One thing that broke my heart, broke it into a million pieces, was one day when someone came to me and said, "You know, Linda, I can't come by your office anymore because I am new here and I would like to stay here,"' Ingram said. 'She said, "I just don't think we can be friends anymore."' Far from getting the help she felt she deserved, Ingram saw that people were blaming her for what had happened.

By 1998, she had stopped working and obtained a long-term disability leave. She sold her house to help pay the bills. She had never been radical about racial issues in the past, but now she became an avid student of racial harassment in the workplace. In the upper reaches of Coke, she had at least one sympathetic ear: that of Ingrid Saunders Jones, a vice president who ran the company's external corporate affairs as well as its foundation and who was African American herself. Jones had been part of Carl Ware's committee, and she knew its conclusion.

Jones had met Ingram through Reverend Roberts; both of them were worshipers at Ebenezer. Jones was also known throughout the civil rights community in Atlanta for channeling support from Coke, invariably in the form of cash, for various causes around town. She ran the Coca-Cola Foundation by 1997, and some people in Atlanta's civil rights world referred to her as 'the bag lady', for the donations Coke delivered through her. It was she who had written the $9,600 check to J. O. Rodgers, the consulting company that Ware's committee used in 1995, with a handwritten note at the bottom of her cover letter, wishing the top executive *a wonderful Holiday Season!* Through her, Coke kept a close relationship with the Reverend Jesse Jackson and with local champions of civil rights.

Jackson had been a thorn in Coke's side in the past, leading a 1981 boycott of Coke products as a last-minute element in his campaign to get Coke to do better by African Americans. While the boycott lasted only about a month, it generated all kinds of unwelcome publicity for the company, forcing a scramble by Coke executives – with Don Keough in the lead – to mollify Jackson. He got the credit for securing changes that had already been conceded by Coke, including a promise to hire more blacks and to give blacks more opportunities to buy bottling companies and distributorships connected to Coke. In the years that followed, Coke gave millions of dollars to organizations tied to Jackson, including his Rainbow/PUSH Coalition and a newer program, the Wall Street Project, which Jackson had created to try to persuade banks and other lenders to increase the numbers of minorities in the financial-services industry. When the Wall Street Project held an anniversary dinner in New York in early 2000, the Coca-Cola Company was listed in the program as one of its biggest sponsors. It had paid $50,000 to be on that list.

Ingrid Saunders Jones recognized that the issues she and Carl Ware had discussed at their retreat in New York still plagued the company. Almost three years after Ware submitted his report to Ivester, she initiated her own discussions with Ivester about racial problems at Coke. In the summer of 1998, when Ivester had been chairman for about nine months, she sent him a memo describing ways to address what she called 'the issue of invisibility'.

Her remarks were clearly intended to separate the emotional from the concrete, something that Ivester advocated. 'There are "facts" on this subject and I will present them as effectively as possible,' she wrote. 'But what I know "for a fact" is that there are also what I call "invisible moments" which are driven by variables that are hard to factualize. Sometimes those "invisible moments" are driven by chauvinism and power . . . sometimes by subconscious dismissal of those who are different . . . sometimes by pure and absolute disrespect . . . and sometimes as a result of a lack of consciousness.'

She closed by proposing 'a process' in which she would discuss her views with Ivester at lunches every six weeks or so. And she offered to supply him with articles, essays, and books that would help fuel their discussions, 'in between our comings together'.

Ivester agreed to the proposal, though it is unclear how often they met. The week Saunders Jones delivered her July 6 memo, Coke's stock price was in the stratosphere, topping seventy-nine dollars a share, reaching new highs on a daily basis. The business in Japan, however, was stumbling through a recession, and in Germany sales were off. In the United States, Coca-Cola was not selling as well as Ivester had hoped, despite a huge marketing campaign, known as the Coke Card that was supposed to entice a generation's worth of college and high school students to start drinking Coke by tying it to movies, roller skating, free concerts, and other activities that summer. There were enormous public triumphs, but at the same time serious private problems remained at Coke. What Saunders Jones wanted sounded fine, as long as Ivester could find the time.

When Ingrid Saunders Jones learned of Linda Ingram's trauma, she was sympathetic, and she lined up people in Coke's sprawling human resources department for Ingram to see, but it turned out not to be so simple. Ingram found that although plenty of people talked about doing something about her situation, no one seemed willing to take any action that would help her. She grew infuriated by all the talk, believing that people were hoping she would just go away. Inside the company, it was well known that people rarely got fired; Coke would simply create a new branch of its bureaucracy that would grow around them, channeling their former responsibilities in another direction and rendering the person obsolete. It was 'the Coca-Cola way', director Donald McHenry said. 'If you stole ten cents from them, they would fire you. On the other hand, if you were incompetent, you just got moved.'

Ingram had seen this plenty of times, and now she worried that it was going to happen to her. She would be condemned to die a slow death inside Coke instead of getting the job switch and the sympathy she deserved. It wasn't long before she decided to do something about it. It was another conversation with a Coke executive, one of the people who was supposed to help her, that clinched the matter.

Ingram had been discussing her case with a human resources manager named Charlene Crusoe-Ingram, who was no relation.

She placed a call to her one afternoon, telling her once more about her situation and pleading for help. Crusoe-Ingram wasn't in, but Linda Ingram left a message that she 'might have to go outside the company' to get what she needed.

'I meant to a doctor,' Ingram recalled.

But at Coke, her message was interpreted as a threat of legal action. When Crusoe-Ingram, who is also black, called back, she was frosty, according to Ingram, and she had a message. 'I tell all of my employees that they need to do whatever they need to do to protect themselves,' Ingram remembered Crusoe-Ingram saying. 'But I and the Coca-Cola Company are not afraid of anything that you could do.'

To Ingram, those were fighting words. And she now had a sort of ally, a person who had been through an experience like hers. One night, reading *Ebony* magazine at her home in the Atlanta suburbs, Ingram had come across a profile of Bari-Ellen Roberts, the lead plaintiff in a 1994 racial discrimination lawsuit against Texaco that ended in a $176-million settlement. The article included Roberts's e-mail address, and Ingram, after lengthy private debate with herself, sat down at her home computer a few nights later and tapped out a request for advice.

'It was really a plea for help,' Ingram would say later. She trembled at the thought of being detected by Coke. 'I was afraid to say what company I worked for, so I said I work for this worldwide company and I am experiencing this.'

Not long after that, Roberts came to Atlanta to promote the book she had written about the Texaco case. Ingram went to a reception at a local bookstore, and when she introduced herself Roberts pressed a slip of paper into her hand. On the paper, Roberts had written the number of her lawyer.

That lawyer was Cyrus Mehri, who had started a small firm in Washington a few months earlier. Mehri had a long history as a challenger of the status quo, starting in the seventh grade, when, asked to write a book report, he chose a book written by Abbie Hoffman. His mother had protested against the Shah while she was a student in Iran, and he had cut his professional teeth by working for Ralph Nader's Public Citizen organization before completing law school and choosing other kinds of targets.

Opening his own practice in the late 1990s, when personal financial success was a prime motivating force in most households, Mehri fervently maintained that the strong had an obligation to help the weak. He founded his law firm on that principle, with a website called findjustice.com, and was constantly on the lookout for cases that might advance it. At the same time, he was practical. He knew that he had to pay his lawyers and his assistants if he was going to make the firm last. And big targets made the best targets when it came to getting publicity for his principles and getting paid for all his work.

When Ingram told him the story of her treatment at Coke, he felt it had all the ingredients of a major, maybe even landmark, lawsuit. Here was an ugly accusation against a beloved product, made by a company based in a city known as a cradle of the civil rights movement. It had all the elements required to become front-page news; it pitted good against evil, black against white. Mehri's eyes lit up. It could be even bigger than Texaco.

He envisioned a class-action lawsuit, one that would seek justice not just for Linda Ingram but for all Coke employees who felt they had been treated unfairly simply because of the color of their skin. He knew from experience that where there was one story like hers, there were bound to be more. Like taxis and seagulls, racial-discrimination complaints seldom made solo appearances. Piece by piece, he began assembling the papers, the precedents, all the building blocks of a case.

Ingram needed company. She couldn't stand alone on this, emotionally or practically. She already knew that she wasn't alone in her worries, just as Carl Ware's report had concluded, though she, like most of the people at Coke, had never seen or even heard of the report. By herself, she spread the word about what she planned to do. She had had conversations with other people who were black and unhappy with their treatment at the company, and dozens more were out there. She needed their help, now, if they were ever going to get the Coca-Cola Company to change.

Whites at Coke heard the rumblings, and many of them shook their heads. They did not think there was racial discrimination at their company. As one person pointed out, 'Everyone is treated equally badly here.' For those who did not receive stock options, the hours were long and the pay meager compared with many other companies in town. The work was demanding and getting more so. Ivester was driven, just as Goizueta had been before him. These were the facts. They didn't see what their black colleagues had to complain about.

In the end, three other employees from the Atlanta headquarters said they would become plaintiffs, too. One was Motisola Abdallah, a secretary in the marketing department, who claimed that she had been denied promotions and made to run personal errands for the white managers she worked for. It was humiliating, and when she complained she was told that her manager 'could not change grown people and their attitudes about race'. She subsequently received an unflattering evaluation, which she felt was in retaliation for her complaints.

Another plaintiff was Gregory Allen Clark, a former prison guard who had been hired at Coke to work security. Clark said he was denied promotions, despite the fact that he held a college degree and had completed some postgraduate courses. He was told at one point that in order to qualify for one job, he had to spend time in lower-level postings first. He noticed that white security officers did not have to do that.

The third person to join Ingram was Kimberly Gray Orton, who spent thirteen years at Coke and rose to director within her division before quitting in late 1998. Orton had worked in Seattle, St. Louis, and New York for Coke before returning to Atlanta in 1992. In 1994 she became a director, one of only four African Americans at that level, which was still middle management. She was charming and funny and popular among the people she worked with, who encompassed various races, backgrounds, and religions. Yet she believed she was underpaid for her work at Coca-Cola, earning tens of thousands less than whites in comparable positions. With a salary of $99,000, Orton concluded that as a director she received less than her counterparts, nearly all of whom were white. Some of the people she supervised, all of them white, also were paid more than she was, she said.

Mehri felt that all of their stories were compelling and showed that they may have been treated unfairly. But each of the stories told a slightly different tale. There were issues of pay equity and curtailed opportunity embedded in the plaintiffs' experiences over time, as well as the outright slurs that Linda Ingram reported. How did they fit together? And how many more similar stories were there, behind the walls of the Coke tower? Here were four unhappy people, in the six-thousand-person citadel that was Coke's headquarters in Atlanta. In terms of the entire company, they were an even smaller proportion. Were these isolated cases or part of a pattern?

He soon got his answer, in that mysterious but helpful way that information often finds its way to lawyers and journalists and others tackling issues shrouded in secrecy. A package arrived in the mail at Mehri's office, a big, bulky one with no return address. When he opened it, he found a printout of the entire human resources database kept by the Coca-Cola Company, with information about job titles, job types, salaries, and years of employment, all there for the lawyer to see. Someone who knew what he was doing had made sure he got vital information about who worked for Coke.

When he had had time to analyze the database, Mehri realized that it was a gold mine. The database showed that blacks were clustered disproportionately in the lowest-paying jobs and further marginalized by being confined to certain departments and roles. They were almost never promoted to top management positions, and they rarely got jobs in operations, where historically the important work of the company – the making of syrup and the selling of Coca-Cola worldwide – was done. Of all the people working at Coke's headquarters in Atlanta, 15.7 percent were African American. But they held nearly 37 percent of the administrative jobs, and only 1.5 percent of the vice presidential jobs. A list of corporate vice presidents in the 1999 annual report included just three blacks out of a total of twenty-three. Of the thirteen senior vice presidents, only one, Carl Ware, was black. And still, nearly four years after his report to Ivester, he represented the all-time high.

Certain areas of the company seemed off-limits to black employees. In the chief financial officer's division, which had forty-two people who helped crunch the numbers and balance the books, only one was African American. Global marketing, with fifty-four people, had just two blacks. The product integrity department, some forty-two people deep, had no blacks at all.

Meanwhile, pay scales appeared to vary based on color as well. The median salary for blacks at Coke in 1998 was $36,296, according to the database, while the median salary for whites was nearly twice that, at $65,531. The gap between the two groups had widened since 1995, when the median for blacks was $34,038 and that for whites was $55,020. There was systematic discrimination going on inside Coke, Mehri thought, casting a shadow across the cheerful image of the soda in the familiar bottle. It wasn't a recent development or a casual oversight. It had been going on for years.

Mehri planned to attach the database findings as an exhibit to Ingram's lawsuit. Now, Mehri thought, *now* he had a case. And it was a strong case. He had Linda Ingram and three other named plaintiffs. He had evidence to show that a kind of institutional discrimination had been taking place for years, restricting blacks to certain areas and suppressing their salaries, compared with whites. And he began working on a third part of his case, collecting affidavits from other blacks at Coke that would support a class-action lawsuit.

Mehri knew that he faced an enormous and lengthy battle. The Coca-Cola Company would not go down without a fight. He wanted to be ready for it. He would hang on to that class-action brief as long as he could, dangling it like a sword above the company's head, to use when he saw fit.

Inside the Coca-Cola Company, among the people who knew Linda Ingram and had talked to her about the problems they had getting promoted or getting raises or getting the attention and respect they felt they deserved, there was a sense that some kind of action was coming. This would not be about the business of selling soft drinks. This would not be about share price, either. This would be about *them*. Their expectancy was like a secret they carried with them as they went about their work. They waited for Linda Ingram to make her move.

Chapter Eleven

Cracks in the Empire

JOHN PHILIS RUNS ONE OF the last soda fountains in New York. His grandfather Soterios, an immigrant from Greece, started the Lexington Candy Shop in 1925, and it still occupies its original real estate, a two-story building at the corner of Lexington Avenue and East Eighty-third Street in Manhattan. When Soterios Philis opened for business, soda fountains with candy shops sat on every other corner in city neighborhoods, from the Upper East Side to Jackson Heights, across the plains of Flatbush and the urban canyons of the Bronx. Everyone loved sweets in America. Still, this was a sharp-elbowed way to make a living. There were so many soda fountains and only so many customers. You had to give people a reason to come to your place.

In the beginning, Philis made sodas and ice-cream sundaes to order, and also sold chocolate-covered caramels, creams, and other kinds of candy from behind a big glass counter that took up nearly half the store. He invested in wrought-iron tables and chairs so people could come in and sit down for a while. This was the way the Lexington Candy Shop functioned until after the end of World War II.

In 1948, the store cut back most of its candy and became a luncheonette, open from early in the morning until early evening. Lives had been altered, and business had to respond. There was more money to be made in the restaurant business than in chocolates, Soterios Philis believed. The postwar world had set new patterns for the way people worked and lived and what they spent their money on. Having a place where a man or a woman with a demanding job could get a quick bite to eat, or take the family for a meal, promised a better future for the Philis family than devoting so much space to sweets.

A half century later, the place does a brisk trade in everything from homemade clam chowder to slices of coconut cake, with extra money coming in from the sale of lottery tickets, candy bars, and cigarettes at a counter in the front. John Philis cooks the roast beef for the sandwiches in an oven at the back and happily hews to a menu that suggests that, apart from iceberg lettuce, vegetables haven't been invented yet. There is no tofu to be found, no trends like Thai seasoning in evidence. The place is warm and toasty in the winter and cooled by air conditioners in the summer. It opens early in the morning for breakfast and doesn't shut its doors until 7:00 P.M., and its customers include the cashiers from the grocery store across the street as well as parents pushing their stroller-bound babies across the old terrazzo floor. The owners are accessible and the waitresses friendly; they tend to remember their customers' names, as well as what they like to order.

From the very beginning, the store sold Coca-Cola, mixing it up with syrup pumped from a container behind the soda counter and carbonated water propelled by a sprayer into the glass. The Cokes could be enhanced in various ways, with cherry flavoring, vanilla, chocolate, and coffee, and there is still a Coca-Cola sundae on the menu, which involves full-strength Coca-Cola syrup spooned over a scoop of vanilla ice cream and topped with whipped cream and a cherry. It is one of the few places that will dispense Coca-Cola syrup on demand. A few pediatricians still send families to the shop to buy a small amount of the stuff because they think it soothes a child's upset stomach like nothing else.

Soterios Philis made his allegiance to Coca-Cola obvious throughout the store. He hung up Coca-Cola posters and nailed a Coca-Cola clock to the wall. He accepted the free glasses that Coke salesmen offered him, and he used Coca-Cola decorations all over the mirrored wall behind the lunch counter. More than that, he refused to serve Pepsi. He liked the taste and the image of Coke better, particularly during World War II, when Woodruff's pledge to provide Cokes to all the GIs, wherever they were, struck him as not only patriotic but the right thing to do.

When he retired, his family stuck by Coca-Cola. They kept it as their cola of choice in the luncheonette, despite regular visits from the Pepsi salesmen. Much of their loyalty had to do with taste as well as with the marketing of Coke versus Pepsi. 'It tastes better than Pepsi,' John Philis says. 'And Pepsi never developed the classic American image that Coke had, and has. It's the classic American drink. It's nonalcoholic, and the image portrayed with it is always one of fun.'

He admits that he may be a little biased. He drinks Coke all the time himself and refers to it as 'nectar of the gods'. He still serves many of his drinks in Coke glasses and curates a large Coca-Cola shrine in the store, filled with commemorative bottles from all over the world, as well as toy trains and trucks bearing the Coca-Cola logo.

With such a deep attachment to Coke, the Lexington Candy Shop might be expected to get VIP treatment from the Coca-Cola system. But Philis says the opposite is true. He claims he received random bills for products never ordered. He says he has been pressured to give up his old-fashioned but appealing practice of mixing Coca-Colas one at a time at the fountain; over and over, Coke representatives have tried to get him to replace his equipment with premixed soda dispensers, the kind found in convenience stores, fast-food restaurants, and bars. They told him all Cokes should taste the same, and they can't be sure, when he mixes one himself, that that will be the case. They wanted him to sell Coke their way.

Philis, who still wears a white coat and a tie to work the soda fountain, noticed the change when the longtime bottler for New York City became part of Coca-Cola Enterprises. Bit by bit, what had been charming about Coke was replaced by a grim focus on the bottom line.

'They used to give away signs, cups, glasses, clocks,' he says. How else would his luncheonette have become so strictly, and obviously, devoted to Coke? 'Now they don't give away anything. You have to buy everything.' There are occasional exceptions. Not long ago, a Coca-Cola Enterprises salesman wanted to give him, absolutely free, some cartons full of thirty-two-ounce cups to hold Coca-Cola. One quart, in other words, in a city of the calorie-conscious and the time-pressed. 'I know my customers,' Philis said, 'and not a lot of them are interested in the thirty-two-ounce serving.'

Starting in 1997, the year Coca-Cola Enterprises acquired a large stake in the New York bottler, the Coke team came in with a new attitude: '*We're* going to tell *you* how to run your business,' Philis felt. Now, when he tries to order syrup as well as canned or bottled Coke, he is told he has to negotiate the prices for the two kinds of Coke separately; they can't be bundled together. So he pays one amount for syrup, and something else for the Coke he purchases in bottles and cans.

As a relic of the way Coke used to be, Philis gets the feeling – from Coke people – that he is in the way. He has trouble understanding that attitude. 'We're all in the same boat,' he said. 'We're all in this together, and they seem to have lost that focus.' He owns shares of Coca-Cola stock but worries aloud that the company is not what it appeared to be in the past. 'They have this arrogance that "we can do anything we want",' he said. 'A lot of it was ingrained, and a lot of it was strengthened by the incredible success they had starting in the 1980s, making millionaires out of so many people.'

You could dismiss Philis's concern as a blip on the screen, since he represents such a tiny slice of Coke's business. But there were other people watching the Coca-Cola Company in the 1990s who had begun to ask similar questions.

One of them was Frank Barron, the third-generation bottler from Rome, Georgia, who had sold his business to the Coca-Cola Company just before the birth of Coca-Cola Enterprises. He watched while so many of the practices he had put in place, from small to large, were abandoned. No more free hot dogs at the local fairs, no more free cases of Coke to grieving families. And no more infiltrating the local power structure as a representative of Coke.

'Look around this room,' Barron said, standing in his office and waving an arm at all the plaques and certificates of appreciation he has collected from charities, civic organizations, and church groups over the years. 'They don't do this anymore.' Ultimately, he believes, the bottling business is a local business, one that wraps itself around every other aspect of life in a small town or a big city, translating its understanding of what is important there into sales of more Coca-Cola.

When Coca-Cola Enterprises took over the Barrons' franchise

in 1986, Frank Barron stayed on as a salaried consultant to Coke. 'It was to keep up my political contacts,' Barron said. It would still be useful to Coke for him to know all the elected officials in his city and state; to this day, he still knows almost everyone, and many of them seem to believe he is still a Coke bottler. But as he watched Coca-Cola Enterprises ignore what he knew to be the foundation of the business, he picked up the phone and called Summerfield Johnston, the head of Coca-Cola Enterprises, to complain. 'You guys have got to get into the local scene,' Barron told him. 'You are getting eaten up!'

The places he had carved out and occupied for Coke, on the local school board and at the heart foundation, were being taken over by Pepsi. At the same time, the new Coke bottlers in Rome were crunching numbers, rearranging routes, and cutting costs. Decisions were no longer being made in Rome; they were made in Atlanta, at Coke's headquarters, and at CCE's offices, with an eye on that year's bottom line. Barron sensed that his carefully crafted business was in jeopardy. He had gotten a good price for the Rome franchise, but this was not a matter of money. This was about heritage, and pride, and the present and the future as well as the past. Didn't the Coca-Cola Company care?

Coca-Cola Enterprises was ten or eleven years old, on the cusp of adolescence, by the time Frank Barron began to worry about it. Like an adolescent, it was growing wildly in all directions. It kept getting bigger, thanks to Coke's strategy; and because of its scale, it put endless pressure on the other independent bottlers that remained.

In 1997, Dick Montag decided he had to sell the Coke franchise that three generations of his family had owned and run in Bellingham, Washington. Most of the Coke he bottled was sold to grocery stores, in chains where the prices were being set by the Coca-Cola Company, working with Coca-Cola Enterprises. An independent bottler had the choice of following along, or not, if a deal with a chain crossed into his territory; but both alternatives had been rendered unattractive by what was taking place inside the giant Coke-created bottler.

'They would offer prices to them that would drive down margins to the point where they were lower than what we had paid for the product,' Montag said. About 80 percent of his business was being affected. He tried to make up the loss through his network of vending machines and other dispensers of cold Coca-Cola drinks, which historically are off-limits for price battles. But he could see how the wheel was turning.

He did not feel extreme pressure to do whatever Coca-Cola Enterprises was promising its customers. But there was subtle force applied to bottlers like him. 'Everything, ultimately, was up to me,' he said. 'But there was certainly "encouragement" to go along with chain buys. It was to our advantage to try to cooperate.'

Montag was one of only four independent bottlers left on the West Coast by the time he decided to sell. In June 1997, he parted with the company that his grandfather and great-uncle had founded after striking out in wilder frontier businesses. They had panned for gold and chopped down timber, but in 1905 selling Coke seemed to them a much better way to make a living. They made the investment, took on the responsibility, and handed it down through two generations. By the time it got to Dick Montag, the world had changed. After ninety-two years, he sold the family franchise to Coca-Cola Enterprises.

The experiences of John Philis and Frank Barron and Dick Montag happened independently of one another, but their stories shed light on the kinds of relationships the biggest Coke bottler formed with the world. After more than a decade, Coca-Cola Enterprises was no longer a mystery but a distinct business force that people paid close attention to. It was designed by Coke, and it was an essential part of Coke. And not long after Doug Ivester replaced Roberto Goizueta, another person had begun to scrutinize the ties between these two elements of Coca-Cola.

Albert Meyer, a soft-spoken onetime accounting professor who had made a name for himself in the world of fraud investigation, was working at a small investment company in Indiana in early 1998 when his boss asked him to take a closer look at Coke.

Meyer was a South African, trained as a CPA, with a full-body belief that accountants had a unique role in business and in life. When he taught accounting, he would never let his students forget it. 'You are the gatekeepers of society,' he liked to thunder from the lectern in his clipped accent. 'You must *never* compromise your ethics.' He was disgusted when he saw accounting firms sign off on paperwork that, on further examination, showed a business run amok. He would make it his business to expose that kind of thing whenever he came across it.

Meyer never intended to be a muckraker – only an accountant. In 1993, he was teaching accounting at tiny Spring Arbor College in Michigan when he offered to help the college prepare its books for an outside audit. Meyer stumbled across a scheme that ended up catapulting him, and the college, into the headlines. His clue was a receipt for a $300,000 wire transfer to a charity called the Foundation for New Era Philanthropy.

Several things bothered him: the size of the transfer, the fact that it had been wired to its recipient (which suggested an urgency not often necessary in the academic world), and the name of the charity. *Odd,* he thought. *Usually these are in the name of a person.* He sent for copies of various government filings, as well as the Philadelphia-based charity's financial statements. He discovered that New Era was persuading institutions to give money on the promise that an unnamed major philanthropist would match whatever they gave. In fact, there was no such arrangement, and the money was being siphoned into private bank accounts controlled by Jack Bennett, New Era's founder. Government regulators soon moved in and charged Bennett with fraud. He was sentenced to eleven years in prison, while dozens of schools and donors lost as much as $200 million that he had collected from them.

Meyer became a hero, a kind of caped-crusader CPA, though he saw himself as simply doing his job. His name was in the newspapers, and his sudden fame brought him a flood of job offers from investment firms. Ultimately, he left Spring Arbor for a job with a company called Martin Capital in Elkhart, Indiana.

He was content there, paid to pore over financial statements in search of good investments for the firm to make. It was an accountant's dream job in many ways. In the spring of 1998, his boss, Frank Martin, asked him to examine Coca-Cola, which was roaring along spectacularly some six months after Goizueta's death.

Martin told Meyer, 'We know everything is fine with Coke because Buffett owns it, but could you just look at the financials and tell us where Coke makes its money?'

As Martin gave those instructions, Doug Ivester, the man who years ago had pledged himself to the accounting life, was thriving in the work of running the Coca-Cola Company. He jetted back and forth across the globe, visiting customers and checking on operations in countries like China, Korea, Germany, and South Africa. Awed competitors claimed he once logged a day that began with breakfast in Chicago, followed by meetings in Atlanta. Dinner was in London, and the next morning he was in Johannesburg in time for breakfast. He liked to be physically present for meetings large and small. He was more peripatetic than a presidential-primary hopeful.

Twelve senior executives reported directly to Ivester, including the heads of the six regions around the world that Coke had devised for reporting purposes. Goizueta may have died, but the miracle had to live on. The two of them had forecast 15 to 20 percent earnings growth for 1998, and 7 to 8 percent growth in soft-drink volume. Those had been the growth targets for years now, and Ivester saw no reason for them to change.

Wall Street, too, believed that nothing had to change. Goizueta was gone, but in his place was his right-hand man, the person who knew best how the phenomenon in Atlanta worked. The analysts gave him an extended honeymoon, and why not? Profits continued to pour in, volume hit all of its growth targets, and the stock continued to soar. In the spring of 1998, Coke shares traded for seventy-five dollars apiece, about twenty dollars more than the day Goizueta died. They showed no signs of going anywhere but up.

Ivester inherited Goizueta's board of directors, and the board was closely controlled at that time, as it had been for years, by a triumvirate consisting of Warren Buffett, Herbert Allen, and Jimmy Williams. All three of them had taken different paths to Atlanta. Buffett had seized upon the stock in the late 1980s for its growth potential. Like his other investments – Dairy Queen, Gillette, Disney, Salomon Brothers, See's Candies – he saw in Coke a beautiful thing: a company that had the potential to increase in value. Buffett often told people, in his trademark folksy style, that if he liked a product he either invested in it or bought the whole thing. A nod like that, or a nod in the other direction, usually produced a market stampede, so well regarded was his judgment. As a result, he had different reporting rules with the Securities and Exchange Commission. Any major stock trades he made could not be made public for three months. He served on the audit committee for Coke, keeping an eye on the books, as well as on the finance committee.

Allen, meanwhile, had logged more than fifteen years as a Coke director by the time Ivester became chairman and chief executive. He chaired the important Compensation Committee, the group that had produced such enormous rewards for Goizueta and Keough and, lately, Ivester. He was not the largest shareholder of Coke, but he was one of the most influential. He was also a member of the finance committee. He had Keough working right in his office in New York, and if he ever needed a second opinion about what was going on at Coke, Keough was more than happy to provide it.

Williams was the least well known of the three outside Atlanta. His name did not appear in headlines, and he did not have a following beyond his hometown. He was Coca-Cola through and through; Coke ran in his veins, as the saying went, as it did for so many Atlantans. Since 1979, he had been a director. He chaired the finance committee and from time to time served as a spokesman for the board. Short and white-haired, with a narrow pink face that had grown craggier with time, he had been named chairman and chief executive of SunTrust in 1991, at the age of fifty-eight, and by 1998 he was retiring, though he would remain on the Coke board. He was also an adviser to several of the enormous foundations in Atlanta and elsewhere that had been built with Coca-Cola wealth, like the Joseph B. Whitehead Foundation, with assets of more than $1 billion, and the Woodruff Foundation, the legacy of The Boss. With $3.1 billion, it was one of the largest foundations in the country.

These were the three men who controlled much of the agenda inside Coke's boardroom. For so long, they had had nothing to worry about. Goizueta had been a master at soothing their concerns, such as they were. He had invited them on junkets to inspect Coke operations in other countries, and he had sent them presents on their birthdays. And although they had joined the boards at different intervals, all of them had been aboard for Coke's marvelous ride across the last decade. All of them had seen their holdings rise and rise for years. They saw no reason that the trend should not continue.

Ivester's earliest strategic move was to offer $800 million to buy Orangina. But he needed approval from the powerful competition commission of France to make the Orangina deal go through. Not to worry, Ivester told his board. There won't be a problem with this. He had already checked it out.

The board liked Ivester, as did the rest of the business world. He was virtually Goizueta with a North Georgia accent, and so completely did they identify the two men that, inside and outside the company, Ivester's name began to be pronounced with a Cuban inflection, the accent on the penultimate syllable. Now he became 'Eye-VEST-er', not 'EYE-vester', as everyone in his family had always pronounced it.

The new CEO shouldered the burden and kept forging ahead. He had plans of his own for Coke, plans that would make the more than 5 million shares of Coke stock that he owned or stood to gain through his stock options worth even more than they already were. He continued to put in long hours at his desk or on the road; weekends were largely dedicated to work, as they had long been, and when he wanted to spend more time with Kay, his wife, he reserved a seat for her on the company plane and they went to visit a Coke market together.

In June, about eight months into his latest role, Ivester had his public debut as chairman and CEO. The occasion was the biannual meeting for Wall Street analysts and money managers that Coke hosted at its offices in Atlanta. The turnout was high, as it always had been, and Ivester began his day by attending a 7:00 A.M. breakfast at the Ritz-Carlton in downtown Atlanta, where the company was highlighting Minute Maid, the juice brand owned by Coke. Minute Maid, where Don Keough had once worked, was enjoying some long-delayed attention from senior management. It was still run out of Houston, but Keough was long gone. Now the person in charge was Ralph Cooper, a twenty-five-year Coke veteran, and Coke had big plans for Minute Maid, starting with the American lunchbox – there would be small juice boxes of Minute Maid orange juice for sale, for the first time – and continuing abroad.

After breakfast, the visitors filed into the Coca-Cola auditorium, and as they entered, an Ivester assistant handed various people Coke bottles that had been painted silver or gold. There were many silver bottles, but only two gold ones. When everyone was seated, Ivester strode across the stage and asked the people with silver bottles to rise. They did. Then he asked the people with gold bottles to stand. And the two did.

Then he explained: The gold bottles represented Coke's share of the worldwide beverage market. The silver bottles represented everyone else's. That was why Ivester felt so comfortable making generous predictions about the company's future growth. Clearly there was a huge market out there that Coke did not yet own, and he was going to make sure that the Coca-Cola Company got at least part of it. One silver bottle at a time would change to gold; that was where he was taking Coke.

The rest of the day was devoted to speakers representing different geographic regions of the Coke empire. Each one, usually the senior vice president in charge of the region, painted the same glowing picture: Coke was growing, would continue to grow, and had never before been so well positioned to capture growth from its competitors. Highlighted again and again was the bottling system that Ivester had done so much to put together: Without such strong partners, various executives observed, Coke's job would be that much harder. The bottlers themselves did not speak; no one had invited them.

At the breaks, everyone poured out of the auditorium into a reception area where every single beverage was a Coke product: Minute Maid juices in bottles; Coca-Cola in cans and twenty-ounce bottles; diet Coke, Sprite, Barq's Root Beer, Fruitopia. They drank, and they gathered in small groups to assess what they were hearing. Outside, the sun beat down, turning Atlanta into the kind of hothouse it becomes in late June. Up the hill from Coke headquarters, at the Varsity diner, customers lined up as usual for their sizzling onion rings and their molten pimento-cheese sandwiches and their Coca-Colas served in large paper cups over crushed ice. Coke products were the only kinds of sodas a customer could get at the Varsity; Goizueta and Ivester, whose pictures hung on a special 'wall of fame' there, had made sure of that.

Back down the hill, analysts were suitably impressed by all they heard. But they would save their highest praise for Ivester, who took the stage in the late afternoon to deliver a speech in which he used a yellow-painted wooden bottle holder, a six-pack container from the 1920s, as a prop. It was an innovation that Robert Woodruff, the Coke legend, had summarily embraced. It was one of the earliest ways of getting people to buy more Coke – with the local bottler's help, that is. They were encouraged to take the six-pack home and keep some Coke for later. It had taken off like a rocket, and Coke was still packaged in six-packs, though twelve-packs and twenty-four-packs were part of the picture, too.

Ivester outlined six reasons that the Coca-Cola Company was an unstoppable force. There were the brands, the people, the bottlers, the marketing, the customers – all celebrated for years by Coke's leaders. But the sixth element in his strategy, the final component in that six-pack, was something that Ivester called mind-set, the thing that had helped carry him through his childhood and the thing that he now was inculcating across this huge, powerful company.

Mind-set, he explained, protected Coke workers from settling for less. Mind-set made sure the company reached its goals. Mind-set was not taking no for an answer and being confident that you were going to achieve whatever you set out to achieve. In this case, it was 2 billion servings a day – not the 1 billion that Coke was already selling all over the world.

'The world will continue to change,' Ivester told the audience. But not to worry: 'The mind-set of the Coca-Cola system enables it to adapt to the environment, to stay focused on long-term value creation, and to build its business to new levels of performance.' He had it, and he was going to make sure everyone else shared it, too.

Everyone burst into applause when he was through. The applause went on and on. Some analysts marveled privately at Ivester's transformation. He seemed polished, confident and at ease, the opposite of the way he had often come across while Goizueta was alive. Some ratcheted up their expectations for the company's growth and profits after the meeting; many of them were already as high as they could go. A few goaded Ivester to raise the company's volume and earnings targets; he declined.

Even before Ivester's speech, there was nearly universal acclaim among the analysts for Coke's performance. Allan Kaplan, the Merrill Lynch analyst who was Goizueta's nemesis, had retired, and the current crop of analysts felt that Coke could do no wrong. 'There was just this phenomenal consistency, and the volume numbers and the earnings were great,' said Jennifer Solomon, the beverage analyst for Salomon Smith Barney. 'And Coca-Cola Enterprises was doing very well as a stock. It went up about a hundred percent in 1997, which was just a phenomenal return.' She concluded, as did almost everyone else, that the Coke empire was running on all cylinders. Problems had been fixed; the future gleamed. 'If even the bottlers were doing well,' she said, 'the whole system must be healthy.'

On the infrequent occasions when volume did not meet expectations, earnings still rose between 15 and 20 percent. Coke seemed to be guaranteeing a certain return on a person's investment. No wonder Warren Buffett was so in love with the stock, declaring all the time in public that he would never sell a single share. 'It was such a powerful business model,' Solomon said. 'They had this huge infrastructure in place that they didn't have to pay for directly. They sold this goop for a dollar a case that it cost them pennies to make. How many businesses have that kind of margin?'

Shortly before the meeting, as the stock price topped eighty dollars a share, Solomon had published a note in which she wondered whether Coke's value had peaked. There was a recession in Japan, one of the biggest profit sources, after all. And Pepsi was starting to show signs of life. The response she got – not from the company, but from money managers and other clients – was vociferous. 'They said, I understand your point, but I don't want to hear it.' One person, a senior executive with a popular mutual fund company, told her she should be fired for 'being negative on Coke'.

Less than a month after the meeting in Atlanta, on the fifteenth of July, Coke stock rose to more than eighty-eight dollars a share. This was an all-time high, and it had been achieved not under the legendary Goizueta but under his chosen heir, Doug Ivester. Ivester, the board, and the rest of the Coke family couldn't have been more pleased. Coke's leadership might have changed, but the success story continued. In fact, as Ivester would say, it was just beginning.

All the while, the world turned, and in some ways, in some places, things were not going so well for Coke. The Japanese economy was in the second year of a deep recession, but this was barely acknowledged at the June meeting. Japan was Coke's fifth-largest market and one of its most profitable; fully 20 percent of the company's profits came from selling Coca-Cola, canned coffee, canned tea, and scores of other products at high prices across Japan. With demand for all beverages slowing, as will happen in almost any recession, Coke's business in Japan was on the rocks. There were also strained relations with many of the local bottlers. But no one at Coke would acknowledge this. Instead, Japan was characterized as a land of 'opportunity'.

Then there was Germany, Coke's fourth-largest market and one of its oldest. A 1961 Billy Wilder film, *One, Two, Three,* had zeroed in on the life of a Coca-Cola executive in Berlin and captured the essence of a Coke man's zeal and ambition – that he would say or do almost anything to sell more Coke. Germany remained a key area for the company nearly forty years later. The Coke bottlers included men like Max Schmeling, a former heavyweight boxing champion. When the Berlin Wall came down in 1989, Goizueta made sure trucks filled with cold Coca-Colas were standing by, and as the East Germans poured across the border, Coke workers handed them the all-American drink. The scene was poignant, especially for Goizueta, and it spurred him to build brand-new plants with huge production capacities in Germany and in other parts of what had been the Soviet bloc. Drawn by the prospect of profit from emerging markets, Goizueta went full steam ahead into places that had had, until that point, very little Coca-Cola. It was part business, part blood feud. He had to be in these formerly Communist countries, Coke at the ready, to show them what they'd been missing.

As always, Coke executives enjoyed unusual access to world leaders, living in a kind of extra-government, the Republic of Coke. In emerging markets in particular, they were welcomed with open arms. They flew into Romania, docking the Gulfstream inside Nicolae Ceausescu's private and luxurious hangar. They watched television with the president of Turkey. They lunched with Deng Xiaoping and offered Nelson Mandela lifts in the company jet.

Germany, though, was not a new market. Sales of Coke there, as in other parts of Europe, had been achieved two generations earlier by building a series of relationships with beer distributors. There is no public gathering place in Germany where beer isn't loved, and Coke was quick to piggyback its own products onto the prevailing beverage system. Soon there were more than a hundred Coke bottlers, each one thrilled with the lifestyle that selling Coca-Cola gave them, in addition to the beer business many of them already had.

It worked for a long time, almost as long as the independent bottling system in the United States. But in the early 1990s, Coke executives grew frustrated with having to negotiate every move with dozens of tiny distributors scattered across what was now a unified Germany. It was the American bottling dilemma all over again: If everyone was selling an identical product, didn't it make more sense to combine so many small players into several larger ones? Ivester pushed for a single bottler for all of Germany, and he got the number down to a handful. He created one giant anchor bottler, with the tongue-twisting name of Coca-Cola Erfrischungsgetranke. Coke owned the entire company at its inception, but by 1997 it had reduced its stake to about 45 percent. This was the German version of Coca-Cola Enterprises, bottling about 60 percent of all the Coke in the country.

Bottling in Germany had been made more efficient, but at a price. 'You had to go against the interests of the bottlers, who had been there for years,' said one former Coke executive. 'And the bottlers didn't want to give up bottling.' It was almost the same situation that had existed in the United States ten or twenty years earlier.

Between declining economic conditions and the rapid consolidation that produced that bottler, sales of Coke in Germany were off by the time the investor meeting rolled around. The weather in northern Europe had been unusually rainy, and that had depressed soft-drink sales further. Germany was a classic example of the situation Coke encountered all over the world: If another beverage was already established as the drink of choice, consumers were fair-weather friends, at best, to a beverage like Coca-Cola. And there was simmering resentment among some of the former distributors at the scorched-earth style with which the giant German bottler had been created. It was a hallmark of Ivester's style – the business of increasing shareholder value demanded it, he might have said if asked – and it had not played so well in one of Coke's biggest overseas markets.

But no mention was made of this at the meeting. Germany was one more stellar example of the remaking of the Coca-Cola system, thanks to Ivester's vision and execution. At least, that is the way it was presented to the hundreds of people in the audience, the people with billions of dollars to invest. No one from the German bottler had been invited to speak.

Next to be spotlighted was the United States. When Jack Stahl, the president of Coca-Cola North America, stepped to the microphone, he described a wonderland of Coke-selling opportunities. There were the sales to be gained from special events, like the Coke Card, which offered free Cokes with various activities like bowling and summer concerts. Elaborate market research had enabled Stahl's division to come up with cards tailored to different cities: Tulsa had one set of enticements, all tied to Coke, and New York had another. He talked of turning the continent into a place 'where Coca-Cola brands are preferred and consumed more each day than the day before, as we connect our brands with consumers' lives in a meaningful way'. Stahl described how advertising and marketing – the act of promoting desire for a Coke and making sure it was always easy to get one – promised even more sales. In 1998, Coke's share of the cola market was 44 percent, compared with 31 percent for Pepsi. But increasing market share was the battle cry that Goizueta, and now Ivester, emphasized across the land. They were discovering that building more market share was expensive, mainly for bottlers. Prices for Coke syrup increased, but prices for the finished product had declined as Pepsi waged a price war, to the point that Coke and Pepsi still cost the same as they had fifteen years earlier. Many U.S. bottlers wondered how they, or Coca-Cola Enterprises, or any bottler anywhere, could go on like this.

At the same time, Coke was urging its bottlers to invest heavily in equipment like vending machines and refrigerated cases. A cold Coke, the thinking went, could be sold for more than a warm Coke on a grocery-store shelf. And the more cold Cokes that were sold, the less the shrinking profits on grocery-store sales would matter. Some bottlers had found that the balance could be readjusted in their favor with such tactics; but still, they had that gnawing feeling as they watched the majority of their products being sold for less than they had spent to make them. All in the interests of market share; Coke wanted to dominate every store, and it would not take no for an answer. It was helping Coca-Cola Enterprises already, with great chunks of capital for vending machines and infusions of marketing support to help beat back Pepsi, and it would do the same for other bottlers as well, though no one from Coke mentioned the financial support at the meeting.

Stahl's presentation was upbeat, a characteristically optimistic Coca-Cola performance. Investors and analysts left Atlanta that day believing even more completely in the Coca-Cola Company's ability to stay on course. There was no reason to question management, no need to ask how the company planned to achieve everything. It had all been laid out for them, as plain as day. Goizueta had created this thing and kept it going for more than sixteen years. Ivester was the man to continue that. They flew out of the city's Hartsfield International Airport at sunset, their ideas about the Coca-Cola Company suffused with a corporate-sponsored rosy glow.

They didn't know that out in Elkhart, Indiana, Albert Meyer had burrowed his way deep into Coke's financial statements and those of Coca-Cola Enterprises. 'He's a crusader,' Frank Martin would say. What Meyer found astonished him. Companies are permitted to report their business dealings separately from affiliates as long as they own less than 50 percent of those affiliates. The definition of 'control', at least in the financial sense, holds that it exists when one company owns 50 percent or more of another company.

However, Meyer saw, though Coke had made a point of owning less than 50 percent of its biggest bottler, it exerted all kinds of control over Coca-Cola Enterprises. The concentrate company – Mother Coke, as many people referred to it – had developed all kinds of ways of getting around the rule, Meyer believed. The bottler's board was populated with current and former Coca-Cola executives. The decisions that were being made – to add franchises often by purchasing them from the Coca-Cola Company, and to ramp up spending for equipment like vending machines – were fraught with conflicts of interest, he thought, and no one was questioning that.

'It was public knowledge,' he said. 'It was all right there in the proxy so Coke could always say, well, we told people in the proxy.' But he was astounded by the extent of the potential conflicts, the control, and the net effect of it all.

Several of the thirteen board members at the bottler had lucrative consulting contracts with Coke. Others were tied to SunTrust, the enormous Atlanta bank that controlled huge blocks of Coca-Cola stock through a series of trusts. At least five had current or former ties to Coke, with enormous holdings of Coca-Cola stock as a result. And what Meyer considered a grotesque imbalance in the business itself had developed, with the bottler staggering under an enormous load of debt while Coca-Cola had almost no debt at all.

'We enter into anchor bottler partnerships because we expect results beyond what we could attain alone or with multiple bottlers,' the Coke annual report stated year after year. Now those words seemed almost ominous to Meyer.

He began to pick apart the amounts of money flowing through the two companies. Coke had next to no debt, while Coca-Cola Enterprises, in the middle of 1998, had more than $7 billion of it. Its interest expense and franchise costs kept going up, while its net income declined. From 1997 to 1998, the bottler's net income fell from $171 million to $142 million, while it paid $701 million in interest, up from $537 million the year before, and its franchise costs – buying Coca-Cola bottlers, either from the families that had held them for generations or, in many cases, from the Coca-Cola Company – ballooned from $11.8 billion to $13.9 billion.

The bottler had been on an acquisition binge for the last three years, almost doubling in size from $7.9 billion in revenues in 1996 to $13.4 billion in 1998. It was nearly the size of the Coca-Cola Company. It had snapped up franchises from east to west, in Europe and Canada and all over the United States, gnawing its way across the land and consuming places that had been in the hands of families until then.

It had spent prodigiously for those, too – often issuing stock or borrowing money to make the deals. The spending could seem compulsive to an outsider. In 1996, Coca-Cola Enterprises paid $915 million for all of the Coca-Cola bottling plants in France and Belgium; another $313 million for Ouachita Coca-Cola Bottling Company, which covered parts of Arkansas, Louisiana, and Mississippi and was formerly held by the Biedenharn family; and $158 million for Coca-Cola Bottling Company West, which included franchises in Minnesota, Montana, North and South Dakota, and Wyoming.

The bill came to just under $1.4 billion, and that was only one year. The following year, the bottler spent $3.7 billion for Coca-Cola bottling operations across Canada, plus the Coca-Cola Bottling Company of New York, and to take full control of a joint-venture bottling company that Coca-Cola had formed with Cadbury Schweppes in Britain.

In 1998, the expansion continued: $1.1 billion to take control of a large bottler known as Coke Southwest, with franchises in Colorado, Kansas, New Mexico, Oklahoma, and Texas; another $975 million for another assortment of Coke bottlers in the United States and Luxembourg.

While the spree might have seemed uncontrolled, executives at Coke and at the bottler successfully argued that owning all those franchises gave the bottler a position of strength. By 1998, Coca-Cola Enterprises controlled most of Texas, all but a scrap of Florida, and huge swaths of California. It owned nearly all the bottling in Canada. It controlled bottling across most of Western Europe. And all of these places were now 'aligned' with the Coca-Cola Company, meaning that programs and strategies would be easier to pull off. That was the way the board saw it: greater efficiencies, more constituents consolidated under one roof – an easier time of it, generally speaking, for the sale of Coca-Cola.

But Albert Meyer begged to differ. The more control the bottler allowed Coke, the less independent it could be and the less reason it had to exist as a separate, publicly traded company, he felt. Forget the rule that owning less than 50 percent means not controlling a company, he said. In truth and in fact, the Coca-Cola Company exercised control over its largest bottler – from the pricing and timing of the sale of the franchises Coke owned to the strategic moves that came afterward. At that time, the Financial Accounting Standards Board was considering whether companies should be required to consolidate their financial statements if one could be shown to control another. Such a change had been considered, and defeated, before; Meyer thought it was high time the regulation was tightened.

He believed that the board of Coca-Cola Enterprises was another means by which Coke controlled the bottler.

Looking at Ivester's portfolio, Meyer decided that there was an apparent conflict of interest. Ivester's holdings of Coke stock, restricted and unrestricted, totalled more than 5 million shares, compared with a measly 53,000 shares of Coca-Cola Enterprises.

Ultimately, the bottler's profit was completely in the hands of Coke, he concluded, through a system of raising concentrate prices and rebating part of that at the end of the year in order to make the bottler seem modestly profitable. There was abundant evidence of self-dealing by Coke, he felt, in the way that bottling franchises were being sold to Coca-Cola Enterprises. 'The bottler was posting a one percent return on assets, which is just absurd,' Meyer said. The system, he concluded, was 'a mechanism for Coke to ensure a high gross margin for itself, and give back just enough at the SG & A line.'

Coke, he said, should be required to report its bottler's finances along with its own – an accounting technique known as consolidation. Doing so, however, would wipe most of the profits off Coke's books. It would have to shoulder the expenses of bottling, the expenses it had rid itself of with the creation of Coca-Cola Enterprises, and while it would have more income, it would also have far more debt.

Meyer believed he had cracked the code. He thought he had figured out what was happening between Coke and its big bottlers – something that few people inside Coke comprehended. No one on Wall Street fully understood the minutiae of the relationship, or the way that money traveled back and forth between the companies. Coca-Cola Enterprises had been presented to them as a better way of bottling and selling Coke. The bottler's rapid expansion was part of the plan. 'Coke was finding growth challenging in the mid-nineties,' Andrew Conway recalled later. 'They overcame that by having cash gains that were spent to drive the business forward.' As far as investing was concerned, Coke and its bigger bottler appeared to perform as a single entity, one tied to the other.

Meyer believed he had figured out the system and that it was flawed. He felt like the child in the fairy tale of the emperor's new clothes. He felt as if he were the only one who knew the truth.

He began searching for ways to publish his discovery. He found audiences, first in *Grant's Interest Rate Observer* and then in *The New York Times*. Under the headline 'Putting Extra Fizz into Profits', the *Times* article appeared on August 4, 1998, describing Meyer's findings. The market makers read it, considered it, and galloped away from Coke stock, knocking three dollars and fifty cents off the share price in a single session. In Atlanta, it was as if an earthquake had rocked the Coke tower.

The chief Coke spokesman, Randal Donaldson, called other reporters to plead Coke's position. There is no case for consolidation, Donaldson and others said over and over. Meyer doesn't know what he's talking about. We own less than 50 percent of this bottler, so we account for our transactions with it by the equity method of accounting. We're as transparent as possible. We have nothing to hide.

On Wall Street, analysts and traders were disturbed by the prospect of consolidation dismantling the Coke miracle, and some sold off what they had. But after the first deflating day, Coca-Cola stock held steady. Executives in Atlanta swarmed the telephone lines, trying for damage control with money managers and individual investors. They did their jobs well. Before the end of September, share prices were edging close to their old levels, and the Coca-Cola Company appeared unharmed by Meyer's pronouncements.

It was the bottler, Coca-Cola Enterprises, that lost some believers for good. Several major investors quietly sold most of what they had, including Putnam Investment Management, which parted with 10 million shares, and Prudential Mutual Fund Management, which let go of more than 6 million. Some of the shares went on the market; others were acquired privately by none other than Coca-Cola Enterprises itself. Citing 'a good price', the bottler bought up 14 million shares of its own stock – borrowing $404 million in short-term paper to do so, though it was already weighed down with debt from its acquisition drive.

Coca-Cola was 'a pretty intimidating company', Martin would say later. 'Nobody was able to tell me that Coke wouldn't seek retribution against our firm.' Meyer's zeal made him nervous. It was a small family company, after all, and he wanted something of it to be left for posterity. 'Nowhere in our mission statement,' he said, 'does it say we should go after elephants with peashooters.'

In the meantime, Meyer had parted from Martin, sold his house in Elkhart and moved to Dallas, where he got a job with David Tice & Associates, a hedge fund. He still investigated Coke's books, but he also found some fresh targets like Tyco, the giant conglomerate, in which he detected accounting irregularities. Meyer published his findings in 1999, sending Tyco's stock into a decline for a short time. It would be three more years before the company's senior management became entangled in an enormous scandal that came to symbolize the excesses of the bull market.

In his new job, Meyer vowed he would keep on examining Coke's financial relationship with its largest bottler. He was not yet finished.

Chapter Twelve

Whatever It Takes

ALMOST A HUNDRED MILES northeast of Dallas and a short hop from Oklahoma's southern edge, Paris, Texas, lies in shade-tree country, though that still means hundred-degree heat in the middle of July. It's not a fancy place, though there is a replica of the Eiffel Tower, topped with a red cowboy hat. People hang their laundry on the line and don't have all that much money to spend on things they don't consider essential. Paris is where Jerry and Leslie Dudley and their seven children decided to settle in 1998, buying a company called Harmar Bottling.

Jerry Dudley was no newcomer to soft-drink bottling, and he took what he knew and built what had been a modest business into a bigger one. He did what a traditional bottler did: He called on stores and restaurants, trying to sell them the brands he bottled. They tended to be happy to see him. Harmar sold Royal Crown cola, 7UP, A&W root beer, Sunkist orange soda, Arizona iced tea, and Snapple fruit-flavored drinks. These were the B team of soft drinks – not Coke, not Pepsi, but still attracting a crowd of faithful consumers. Selling RC cola gave the Dudleys an automatic niche, since it has long been cheaper than either Coke or Pepsi. Where a twenty-ounce bottle of Coke sells for ninety-nine cents, the same size RC often costs sixty-nine cents. And while RC's market share is far smaller than either Coke's or Pepsi's, there are nevertheless thousands of people in and around Paris, Texas, who will buy it.

Two years after they bought the business, the Dudleys could have congratulated themselves. Everything was going well. They had plenty of demand, and they were supplying all their customers. Their days were long, but they were making money, and that was a happy thing.

Then everything took a turn for the worse. It happened shortly after the Paris Coca-Cola bottler, which had been a small independent company, was acquired by Coca-Cola Enterprises.

'Our Royal Crown business fell fifty percent,' said Leslie Dudley. 'Then it got to be down closer to seventy, seventy-five percent.' In their relatively small business, selling fewer than 2 million cases a year, the pinch was noticeable and sharp.

The Dudleys tried to find out what was happening, and soon they discovered that across the Paris region stores were coming under the influence of new, aggressive calendar marketing agreements forged by the Coca-Cola Company and its biggest bottler. The agreements, long a fixture in food and beverage retail, had become increasingly hard-nosed when it came to competing brands. Coke led the trend; Pepsi, anxious to keep up, followed suit. The Dudleys and other sellers of Royal Crown, traditionally the cheapest of the three colas, were getting squeezed out of markets that had long been theirs to share with the giants.

'When CCE came in, they would penalize the stores if they didn't go along with their program,' Jerry Dudley recalled. 'We could talk to the stores and offer them a promotion or a deal, but then they'd say, "Well, I'd like to help you, but we have a deal with Coke right now."' Those deals were great for Coke but hideous for its competitors; Coke got first choice of everything, from the signs to the vending machines to the space in the refrigerator case.

Miles away in Houston, a lawyer named Tom Stanley was hearing similar stories. He had discovered the marketing agreements literally by accident, with the crash of a bottling truck.

Stanley had a friend named Stuart Wright, who lived in Louisiana and had a law practice there. The driver of a Royal Crown truck had been involved in a wreck, and the other side was suing for personal injury. Wright had been hired to defend the owner of the truck, a Royal Crown distributor named Jimmy Carneline, who lived in the town of Many, Louisiana.

Carneline, by way of claiming he couldn't afford to pay anyone a huge settlement, started telling his lawyer how business had deteriorated recently. He was puzzled as to why. He couldn't get his sodas on store shelves, even in places where he had been welcome for years. And there hadn't been any problems, either on the delivery side or the product-quality side. That was in 1992, two years after the Dudleys, whom he knew through their Royal Crown connections, began having difficulties.

Wright called Stanley, who had a specialty in antitrust cases, and asked him to talk to Carneline, the third generation of his family to distribute Royal Crown cola. Stanley knew all about Royal Crown cola, though he himself had grown up on even cheaper Double-Cola. Across the South, Royal Crown is often mentioned in the same breath with Moon Pies: confections made of chocolate, marshmallow, and graham cracker that are sold in roadside stores and supermarkets all over the South. RC was always cheaper than Coke or Pepsi and went well with Moon Pies, peanut rounders, and other sugary stuff people liked to buy. Stanley, who studied law at the University of Texas and keeps all kinds of Longhorn memorabilia around his office in a 1920s downtown Houston tower, agreed to talk to Carneline.

They sat down together, and Carneline told his tale of woe. Lately, he said, he wasn't allowed to advertise in some stores. His space on the shelves had been cut back to a small fraction of its former self. He was not permitted to put up signs that said anything at all about RC – nothing about the price, nothing about the serving size, nothing with the name on it at all. Stanley was captivated. Carneline showed him copies of some of the marketing agreements signed between stores in his territory and the Coca-Cola Company's biggest bottler, Coca-Cola Enterprises.

Stanley asked Carneline if the agreements were unique to his part of the country. Carneline shook his head. 'No,' he told the lawyer, 'they're doing it everywhere.'

Carneline gave Jerry Dudley's phone number to Stanley. Other distributors, in Louisiana, Oklahoma, Texas, and Arkansas, also came forward, drawn by the prospect of justice. They all said the same things: We can never get any ads. And we never have any complaints about our products, but our space keeps getting reduced. We can't put up signs. In short, we can't do anything we need to do to be competitive.

The uneven rectangle formed by East Texas, southern Arkansas, and western Louisiana at that point was still a mix of small- and medium-size grocery chains, with names like Brookshire's and Big Star and Piggly Wiggly. The more restrictive marketing agreements seemed to cluster themselves around the larger national or regional chains, whether they were supermarkets or convenience stores, Stanley remembers. 'If you went into a local chain, you saw a much more competitive environment,' he said. That was the old-fashioned kind of drink aisle, in other words, where there was a wide assortment of sodas made by a variety of companies and no clear domination by one brand or another.

That, too, would change. By 1997, as one of the Royal Crown distributors put it, 'Coke had agreements with stores in places you couldn't even get to with a telegram.' The marketing agreements, setting out the terms for advertising, shelf space, and signs and refrigerator space, grew more restrictive at the same time. They were legal, but Stanley increasingly believed they were unfair. 'Every time the RC or Pepsi bottler would come up with some ingenious way to get around the agreement, it would be changed to cut that loophole out,' he said. As a cola drinker, he had never paid much attention to what he saw for sale in a store. Now he examined the products on display – how they were displayed, especially – everywhere he went.

In 1994, one Royal Crown bottler, Thomas Edelman of Monroe, Louisiana, decided to advertise on billboards, promoting his products at two regional convenience store chains called Handy Mart and Delta Mini-Mart. In return, the chains said he could sell ice-cold drinks at the front of the store, which worked out nicely for Edelman. But two years later, the chains came to him and said he could no longer do that. Ouachita Coca-Cola Bottling, the local Coke bottler owned by a descendant of Joseph Biedenharn, the Mississippi candy merchant who was the very first person to sell Coke in bottles, had been purchased by Coca-Cola Enterprises, and the giant bottler declared that ice barrels – the kind Edelman used – were a form of advertising and violated the chains' agreements with Coke. That was the end of Thomas Edelman's program; his sales dropped 30 or 40 percent almost overnight.

Then there was Bruce Hackett, a Royal Crown distributor from Monticello, in southern Arkansas, who had worked for the local Coke bottler there for nearly a decade. When he quit in 1994 to start his own business, he found himself in the soft-drink version of the Bermuda Triangle. The Coke bottler was sold to Coca-Cola

Enterprises, Coca-Cola Enterprises had fierce new terms for its marketing agreements with stores, and Hackett, who had looked forward to being his own boss, had nowhere to go. The banner signs he had invested in, to put along the side of the road near convenience stores where he was selling RC, ended up in a bin in his basement. He wasn't allowed to advertise his drinks, he was told by store manager after store manager. Only Coke could advertise. He ended up lending the signs to friends who were holding fund-raisers at the local Baptist church. Instead of letting people know that they could get a twenty-ounce RC down at the convenience store for sixty-nine cents, Hackett's signs appeared along those Arkansas highways and byways with FISH FRY, NEXT LEFT spray-painted on the reverse.

'The typical person has no concept of the techniques used by the dominant suppliers in the grocery industry,' Tom Stanley said. 'They think, if you don't see it, it doesn't exist.' And in stores all over Arkansas and Texas and Louisiana, shoppers couldn't see the Royal Crown cola, or the 7Up, or the other drinks that weren't Coke or Pepsi products. If they were for sale at all, they might be relegated to an obscure corner or a bottom shelf, the so-called Coffin Corner. They would never be front and center.

Stanley, who had come to believe that Royal Crown was off the market because he never saw it anywhere, felt he had a good case. In 1994, a year in which the sales of Coca-Cola concentrate had never been higher, he filed a lawsuit against Coke, Pepsi, and both their respective bottlers, contending that they had hampered competition with their marketing agreements and caused damage to his clients, including Jimmy Carneline, Bruce Hackett, and the Dudleys.

The case was filed in state court in Daingerfield, a small Texas town bisected by freight-train tracks where another lawyer friend of Stanley's, Nelson Roach, had his practice. Roach was an imposing figure, six-foot-four with a loud laugh and a passion for riding his motorcycle across the Texas hills. He had made a specialty out of suing on antitrust claims against powerhouses like Microsoft, and now he took on Coca-Cola. He was not shy, and he enjoyed putting on a show. In the courtroom he would drop to his hands and knees while questioning a witness, trying to show the jury just how a person would have to shop if he or she wanted to find RC in a store where Coke or Pepsi had one of its marketing agreements in place.

The lawsuit, which alleged violations of Texas antitrust laws, took six years to resolve, a period of time in which Jimmy Carneline dropped out for health reasons, the charges against Pepsi were settled, and Coca-Cola Enterprises grew larger and larger. It continued to be the biggest Coke bottler in the world, its power centralized in Atlanta but its influence stretching from Los Angeles to Maine and across the Atlantic to Great Britain, France, Belgium, Luxembourg, and the Netherlands. It remained the prototype of what Coke wanted: a big bottling company, supremely dedicated to Coke's interests.

That bottling company was still a good idea, in Don Keough's opinion. And until the end of 1999, it was still run by Henry Schimberg, the master competitor brought into the company in 1991.

Schimberg insisted that a big bottler could be run along the lines of a small one with good teams of field people in place and a strong focus on a common message. The elimination of the small independent bottlers was no big deal to him. This was the modern era, and everybody in the Coca-Cola system was supposed to be working to increase shareholder value, no matter what. Size could guarantee effectiveness, he maintained. 'I expect all of our people to live in the marketplace,' Schimberg said at an industry conference early in 1999. 'That's the culture of this company.'

Since his arrival, Schimberg had emphasized that analysts who covered the stock should look at the company's annual cash operating profit growth. If cash operating profit grew by 10 to 15 percent, for example, that would be a reliable indicator of the bottler's success as a business. While bottling was heavy with expenditures – for factories, trucks to deliver the soft drinks, personnel, and equipment like vending machines – those were not supposed to be as important as cash operating profit. As the bottler expanded rapidly from 1995 to 1998, it became increasingly complicated to measure the performance year to year. Coached by Coke executives, stock analysts contented themselves with the cash operating profit number, also called EBITDA, a number that showed that the company was growing every year, even if profits were hard to come by.

'Coca-Cola was able to condition the financial community to value its bottlers on an EBITDA basis,' observed Andrew Conway, 'without any regard for returns on invested capital.'

Meanwhile, the nation's tastes had shifted, and Coca-Cola was no longer growing. Market share remained about the same, but other drinks – bottled water, lemonade, fruit drinks, herb-enhanced drinks, and iced tea and coffee – picked up followers who once might have been Coke drinkers. It was hard to say what caused this. Some believed tastes simply had changed, and now Coca-Cola and Pepsi-Cola were too sweet for many consumers. The fulfillment of labeling requirements made it absolutely clear that a twelve-ounce can of soda held not just brown liquid, but 120 calories – compared to zero for bottled water.

And the sodas themselves had changed as well. 'People will come up to me and say, "When I was little, I used to love these drinks, but they don't taste the same anymore,"' Jerry Dudley said. 'You know what? They're not the same. They used to be made with real sugar. We'd haul these big sacks of sugar up and dump them into the mix. Now it's high-fructose corn syrup.' One bottler in Dublin, Texas, continued to make Dr Pepper with cane sugar. 'People drive in for miles,' Leslie Dudley said.

In meetings, Coke executives exhorted Coca-Cola Enterprises executives to develop programs that would 'drive Coca-Cola volume'. For at the heart of every business move the company made was the realization that Coca-Cola was no longer everyone's drink of choice.

Inside Coke, a plan had been created that would improve the odds. It was like a game of poker, based on the immense national renown of Coca-Cola. With that single brand, Coke was like the dealer, holding all the aces.

The plan was not unlike the exclusive contracts that Coke had signed with airlines, baseball stadiums, movie theater chains, and hotels. Those contracts promised that only Coke products would be served, and often gave signing bonuses to organizations that agreed to them.

Here the doctrine attached itself to supermarkets and

convenience stores – places where people shopped for the basic elements of survival. Supermarkets had a running love-hate relationship with Coke and Pepsi as it was. They rarely made money on the prices they had to charge through most of the 1990s – price wars between the two, as well as the emergence of good-tasting store brands, or generics – had pushed the price of Coke and Pepsi down. Two-liter bottles of either brand typically sold for sixty-nine or seventy-nine cents 'on special' in many areas; over time, the price of a grocery-store Coke or Pepsi had fallen below its 1970 levels, adjusted for inflation.

Still, the store owners always had both Coke *and* Pepsi, because that got people to come in and created the potential for them to buy other things as well – things that weren't on special every other day. The notion of confining themselves to one brand ran counter to most store owners' business sense. They ran special ads touting the low price on Coke one week, Pepsi the next; the drinks were known as 'loss leaders' that, though not profitable themselves, got people in the door.

Sometime around 1990, Coke executives decided to promote a series of programs that would exclude competing brands, gambling that the power of the Coca-Cola brand would persuade store owners to go along. They knew that people didn't love cola as much as they used to. Part of the reason was health concerns: all that sugar and caffeine. And part was that by the early nineties there were so many other choices for the thirsty that colas could be overlooked.

Coke began to propose marketing agreements to stores that were almost laughably restrictive in their language. A store that wanted to sell Coca-Cola could not do so unless it agreed to certain terms, ranging from granting Coke the exclusive right to hang signs in the store (meaning no one else could put up a sign promoting or even mentioning any other kind of soft drink) to setting proportions for vending machines (in one agreement, Coke had to have two vending machines for every machine set up by a rival company). A store had to grant 60, 70, 80 percent of its shelf space to Coke products, and deals were made for 'doors' – the glass-fronted refrigerator cases, which Coke claimed almost in their entirety. Coke would ask for six of the store's eight doors, or the middle third of all the doors, and usually the company got what it wanted.

Why would store owners agree to these kinds of arrangements? Some of them received cash signing bonuses. Others got rebates on the price per case of Coke and other Coke products. And in many instances they were afraid – either of having no Coke to sell (it was, after all, still the nation's top-selling soft drink) or of having to sell it for more than their nearby competitors, which would jeopardize their business if they were small and frustrate their shareholders if they were large.

As more Coca-Cola bottlers were bought up by Coca-Cola Enterprises, Dr Pepper, the spicy cherry drink owned by Cadbury Schweppes, became part of the equation in places like Texas, Arkansas, and Louisiana. Many of those independent Coke bottlers had agreements to package and sell Dr Pepper as well. And as their franchises passed into the hands of Coca-Cola Enterprises, the bottler realized that in some areas it now controlled two of the top-selling sodas. It could demand even more concessions from its customers.

Some of the calendar marketing agreements were truly excessive. 'Coca-Cola products will occupy a minimum of 100 percent of total soft-drink space,' read one, signed between Coca-Cola Enterprises and an Arkansas drugstore chain, USA Drug, in 1998. In north Texas, the program was known as Operation RED, with RED being shorthand for 'Retail Execution to Drive Volume'. The objective was to increase volume and profits for store owners, according to the documents. But it appeared just as likely, if not more so, to increase volume and profits for Coca-Cola and its sprawling bottler. Unlike supermarkets, convenience stores were not gripped by price wars. And since the sodas were sold cold, they commanded a higher price than warm ones from a supermarket's shelf would. The country's 120,000 convenience stores are 'a beverage laboratory', said Lindsay Hutter, a spokeswoman for the National Association of Convenience Stores. And to Coke they were also vending machines in giant, walk-in format. Every soda sold in a convenience store, at ninety-nine cents to $1.09 for a twenty-ounce bottle, carried a hefty profit for Coke. Texas was the national leader in convenience stores, with 12,500 to California's 9,000. Thus Texas became a prime battleground for Coke's plan to capture as much of the convenience store and supermarket soft-drink business as possible.

This was what the Dudleys in Paris, Jimmy Carneline in Louisiana, and Bruce Hackett in Arkansas each discovered separately, inside convenience stores and supermarkets, and that discovery formed the basis of the lawsuit they filed in 1994.

Coke executives said they were merely asking for the same kinds of things everyone else wanted. 'We have always tried to conduct our business operations with the highest integrity and compliance with all laws and regulations,' a spokeswoman for Coca-Cola Enterprises, Laura Asman, said.

Some felt the trail of documents and testimony might suggest otherwise. When the lawsuit finally came to trial, Tom Stanley put Bruce Hackett on the stand to describe how, when he worked for Ouachita Coca-Cola, he was specifically told not to demand such exclusive terms. And Stanley quizzed a Coca-Cola Enterprises employee named Scott Holloway to find out why the company had paid a $2-million signing bonus to the Brookshire's supermarket chain. 'Was it so CCE could promote the products the way CCE wanted to promote them?' Stanley asked.

'Yes,' Holloway replied.

Coke saw that as logical. 'We are spending a lot of money with retailers on marketing,' declared Polly Howes, another spokeswoman, 'and it doesn't make a whole lot of sense to provide retailers with money to promote our products if, when you go into the store, it doesn't look like you are the featured product.' Promoting many different products, from different companies, was not a good idea, she added: 'It sort of devalues the category.'

It was not just happening in Texas, Louisiana, and Arkansas. In Tucson, a longtime independent bottler named George Kalil complained that his business was being eroded by agreements that Coke had arranged with various stores in the area.

Kalil is a towering figure in the beverage world, with a huge form that tapers as it nears his gleaming bald head. He moves slowly and speaks slowly, but there is nothing sluggish about his opinions when it comes to the soft-drink industry.

For years Kalil had felt manipulated by local Coke practices, including something called the 'clean agreement', in which he was prevented from advertising his products. 'They would go to a grocer in Phoenix and tell him that if he did not run a Kalil Bottling ad for RC and 7UP during the weeks the Coke ad was running, they'd give him an extra 40 cents back per case,' he said. Kalil also sells Sunkist orange soda, A&W root beer (both made by Cadbury Schweppes), and Welch's grape soda. All three are leaders in their categories in Arizona, but Coke found a way to foil that, he said.

'They went to convenience stores and said, "If you want our best package, we want all of those businesses,"' Kalil said. To sell Coke, in other words, a store had to sell Barq's root beer, Minute Maid orange soda, and other flavors that Coke makes. And competing flavors couldn't be on the shelves in some instances. The company got space this way for POWERade, its struggling rival to Gatorade, at the expense of Gatorade, the nation's top-selling sports drink. 'They are taking a good product and tying a dog product onto it,' Kalil said, 'tying everything together.'

In the summer of 2000, the lawsuit brought by the Royal Crown bottlers and distributors in Texas came to trial. The jury returned a guilty verdict against Coke and its bottler for breaking state antitrust laws through the terms of their marketing agreements and ordered them to pay $15.6 million in damages and fines. Coke filed an appeal; the verdict would stand.

Throughout the trial, the Dudleys lived in their mobile home, parking it at a state park in Daingerfield. They sat in the courtroom all day long, Monday through Friday, and sped home to Paris as soon as the proceedings adjourned for the weekend. 'We'd come home and work at the plant until Sunday afternoon,' Leslie Dudley recalled. 'Then we'd wash clothes and go back. We did this for eight weeks. It was something we believed in.'

Chapter Thirteen

Wonderful World

COCA-COLA WAS THE centerpiece of the Coke empire, but by the summer of 1998 Doug Ivester was trying to introduce a product most alien to traditional thinking at Coke. That product was plain water.

Bottled water was the fastest-growing segment of the beverage business, and companies that owned a lot of water brands were having a field day. Pepsi had taken the dare, too, and started a brand called Aquafina that was a deliberate departure from the typical Alpine-spring water label. Instead, Pepsi had decided to take ordinary tap water and purify it in its bottling plants. The raw material was about as cheap as any could be, and the Pepsi bottlers were ecstatic. They had seen how many women reached for the bottled water instead of the diet drinks, and how they chose water for their children instead of cola. They knew it was the right move.

At Coke, however, Ivester struggled with the notion. He wanted to find a way to sell bottled water that would not alter Coke's relationship with its bottlers as a seller of concentrate. Coca-Cola Enterprises, seeing the potential in sales of bottled water, entered into agreements to distribute Naya, from a company that bottled spring water in Canada, as well as Evian, which collected water from Evian-les-Bains in the French Alps.

Ivester wanted to do bottled water his way. Finally, in early 1999, he got his arms around it. Bottlers would filter ordinary municipal water in their plants, just as their counterparts at Pepsi were doing. But it had to have something else – something only the Coca-Cola Company could provide. Ivester decided that a dose of mineral salts, including potassium chloride, had to be added to the water. The minerals amounted to a concentrate that the bottlers would have to buy from Coke. There. He had done it. In the spring of that year, Coke bottlers began selling Dasani.

It was an unusual concession. Within the Coca-Cola Company, the hardest push was still on selling the flagship soft drink, Coca-Cola. With the highest margins of any product the company made, Coke really was it. Inside the company a fresh struggle developed, between those who thought Coke needed to diversify into other kinds of drinks and those for whom Coca-Cola was, as Don Keough liked to say, 'the alpha and the omega'.

Even before he settled the water project, Ivester had his hands full. By late August 1998, Pepsi was complaining endlessly to French officials about the Orangina deal. At the same time, a massive disappointment was unfolding in the former Soviet Union, where, a decade before, Goizueta had directed a huge buildup of plants and fleets to serve what he was sure would be one of Coke's biggest markets. Coke had waited a very long time to have a piece of that Russian soft-drink business, and when the time arrived the pent-up energy and enthusiasm had been poured into cities like Moscow and St. Petersburg, with heavy investment to build plants and buy up bottlers. There had been stellar results: By 1997 Coke outsold Pepsi by a ratio of two to one. It was yet another humiliating defeat for Pepsi, and one more way for Coke to put Pepsi in its place – far, far behind the Coca-Cola Company.

But as the ruble collapsed at the end of August, Ivester had to recognize that Coke had a problem. A lot of the machinery lay idle; supply had always exceeded demand, but now most of the demand that had been there dried up. People who felt suddenly poorer didn't want to spend money on expensive American soft drinks. They dropped other products, too, like American cigarettes, and generally retreated as consumers of nonessential items.

With these fires burning, Ivester saw that for the first time in quite a while, Coke would not meet its volume targets for the quarter. He knew he would have to manage this smoothly and without appearing the least bit flustered. He was the heir to Goizueta, and what would Goizueta do? He, Doug Ivester, would do the same thing. There was disappointment coming, but he would not disappoint. He would find a way to manage it.

In early September, he called a meeting of all the Wall Street analysts who covered Coke in New York. At the gathering, held in the aerie of the Coca-Cola Building on Fifth Avenue, Ivester informed Andrew Conway, Jennifer Solomon, Emanuel Goldman, and the others whose jobs required them to follow the trajectory of Coke that the company, hurt by an unexpected decline in its Russian business, would not meet its earnings and volume goals for the third quarter.

Such an event had not happened in years. The analysts were surprised but somewhat cavalier. Lots of companies had taken a bath in Russia, recently and unexpectedly. R.J. Reynolds, the second-biggest cigarette maker in the world, was one of them, and so was Long-Term Capital Management, the legendary hedge fund that had bet big on the ruble and lost. The Russian economy, propped on too much debt, caved in when bondholders decided to get out. Coke's prospects dimmed, and so did those of Reynolds. Long-Term Capital would have imploded were it not for the intervention of several major lenders, including the Federal Reserve Bank of New York, which decided it had too much to lose. Coke didn't have those kinds of friends.

Still, the company was large, complex, and operating in more than two hundred countries around the world. A punch to the gut in Russia, in theory, could be offset by a surge in business from somewhere else.

Yet as he scanned the Coca-Cola horizon, Ivester couldn't help but notice pockets of trouble almost everywhere. Indonesia was in recession. Japan was in a depression. Business in Europe was off, because of bad weather and nervousness over the Russian situation. The former Yugoslavia was in pieces and at war. Latin America had its own set of crises. India was a hodgepodge of bottlers, still trying to sort out the market. China, the final great hope of the Coca-Cola Company, was doing fine; but compared with the other, better-developed markets around the globe, China's volume was still very small. Too small to make enough of a difference. Like Africa, China had lots of people, but not enough of them spent enough of their money on soft drinks. Not yet.

But wait. There were still things an executive like Ivester could pull out of his pocket, things that could turn the business around. Coke had a long and checkered relationship with Cadbury

Schweppes, the London-based maker of soft drinks like Schweppes and Canada Dry ginger ale, tonic water, and other mixers, as well as Dr Pepper and 7UP. In the South, where Coca-Cola and Pepsi-Cola had such strongholds, Dr Pepper was one of the few other drinks that challenged them. It was officially a spicy cherry drink, but to consumers it fell pleasantly between a cola and a fruit-flavored drink. Coke had wanted Dr Pepper for years. In the 1980s it had tried to buy it, only to have the notion rejected by the Federal Trade Commission, an agency long suspicious of the soft-drink giant. The commission had ruled that buying Dr Pepper would give Coke too large a share of the market. Wherever possible, Coke would try to put Dr Pepper into its system by urging Coca-Cola Enterprises to buy local Coke bottlers that also handled Dr Pepper. It was the best way to capitalize on another company's brand if the law stood in the way of owning it.

Cadbury Schweppes, meanwhile, was a company with a split personality. The Cadbury side made candy: chocolate bars, fruit gums, licorice, and other sweets that sold well all over the world. The Schweppes side was iconic, begun by Jacob Schweppe, the entrepreneur who was among the first to commercially produce artificially carbonated water in the eighteenth century, but it was not growing vigorously. Schweppes brands continuously finished third or worse to Coke and Pepsi almost everywhere in the world. In the United States, they lived a dangerous life, distributed by both Coke and Pepsi bottlers as well as independent bottlers in parts of the country. They needed Coke and Pepsi, but they also resented them in a kind of soft-drink version of the Stockholm syndrome.

Maybe the time had come for Cadbury Schweppes to rethink its future. Ivester had planted the seed in meetings held months earlier. He summoned John Sunderland, the chief executive of Cadbury Schweppes, a man who was the British incarnation of Ivester in his quest to build shareholder value. Sunderland was a Thatcher disciple who detested the sloth that characterized certain Englishmen's attitudes toward work. Like Ivester and Goizueta, he believed that business had to be waged in the interests of the shareholders. He espoused concepts like efficiency and maximizing return on investment. He was not averse to taking chances in business, but they had to be calculated ones. He urged his managers

to take risks, too, and to make the point at a meeting in the Alps
one day, he strapped on paragliding gear. Mortally afraid of flying,
he leaped from a craggy mountainside, gliding to a perfect landing
on the grass far below. He said later that he would never do it again.

Sunderland had dealt with Coke extensively. In 1987, the two
companies had formed a joint bottling venture, which they called
Coca-Cola Cadbury Schweppes Bottling. True to its pattern with
other big bottlers, Coke kept a 49 percent interest in the company.
Cadbury held the rest. The arrangement meant that Sunderland
had to rupture Cadbury's longtime ties to Pepsi, bringing to a halt
a thirty-two-year relationship.

His company soon found itself confronting immense and endless
tension with its new partner. Coke, the minority owner, kept
pushing for volume at all costs; at board meetings, the directors
who represented Cadbury refused, arguing that soft drinks should
be sold only if they were profitable. It was a classic confrontation,
the divided soul of the soft-drink business, and neither side wanted
to give in.

The Coca-Cola Company, led by Goizueta as the joint venture
began, had already embarked on a plan of attack against its
competitors that called for it to be the largest player in every
country, in every market, and in every venue. That involved
increasing volume, so that Coke sold more of its concentrate and
could meet its growth projections. Everywhere, in all kinds of
places, Coke salesmen argued with store managers about how
many feet of every shelf they were entitled to. They practiced a
unique logic, insisting that if they had a special one week, the soda
they sold through the special should be counted when determining
what their future allotments of shelf space should be. In most
grocery stores, shelf space alternates between competing companies
week by week. But Coke didn't want to put up with that. It
wanted shoppers to see an aisle dominated by its two-liter bottles
and its twelve-packs of cans as far as the eye could see. The process
was so wearying that some store managers gave up and let Coke
have its way.

The strategy may have put more Coke on display, but it also
drove down prices on those bottles and cans. Supermarkets didn't
mind holding a special on Coke every week or so, but the bottlers

who collected diminishing amounts for their products certainly did. The long-range plan called for the volume and the low pricing to weed out most competitors, which would allow Coke to raise prices eventually – by as much as it wanted. But Coke's bottlers, by the late 1990s, were protesting loud and hard. They needed to make more money.

This wasn't working for them, the bottlers informed Coke. It was not just the small bottlers who protested. It was also Coca-Cola Enterprises.

The price of a Coca-Cola two-liter bottle had stayed below a dollar for the better part of two decades. When prices should have gone up and stayed up, in the late 1980s, the plan to build volume was in full swing, and it prevented the price rise. The trend didn't change, and by the fall of 1997 bottlers everywhere were in full howl. None howled louder than Summerfield Johnston, the chairman of Coca-Cola Enterprises, who had signed on for the Coke program by agreeing to the new contract twenty years earlier but now, *now,* just wished he had left well enough alone. His net worth had soared with the price of Coca-Cola Enterprises stock. But he, like most bottlers, worried that without price increases, not one of them was going to survive.

Meanwhile, Ivester had another plan that would help Summerfield and other bottlers whose equipment lay unused or underused all over the world. He wanted to buy the Cadbury Schweppes brands in most countries.

He was confident that this deal would be a natural fit. Inside Cadbury, Sunderland had already reached the conclusion that his company would be better off buying up competitors in the highly fragmented worldwide candy and chocolate business than it would be battling Coke and Pepsi in the soft-drink arena. While there was nostalgia involved in the soft-drink brands, Cadbury executives had to keep shareholder interests in mind. They saw more growth in becoming a pure candy empire, and they needed cash to do it. So they approached both Coke and Pepsi and offered to sell their brands, everything outside the United States.

Cadbury's moment of truth had come earlier in 1998. It had come in Morocco, one of the few African countries where Cadbury Schweppes did well with its soft drinks compared with

Coke. Unexpectedly, Cadbury's London headquarters received word that the longtime bottler in Morocco would be working with Coke from then on. It was a major setback, and it was, as one longtime observer of both companies said, 'an unbridled exercise of dominant power'. At Cadbury, management felt there was nothing it could do. Coke had done this and was sure to do it again. It was time to get out of the soft-drink business.

Cadbury offered its brands around. Pepsi was interested in only a few pieces of the business, but Coke wanted the whole show. Cadbury was eager to shed everything except its hugely lucrative United States business, where it sold Dr Pepper and 7UP. Coke would not be able to buy that anyway because of antitrust rules.

Coke and Cadbury held their talks and settled on a price. And at an early-morning meeting in New York in December, where he was forced to announce more bad news about Coke's volume growth, Ivester also triumphantly announced that Coke would spend $1.8 billion to buy Cadbury's brands everywhere except the United States, France, and South Africa. The move would add business for the bottlers in much of the world, including the United Kingdom. While he also revealed that Coke's volume and earnings growth were well off their targets, for the second quarter in a row, analysts and others paid more attention to the Cadbury acquisition, the largest Coke had ever made.

It was a brilliant plan. It promised to give international bottlers, including Coca-Cola Enterprises, more products to sell. It would improve returns on capital for the bottlers by increasing the demand on their factories with these additional brands. Coke would pick up additional market share with all of the former Cadbury products and would collect more money from syrup sales on those products as well. Win–win, the analysts said.

There was just one small problem. And it radiated from a point about thirty miles north of the Coca-Cola Building where Ivester made the announcement – at PepsiCo headquarters.

Everything that Orangina had represented, in terms of Coke's assault on the rest of the soft-drink business, was magnified in the Cadbury deal. At least that was what Pepsi lawyer Bob Biggart thought. He convinced Rob Sharpe that this was the case, and they took their beliefs to Roger Enrico. Enrico, already pleased with the results from their Orangina campaign, gave them permission to wage the same battle with the European Union.

Again, Pepsi lawyers argued politely to all who would listen that Coke was a threat not just to Pepsi but to all competitors, present and future, if it was permitted to buy these brands. 'This is not about the cola wars,' they would insist. 'This is about freedom.'

The words rang true with at least one man, Karel van Miert, the head of the European Community's competiton council. And when the plan was announced, he was enraged that Coke had not filed any kind of notice with the commission – something it was required to do, Van Miert said, though Coke executives would say they thought they did not have to. To them, their market was still below the threshold required for filing, though they calculated their business in terms of concentrate sales, while the European officials tended to include bottling as well.

Either way, Coke soon had a very large problem on its hands. Van Miert went to reporters, scolding Coke for its arrogance. 'They thought they could pull the wool over our eyes,' he huffed. 'Coca-Cola should learn to respect the rules like everybody else.'

Newspapers across Europe vilified the company for believing it would be able to run roughshod over the European Community regulations.

Now Ivester, his plans stalled, had to be a little worried. From New York, there was a drumbeat of worry, too. Don Keough, watching from his perch at Allen & Company, saw the latest publicity about Coke as a bad thing for the company.

Chapter Fourteen

Zeus Works for Pepsi

KEOUGH TOLD HIMSELF HE wasn't going to get involved. Sure, he had some concerns about what he saw happening in Atlanta. He'd had them for years. Sure, he'd been hearing from bottlers. But he didn't want to call Ivester. He preferred to stay out of it, he told everyone.

Keough had long had his doubts about Ivester's qualifications when it came to leading a massive corporation like Coke. Now, with the cracks in the façade from Orangina, from the publicity about the system's accounting issues and the rumbling from the European Union, he worried that Coke might be edging toward real trouble. Those cracks imperiled the image of the company he had worked so hard to create. In spite of himself, he thought it might be a good idea if he and Ivester talked. He decided to invite the younger man to lunch.

Keough was not the only person who sensed that Europe might be difficult for Ivester. People from countries with old, polished civilizations might be put off by Ivester's brusque, all-business approach to life, and Keough had seen that before. He had been instrumental in assigning Ivester to run the European division back in 1989, and he had seen what could happen when the tightly focused business culture that Ivester embodied ran up against the culture of monarchs, dynasties, and the three-hour lunch.

Ivester saw the Cadbury Schweppes brands as the answer to a number of issues facing Coke. There was a willing seller and a willing buyer. It all seemed ideal.

Then the fireworks began.

Coke had not submitted the plan to the European Union because, it reasoned, without factoring in the bottling, the company had a less-than-dominant share of the total beverage market. *We don't sell*

Coca-Cola; our business is the concentrate. Van Miert, Belgian, disagreed and ordered Coke to submit its deal for review at once.

Van Miert was a fierce patriot, a Belgian first but a European second, who appeared to some to resent the buying and selling of European companies by larger American firms. Within Europe there were strong currents of anti-American fervor, intensified by issues like the conversion of local currencies to the Euro, the spreading consolidation of small companies like department stores and packaged-food makers, and other signs of high-speed modernization. Van Miert's opinions were valued by many regulators in the individual countries of the European Union, though his power did not extend to decisions like the French regulators' determination on Orangina. He reflected a trend of the times, a trend that worked against American companies like Coca-Cola.

Ivester was surprised at the European Union's reaction. In his opinion, Coke had abided by its laws. He had had Coke's lawyers read all the relevant laws, and he was sure the company had met its obligations. He obediently set the application in motion, and he and the lawyers waited for the approval they were sure would come.

Rob Sharpe had been busy, too. Back in Purchase, New York, he and Biggart had been frantically compiling studies and market-share analyses into a thick black binder. They distributed copies of their data to anyone with even a remote connection to the regulatory hearings in Europe: first in France, for the Orangina case, and then in Brussels, where the European Union had its headquarters.

Biggart began circulating documents and charts to lawyers involved with the hearings. Maybe Coke wasn't concerned about what Pepsi was doing. Maybe Coke executives were simply following the strategy they laid out behind closed doors in Atlanta. But Pepsi had a plan: to be a kind of Cassandra of the soft-drink industry, alerting the rest of the world to the reasons they needed to be concerned about Coke.

Sharpe and Biggart organized teams of lawyers in many of the two hundred countries where the Coke-Cadbury deal was to take effect. They directed them – politely, of course, and without appearing to care too much about Pepsi – to meet with regulators to inform them that Coke's overwhelming dominance of the soft-drink market was not going to be good for anyone.

'We went in and said, this is about what is fair in the market-place,' one lawyer said. 'This is not about just giving access to us, but to everybody.'

In Australia, the national competition authority voted to reject the deal, saying Coke would end up with too much of the soft-drink market. In Mexico, the competition council voted unanimously against Coke's acquisition of Cadbury, saying it would concentrate too much power in one company's hands. In Canada, the deal ran aground for the same reason. And in the European Union, Pepsi scored its clearest triumph. There was no final vote, only ominous warnings from Van Miert and others about the deep unlikely prospects of the deal's winning their approval.

Ivester decided to cut Coke's losses. The deal would be recast, he announced in the middle of April, to eliminate most of the countries in the European Union. The price would shrink to about $1 billion, and while Coke was disappointed not to have the whole package, it was still much of what the company had been after. Coke would still sell Dr Pepper in much of the world, along with brands like Canada Dry and Schweppes. The deal would add, as Ivester had always hoped, to the portfolios of bottling companies all over the planet, extending Coke's influence in all sorts of markets.

In New York, however, Don Keough seethed. What had gone on? Why hadn't the Coca-Cola Company been able to push its agenda through? Where were Coke's men on the ground through all of this, the ones who went to cocktail parties with the members of the regulatory agencies and invited them to play golf and saw them on the ski slopes?

There were still just under thirty thousand people working for the Coca-Cola Company all over the world. But they tended to defer to Doug Ivester, who liked to be in charge.

He was merely following the example of Coke's other leaders, men like Asa Candler, Robert Woodruff, and Roberto Goizueta. Ivester wanted to do things himself. He logged thousands of miles in the corporate jets, visiting markets from Asia to Africa and personally overseeing even small moves. 'He believed he could do everything better than anyone else,' said a former PepsiCo executive. He was in more countries than the pope or the president. He seemed to be everywhere.

Wherever he was, Ivester could monitor the movements of various Coke markets on his computer, which tapped into an enormous database of sales – when someone bought a Coke, and where, and for how much – that was constantly updated. He loved e-mail, interrupting his own conversations sometimes so he could read his new messages. Even the most senior executives, the ring of presidents just below him on the corporate ladder, had to check in with Ivester constantly; three or four e-mails a day on various issues, even if the other executives were right down the hall in Atlanta, was the rule. If they were on the road, he wanted to hear from them six times a day. They heard from him, if he didn't get those messages as often as he liked.

He believed he was in close and constant touch with the world of Coca-Cola. But he would learn that, as thorough as his planning was, sometimes a Coca-Cola bottle could contain surprises.

By springtime of 1999, only a year and a half after he took over from Goizueta, Ivester was diligently trying to stem problems on five continents. Emanuel Goldman, the analyst for ING Barings, would put it more graphically. 'It's as if Zeus is hurling thunderbolts at Coke,' he said, 'and Zeus works for Pepsi.'

Only Africa, where Carl Ware was in charge, beamed like any kind of bright light for Coke, except that sales were turning sluggish in South Africa, one of the company's ten biggest markets. The rate of growth in Africa outpaced that in Asia for the first part of 1999, something that had not happened before.

Ivester busied himself with solving this multitude of problems. Doug Daft, the senior vice president in charge of Asia, scheduled frequent meetings to update him on the region's progress, and Ivester suggested various techniques, such as selling Coke in Indonesia in smaller bottles to keep it affordable despite the economy. The sun would come out; he was confident of that. He would have to work hard, though, to make sure it did. He busied himself at his desk, the e-mail messages chiming as they arrived at the rate of one or two every minute.

And then came a blow that he had not been expecting. Linda Ingram, along with three other employees, filed a lawsuit in federal court in Atlanta. Together they accused the Coca-Cola Company of systematically discriminating against them because of the color of their skin.

Cyrus Mehri had organized everything about the lawsuit, from the allegations to its timing. He approached a *New York Times* reporter in the paper's Washington bureau, Steven Holmes, and offered to give him the story a day ahead of all the other news organizations, meaning the *Times* would be able to print it before any competitors could. Holmes read the documents, interviewed Mehri, and wrote his story. It appeared in the national news section on April 23, 1999.

Racial discrimination lawsuits are filed all the time, against all sorts of companies. But this one was directed at a company with a reputation for supporting minority causes through the years. Its product amounted to refreshment – a moment of pleasure – with no downside as far as anyone knew. Besides that, it was a southern company, and the lawsuit served to undermine all those claims of southern progress when it came to race relations. It had all the ingredients of a great story.

The following morning, *The Wall Street Journal, The Atlanta Journal-Constitution, USA Today,* and a host of other newspapers leaped on the story. The allegations of Linda Ingram, Motisola Abdallah, Gregory Clark, and Kimberly Orton flashed around the world. For a generation, Coke had worked to improve its image among members of the black community. Faced with Ingram's accusations, the company tried to hold that ground.

Ivester remained calm. The allegations were incorrect, he said, and time would prove that Coke had done nothing wrong. From the twenty-fifth floor, he vowed to fight the lawsuit. There would be no settling these claims. He had the company's honor, and its image, to protect. There were few things worse for any company in the late 1990s, trying to peddle its products to people of every race and creed all over the world, than to be accused of discrimination.

He ordered up an e-mail, his favored form of mass communication, to be sent to every Coke employee in the nation. In it, he assured them that the lawsuit contained 'significant errors of fact', and he encouraged them to come to him with any problems of their own. 'Our company has always endeavored to treat our customers, our consumers, our bottlers and, perhaps most importantly, our employees with fairness, respect and dignity,' his e-mail said. 'It is because of that background that the lawsuit is so troubling to me.'

A month later he sent out another communiqué, this one announcing that he had formed a special Diversity Council that would report to him on matters like the kind that had spawned the lawsuit. He also positioned himself as the channel through which any needed changes would come. 'I will personally increase my own efforts to open the lines of communication with all constituencies,' he wrote on May 25. 'I will hold regularly scheduled meetings with small groups of associates to listen to their thoughts, concerns and opinions. These meetings will take place over the weeks and months ahead, and will help us determine what actions are appropriate for us to achieve our goals.' To help him, he added, he was forming this Diversity Council. It would be led by two of his trusted lieutenants. One was Jack Stahl, the senior vice president for North America, who was busily trying to restart sales in the United States and Canada. The other was Carl Ware.

Careers had been derailed at Coke over smaller matters. Ivester must have realized the stakes. But he was convinced that the lawsuit was winnable for Coke. There was no overt or intentional racial discrimination at the company, he believed, and anyone who said there was was just plain wrong. People were not held back because of their color. They were evaluated on the basis of their performance, and not always fired if they failed. 'It's genteel,' Donald McHenry explained later. 'It's a they-don't-want-anybody-to-go-away-mad kind of thing.' That's the way it was. That was the company Ivester knew. Those were the facts.

Ivester firmly believed that Coke would emerge from the lawsuit unscathed. 'The Coca-Cola company did not spring into full-blown greatness overnight,' he told Coke workers sprinkled from Oregon to Maine in his May 25 memo. 'It did thousands of little things well, and those thousands of little things over many years – taken together – created greatness.'

Meanwhile, he ordered the company's lawyers, led by Joseph Gladden, the general counsel, to mount a tenacious defense. They created a war room where employees sifted through thousands of human resources documents. Trolleys filled with cartons of records came and went from the war room all day long. No one could get inside without a special security badge.

But Mehri, too, had a lot on the line. He had contacted half a dozen law firms on the East Coast, trying unsuccessfully to find someone to partner with so that he would not have to oversee everything from Washington. Every single firm turned him down. He knew then that he would have to see the lawsuit through all by himself. So he took out a seven-figure loan to keep the office running and prepared himself for a long, hard, and lonely fight.

Within Coke, reaction to the lawsuit ranged from disbelief to silent cheers. One of the sympathizers was Larry Jones, a part-time minister who joined Coke in 1985, a few days before the introduction of New Coke. Jones worked in the benefits office and knew well how Coke's wealth was spread around. He had noticed, for example, that when he organized seminars for people receiving stock options – and those seminars were standing room only – there were almost no black faces in the crowd. 'You could count them on one hand,' he said. He had noticed, too, how many of his black friends complained that their performance evaluations had been unfair or found out that they were earning less than whites in their department who had the same kind of job and sometimes less experience.

Jones had believed that Coke had a problem for a long time. He was a company man, so he decided to address it through company channels. He was such a company man that he scolded his children if he caught them drinking anything that wasn't a Coke product. He did not know, at that time, about the report Carl Ware had submitted in 1995. He plugged away at his job, still hearing complaints from other blacks. Then, on a bright spring day in 1999, there came Linda Ingram and her lawsuit. Jones would have to keep an eye on this.

The lawsuit also gave Jesse Jackson a new reason to include the Coca-Cola Company in his life. Since his boycott of Coke products in 1981, Jackson had been busy. He had twice run for president, and while his campaign did not get him the Democratic party's nomination, he had succeeded in getting some of his ideas included in the platform. He had started new nonprofit organizations, often with financial support from Coke and other companies, and he maintained ties with civil rights leaders around the country from his headquarters in Chicago.

Because of his relationship with Coke, he found himself in an unusual spot with the lawsuit. The company had been his benefactor for nearly two decades, ever since the unpleasantness between them ended. Now, though, there were allegations of a most serious kind coming out of the building. What should he do – for the workers at Coke, for the Coca-Cola Company, and for himself?

He had to navigate this one carefully. He was able to activate some of his friends in the civil rights movement in Atlanta, encouraging them to praise Coke's past record while not saying anything that committed them in any way about Coke in the present. Then he made a move that few others immersed in the civil rights cause could have conceived and carried out. He arranged an encounter behind the scenes, one that would have a profound effect on Cyrus Mehri as the case wound its way through the courts.

Jackson was friendly with a personal-injury lawyer from Stuart, Florida, named Willie Gary. A prosperous, well-known black litigator, Gary had come up from nothing, not unlike Doug Ivester, whom he had met earlier in the year when both were receiving awards from the Horatio Alger Society in Washington, a group dedicated to the idea that anyone can make it in America as long as he or she is willing to work hard. The group holds a lavish dinner once a year in Washington, honoring a dozen people, male and female, black and white, many of them from the business world. Along with the dinner there is a weekend retreat for the honorees and their spouses, at which they visit with one another and deliver inspirational remarks to high school students who are struggling to make something of themselves.

In 1999, both Doug Ivester and Willie Gary were millionaires many times over, and both of them had been selected to receive the Horatio Alger Award. For Ivester, who spent weeks preparing an essay about his origins and his philosophy of life, this was a highly emotional moment, one that he could only have dreamed about as a boy. His father and mother, Buck and Ada Mae, attended the awards banquet, which included a video of all the winners, their baby pictures showcased along with their later accomplishments. One person who was there remembers tears springing to Ivester's eyes as Buck threw an arm across his shoulders and told him, 'Son, I am proud of you.'

Gary took the award more or less in stride. He had built himself a law business that turned rivals pea green with envy and he relentlessly advertised how successful he was. His headquarters was a waterfront complex on Florida's Atlantic Coast, where his cars – among them a Mercedes, a Bentley, a Rolls-Royce, and a limousine with tinted windows – were usually parked out front. Inside he had decorated the place with everything that he believed an accomplished lawyer ought to have, from an elaborately carved working fireplace in his office to a mahogany-paneled jury room where his witnesses could prepare both to give evidence and for the possibility of a harsh cross-examination.

Prospective clients received a kit prepared by a public relations firm, detailing Gary's track record, which included photographs, reprints of newspaper articles, and a color video that showed him bounding into a room while the theme song from the movie *Rocky* throbbed in the background. The video not only included a tour of his office but also made its way through the seventeen-bedroom house that he lived in, built with some of the money he took home from his trials. Then there was the Willie Gary airplane, *Wings of Justice*. At first it was a Gulfstream with gold-plated hardware in the bathrooms. Then Gary replaced it with a customized Boeing 737 that had equally elegant hardware and two galleys. He used the planes to get himself all over the country in time to deliver the kinds of stirring and highly emotional closing arguments for which he was famous.

His biggest triumph, by the time he won the Horatio Alger Award, was a multimillion-dollar award to the owner of a Mississippi funeral home who sold his business to the Loewen Group, a fast-growing empire of funeral homes, and then objected to the way Loewen tried to capture other businesses from him afterward. Though the award was eventually reduced, it remained the largest in Mississippi history and helped turn the national spotlight on Gary.

He was riding high in 1999. His penniless upbringing with half a dozen brothers and sisters, the days when he walked to school without shoes because he owned none, the panic over not having enough money to pay for college – all of those things had been reduced to exceedingly marketable memories. He was reaching beyond a life in the law now. He invested in a cable company that he named Major Broadcasting, hoping to create his version of the Disney Channel for black audiences, where all the programming would be wholesome and family-friendly or focused around sports. He made himself a talk-show host and began seeking advertisers, as any self-respecting cable executive would do.

His history with Jesse Jackson stretched back to those misty days when he had had nothing. Gary was the son of a migrant worker who picked beans, melons, and other crops in an arc that started in Florida and made its way up into the Deep South year by year, following the harvest. His schooling was haphazard, but he turned out to be a talented football player and he talked his way, more or less, onto the team at Shaw University in Raleigh, North Carolina, after losing a scholarship at another college.

Sometime during those years he met Jackson's wife, who grew up in the same area, and they remained friendly. As Jackson, the self-appointed bearer of the civil rights agenda begun by Martin Luther King, Jr., ascended in the American scene, he often heard from Willie Gary. They were friends, and they liked to help each other out. When Jackson learned of the racial-discrimination lawsuit that had been filed against Coke, he arranged for Willie Gary to speak with Doug Ivester.

They got together again in early 2000, at a moment when the lawsuit still simmered but had ceased to be front-page news. Ivester had been dispatched to a dinner in New York, held to mark the anniversary of Jackson's Wall Street Project, and while he was there Jackson brought Willie Gary by to say hello.

Jackson's intent, he would say later, was to provide Coke with the kind of help that only Gary could provide. Perhaps it would be good marketing to have Gary on Coke's side. Perhaps Gary could bring something to the table that no one at Coke had thought of. But at that moment it was Coke that he tried to help, Jackson would later say.

Nothing came of the meeting. Ivester went home to Atlanta from New York, and Gary got back into his plane, with its luxurious bathroom fixtures and its supersized kitchen, and returned to Florida. It was probably the last time the two would speak. But it was not the last time that Willie Gary or Jesse Jackson would have contact with the Coca-Cola Company over the discrimination lawsuit. Their association was just beginning.

Chapter Fifteen

Headaches in Belgium

IN 1999, ODILON HERMANS was headmaster of the small but rigorous St. Mary School in Bornem, Brussels, a middle school in a well-off suburb. Tuesday, June 8, was the second day of examination week, and some of his students, he knew, were nervous. But he had never seen nervousness take such a violent form before. They complained of dizziness. Some said they felt nauseous. A few vomited and asked to go home.

Hermans sent one or two boys to a nearby hospital to be checked; for all he knew, a virus had settled over the school, spreading through the students, who were all between ages eleven and thirteen and who had been pushing themselves hard in recent weeks, preparing for their tests. Then he sent a few more boys, and some girls, to the hospital, and then several more. By the end of the following day, thirty-three of Hermans's students had visited hospitals in the area, all complaining of the same symptoms. They all had headaches, nausea, discomfort; some had vomited, and at least one developed a condition that his doctors would describe as 'an excess red blood cell count'.

Hermans had never experienced anything like it. He and his assistants quickly surveyed the school, looking for signs of food poisoning. What else could have caused so many students to feel ill? They found nothing wrong in their kitchens and nothing amiss with any of the faculty. And then someone realized that the students had been drinking Coca-Cola just before they began complaining. The Coke, in twenty-centiliter glass bottles, arrived at the school in cases shipped from a bottling plant in Antwerp, an hour or so away, and some of the students had been trying to win a contest that involved messages under the cap. Many of them had drunk, or at least opened, several Cokes apiece.

Hermans called the plant and told management what was happening on that Tuesday. Several managers came to the school before evening, saw that several bottles of Coca-Cola remained in the cases that had been delivered earlier that week, and decided not to take them away. Hermans wanted the Cokes out of his school, however, and he called the company again the next day, and again on June 10. Finally, on the third try, someone came to retrieve the cases of Coke. Hermans was a little surprised they took so long. 'We had to push them a little bit,' he said. He had no idea what had been unleashed.

At the time, Belgium's government was convulsed by a separate crisis over food safety. In England, mad cow disease, traced to animal feed, had caused a panic among consumers and a handful of deaths. In Belgium, cancer-causing dioxin had been detected, also in animal feed, a few weeks before the problems at the St. Mary School appeared, and millions of Belgians were consumed with fear that they and their children had been contaminated. Eggs, chicken, beef, pork, and cheese were all suspected of silently spreading the risk. Belgians blamed their government for doing too little in the way of inspecting foods before they wound up on store shelves.

In Brussels, where Coca-Cola executives shared an office building with executives of Coca-Cola Enterprises, owner of the Belgian bottling franchise, there was relatively little furor on June 8 over the sick schoolchildren in Bornem. Coincidence, they said. Not the Coca-Cola. The Coca-Cola Company had spent the last ninety years assuring the planet that its product was pure. Everyone at Coke believed that, and they had convinced much of the rest of the world, too.

Purity had been a selling point for Coke from the beginning. Asa Candler had insisted to all that the drink was clean and safe, when he wasn't insisting that it could cure headaches and ennui. His worry about what might happen to Coke's integrity if someone put it into bottles had mostly centered around the fear of contamination, but improved technology and assiduous marketing soon took care of that. People came to believe that a bottle of Coke was the same wherever they went and that they could trust that what was inside would not harm them.

The National Association of Carbonated Soft Drink

Manufacturers, later the National Soft Drink Association, staged a campaign during the early 1920s to convince people that bottled soft drinks were reliable and clean. It included the adoption of a code of ethics for the bottlers, ratified in 1923, which included such promises as 'I pledge myself to use nothing but the purest of standard ingredients in the manufacture of my products.' The effort peaked in 1924 with an event called Bottled Carbonated Beverage Day, in which bottlers all over the country tried to persuade people to believe in their products, using radio advertising and every other means at their disposal. In Baltimore, bottlers chartered a plane to drop leaflets over the city, each paper missive hailing the healthfulness of bottled soft drinks.

While the carbon dioxide in a sealed soft drink effectively halts the degeneration of the ingredients, early bottled drinks were not known for their cleanliness. Bits of straw, hair, broken glass, feathers, ash, sawdust, and cigarette butts were among the undesirable elements people came across while drinking a bottled beverage in the late 1800s. Through the early part of the twentieth century, bottlers cleaned their empty bottles by hand, filling them with lead shot to help scour every crevice. Sometimes people came across leftover shot – invisible in a concoction like Coca-Cola – when they were nearly done with their drinks.

But with the help of machines like the Dixie Full Automatic Filling & Crowning Machine, manufactured by Crown Cork & Seal in Baltimore circa 1925, and correspondingly large machines to clean and sterilize bottles upon their return from the market, all set up inside dedicated bottling factories, many of the hygiene problems had been eliminated by the mid-1920s. The soda-drinking public was actively encouraged to suspend its squeamishness. Besides, Coke sold in bottles was convenient, could be enjoyed anywhere, and cost the same – just one nickel – as Coke served at soda fountains.

Purity could be a double-edged sword, as Coke discovered after the passage of the Pure Food and Drug Act in 1906. The law was the result of a twenty-year campaign by a career bureaucrat named Harvey Washington Wiley, who was suspicious of many mass-marketed foods and beverages. Wiley, an opponent of 'unpure' food, which he defined as anything that contained additives that were bad for people, began to pursue the Coca-Cola Company. It was not the cleanliness of Coke that worried him; it was one of the ingredients.

Wiley was morally opposed to caffeine, testifying before Congress in 1902 that it was a poison and a habit-forming drug. He apparently tolerated the presence of caffeine in coffee and tea because the stimulant naturally occurred in the beans and leaves. But when it came to Coca-Cola, he maintained, caffeine was an ingredient, added to the formula by choice. That, and the fact that it was marketed as a sweet drink, suitable for children, turned Wiley into a possessed man bent on taking down the nation's most popular soft drink.

In 1909 he ordered federal agents to seize a shipment of Coke syrup just outside Chattanooga, and he charged the company with marketing and selling an adulterated beverage that contained the dangerous element caffeine. In fighting the charges, Coke hired a fledgling psychologist named Harry Hollingsworth to conduct a study on the effects of caffeine. He concluded that it was a mild stimulant with no secondary fatigue or depression. The case, tried in Chattanooga, was dismissed after several weeks of testimony, including that of Hollingsworth. It marked the first time Coke hired professionals in other fields to help convince the world that it was right.

Even with Wiley's crusade laid to rest, Coke still had to confront periodic accusations that there was something wrong with Coca-Cola. Teetotalers spread stories of men going home besotted after drinking a few Coca-Colas, and more than once, federal authorities reported breaking up rings that were adding their own stimulants to the Cokes they mixed inside seemingly innocent-looking pharmacies. The biggest drag on Coke's image, however, was the persistent claim that a dead mouse had been found inside a Coke bottle, horrifying to not just the person drinking that Coke but also to everyone who heard about it later.

The claim appears to be nearly as old as bottled Coke itself. In 1914, a man in Mississippi sued the local Coca-Cola bottler over the discovery of a rodent in his Coke. The man won, and the bottler appealed but failed to overturn the verdict. The judge, clearly amused by the details, wrote, 'A "sma' mousie" caused the trouble in this case . . . drowned in a bottle of Coca-Cola.' Dozens of similar cases followed, all of them alleging the same unappetizing discovery. No one – not Coke, not its bottlers, and not the injured parties – argued about the existence of the dead mouse. Instead they debated who should bear the responsibility for it and what the compensation should be for what another judge, also seemingly entertained by the case before him, referred to as the plaintiff's 'mental aversion . . . to ratty nourishment'.

Rat and mouse stories proliferated over the years, usually involving a Coke, or a Pepsi, occasionally a 7UP, but in every case the details were more or less the same: Someone enjoying a harmless, pure, and refreshing soda found, once the bottle was empty, that he or she had not been drinking alone.

Such stories reflect fears about industrialization, some experts believe, as well as the storyteller's desire for importance. Sometimes different versions developed and were passed along to listeners, who, when it was their turn to feel important, combined them in the retelling for optimum dramatic effect. Money may have been a motivation in some of the lawsuits; most of them targeted Coca-Cola, the biggest name in soft drinks. One study found that, of forty-five suits brought to trial, all but six of them were filed against the Coca-Cola Company, and most of the plaintiffs won some kind of financial redress. One plaintiff walked away with fifty dollars in a 1953 case, while another collected $20,000 in a case decided in 1969.

Most of the claims were against independently owned bottlers, and the bottlers, in their rush to preserve their business, appeared eager to settle the claims and move on. That may explain the proliferation of the lawsuits, since nobody loves a lawsuit like a person, or his lawyer, who is pretty sure there is a reward waiting for him on the other end. But the local bottlers, with their expensive investments in plants and trucks and other equipment, couldn't stand the thought of their livelihood drying up over a mouse, and they no doubt wanted to bury the controversy – and the mouse, if there was one – as quickly as possible.

Decades later, the situation in Bornem presented similar issues. But the bottler was no longer small and local. And this time, it was much slower to respond. While the Coca-Cola Company announced an investigation into the complaints from the school-children, the bottler, according to Hermans, did not seem to want to retrieve the offending bottles or to actively engage the school or its students in a discussion of what might have gone wrong. Even more remote was the possibility of Coca-Cola Enterprises paying to make the problem go away.

Some saw this as the profit motive at work; for the Coca-Cola Company, which had already sold the syrup to its bottler that created those sodas, destroying them had no impact on its bottom line. For the bottler, however, every Coke in Bornem that went unsold was a nick at its profits. And those profits were under unrelenting pressure already, from the interest payments on the debt that resulted from the huge expansion undertaken over the previous three years, combined with the need to please Wall Street and the overall company's struggle to grow in the American soft-drink market.

Despite the 'alignment' that both the Coca-Cola Company and its biggest bottler liked to boast about, they were visibly at odds after the news of the suspect bottles of Belgian Coke surfaced. Yet they would separately deny that there was much of a problem to begin with. When Ivester, traveling in France, asked for a briefing, he was told that the situation was 'not serious'. He boarded the Gulfstream again, settled into his seat, and returned to Atlanta. First, though, he assigned Anton Amon, Coke's senior scientist, to oversee the matter, along with William Casey, president for Europe.

To the bottler, the complaints from the St. Mary School were not terribly serious in the scheme of things. With millions of soft drinks being produced every day, mistakes happened nearly every day, too. Glass bottles got chipped, and no one knew where the chips fell. Cans were loaded mechanically into pallets, and there could be odd liquids or solids on the pallets that no one had approved. The trucking, meanwhile, added another variable to the finished Coca-Cola product; all kinds of things, like rain and snow and excessive heat, could befall a can or bottle on its way to the grocery store shelf. The miracle of Coca-Cola was that it managed to be so pure so much of the time. Careful management and stringent control had combined to eliminate much of the hazard to people's health. But life was full of surprises, and in soft-drink production, as in every other factory operation, there was no way to eliminate all the problems all the time. Any bottler could tell you that.

Ivester flew home in the Coke jet. This was, after all, the bottler's problem to fix. In Belgium, meanwhile, another batch of children had complained of feeling sick on June 10. This time, it was not bottles of Coke from the Antwerp plant that were to blame but cans of Coke and fruit-flavored Fanta manufactured at a giant new facility in Dunkirk, on the French coast. The cans smelled of some kind of rank substance, and the children who drank from them, after buying them from a vending machine at their school in Bruges, a tiny Flemish masterpiece of a town just outside Brussels, said they had headaches, nausea, and other unusual feelings of discomfort. Instead of providing a pause that refreshed them, these drinks, they said, sent them to the hospital.

Three days later, on Sunday, June 13, Belgians went to the polls and voted their government out of office. The new government, anxious to reassure people about the safety of their food supply, reported for work on Monday. Officials, apprised of the Bornem and Bruges incidents immediately ordered Coca-Cola Enterprises to remove all of its sodas from stores. Vending machines were off-limits until Belgian health officials could inspect all of them.

The Coca-Cola Company was powerless to do anything but wait for the political chaos to subside. Store owners began pulling cans and bottles of Coke products from their shelves, and executives from Coca-Cola Enterprises began ordering their workers to collect them. The recall began in Belgium but soon spread to other nearby countries. The recall became the biggest product recall in company history, bigger than anything that had happened in Europe or any other part of the world since Coke began to be served.

The Belgian market had been one of the more successful in Europe, with Belgians consuming 260 servings of Coke products apiece every year – far more than the French, with 96 servings, or the Germans, who logged 200 per person at the end of 1998. Coca-Cola Enterprises featured the country with full-page color photographs – staged in cafés that appeared to serve only Coke –

in its annual report in 1998. Per-capita consumption, the measure of a country's performance for Coke and a building block in worldwide market share, was 'among the highest in Europe', the report said.

But now Belgium was giving the Coca-Cola Company a big black eye. Not only were sales suffering as a result of the recall but the mighty Coca-Cola image was harmed as well. The news of the Cokes that made children sick – a gripping headline if there ever was one – traveled at lightning speed across the world. The electronic media that Coke executives always harnessed so well to convey their marketing messages now reared up and fed the rumor that Coke was unsafe. Consumers began calling their governments in places as far away from Belgium as Singapore, asking if they should avoid drinking Coke. Belgian television carried images of store owners dumping huge quantities of Coca-Cola, and those images were picked up and shown around the planet.

This was a force so large that no one, not even the world's master marketers, could find a way to stop it. And what was already bad from Coke's point of view was about to get even worse.

Coca-Cola Enterprises had initially been ordered to remove its vending machines before the election. But not all of the machines could be removed, in part because workers went out to do the work over the weekend, discovering, once they arrived, that many buildings were locked. That was the explanation offered by Randal Donaldson, Coke's chief spokesman in Atlanta. The company's explanation for its failure to remove the machines did not satisfy government officials, particularly Luc van den Bossche, the chain-smoking career politician who became minister of health in the cabinet formed on June 13.

Van den Bossche now invoked his power to ban the company's products from the marketplace across Belgium. There was no longer a voluntary recall by the Coca-Cola Company; now, by government decree, he informed officials of the European Union, as well as French government ministers, of the steps he had taken. And he set up a telephone hotline for people to call if they felt ill or had any unusual reaction after drinking Coca-Cola, Fanta, or any other Coke product. More than 240 people made the call.

It was an extraordinary development for Coke. Millions of cans and bottles were taken off store shelves as television cameras rolled. But this was only the beginning.

Fear of Coca-Cola spread across Western Europe. France ordered the company to shut down its manufacturing plant in Dunkirk, because that was where the Cokes that the children in Bruges drank came from. Coca-Cola Enterprises, the owner of that plant, did so. Luxembourg banned Coke products a day after Van den Bossche did. In the Netherlands, Coke products shipped through Belgium were banned. And then Coke, trying to stanch the damage, came forward with its explanation of what had gone wrong.

Company spokesmen said tainted carbon dioxide, the gas that provides the bubbles in a soft drink, had caused the odd, sulfuric smell and unpleasant taste in the bottles of Coke from the Antwerp plant. And the substance on the cans from Bruges and elsewhere was identified as a creosote-type chemical compound, which Coke executives said appeared to have originated from the wooden pallets that transported the cans from Dunkirk. The compound did not meet the system's specifications for wooden pallets, the company said, but it had been used anyway by the Australian company that manufactured them for Coca-Cola Enterprises.

There. That was that. The sources had been identified, and the company felt it was now in control of the situation. But its official explanation of the problem, released on June 14, did not stop the surge. The same day, forty-two children from the Belgian town of Lochristi were sent to area hospitals after they said they got headaches after drinking Cokes.

Trying to ease worries, Coke spokesmen insisted that their products were fine. 'It may make you feel sick,' Rob Baskin, a spokesman in Atlanta, said on June 15, as eight more children, this time from Kortrijk, Belgium, were rushed to hospitals, throwing up and complaining of headaches, 'but it is not harmful.'

Doug Ivester, meanwhile, remained in Atlanta. The issues with the Cokes the children drank had been explained, and technically this was a bottler problem, not a syrup problem. Still, there were suggestions that the 'secret formula' was to blame. The bottler was lying low, and in Europe's newspapers pressure mounted for Ivester to apologize to the Belgian schoolchildren who said they were sickened by drinking Coca-Cola. There was no shortage of hostility toward Americans and American companies at the time; the United States had refused to lift quotas on beef exports, bananas, and other tariff-sensitive goods. Europeans were angry, and they vented their frustration on the Coca-Cola Company. Belgians were even angrier. First the food supply, now the Coca-Cola. It was too much to take.

Don Keough, hearing all of this, got on the phone with Ivester. 'You ought to get over there right away,' he told him. Ivester was in Belgium as they spoke.

Keough saw it this way: 'They think they're sick, and their parents think they're sick. It's the intuitive way to deal with it.' Goizueta, he thought, would have flown to Brussels immediately.

Meanwhile, Coke's attempts to take control of the situation on the ground failed one by one. 'It changed on a daily basis,' remembered one Coke executive, who worked on Belgium nearly twenty-four hours a day for several weeks in June. 'Our people in Belgium whispered in our ear that something like that might happen. But our sense of it was that we had been forthright in our plans, we had shared all the information from our testing data, and there just wasn't a problem.'

No problem, so the commotion ought to go away. Nevertheless, the press in Belgium and abroad took the Coca-Cola Company to task over the flawed sodas. And that became the problem – more so than the incident itself. Coke had skillfully selected and marketed an upbeat image for itself all over the world for the past 113 years, and now here was the world relaying an entirely different and unwholesome image, broadcast everywhere for all to hear. Other forces – not the Coca-Cola Company – were suddenly calling the shots. There may have been truth to what they were saying, and maybe not. It hardly mattered; the information, regardless of its quality, had developed a life of its own. Ivester, the Coke executive who best understood the power of high-tech communication, could only watch as news flashed around the world, from Belgium to New York to Tokyo to New Delhi, condemning the company's slow response to an issue that struck at the heart of its business. And then the matter took on epic proportions. It became all about the safety of packaged food: If you can't trust the Coca-Cola Company, what company can you trust? Reporters and editorial writers asked the same question, over and over, in different ways and in different languages, all based on what had happened in Belgium.

The Belgian government had been completely replaced, though a few characters from the coalition's old lineup remained. Van den Bossche was the minister put in charge of the Coca-Cola situation. As custodian of the country's health, he could not allow Coke back on the shelves without a thorough investigation, he told Coke executives stiffly. He would not be rushed. He would have to be convinced, he said through plumes of cigarette smoke, that Coke was safe to drink before anyone in his country would be able to buy it. 'I do not negotiate,' he informed the world. 'I decide.'

Days rolled by. No Coke was being sold in Belgium or the Netherlands or Luxembourg. In France, it was for sale in many places, but it wasn't exactly flying out of the stores. In Atlanta, the executives of Coca-Cola Enterprises felt like screaming.

Keough's image floated across the minds of Coca-Cola executives assigned to manage the Belgian mess, as well as some of those watching from afar. They did not necessarily think it was a crisis for the bottler to solve; to them, the whole Coke brand was in jeopardy. The division of labor did not matter anymore, now that the whole Coca-Cola system was on the line. 'Don Keough would have been in the hospital, talking to the families, and they would have applauded him as he left,' said one former Coca-Cola Company executive.

But Keough was not involved, except as an observer and a Coca-Cola shareholder. He stayed away, answering his phone when it rang but not going anywhere near the crisis except for one call to Ivester.

Inside Coke, some veterans thought that what was missing, oddly enough for a company so preoccupied with control, was a person seen to be more in charge. 'You needed a czar,' said a former executive, who worked closely with Ivester during this period.

The French and the Belgians complained that Coke could not tell them enough about the tainted Cokes, either where they came from, or what was really wrong with them. The company stubbornly stuck to its explanations of what had happened, in Antwerp and in Dunkirk. Then, to back up its position, that there was really no danger to consumers, the company commissioned a study from an expert at the University of Utrecht in the Netherlands, which appeared on June 21 and concluded that the amounts of unhealthy chemicals present in the sodas he tested were unlikely to have made anyone ill. There were those bottles of Coke and diet Coke from the Antwerp plant, 'of which the content had an off-odour', the scientist, Robert Kroes, reported. Analysis showed the presence of hydrogen sulfide and carbonyl sulfide 'at very low quantities just above the detection limit', which perhaps accounted for the smell, since both are known for their 'rotten-egg odour', he wrote. However, he concluded that even if a person drank the sodas, he or she would consume less carbonyl sulfide than was present in a serving of cooked meat.

For Ivester, the crisis was a test of his abilities as chief executive for which nothing in his past had prepared him. And while he cared deeply about the welfare of the children who seemed to have become sick, he was perceived as finding it difficult to convey that. He had no forum and was forced to remain behind the scenes. He enlisted Coke's best people to help, but their progress was slow.

And time was working against him. With every hour, new developments in the story – more children who said they felt sick after drinking Coke, another country that was warning citizens not to drink Coke – emerged. With every round of bad news, the pressure on Ivester increased.

By the sixteenth of June, he had issued an apology, even though he was far from convinced that there was anything significantly wrong with the Cokes in Belgium. Later he would say that he had been urged to 'take a lower profile' by the Belgian health minister and others in the government. 'Let us handle this,' the Belgians, led by Van den Bossche, told Coke executives, according to another person who participated in the discussions. If Coke wanted its Belgian business back, it would have to listen. To the Belgians, that is. And so Coke did.

Ivester's apology, designed as part of Coke's marketing plan, did not go over especially well. He issued it from Atlanta, and it was a statement thoroughly vetted by Coke's lawyers to avoid any suggestion of guilt. 'We deeply regret any problems experienced by our European consumers,' Ivester said in his statement. 'The Coca-Cola Company's highest priority is the quality of our products. For 113 years our success has been based on the trust that consumers have in that quality. That trust is sacred to us.'

German officials, meanwhile, were emptying store shelves that held Cokes bottled in Belgium or France. Consumer groups there complained that Coke appeared to have been less than direct and not plausible in its explanations of what had gone wrong. Now Coke's largest European market, its fourth-strongest source of profits, had been covered by the same cloud that refused to leave Belgium. And eighty people in France had reported nausea, fever, and headaches after drinking Coca-Cola.

On June 18, Ivester got into the Gulfstream and flew to Brussels. There he telephoned James Burke, who had been chairman of Johnson & Johnson during the Tylenol tampering crisis in the early 1980s, and talked to him at length. He remained baffled by the public reaction, which seemed to be based on very little evidence that anything was actually wrong with the soft drinks. There were no hypodermic needles in the cans, as Pepsi had had to contend with in the early 1990s. There was no one seriously ill, no one dying. Nevertheless, in Spain, the authorities were recalling thousands of cases of Coke, and the German government was telling consumers to read can and bottle labels carefully, to make sure Cokes they drank had been bottled in Germany, where, they said, it was still safe.

June 21 arrived, and Coke products were still banned. Ivester decided it was time to communicate with all Coca-Cola employees everywhere about the situation. He composed a memo with the help of his public relations team and sent it out to every one of the 29,000 people working for Coke. First he outlined the issues that had been present in Europe before the tainted Cokes were reported: mad cow disease in England, dioxin problems in Belgium, a general distrust of genetically modified foods across the region. 'Now, in the midst of this environment, our system's quality-control processes in Belgium faltered,' he wrote. 'There were two separate, unrelated instances, coming two days apart.

During my time with the company, I can recall no other time when such a situation has occurred.'

But all that was behind the company now, Ivester continued. 'I have personally tasted the products and held the packages involved with no adverse reaction,' he told his troops. There was nothing to worry about. Still, 'I have personally apologized to the highest government officials,' Ivester added, 'and will issue a public apology to the people of Belgium.' That he did, in newspaper advertisements the following day. 'My Apologies to the Consumers of Belgium,' the headline read, beside a picture of a smiling Ivester.

At a press conference held to announce that Coke had been approved for sale again, he picked up a bottle of the offending soda and drank from it. Nothing happened to him.

The messages coming out of Coke had to be tightly controlled, and the word from Atlanta was that Coke could acknowledge the breakdown in its quality management but only as an isolated incident, traceable to specific causes. At least one person found this shortsighted. 'When you have a billion servings a day, you have quality issues,' said the former executive. 'People operate the machines. People make mistakes. The machinery breaks down.'

It was not a broken product but a broken promise that Coke now had to face down, in Ivester's view. That was a subtle distinction, but broken promises could be massaged into oblivion by asking people for their forgiveness, using the right words and the right body language, and then the product, which had never had anything wrong with it, according to Coke, would return to the place where it had been all along: on the shelves, in the stores, in the hearts and minds of consumers.

The ads, the demonstrated humility, and the passage of time all combined to help Ivester and Coke climb out of their predicament. On June 23, Van den Bossche agreed to allow Coke to be sold once again in Belgium, subject to conditions, including tighter quality controls, that Van den Bossche announced he had decreed.

Two days later, all the other countries that had banned or refused Coke products from Belgium or France relaxed their rules, although vending machines remained shut down in Belgium, and the French government continued to investigate the source of the chemical in the Dunkirk plant.

The incident may have been a legitimate health crisis, or it may have been an extreme, sustained version of the mouse phenomenon, which bothered many people, may have affected some of them, and never could be fully confirmed or denied. Some of the children from Bornem remained hospitalized or apparently ill into the summer. There was no specific name for the illness they had, and no traceable cause. Other children recovered immediately.

The damage to Coke and to Coca-Cola Enterprises could not be calculated immediately. In July, the bottler reported that it spent $103 million to remove and destroy recalled products, denting its results for the quarter. Schimberg insisted that without the recall the bottler would have increased its cash operating profit growth by 6 percent. But the recall was not imaginary, and it pushed down profits by 6 percent.

The Coca-Cola Company, which would spend an additional $50 million on marketing in Belgium in the months that followed, circulated a report it commissioned in which it was suggested that the illnesses attributed to drinking Coke or Fanta in Belgium were psychosomatic. The trace amounts of substances found in the drinks or on the outside of the cans, the report said, were too small to have made anyone sick. No one formally argued with the report; later, a report in the British journal *Lancet* seemed to back it up.

The Coca-Cola machine was up and running again by July 1, the day Coke ran another ad in the Belgian newspapers, promising to 'bring Coca-Cola back to you and your family over the next few weeks'. New shipments had been ordered, and a promotion set up in which Ivester promised to buy every Belgian a Coke.

It was a single, unanticipated, unfortunate breakdown, Ivester told himself and others, compounded by the government upheaval that happened to coincide, unluckily enough, with the complaints about Coke products. It would not happen again. He had made sure of it.

But in New York, where he watched the situation get worse by the day before it finally, *finally* seemed to get better, Don Keough was livid. This was the Coca-Cola Company, for God's sake. His phone began to ring, with bottlers and former Coke men checking in to complain and commiserate. He made a few calls himself.

Life proved full of unexpected developments at the Coca-Cola Company. A jittery public now questioned its Coke, not just in Belgium but in points far afield, like Singapore, where people voiced anxieties about a drink that had once seemed more benign than water.

And on June 29, Ivester was to find that there was always the possibility of something else going wrong. That was the day the company was ordered to recall thousands of cases of Bonaqua mineral water, a Coke brand, bottled at a plant in Poland, after mold was found growing inside some fifteen hundred bottles. Coke officials declared the mold was not dangerous. The Polish government said it could cause digestive problems. Overnight, the bottles disappeared from the shelves.

Chapter Sixteen

A Letter in the Mail

KEOUGH FOUND THE LATEST European episode very troubling, and this time he felt some blame had to be taken by Ivester. Sure, the Belgians had been up in arms even before a single problematic drink had been found. And sure, the publicity around the recall had made it seem even bigger than it was. *It didn't matter.* Ivester, Keough felt, should have found a way to get the Coca-Cola Company out of the mess: not two and a half weeks later but *right away*.

He saw problems for Coca-Cola everywhere, not just in Belgium. Time had run out, he decided, for the kind of economics that Ivester had been so good at in the past. The game he had been playing had hit the wall, he thought, and the company was going to have to do things differently.

There were people who called him to tell him of their displeasure with the Coca-Cola Company, and Keough couldn't stand hearing that. If only Goizueta were around, or if he, Keough, were in the driver's seat, then he felt things might have been handled better.

Pretty soon he shared his opinion with other people. Herbert Allen was right next door, and he had some discussions about the situation with the man who had installed him as the chairman of his own company. Keough had not yet had that lunch with Ivester, and now Allen suggested they all have dinner. They put a date on the calendar.

During dinner at a restaurant called Abruzzi, Ivester seemed at ease and denied there was any trouble at the Coca-Cola Company. It was friendly, entirely free of animosity, and they discussed the company. Ivester took the long view of Coca-Cola's future, and he wasn't worried. After that, Keough told Allen he was checking out.

He would no longer be involved, he said, in what went on at the Coca-Cola Company.

Keough had a separate conversation with Warren Buffett. It was not what Keough would call 'a heavy chat'. He happened to be somewhere with Buffett and other people from Berkshire Hathaway one day, and Buffett – *not Keough,* Keough said – brought it up. Buffett murmured something about life being a little rocky at the Coca-Cola Company, a little tougher than usual. But Buffett had had his money in Coke for more than ten years, and he took the long view. A few bumps were nothing to get excited about, he may have told Keough, and that was the end of the conversation.

But lots of people had Keough's phone numbers in Atlanta and New York, and similarly, he had kept up with lots of bottlers and customers in the years since he had ceased to be the president of the Coca-Cola Company. He had several contacts at *Fortune,* all people he'd worked with successfully in the past to get a Coca-Cola message into the glossy pages of the magazine. Now he picked up the phone to speak to some of them. He unloaded a torrent of information about how he felt the Coca-Cola leadership had stumbled, in Belgium and elsewhere, and what it would take to make Coke a mighty brand again. This was awful, he fumed. The management of Coke was a bit of a mess.

Keough was a man who thought in terms of the big picture, the interaction of Coca-Cola with the rest of the world. Now he cataloged everything that he felt was wrong with the company, piling up Belgium, Cadbury, Orangina, the lack of a president. Ivester had to take notice of his own mistakes, and fix them, *before it was too late*.

Keough knew how to play the public relations game probably better than anyone at Coke since Woodruff. He had been the secret weapon that Roberto Goizueta used to his advantage when he needed to win over an irate customer or smooth over an unhappy truth. 'You need someone like that,' said one former executive. 'And he was good at it. He was good at making people think they were important.'

Keough matched the essence of Coke's marketing power, measure for measure. Over the years, Coca-Cola had made itself all things to all consumers. It could be global; it could be specifically patriotic. It could be all about families, and it could be all about the individual. It could embrace Santa Claus and Ramadan without missing a beat. 'It's just a small moment of pleasure,' Keough liked to say. Listeners would agree; it was just a soft drink, a quick hit in a bottle or a can – everything and nothing at the same time.

But to Keough Coca-Cola could never be nothing. It represented everything that he had worked for, and just about everything that he believed in, as well as most of his personal fortune. Coke for him was a consuming entity, a door through which he had entered a world he found impossible to leave. Some executives compared the annual planning sessions in Atlanta, which were so important that managers from every corner of the planet would fly in to spend several days plotting strategy for the next year, with a meeting of the College of Cardinals. Keough would not have taken issue with that imagery.

He knew that reporters assigned to cover the company were invariably frustrated by the information coming through its official channels. Coke kept itself closed up and closed off, like a barnacle at low tide, and contact with reporters was emphatically discouraged throughout the ranks. Almost no one would risk an unsanctioned meeting with a reporter, and the sanctioned ones were always attended, either in person or on the telephone, by a senior person from the public relations department, which had a certain stifling effect. One public relations executive was known to breathe heavily into the telephone, a never ending reminder of their official presence.

So someone like Keough, offering delicious tidbits that illustrated concerns about leadership inside Coke, was hard to resist. It was a good story – maybe even a great story. His willingness to reach out to the press made him highly unusual among the people connected to Coke, and it gave him a power that he enjoyed. He used it sparingly but whenever he felt he should.

This was one of those times.

Something even bigger than Belgium had helped to make up his mind. It was not a television report or an analyst's comment that broke the camel's back. It was a small exchange between two powerful men that went badly, at least according to one of them. It involved a lunch, and an innocuous-looking letter – written by Don Keough.

When all the dust from the biggest product recall in company history had settled and Coca-Cola was back on the shelves and in the vending machines across Belgium, and in France and Luxembourg and Germany and the Netherlands and all the other places where it needed to be, Keough decided to give Ivester some personal advice. He asked for a time when they could sit down for lunch.

It was not an easy decision. Watching from the sidelines was what Keough had told himself he needed to do. This was Ivester's moment, to make or break, and Keough was not going to get involved. Sure, he talked to people when they called him or when he ran into them on a plane or at a party somewhere. But he had an interest here, as a shareholder and as a former president of Coke. He wanted to help Ivester put out the fires that were consuming Coca-Cola, at home and around the world. Keough had an interest in the company's fate, too.

About two weeks after the Belgian authorities relented, the two of them met for lunch in Atlanta. Ivester had chosen the location, the Capital City Club, a square brick mansion on Peachtree Street in the heart of downtown. It is one of a few vintage buildings left in the area, and it was a place that Goizueta, possibly recalling his vanished life in Havana, had always loved.

Ivester sat down at a table for two, in the dusky cool of the club, to break bread with Keough. It was July 12, so they discussed the searing heat outside. Then they talked about their families, and finally they got to the Coca-Cola Company. Keough brought up several issues that were concerns of his and others; he always did maintain that he was obligated to pass on feedback he got to those in power at Coke. Ivester was polite and, as usual, not much for chitchat. He mostly listened while Keough talked. When lunch was over, Keough wasn't sure he had gotten Ivester's attention. He certainly hadn't gotten a vow of cooperation or any other indication that Ivester agreed with the most important points he'd raised.

So ten days later he pulled out a sheet of his writing paper, embossed with his full name across the top, and opened the middle drawer of his desk to retrieve a pen. Grasping it in his freckled hand, he began to write.

In his looping handwriting – he would have the secretary type it later – he wrote that he sensed that a number of the innovations that Ivester had put in place since his own retirement had not necessarily been great for the Coca-Cola Company. Let's start with the bottling system. While Keough had cheered the creation of Coca-Cola Enterprises, he did not think that the model had to be duplicated the world over. These days, there were nearly a dozen Coca-Cola Enterprises clones, growing larger and hungrier every day. These companies required special care and feeding. Everyone who fully understood them knew that. Too many of them would drag the Coca-Cola Company's profits down. And bottlers that got too big could lose that all-important connection with their local markets. Keough worried about that.

There had already been negative reports about the state of the modern bottling system. In May 1999 *The New York Times* had published an article that highlighted the $1.2 billion in marketing support and other money that Coke had given to Coca-Cola Enterprises in 1998. Albert Meyer, still digging into the finances of the Coke system, had found that subtracting the marketing support Coca-Cola Enterprises received annually from Coke would produce numbers showing that the bottler wasn't getting more profitable but was instead weakening under its load. Cash operating profit, the number that investors were instructed to examine by Coca-Cola Enterprises management, actually had declined as a percentage of revenues, Meyer concluded. It had fallen steadily, from 8.9 percent of revenues in 1995 to 5.7 percent in 1998. As the bottler got bigger, adding more territory, its profitability had waned.

Then Meyer made another interesting discovery: If the amount of marketing support that Coke gave the giant bottler was added back, cash operating profit rose year by year – always by 14.8 percent, except once, when it was just 14.7 percent. 'Maybe somebody made a calculation error,' he said.

The problem was that over time the marketing support had had to keep rising to make that number happen. The company had paid

$343 million in marketing support in 1995 and increased that figure every year. The nearly $900 million paid in 1998 was the largest sum yet, and Meyer predicted that Coke would have to keep adding to it to make Coca-Cola Enterprises presentable to investors.

Elsewhere in the world, Coke had spent another $640 million to help out other big bottlers. And this seemed incongruous. 'The bottlers were supposed to be Coke's engine of growth,' the *Times* article noted, 'not parts that need copious refueling.'

At Panamerican Beverages – the Latin American anchor bottler left with $1.1 billion in debt after Coke sold it the Cisneros operation in Venezuela – and at Coca-Cola Amatil – where Norbert Cole, the former chief executive, was suing Coke over the breakup of the giant bottler into two parts the year before – Coke seemed to be calling the shots, which translated into problems for the bottlers.

A Merrill Lynch analyst, Doug Lane, issued a rare midday report refuting the issues discussed in the article. Lane's report described a much rosier situation at Coke, noting that the price per case of the support had decreased at Coca-Cola Enterprises, and adding that the 'infrastructure spending', more than $340 million that Coke spent on its effort to get more vending machines into the marketplace in North America and Western Europe, was going to be less the following year. But that hadn't soothed everyone. In May, the shares traded at about seventy dollars apiece. Now, in July, they were holding at about sixty-three dollars per share, and someone like Keough, who had most of his wealth in Coke stock, would not be happy about that.

Bottlers had always professed their love for Keough, and indeed he had spent long stretches of time with them, urging them to consider the changing world of Coke and exhorting them to greatness in speeches like the one he gave for Coke's hundredth-anniversary bash. Bottlers were the company's critical link to the consumer, and bottlers had to be regarded in that light. He had been the one Goizueta picked to hail the bottlers at the hundredth-anniversary birthday party, and he had done a spectacular job. They had walked out of the huge civic center in Atlanta feeling on top of the world all those years ago.

Now, in his communiqué to Ivester, he described the process of consolidating the bottlers from hundreds to a handful as a creation that had necessarily required destruction. This had been their revolution, and it had not been without its miseries. *We knew it would be a painful process,* Keough wrote. *You can't make an omelette without breaking some eggs. Well, we broke a lot of eggs.*

In his time as Coke's president, he had backed that first anchor bottler, the one now headed by Summerfield Johnston, Jr., a man he had known for decades. Keough had flown him around the world to help Johnston understand the inner workings of Coca-Cola; they were on the same side, like soldiers or brothers. That bottler – well, that one was fine. But as he examined the state of Coke's other giant bottlers, his conclusion was that Ivester had gone too far. He would help him now. He would give Ivester his recipe for success.

Here his writing reflected the spirit of a true Coca-Cola loyalist. He had helped lead the revolution, and he wanted to make sure it had a happy ending. *The following truths become self-evident,* Keough wrote. The bottlers from the beginning were *a large group of small, unsophisticated businesses throughout the United States,* turning to the Coca-Cola Company as if it were the sun – for *light, for guidance, for everything.* As a result, Coke became *banker, lawyer, land purchaser, construction adviser, plant designer, architect, supplier of everything from uniforms to regulatory guidelines, and lobbyist,* providing services that Keough, who once had to track down a specific kind of light bulb for a bottler's sign, knew all about. *The company became a great teaching machine, catalyst, hand-holder and baby-sitter,* he wrote. He believed that much of that was continuing, and now it had to end. Much of what Coke did could be handled by the bottlers; there were redundancies and wasted efforts, and he did not like what that was doing to the company's costs.

By now he was more than halfway through his letter.

As he cast his eye across the empire that had once answered to him, Keough considered the Coca-Cola Company's domestic headquarters in Atlanta. The bureaucracy of technical experts, administrators, midlevel managers, and marketing specialists had grown unwieldy. All of those people had jobs, Keough recognized, but not all of those jobs were important. Some of the planning and the fieldwork could be done by the big bottlers. And the marketing – too much of the local efforts had been centralized over the years. Bottlers could certainly do more of that, which would save Coke money, too.

And above all, there was this problem: Coca-Cola, the brown soda at the core of this empire, the company's ultimate reason for existing, was not getting the attention it deserved, and therefore it was not growing. Since 1984, sales of cola had been flat or falling, and no one at Coke or Pepsi had figured out a way to reverse that trend.

Pepsi, after a couple of stumbles that cost its marketing head his job, had created a campaign in 1998 called 'The Joy of Cola', featuring a child actress, Hallie Eisenberg, in various cute situations, including one based on Marlon Brando's character in *The Godfather*. Aware that this new campaign was getting noticed by consumers, Ivester had ordered up a new one of his own. He had approved other commercials that were centered around the 'Always' theme that Peter Sealey had come up with in 1993. But as far as a new theme, a new rallying point for everything Coca-Cola wanted to be – well, Ivester had not come up with one, and neither had Sergio Zyman before he left.

But now there was one in the works. It was called 'Enjoy', which Coke executives insisted was similar to Pepsi's campaign only by coincidence. It introduced the word as a replacement for 'Always', and it focused on the taste of Coca-Cola – properly served ice cold, which Ivester proposed emphasizing with taste tests and glass bottles, nostalgic though they were.

The new campaign was scheduled to be unveiled in October, and Charlie Frenette was supervising it for Ivester.

From where Keough sat, whatever Ivester was doing wasn't enough. Coca-Cola, he believed, was the central purpose for everyone working at the Coca-Cola Company, and they had better not forget it. Profit margins aside – but not too far aside, for the shareholders' sake – Coke was *it,* their reason for being, and they needed to work harder to make sure Coke sold better, and faster. That was where the money was.

The honking of the traffic moving fitfully down Fifth Avenue drifted up to the ninth floor, interrupting Keough's thoughts. He put down his pen for a moment. He was not just worried about his own fortune, considerable though that was. He was fretting about his legacy. What was the point of all those years on the road, those days and nights in the air, those thousands of lunches and dinners and cocktail parties and bar mitzvahs and hearty laughs at other people's bad jokes, if everything he, Don Keough, had accomplished ended up unraveled?

He didn't want to be forgotten. Other people had noticed that within Coke the name of Keough was seldom uttered. One executive, wandering through a conference room that displayed pictures of all Coke's former leaders, was surprised to see no portrait or even a photograph of Keough. True, he had never been chairman. He had lost that sweepstake by a nose. But many people believed that he had been indispensable at a critical time for Coke, during all those years that Roberto Goizueta was alive.

Keough hated feeling irrelevant. Some people at Coke believed that he had never recovered from losing his bid for chairman to Goizueta. The same people thought that, in pushing Goizueta to pick John Hunter as his successor, Keough had been trying to vindicate himself. When Ivester got the nod instead, it reinforced the sense that the financial wizards reigned supreme at the Coca-Cola Company. Keough was not a financial specialist and never would be. He was the consummate salesman, clearing the way for Coke into all sorts of places. He had deserved to be the supreme leader of Coke someday, *and that day never came.*

He resumed writing. He was close to finishing. This letter of his was a Keough encyclical, calmly and gracefully worded, a chapel-quality reflection on the historic image of Coca-Cola, filled with suggestions on how to take the flagship soft drink and point it in the direction of even greater prominence in the future. Ivester, Keough told him, had the opportunity of a lifetime, to make Coke supremely important to the world, and to refocus the company on selling Coca-Cola. He went on, in an urgent and often poetic tone, to discuss why Coke was essential, what it meant now to bottlers and consumers and all that it had meant for more than a hundred years. Coke was, he wrote, *the alpha and the omega,* the reason for every hour of every day that he and Ivester and Goizueta and everyone else spent at that company. If Ivester could turn its fate around, he would leave a lasting mark on the company and be remembered as not just a good leader but as one of the great ones. On every page Keough displayed his sentimental attachment to Coca-Cola, delineating his own fundamental connection to a product he loved. It was Mother Coke, bubble-filled giver of life; it was the sweet dark object of his affection. He was a bard in the best Irish tradition as he drew to a close, a man singing the praises of his beloved sugar and water and gas.

The Coca-Cola Company needs to reinvent itself, he wrote. Instead of the 29,000-person swollen operation that existed on that hot July afternoon, it needed to become *lean, highly specialized and focused.* It had to reinvigorate the world's interest in Coca-Cola. And the time to move was now, rapidly, in a way that Coke was unaccustomed to.

History indicates we move slowly, he wrote. But there was no time to waste. *Yes, some eggs will be broken,* he concluded. But if no one did anything quickly to turn the company into a new, improved version of itself, *the sheer weight of the company will take the joy, the life, and the magic out of the Coca-Cola Company and crush it.*

Ivester received the letter within a couple of days and wasted no time writing back. He had his secretary type a short, succinct response. There were one or two sentences, compared with the three single-spaced pages that Keough's secretary had sent.

Ivester's reply to the Keough epistle was a simple 'Thank you for your input,' or words to that effect. His secretary put it into an envelope addressed to Keough and stuck it in the mail.

The letter was Ivester's honest, instinctive reply.

Some of Keough's friends sensed that he had grown increasingly worried about the company's future by the summer of 1999. 'He put so much of his life into the Coca-Cola Company that he doesn't want to see it fail,' one said. That letter to Ivester was Keough's blueprint for Coke's survival and, by extension, Ivester's survival, too. He wanted to help.

When they had that lunch together, on July 12, Keough concluded that Ivester was not about to listen to him. Ivester left the table at the Capital City Club to go back to the chairman's office, to sort out the knotty problems of the soft-drink business, at home and abroad, from behind the throne he alone occupied. But Keough, when he had dabbed his mouth with the napkin one last time, had more time on his hands.

He returned to New York, and as he did so he knew that despite what he had tried to do, it appeared Ivester was determined to forge ahead on his own. And that made Keough angry. Keough believed in accepting help, particularly if it was well intentioned. Ivester clearly didn't, Keough thought. Keough liked to talk. Ivester didn't.

In late July, *Fortune* came out with a cover story that trumpeted the miserable state of the Coca-Cola Company. It was a big shift in tone for the magazine, which had long been a supporter of the new Coca-Cola Company. Seven months after Ivester got the top job, *Fortune* had featured him on its cover. He was beaming and holding a bottle of Coke, beneath a headline that called him 'The Coke Machine'. There were more compliments inside.

'If Goizueta was a man obsessed with the success of Coca-Cola, Ivester is even more so,' the magazine declared. 'If Goizueta will go down in history as the quintessential late-20th-century CEO, Ivester may give us a glimpse of the 21st-century CEO, who marshals data and manages people in a way no pre–Information Age executive ever did or could.'

This time, *Fortune* was a lot less flattering. The article discussed problems large and small at Coke – like the little-known irritation of the Walt Disney Company over a Coke deal with Universal, the well-documented outrage in Europe over Coke's behavior toward the regulators and the company's failure to seize control of the situation in Belgium – and laid them squarely at Ivester's door. It even crabbed about Ivester's failure to name a second-in-command – alluding to board unhappiness over that, even though the Coke directors had told Ivester there was no rush.

Ivester had been interviewed for the article. He came across as testy and was described as being somewhat in denial. Even worse, he had been photographed looking tense and pale, like a hunted man. 'If Ivester is astute,' *Fortune* wrote, 'he'll learn from his missteps and try to see the world more the way others do. If he's lucky, investors will regard him and the Coca-Cola Company rationally: down, but likely to bounce back. If he's lucky and astute, he'll be compared favorably with Roberto Goizueta someday.'

Keough wanted only what was best for the Coca-Cola Company and the shareholders. He personally understood how shareholders felt, watching the stock price plunge from nearly eighty-nine dollars to somewhere in the low sixties these days. This was not the script he and Goizueta had put together. The share price was supposed to just keep going up and up and up. Here was one more example of how he felt Ivester had failed.

The *Fortune* article appeared a day or two before Ivester held a large meeting in New York for analysts and reporters. He had promised to address lingering questions about the Belgian crisis and, more important, to describe the company's prospects going forward. The meeting, in the Essex House on Central Park South on a hot, humid mid-July morning, was a classic Coca-Cola offensive, with plenty of PowerPoint graphics showing the countries where Coke outsold its competitors in the soft drink industry, and others showing anticipated rates of growth over the next few years. The world was painted red, still, though in several key regions, including parts of Asia and Latin America, Coke acknowledged that growth was flat or declining. This world did not resemble the sunny picture described a little more than a year earlier, when Ivester had given his six-pack speech to all the analysts assembled in Atlanta.

Ivester and his associates, including James Chestnut, the chief financial officer, put on a brave front. Things were bad, they admitted, yes; but they were also going to get better. With a little time, all the kinks in Japan, Germany, the United States, Venezuela, Brazil, Eastern Europe, and now Western Europe would sort themselves out. The company was moving aggressively to fix everything, and it would get the job done.

Business almost everywhere had deteriorated rapidly and suddenly, Chestnut told the analysts, in an unusually frank appraisal. 'It's almost as if it fell off a cliff,' he said. The recovery, he added, would not be so rapid. The business would take an unspecified period of time to ascend to its old heights.

When would things return to normal for the Coca-Cola

Company, someone in the audience wanted to know. Chestnut had to come up with a good answer. He paused, swallowed, and then announced, in his clipped, faintly Celtic monotone: 'I don't think the world is ever going to be normal. I think we're in a permanent state of change.'

Keough, from his perch four blocks south, must have thought that was pretty astute of Chestnut.

Ivester applied the same techniques with the analysts that had always served him, and Goizueta before him, so well. He strode briskly around the front of the crowded room, and he appeared robust and confident. He spoke assertively, sometimes brusquely, about prospects in all kinds of countries: the hundred ways to sell more Coca-Cola that took into account local concerns about rising unemployment, falling currency value, cheaper competitors, and health issues. A listener could easily conclude that the European recall had been a mere blip on the global Coca-Cola radar; all was well inside the empire, and everything would continue as it always had, with Coke the supreme soft drink on the planet.

Goizueta had known that an invincible image was the Coca-Cola Company's most potent weapon, against competitors and against doubters. And Ivester knew he had to keep that going, even though the image had been battered by what happened in Belgium. He maintained the same optimism that had colored most of his dealings inside and outside the company ever since he arrived there. He was sure that wherever he went, a Coke in his hand, he would be welcome. And so far that had always been true.

He believed that dispensing Coca-Cola was not just a matter of providing beverages to a thirsty planet, though that was important. He maintained, as had Goizueta before him, that someone who sold Coke in a place was initiating a chain reaction of positive economic events that would involve and affect hundreds of people by the time it was through. A person bought a Coke from a vendor; that vendor pocketed the money and put it toward the purchase of more Cokes. Eventually the vendor could buy a bigger bicycle, or a larger ice chest. And that, in time, could become a store. All along, the people who supplied this vendor – with ice, with electrical power, with paper napkins, you name it – were also going to benefit. And if the vendor got big enough, he might need someone to build awnings and signs for him, and then someone to create advertising for him, and someone else to do his bookkeeping. It was like a snowball in a cartoon, gaining momentum and size as it rolled, and at the center was a bottle of Coca-Cola.

So as he stood before the analysts in the middle of July, Ivester was still a confident man. He had had his share of stumbles, and he could have been depressed about them. But he wasn't. He knew what the Coca-Cola Company needed, for the shareholders' benefit, and he was going to make sure the Coca-Cola Company got it.

Even as he described a world in which soda sales had gone flat, from Japan to South Africa to Eastern Europe and the United States, Ivester still seemed chipper. The short term was unpleasant, he would grant that. But the long term was as rosy as ever. The world belonged to Coca-Cola. It had for decades now, and that was never going to change.

He discussed Belgium, saying he thought he had been criticized even as he was trying to do what the Belgian officials wanted. 'I could have taken this minister on publicly,' he said. 'I chose not to do that.' Overall, he admitted, in response to an analyst's question, 'there were a few things we would have said a little differently, some nuances.'

Earlier in the week, Coke's offices in several European cities had been raided early in the morning by officials of the European Union. They said they were looking for documents that might help them in an investigation into Coke's competitive practices on the Continent. Pepsi had blown the whistle, years earlier, on some of Coke's practices in supermarkets, and the regulators had not ignored them.

A dawn raid was not good news for any company. But Ivester played it down. 'It's a pretty routine thing,' he said, insisting that many American companies were being targeted by the E.U., a result of politics, for the most part. 'I sort of expected it, that as this wave was going through, somebody would say, oops, we forgot Coca-Cola. It's not something I'm very exercised about.'

The analysts seemed surprised. To them, the raid was one more sign of Coke's troubles abroad. The *Fortune* article had accused

Coke of acting 'arrogantly, urgently, intensely' in Europe – some felt a reflection of Ivester's personality, according to the magazine. Maybe all the blunders weren't just bad luck or coincidence. Maybe Ivester wasn't the right guy for the job. *Maybe Roberto had made a mistake.*

Ivester had read the article and obviously had it on his mind. He referred to his photograph in the magazine and insisted, in an attempt at levity, that the editors of *Fortune* had sorted through hundreds of negatives before finding a picture that was truly hideous. It showed him looking drawn and tired, peering anxiously into the camera lens. He looked like a wolf in a cage. Or a trap. It was 'the worst picture of me', Ivester said.

Chapter Seventeen

Obviously Unhappy

THE REST OF IVESTER'S summer continued to be long and hot and difficult. He had to get the stock price up. But how? The whole world, it seemed, was cutting back on Coke. The huge demand everyone had anticipated wasn't there. This had never happened before. Certainly not to Goizueta, who had spent all those years building and reinvesting and planning for a bright and bustling future. Now that the future had arrived, Goizueta wasn't around anymore. All those plans he had made – the gleaming new plants in Russia, the giant bottlers based in Australia and Atlanta, the deals with partners and governments in countries like Angola, China, and South Africa – weren't working out according to the blueprint. 'He encouraged us to paint by numbers,' Ivester had said of him, at a memorial service attended by thousands of employees in Atlanta a few days after Goizueta died. But now, it seemed, they had no numbers. They had no growth, or not as much as they wanted. He knew what that would mean for the stock.

He wasn't about to give up. He held meetings, flew to points abroad. He was terribly busy. He worked all the time now. There were no breaks to speak of, and he wasn't getting any from the board. In fact, word had seeped into the newspapers that some directors were upset that he had not named a second-in-command, a Keough to help him with the demands of the job.

He didn't confront anyone. He didn't flatly say that he wasn't going to do it. But he didn't pick anyone to be president of Coke. When pressed, he would explain that having six eager senior vice presidents served his needs better than naming a single person to be president. Name a president, and the other senior V.P.s could lose their starch, their edge, their competitive fire. He was also fond of saying that with six people reporting to him directly, he had a better understanding of the business than he would get otherwise. A president, he frequently noted, would be a filter. 'I don't need a filter,' Ivester always added. It drove Keough crazy whenever he read that in the newspaper.

But looking at the troubled world of Coke, it was not illogical to suggest that Ivester needed a strong person at his side. He could have chosen anyone. There was Jack Stahl, still running Coca-Cola USA, who was young but attractive and well spoken and clearly in line for big things at the company. 'I loved Jack Stahl,' said one executive, a man not in the soft-drink business, who worked with him on a deal. Stahl appeared bland and non-confrontational, but in business he was direct and, like Ivester, if he was displeased about something he handled it quietly and with some regard for the other person's dignity. 'There were many times when I worked for Jack that I got called on the carpet,' said one former Coke executive, 'and instead of thinking, "What an SOB", I walked out of there thinking, "How could I have let him down?"'

Stahl was also popular with the analysts, who had first gotten to know him when he was Coke's investor-relations guru in the early 1980s. Emanuel Goldman, the senior man among the analysts covering Coke, had explained everything he knew about the business to Stahl back when Stahl first took that job, and Stahl graciously acknowledged that, often before a crowd, from time to time. It helped to have someone like Manny Goldman, who had moved from job to job among the top Wall Street firms, on your side. He was fond of giving interviews and nearly always said something that wound up in print.

Other possibilities included Neville Isdell, a towering Irishman who had grown up in southern Africa, the son of a police officer, and bounded through various Coca-Cola positions to end up a senior vice president by 1996. That year, he resigned from the company to take a job with Coca-Cola Amatil, the sprawling Australian-based anchor bottler then on the verge of splitting in two. Isdell became the head of the new half of Amatil, another anchor bottler called Coca-Cola Beverages. When it went public on the London Stock Exchange in July 1998, when the Coca-Cola Company's financial success seemed unstoppable, Isdell expected to be sitting on top of the world. Less than a year later, the stock was in tatters, with a war in Kosovo, a depressed Russian ruble, and a general slowdown in soft-drink consumption ruining the grand vision for the bottler that Ivester and Isdell had shared.

It would not have taken much to persuade Isdell to come to Atlanta and become the president of Coca-Cola. And there were quite a few people who thought he would be an excellent choice. 'He was a warm, gracious, inviting personality,' one former executive said. 'Where Doug was uncomfortable speaking publicly, Neville was a natural. If you had never met Keough, you would say that Neville was the greatest speaker in the world.'

But no, Neville Isdell was not going to be Ivester's choice. The chairman and chief executive of Coke preferred to keep his options open a little while longer. With the problems at Coca-Cola Beverages, he couldn't move Isdell now. Besides, he believed he had plenty of time to figure out this issue.

Ivester, impatient himself with failure, must have known the long knives had been unsheathed. First there was the stalled Orangina transaction, then the scaled-back Cadbury deal. And the Belgian episode – the biggest recall of Coca-Cola anywhere, ever – had been another strike against him. But in every case, he could argue, or have others argue on his behalf, this wasn't his fault.

But he didn't. He did not appeal to his friends among the Coke directors or suggest that someone speak on his behalf. He maintained his own sturdy faith in Coca-Cola – that it was the greatest, best-loved brand in all the world. This was a rough patch, but Coke would be fine. He was telling the truth.

In September, Ivester agreed to an interview with a Brazilian newsweekly whose reporter flew to Atlanta for the session. The publication, *Veja,* was widely read in Brazil, and Brazil had been a tantalizing but problem-plagued market for Coke for some time. Ivester believed that the Coca-Cola Company was at a disadvantage there when it came to competing with cheaper sodas, known as *tubainas,* that were locally produced and distributed. The owners of the *tubainas* filled up any old bottle with their flavored drinks. And they did not pay the kinds of taxes that an American company had to pay, Ivester often said, and he pressed the Brazilian government officials he met with to repeal that tax. Without an even playing field, he believed, Coke would always have to struggle in a market like that. As it was, the company was paying $1.5 billion in marketing support to its bottlers in Brazil, spread over several years, to help offset the most recent downturn in sales. Brazilian workers would buy a Coke at the beginning of the month, when their paychecks came in, but midway through the month they were drinking *tubainas* exclusively. Were it not for those competitors, Ivester must have fumed privately, Brazil, the country with the fourth-largest population on the planet, would belong to Coke, too.

When the request for an interview came along, he was ready to consider it. Clearly, it would help to have the chairman and chief executive of the Coca-Cola Company talking in print about his company. He could discuss Coke's plans for the future, and detail some of the reasons that Coke was so strong in so many markets, and deliver – courtesy of someone else's publication – the kind of message to the Brazilian consumer that Coke would otherwise have to pay mightily to send out. So Ivester consented to the *Veja* request. He would sit down in Atlanta with one of its reporters, whose name was Euripedes Alcantara.

The day arrived, and Ivester seemed to have made the right decision in allowing the interview. It was boring, mostly, filled with predictable questions and even more predictable corporate answers. The reporter asked one question about Coke's place in a world where people were increasingly concerned about health. Ivester was primed to answer that one. He loved taking on questions about whether Coca-Cola was good for people. For the record, he would always say that it was. In an interview with *The New York Times* in 1998, he had asserted that by selling Coca-Cola across Africa, the company was actually performing an important public health service. 'Fluid replenishment is a key to health, and when you have a population that has appropriate fluid intake, what you find is they have a lot less kidney problems and kidney disease,' he said. And he did indeed seem to believe it, although the World Health Organization did not even list kidney disease on its long list of Africa's problems. He had spent time with scientists, he said, who understood kidney problems, and 'some of them will tell you

Coca-Cola does a great service because it encourages people to take in more and more liquids.'

Now he addressed the question for Euripides Alcantara. 'First of all, we have a very healthy product,' he declared. 'Of course, our beverage contains sugar, but sugar is a good source of energy, of vitality, not to mention that it is a source of foreign exchange for exporter countries.' Brazil was one of these sugar-producing engines of the world, as Cuba had been when Goizueta lived there. But in many places Coca-Cola was no longer made with cane sugar. That ingredient had been replaced under Goizueta, who saw high-fructose corn syrup as an acceptable substitute, not to mention one that saved the company millions of dollars a year.

'Coca-Cola is an excellent complement to the habits of a healthy life,' Ivester went on. 'Naturally, people need to exercise and follow a balanced diet.' But concerns about health didn't seem to have stopped anyone from imbibing the world's most popular soft drink, he added. These days, he told Euripedes Alcantara, 'people drink more Coca-Cola than in any other period in the past.' That, indeed, was true.

The reporter asked Ivester about the company's adventures in Belgium, and about prospects for growth. Ivester responded to both predictably. And then, tape recorder whirring, Alcantara asked another question: about an obscure new technology he had heard Coke may have been testing, a technology focused around the vending machine.

The vending machine was a subject close to Ivester's heart. The company sold about 11 percent of its products through vending machines, known in Coke parlance as 'cold-drink equipment'. The potential in being able to sell ice-cold Cokes to a thirsty public had first dawned on a Coca-Cola bottler named George Cobb, who turned his idea into a contraption that he field-tested in 1910. Cobb was an Opelika, Alabama, native, the son of a country dentist whose patients brought him kindling and sweet potatoes as payment for his services. He named his machine the Vend-All Nickel in Slot Vending Machine and received a patent on it two years later. Depositing a nickel would release a catch that held down the machine's lid, and once open, a person could help himself to a bottle of Coke. The container held a dozen Coca-

Colas, along with a chunk of ice, and Cobb sold several of them to his fellow Coke entrepreneurs. Cobb, whose bottling franchise was based in West Point, Georgia, in the southwestern part of the state, went on to become one of the most successful bottlers in the entire Coke system. 'A Coca-Cola bottler with all of his family and loyal employees is one of the strongest business influences in any community,' he once wrote, 'and what a tremendous asset to the Parent Company!'

It was not until 1932 that the Coca-Cola Company officially approved coin-operated vending machines. Two years earlier it had endorsed mechanically refrigerated coolers as a way to 'improved serving of the bottled product', and in 1929, the year of the market crash, Coke had approved a refrigerated tub from which stores and other places could sell bottles of Coke. These tubs, known as open-top coolers, made it possible for Coke to be sold front and center. Bottled Coke got to 'move from the back room and the meat case to the front door of countless retail establishments', Coke noted in a history published in the 1960s. It was a good thing, too, as the popularity of the automobile made gas stations and other roadside stops great places to sell bottles of Coke.

Ivester liked vending machines because they had so far proved immune to the kinds of price wars Coke waged with Pepsi in supermarkets and other places. A vending machine sat mute outside a gas station or inside a teachers' lounge. It could be damaged and broken into, but by and large once a price was set and posted on the front, that was the amount a bottler could expect to collect for a twelve-ounce can of Sprite or a twenty-ounce bottle of Coca-Cola. They were usually cold, too, and people seemed willing to pay a little more for that. A cold Coke from a vending machine cost anywhere from fifty cents to $1.25, depending on the area of the country. A warm Coke, in a six-pack or a big bottle, purchased in a grocery store, cost less.

But Ivester's vision extended beyond the vending machine in its present form. Wireless technology was quickly approaching the point where it could be installed in the machine and programmed to communicate – with headquarters, with drivers, even with consumers – about the drinks it contained. Headquarters could find out which drinks were selling, and at what times of the day or night. Drivers would be contacted by wireless transmission that a machine was running low on Coke or Sprite or Fruitopia, so they could come along and replenish it. Consumers, meanwhile, could be called up, on their cell phones or pagers or wireless PDAs, and enticed to buy a Coca-Cola ('Ice-cold! Refreshing! A simple moment of pleasure! Enjoy!') at any moment.

Yes, he had great plans for vending. So when Euripedes Alcantara asked him a question about it, he responded with all sorts of information.

The reporter mentioned that he had heard that Coke was testing a new kind of vending machine, one with the electronic capability to change prices based on the weather. Ivester nodded. It was true, he said.

What kind of a trend is that? Alcantara asked.

'This is a classic situation of supply and demand,' Ivester replied, coolly and logically. 'If demand increases, the price tends to increase. Coca-Cola is a product whose utility varies from moment to moment. In a final summer championship, when people meet in a stadium to have fun, the utility of an ice-cold Coca-Cola is very high.

'So,' he continued, 'it is fair that it should be more expensive. The machine will simply make this process automatic.'

Alcantara dutifully wrote all this down. The interview was published in *Veja* in October, under the headline 'The World Is Thirsty'. Someone in America got his hands on a copy of the magazine, which publishes in Portuguese, and translated the article into English. The person took the translation to the nearest fax machine and dialed up the numbers of friends in competing soft-drink companies as well as reporters for major American news organizations.

And then the world of Coke was swallowed up in a hurricane of its own creation.

From coast to coast, and in virtually every country where Coca-Cola was sold, everyone heard about that vending machine. While a Coke spokesman in at least one newspaper article was careful to say that the machine had been tested but not installed in any country, people didn't care. As far as they were concerned, Coke was willing to raise prices for its drinks in hot weather – gouging its loyal customers as much as it could. Comedians like Jay Leno told jokes on late-night television about the Coke machine, at Coke's expense. Cartoons appeared, critiquing Coke. Editorials blossomed in newspapers large and small, lambasting Coke for believing it could exploit people's thirst. 'Ah, capitalism,' snorted one. 'Imagine this scene: It's July. It's ninety-four degrees. You're at the pool with the kids and everyone wants a drink. You fish in your wallet for the right change and head across the baking concrete to the drink machines. You feed in your quarters and – What's this? The price just went up a dollar?'

Television stations sent crews to interview Coke executives like Rob Baskin, whose job in the public relations division had just become a lot harder. The image of the Coca-Cola Company as benevolent, patriotic purveyor of a simple and refreshing drink, an image so carefully cultivated over the past 113 years, disappeared almost overnight. In its place came a greedy, grasping substitute, no friend to the consumer.

Ivester did not seem distressed by the situation. 'I went in to Doug, and I said, "This one is going to hurt us a little bit,"' said one former executive. 'And he said, "Well, you know it's true."' The executive said, 'Yes, I know it's true, but we wouldn't do it.' Ivester pointed out that the company had the technology, so he had merely illustrated the cutting-edge strength of Coca-Cola. He didn't see much of a problem. 'It'll blow over in a day or two,' he told his colleague. And then he turned back to his desk.

But it didn't blow over in a day or two. Political cartoonists continued to skewer Coke. Newspaper columnists railed against the arrogance of a company that thought it could use the weather, and a basic human need like thirst, to make even more money for itself. The tumult was unmatched by anything in recent Coca-Cola history, certainly not since the launch of New Coke fourteen years earlier. Television stations picked up the story and let everyone, everywhere, know that these were the Coca-Cola Company's plans. This was what those suits in Atlanta considered fair play. Where was the love?

'There were a thousand cartoons,' said a former Coke executive who collected them for history's sake. 'I am not exaggerating. *A thousand cartoons*. It wouldn't go away.'

Coke issued a statement insisting that the machine, as described, did not exist. But experts announced that the technology was already available for communication between vending machines and companies that owned them, and it was merely a matter of deciding on the application, not a matter of developing the software.

Ivester had been under other pressures at the time the vending-machine story appeared. He was still thinking about whether to choose a deputy. And he had to worry about the price of Coke's concentrate – in 1999, as in 1886, the central, fundamental source of profit for the company.

First, he wanted to streamline the command by naming three people to report to him.

Ivester didn't want to anoint someone as his lone deputy, concerned that, for better or worse, being number two would define the person going forward. He no doubt also didn't want to have to worry, on top of everything else, about the sometimes difficult relationship between a CEO and their deputy. For all the years that he had watched Keough and Goizueta interact, he had seen how difficult it could be to have two strong personalities sharing the Coca-Cola pinnacle, and he probably worried about how he would fare if he put himself in the same position.

So he came up with an approach that solved many issues at once.

When Ivester had been president of Coke, there had been virtually nothing standing between his vision of the company and the attainment of that vision. Some claimed that Ivester was extremely ambitious, and that Goizueta, running out of energy by the mid-1990s, had allowed himself to be elbowed out of the way. But what happened with the two of them was by design, and not the result of Ivester's ambition. 'After 1991 or so,' says one Coke executive, 'Goizueta had moved away from managing the business to being a role model for the business and for the rest of America.'

That role was the role of a lifetime, and it suited Goizueta exquisitely. He took on speaking engagements, got on the airplane to points far and near, presided over events like the swearing-in of newly naturalized citizens. He began working on a bequest to the thirsty planet, which would be his thoughts on corporate governance.

Ivester could never hope to follow that act. But he knew he could become a symbol of another sort. He could be the cool, collected über-executive, the kind of manager who let nothing about his company get beyond his control.

That explained his relentless schedule, and his frequent travels to make decisions in markets far from Atlanta. It explained his fervent bid to redesign the bottling system so that it would be better aligned with Coke's plans. And it explained his decision not to insert another person between him and the rest of the company. Naming a president would interrupt the flow of information, which enhanced his ability to control the business. Ivester enjoyed the power that came with being chairman, but he was all for efficiency, too. Adding someone who would compete with him for attention, power, and credit would be foolish. It could slow him down and might even knock him flat. He had seen how it all worked, and he had to be careful.

One of the analysts had asked him, back at the meeting in New York in July: Would he name a president soon?

'I personally don't feel the need to do that,' Ivester said. 'My time allocation is strategic. I don't feel like I need a filter. The way the business operates today, you need less hierarchy, not more.'

He decided to reorganize the senior ranks, giving over many of his responsibilities to a trio of senior vice presidents – all of them men he felt he could trust. Instead of having twelve people reporting directly to him, he would deal directly with only those three. They were all longtime Coca-Cola Company executives, all used to his style and his work habits. The first was Doug Daft, who had spent years abroad selling Coca-Cola in difficult places like Indonesia and China. Daft was known internally as a kind of eccentric professor, and indeed he had once been a math teacher, which helped make the image stick.

His spectacles and tufted hairstyle gave him an owlish appearance, but he was also known to be a keen competitor. He was an operations man, a protégé of Keough's, who infinitely preferred to be away from Atlanta and out in the field. When Goizueta had informed him in 1991 that as head of Coke's operations in the Far East and the Middle East, he'd be expected to live in Atlanta, Daft acquiesced reluctantly. He kept an apartment in London and a ski house in Switzerland. He also had a weekend place in Williamstown, Massachusetts, not far from a house owned by Herbert Allen, who had graduated from Williams College.

For Daft, Coca-Cola had always meant sports. The association had begun when he was a young boy growing up in a small Australian town and the local Coke bottler brought cricket stars and other athletes around to sign autographs for the wide-eyed children. Ken Rosewall, the Australian tennis star, came to Daft's school once, and he never forgot it. 'I don't remember my first Coke,' he would say, 'but I remember what Coke represented.'

Daft and Ivester seemed to get along. With Asia such a huge market for Coke, they needed each other. Still, while Ivester was ascending, Daft had concluded that his own career had plateaued. He would never be the man running the Coca-Cola Company. He had spent close to twenty-five years there by the time Ivester was named president, and his loyalty to the place was deep. Once, in the 1970s, he had left Coke to open a liquor distributorship in Australia. He had come running back to the Coca-Cola Company a year later. There he had remained, amassing millions of dollars worth of stock options but always remaining just below the top in terms of salary, and in terms of power. He did, however, see a lot of Herbert Allen when both were in Williamstown.

Keough liked Daft because he went out and did whatever he was asked to do and didn't demand a huge round of applause afterward. In some ways, he was as quiet about himself as Ivester. He seemed even-tempered for the most part, but people who crossed him found he could be unpleasant at times. He once excoriated a local marketing executive at a meeting in Tokyo, causing the man to break down in tears when he got back to his desk. 'Japanese people can't take it when your boss yells and screams and calls you names,' said Ben Kitay, a vice president in Tokyo at the time. 'You just don't do that in Japan.'

The second executive Ivester tapped was Jack Stahl, the president of Coke's North American business. North America, as Coke liked to refer to the business that was mostly in the United States but included Canada, had been bogged down for years by a price war with Pepsi in the supermarkets that Ivester was still trying to fix.

Stahl had joined the company's investor relations department in 1979, around the same time that Ivester had come over from Ernst & Young. The two had little in common before they arrived at Coke, but once united, they shared a love of numbers and a desire to see Coca-Cola remain the top-selling soft drink in the land. Stahl willingly exhorted bottlers to increase their market share, even if that meant shrinking profits along the way. Soon enough, everyone figured, Coke's dominance would enable it to raise prices and all would be well. So deals of all kinds were struck across the land: to provide services like marketing to clients as big as Burger King, to increase Coke's share of joint advertising programs in supermarkets where Coke wanted Coca-Cola to be king. Stahl participated in all kinds of plans that were meant to make Coke the biggest soft drink ever.

The final member of the new management tier was James Chestnut. Slender and dark-haired, his face distinguished by a thick mustache in a company where any kind of hair below the eyebrows was frowned upon, he had worked for Coke all over the world. His accent was difficult to trace – Scotland? Australia? A little of both? He had bonded with Ivester in their quest for control of the financial vicissitudes of the business. He succeeded Ivester as Coke's chief financial officer after Ivester stepped out of that role. It was still one of the most important jobs at Coke. The stability of the company that Goizueta, Keough, and Ivester had engineered eighteen years before depended on it.

Chestnut projected the kind of confidence before analysts and investors that the company needed. He was not as elegant as Goizueta and not as imposing physically as Ivester, but he could answer questions put to him with a wealth of carefully chosen detail. He helped convey Coke's messages to the world, and for most of his career, those communications had gone flawlessly.

The trio would keep their own responsibilities and oversee other areas in Ivester's place. Tim Haas, the president of Coke's Latin American business, now reported not to Ivester, but to Jack Stahl. Haas had had a tough time of it lately. Coke's prospects had dimmed in Brazil, Colombia, and Venezuela almost overnight.

Currency issues, over-investment and political instability had eroded what once seemed like surefire markets for Coca-Cola.

It appeared that, to Carl Ware, the change was not a positive one. He never came out and said anything about it publicly. But within a week, Ware had made up his mind to leave the Coca-Cola Company. He announced his plans in early November. People in the public relations office at Coke had just finished congratulating themselves on how well received the reorganization had been; then they had to scramble to deal with a new issue. The only black senior vice president the Coca-Cola Company had ever had – the head of the Diversity Council – was quitting, in the middle of Coke's attempt to defend itself against racial-discrimination allegations.

Though Ware was quitting, he was persuaded to call his departure a retirement. He was just fifty-six years old. Retirement had always been the preferred term at Coke; age was never a factor. It was what athletes did when their knees began to go. In the executive suite, it implied a measured, tactical move: to see more of the children or play more golf.

Working with Ware, the company came up with a mutually acceptable statement to describe what he was doing. 'This decision reflects thinking I have been doing for some time,' Ware announced. 'I've always made choices based on setting priorities, and my decision to leave the company is indicative of that.' He added: 'Personally, I want to be able to spend more time with my wife, my son, and my grandchildren.'

Across Atlanta, civil rights leaders began buzzing about Carl Ware. Here was the top black at the Coca-Cola Company, and he was retiring? They didn't buy it. Many assumed, however wrongly, that Ware had been pushed out. Look at that company, people said. Its employees were already suing it, saying there was no hope for promotion and good pay if a person happened to be black. Now, they said, what happened to Carl Ware just proved it.

Six months earlier, Ware had gone before the cameras and the reporters to assure the world that the lawsuit was wrong, and Coke was right. 'He was that black face, if you will, that Coke tried to put on their policies,' said the Reverend Joseph Wheeler, who was active in Atlanta's civil rights community and was surprised when

Ware resigned. 'They would put him on television, and they would try to make it seem like the complaints don't have merit.' That was before anyone outside the company knew about the 1995 report that Ware had put together, describing the plight of black executives at Coke.

'Coke is known for making deals,' Wheeler said. 'But this is really a serious issue. It's interesting to watch the Coke officials dance around this.'

They danced long and hard. With the dots connected, it was not good for Ware to go. The official announcement from the Coke press office said that Ware would remain the head of the Africa division until the end of 2000. 'We are fortunate,' Ivester said in the statement, 'he will remain with us for the next year to ensure a smooth and successful transition of the leadership of the group.' But he was not quitting, everyone in the front office at Coke would insist. He just wanted to retire.

Cyrus Mehri, the lawyer for the four plaintiffs in the racial-discrimination lawsuit, observed the activity with quiet delight. Mehri had finally succeeded in obtaining help with his lawsuit from Bondurant, Mixson & Elmore, a top Atlanta law firm where one of the partners was Emmet Bondurant, the lawyer who had sued Coke on behalf of Bill Schmidt and other Coke bottlers a generation before. Thanks to Carl Ware, Mehri thought, he had Coke where he wanted it. He couldn't have written a better script himself.

The lawsuit was by then in its seventh month. The two sides had gotten partway through the discovery process, with Mehri angrily filing motions that contended Coke lawyers were purposely destroying documents that described the hiring and promotion processes inside the company. The case was large and cumbersome and complicated. At times, Mehri asked himself whether it was going to succeed. He knew he had the human resources data to back up his clients' claims. But he had never gone up against a giant like Coke. They could afford more lawyers for their defense than he could ever hope to muster. Until the retirement of Carl Ware, Mehri had been having a bit of a confidence crisis.

Now he pulled himself together and began to pursue other paths that he had almost forgotten about. He continued the work he had begun on an enormous class-action brief, compiled from the accounts of dozens of African Americans who worked for Coke or who had recently left Coke. He and his assistants put everything into a file, and the file grew. By the time they were done, the documents for the brief would fill thirty boxes. And the brief itself would function as a wild card in Mehri's strategy against Coke.

Keough sat up and took notice when the Carl Ware retirement was announced. Keough knew how Coke could be harmed if its constituents in the African American community were unhappy. Coke sold a huge proportion of its products, especially Sprite, to blacks; entire advertising campaigns had been constructed around NBA players with just that purpose in mind. He thought Ivester's move was a terrible one. The board had not signed off on it, since the reorganization had not required approval. To Keough, this was one more example of the problems plaguing the Coca-Cola Company, *ever since Roberto died*. He heaved a great sigh. He climbed out of his padded leather chair and walked around the corner to see if Herbert Allen was in.

Ivester, meanwhile, was looking at the world differently. To him, the Carl Ware problem had been wrestled to the ground, with a minimum mess. Ware was staying for another year and meanwhile, Ivester had one more thorny issue to tackle. That was the matter of Coke's concentrate price.

For a dozen years, Coke had negotiated an annual concentrate price increase with its biggest bottler, Coca-Cola Enterprises. In 1998, there was one major difference. Earlier in the year, the bottler, along with the other American bottlers of all sizes, had received permission from Coke to increase prices at the supermarkets. It was a major step, intended to stem profit losses by the bottlers, and it held deep ramifications both for the bottlers and for Coke.

The bottlers raised prices by 3 percent in some markets, 6 percent in others. It was expected, of course, that shoppers would hesitate over this. The sixty-nine-cent, two-liter bottle of Coke had been part of the scene for too long.

But Coke didn't want consumers to hesitate too much. That would cut into the volume growth in terms of the Coke syrup sold to bottlers. And the bottlers didn't want consumers to hesitate, because that would leave them with millions of cases of Coke and other soft drinks that had nowhere to go.

So the price increases were agreed upon and put into effect. And then a strange thing happened. People balked, but not the way Coke thought they would. They did not want to pay more for Coca-Cola, but they went right down the aisle and picked out bottled water, fruit juices, bottled teas, and energy drinks – all of which cost more than Coke.

The price increases began in March. By the time November 1999 arrived, Ivester had made his decision on the concentrate price. Instead of raising it 2 or 3 percent, in line with consumer price increases, he would raise it a whopping 7 percent. He felt he had to. It had been a tough year, and he had the earnings of the Coca-Cola Company to consider – earnings that were supposed to grow every year by double-digit rates.

The ability to raise concentrate prices was all Coke's, exerting an enormous and unavoidable influence on bottlers. 'CCE cannot control its own destiny from the standpoint of concentrate price increases and marketing funds,' said Richard Larson, a former executive at the bottler. 'To a large extent, our profitability is controlled by the Coca-Cola Company.'

Ivester knew that his plan would be unpopular, and that he would run some risks in pushing it through. The biggest of all would be from the biggest bottler of all, the Coca-Cola Enterprises that he had created some thirteen years earlier. At the helm sat Summerfield Johnston, a man sufficiently legendary to command such a beast. And Johnston was already angry at Ivester over something else.

In May, Henry Schimberg, the bottler's chief executive, had announced plans to retire about three months ahead of schedule. It surprised many analysts, who had expected him to hang around as long as possible. Schimberg and Johnston shared the credit for taking Coca-Cola Enterprises from the soft-drink equivalent of the doghouse all the way up to a special spot in investors' hearts. Until 1999, Coca-Cola Enterprises' stock had been soaring, right there with Coke's. It had risen and split multiple times, just like Coke's, and people at the company were regularly admonished not to sell any of it.

With Henry Schimberg leaving, Coca-Cola Enterprises would need a new chief executive. And Summerfield wanted his son, Summerfield III, to take over. But as the largest shareholder, Coke had control over that choice. And Ivester said he preferred to elevate someone else.

Summerfield Johnston, Jr., was furious. Instead of Skeeter, Ivester chose John Alm, a slender former accountant who may have reminded Ivester, at least a little, of himself. Alm brought a sense of humor and a sharp skill with numbers to the company. He had been working there for many years. He was not an unlikely or inappropriate choice.

But Summerfield Johnston didn't like it. He was breathing fire. His Coca-Cola stock had already declined by close to 30 percent. He was the second-largest shareholder in Coca-Cola Enterprises, after Coke itself, and after the Belgian recall and other unflattering developments, the market value of that stake had been sheared in half. Then came the news about the concentrate price going up twice as fast as usual. That was the last straw, Johnston decided. Ivester had to be stopped.

For the bottlers had grown up. He stood at the helm of the biggest one, and he wasn't going to take this. 'If you're up on a ladder and it's beginning to fall, you sure want somebody to stop it,' he would say. 'You're not going to sit there and just let it go down.'

He missed Roberto, and he missed Don Keough, who had been gone for years. In his opinion, those two had taken a lot of what was good about the Coca-Cola Company with them when they left. Keough 'understood our business', Johnston said. 'He was always very close to the bottlers and very sympathetic.' After Keough left Coke in 1993, Johnston thought things in general had started to deteriorate. Here came the rapid acquisitions of new territories; here came the huge debts; here came the unsuccessful plan to raise prices in the marketplace and now the leap in concentrate price that was sure to hurt bottlers further.

Johnston still heard from Keough on a regular basis, and now Keough started to hear from Johnston. So did some other key people at Coke. 'I was obviously unhappy,' Johnston recalled. 'I had a lot of discussions with everybody.' He was friendly with several board members and let them know how he felt, too. 'I've never been noted for not saying what I think,' he said.

The huge bottler that Ivester had thought up began to lash its tail, and the effect was not good for Coke.

'I can assure you that we don't control CCE,' a senior Coke executive would say later. And that became apparent. The model that had been put together in 1986, while contemplating uninterrupted good times, was coming apart. No one had prepared for the downside of creating a massive bottler: that if that bottler got angry, it could cause big problems for Coke.

Johnston went to Keough and poured out his lamentation. Keough listened, nodded sympathetically, told him he'd see what could be done. Later, he picked up the phone.

Chapter Eighteen

Enjoy

DAWN WAS BREAKING OVER Atlanta as Doug Ivester flew to Chicago. It was a Wednesday, the first day of December, 1999. He was tired, but he held his chin high.

It had been two years and six weeks since Roberto died. He had been pitched with little warning into a role he felt ready to take on, only to have the world unravel around him. Like a prizefighter, he felt he had outlasted his opponents, the tangible and the unseen, all of them. He had steered the company through a truly terrible year, with public relations disasters on almost every conceivable front, but now the worst seemed behind him. The latest volume estimates, which he would be releasing shortly, suggested a vast worldwide improvement in Coke's fortunes, with consumption going up just about everywhere.

On Wall Street, the analysts who had been watching with increasing alarm breathed sighs of relief. The stock, hovering below sixty dollars for weeks, popped back up and seemed to be holding at about sixty-seven dollars a share. The analysts thought that after a horrifying ride through previously unimaginable turbulence, the old Coca-Cola Company, the one they had all fallen in love with so long ago, was back.

Ivester was on his way to a morning meeting in Chicago with executives of McDonald's, the biggest fast-food chain in the world. The McDonald's account was the single largest customer for Coke's fountain business, and Ivester always saw to it that he met with the McDonald's brass himself. This meeting was for the board of Ronald McDonald House, a children's charity that was a high priority for everyone connected with the golden arches. Ivester was also keenly aware that Don Keough sat on the McDonald's board of directors and was in constant contact with its other members.

Though Keough had been pried loose from the Coca-Cola Company, he remained involved with other institutions tied to Coke. When there was a McDonald's event on the calendar, Ivester took care of it himself. From a business perspective, and from a personal one, he could not afford to let anything go wrong at McDonald's.

He arrived in Chicago aboard one of the Coke jets, his breath puffing white in the wintry air as he made his way to the meeting. It went smoothly and was over within a couple of hours.

Around lunchtime, two more private jets touched down in Chicago. One came from the west, the other from the east. One held Warren Buffett; the other belonged to Herbert Allen.

After lunch Ivester's driver took him back to the airport. They passed the city, where the waters of Lake Michigan were the color of slate and a metallic glow lingered along the skyline. Ivester had been to Chicago plenty of times, and he rarely had time to spare, to take in the art museum or a Cubs game or anything beyond his business there. On this trip, as usual, he had many other issues demanding his attention, and he could not hang around. Before he could return to Atlanta, though, he had one more appointment to keep.

Ivester had gotten a call from Allen earlier in the week, asking if he and Buffett could meet with him. When Ivester had said he would be in Chicago on the first of December, Allen had said they'd meet him there.

Allen had mentioned no particular agenda for the meeting, but that hardly mattered. When two of the most influential members of the Coke board, who were also two of Coke's biggest shareholders, wanted to meet with him, it was his obligation to find the time. So the chairman and chief executive of the Coca-Cola Company walked into the office inside the executive jet hangar where they had agreed to meet, gave a cordial salutation, and listened to what they had to say.

Unlike Goizueta, who had supreme finesse when it came to encounters with Coke's directors, Ivester had never made dealing with the board a separate priority. He considered himself the board's employee, as well as its chairman, and always held that he served at the pleasure of the directors. To keep his job, he reasoned, he had to meet the expectations of shareholders – by increasing shareholder value – and that, too, was what the board desired. He had once acknowledged that increasing shareholder value, that mantra of the company for the sixteen Goizueta years and the ones that came after, occupied his thoughts 'twenty-four hours a day, seven days a week'. Building, strengthening, and solidifying the Coca-Cola empire was the way to accomplish that, he had long believed. That was the way he did his job.

The board's other eleven members, though, were a group handpicked by Goizueta that Ivester had inherited. There was no one that he had selected since he had become chairman, and perhaps that mirrored his belief that the board wasn't broken, didn't need fixing. Indeed, his alterations to the board had been few – deciding not to renew Don Keough's consulting contract in 1998, which meant that Keough, who had not been a director since 1993, no longer sat in on the meetings. Another was instituting a period of time at the end of every board meeting during which he would leave the room so the others could discuss whatever was on their minds that might pertain to his leadership of the company.

For two decades Ivester had been appearing before many of these directors to present a plan, describe a strategy, detail a success. Over the years they had applauded him at the same time they applauded Goizueta, and after Goizueta was gone they had applauded him as a solo act. He had not perceived a need to stroke them, to send them presents, and to organize upbeat field trips to new markets abroad, as Goizueta had done – in part because all that had taken place already, and because his tenure at Coke had been largely one of preserving the status quo. He had been like a fireman, responding to emergencies when they erupted, in places like Belgium, Atlanta, the Far East. He had not altered the vision.

Goizueta had been an oracle before the board, pronouncing the present a success, declaring that the future would be an even greater one. Ivester had been the one who quietly addressed problems and solved them for Goizueta when Goizueta was alive, while Goizueta was drinking his Cokes over ice or laughing with Buffett or strolling out of the tower at four-thirty every afternoon. He had contributed to the illusion that Goizueta possessed infallibility, unheard of in a modern American corporation. And then, after Goizueta died, he had continued to fix everything – for himself and mostly by himself.

The board had been pleased and had shown its pleasure in various ways. The year Goizueta died, Ivester got a $2 million bonus that included an extra $635,000 given at the board's discretion. The award was for that year's earnings and volume growth, which had continued unchecked, and for what the company's proxy statement called 'the smoothness of the transition of leadership'.

There in that hangar in Chicago, Ivester might have thought that Coke's directors planned to congratulate him on some minor success within the company recently, maybe those new volume numbers that seemed so much brighter. Or maybe they had an idea about an acquisition they thought he should make. Buffett was famed for his dealmaking, and so was Allen. Both of them were tuned in to the inner workings of the Coca-Cola Company, and both of them had enormous vested interests in the company's success: Allen with more than 9.5 million shares of Coke stock, Buffett with 200 million. Buffett's Coke holdings were worth more than $13 billion that December afternoon, about $4 billion less than they had been a year and a half earlier.

Ivester stood before them in his winter coat: pale, but with the scars of the past year hidden, his demeanor still exuding the confidence he was famous for. They could have asked him any question at all and he would have answered it with poise and self-assurance. That was his hallmark, and he had never failed in that. He had just been through an unbelievably awful period, with failed deals, a racial-discrimination lawsuit, a huge product recall, and tarnished images, Coke's and his, to show for it. He had taken the hits for that on his own. And the company was going to be fine. He was proud of that.

This, Buffett and Allen observed, was the chairman of the Coca-Cola Company, the man who had succeeded the great Roberto Goizueta, their hero, who created a new Coca-Cola Company from the winking embers of the old one. Neither of them had been part of the old one. They had come along as the miracle began and enjoyed every minute of the ride. One of them was midwestern in his sensibilities; the other one a New Yorker. Together they controlled about $14 billion worth of Coke shares, and they needed, wanted, expected to have the Coke success story continue.

Perhaps they reflected on Ivester's achievements for a moment, noting that he had solved all kinds of thorny problems, like the U.S. bottling situation, for Coke. Perhaps they did not.

Moments into the meeting, it was clear that they were not there to pay him compliments. They never sat down, never even removed their overcoats. In tones frostier than the air outside, they told him that they had lost confidence in him. 'I felt I had the obligation to tell him,' Allen said later. 'Warren felt the same way.'

They made it clear that they wanted him to leave the Coca-Cola Company. It was something of a gamble. There had been no vote by the full board of directors, and if Ivester had decided to challenge them, they could have been humiliated before their fellow directors. But given information like this from two shareholders with so much clout, not many company chairmen would choose to stand and fight. And Ivester did not want to tear the company apart.

So he stood silently, their words coursing swiftly through his brain. Never in the history of Coke had a company chairman been fired. When Coke was a place ruled by one man, such things could happen with other executives. Candler or Woodruff might have expressed displeasure with someone, and that person might have been sent packing, but never had members of the board of directors of the Coca-Cola Company actively unseated a leader of Coke. It was unprecedented.

He might have turned white, or red, or developed pink spots high along his cheekbones as he checked his feelings and clung tightly to his composure. Some men might have argued, and some men would have gotten angry, perhaps raised their voices inside the closed room. But Ivester showed next to no emotion, and said he would oblige. That was the kind of man he was. 'I think he was shocked,' Allen said. 'He didn't think he could run the company without the support of the two of us.'

Ivester was shocked, all right, but for a different reason. He had guessed that something like this might happen – clandestine meetings almost never meant good news – and had told his wife,

Kay, of his suspicions the night before. When the meeting was over he called her and said, 'I was right.'

He could not believe that they would fire him without the consent of the rest of the board. They even had a separation package worked out for him, which included a very large amount of money, and Allen told Ivester when to hold the board meeting at which he would announce he was leaving.

The three of them said good-bye and went their separate ways, each to his own jet and each holding separate opinions about the effect their brief conversation would have on the Coca-Cola Company, the place they all worshiped, the owner of the world's best-known brand and the fuel for their dreams of wealth and power.

By the time Ivester got back to Atlanta, the sky was fading. From the window of his jet, he looked down on the lights twinkling on across the city, a city he had flown from as the ruler of the Coca-Cola Company only that morning and where he knew he would no longer be regarded with the same respect once word of his fate got out. He had sometimes thought about what it would be like to leave the Coca-Cola Company, to no longer have it in his life. And now, after twenty years there, he saw that this was how it would happen. He had not expected the reel to end like this – before the story was complete.

He would spend the next two days working out the details of his severance package with Allen, who oversaw compensation for Coke's senior executives. He agreed to stay on as long as the board wanted, in his belief that the Coca-Cola Company should come first. He was not rapacious, and not self-centered. He had always tried to make decisions based on what would be best for the company, and this time was no different.

By the evening of Friday, December 3, he had begun to tell his close friends at the company about his fate. Each person he told reacted the same way: with astonishment. Doug Ivester was no fly-by-night executive hired from the outside to run a company. He was a true Coca-Cola man, the kind who bled Coca-Cola red, as they liked to say at Coke. He had been tapped by Roberto Goizueta, the designer of the company as the world now knew it. Goizueta, the Coke deity, had thought Ivester had what it took to run the company. Now he would have to pack up and go, just like that. He made everyone he told keep the news under their hats until Monday, when the board would announce his departure. That Friday afternoon, Coke stock closed at $68.31, a high for the year.

He would say nothing about how he had received the statements from Allen and Buffett, or how he had taken them. He was businesslike, as always. He kept the company's best interests in mind, refusing to whine or complain about what had happened to him, and he carried out the wishes of the Coca-Cola Company right up to the end, even going along with the wording of the official announcement, settled upon by Allen and Jimmy Williams, that he had decided 'to retire'. It was an odd choice of words. He was just fifty-two years old.

His replacement would be Doug Daft, who would say he heard the news that Friday, from Ivester himself. Daft described their encounter as 'emotional', and for days afterward, he would radiate seemingly genuine shock that he had been chosen as the new leader of the Coca-Cola Company. He had, after all, been passed over by Goizueta and the board years earlier. He had had no right to hope that he would have a turn running Coke. And now, here it was – completely unexpected, Daft told everyone. 'There weren't a lot of choices,' Allen observed later.

Over the weekend, someone told Jack Stahl that Ivester was leaving. Stahl, one of the top three deputies to Ivester, seemed unable to comprehend the news at first. It was the equivalent of an assassination at Coke, except there was no blood and no corpse. Instead, a healthy man would be walking out of the building for good, driven out by forces no one had seen coming.

One by one, everyone else got the word. Ralph Cooper, a thirty-year veteran of Coke who had worked in Europe and ran the Minute Maid division from Houston, found out on Sunday. So did James Chestnut, who had long been close to Ivester and Daft. Everyone was shocked.

A special meeting of the board was called that Sunday. Several directors did not know, until the meeting began, why it was being held. Allen and Buffett presented Ivester's departure as a choice he had made; 'Doug wants to resign,' one person involved in the discussions remembered one of them saying during the meeting. Many of the directors were stunned that the Coke chairman was quitting.

The successor had been chosen. The company would have to move on. The meeting, conducted in Atlanta but with several directors piped in by telephone, ran longer than anyone expected. Eventually, the board agreed to announce the following morning that Ivester was leaving.

The rest of the world got the news on Monday, December 6, about half an hour before the stock market's opening bell. The announcement rolled across the ticker, and over the television screens, and across the airwaves all over the country, and the world.

And then all hell broke loose.

Ivester had taken his dismissal stoically, but it would not be that way in the rest of the world of Coke. His departure rocked the company, alarmed Atlanta, unsettled Wall Street, and rippled through the rest of the country and the world. No one had anticipated this. As difficult as the last year had been for Coke, no one expected that its chairman would lose his job — or quit his job — over it. Next to no one believed that Ivester had given up voluntarily. He was youthful, he was energetic, and he clearly loved his work, even during its bleakest moments. Besides, everyone at Coke, starting with him, was conditioned to take the long view. Why should he be out after barely two years on the job? What was Coke thinking?

It caused an enormous commotion. In New York, Andrew Conway stared in disbelief at the statement from Coke that filled his computer screen, headlined 'M. Douglas Ivester Announces Plan to Retire'. On the other side of town, the owner of the Philadelphia Coca-Cola bottling franchise, Bruce Llewellyn, was also stunned. He knew and admired Ivester as the architect of Coke's global strategy, and he had had no inkling that he was in danger. Reporters, hearing the news from colleagues as they hung up their coats, thought it was some kind of untimely April Fool's prank. No one had seen this coming.

Questions were lobbed at the company all day from all directions, but everyone at Coke stubbornly stuck to the script. Ivester, perhaps the most dedicated executive in the history of the

Coca-Cola Company, a man in the middle of carrying out his predecessor's vision for that company, a man known for flying halfway around the world to supervise a decision he felt needed his close attention, had had enough. He was retiring, they said, and the board of directors had reluctantly accepted his decision.

To explain all this to a skeptical world, Coke enlisted Jimmy Williams, whose loyalty to Coke was bred in his bones. He was a southern gentleman who had watched Atlanta grow up with the help of the Coca-Cola Company. He had been on Coke's board for nearly two decades, and he oversaw trusts that relied on their millions of Coca-Cola shares for income that led to good works. He had been present when Roberto Goizueta took his first trip to Ichauway and learned to shoot by firing at Coke cans lined up along a fence. Now he knew he had to do whatever it took to get the message Coke wanted across.

'Doug has informed the board of his desire to retire,' he said in a statement he would repeat verbatim to reporters in interviews throughout that day, 'a decision the board has reluctantly accepted.' There was even a quote that the company issued from Ivester himself, though he would not be available otherwise to speak to reporters about what had happened. It was couched in careful language and contained as much mystery as information.

'After extensive reflection and thought,' the Ivester statement read, 'I have concluded that it is time for me to move on to the next stage of my life and, therefore, to put into place an orderly transition for this great company.'

The company announced that its next chairman and chief executive would be Doug Daft. At fifty-six, Daft was four years older than Ivester. He seemed thunderstruck, awed, discombobulated by his fate. In interviews, he would express pure amazement that he was going to be the next chairman and chief executive of Coke. Few people outside the Coke tower had ever heard of him. He promised no rapid changes at the company, and people believed him. He had been no more than an also-ran when Goizueta was looking around for a successor to groom. His designation by the board as chairman-elect only increased the surprise around Ivester's departure.

Daft would insist later that he was oblivious to whatever

machinations had vaulted him into his new role. Keough, though, was quickly on the telephone praising Daft to reporters, analysts, and anyone who would listen. 'The fellow is the right man at the right time at the right place,' Keough told one reporter. 'He's going to have a lot of fun with it, when all is said and done.' Someone else lined up Daft's son to provide cheerful insights about his father. The Coke machine, stalled momentarily by the abrupt departure of Ivester, began to hum.

Daft insisted that he had been kept in the dark about the activities that led to his remarkable ascension. He said he didn't know what the board had done, or what role Keough might have played, or even what led to Ivester's departure.

'I don't necessarily know what happened,' he would say, more than two years later. 'I don't know, and I don't want to know. There were tensions, obviously. I really don't know what was in people's minds.'

The news that Ivester was leaving washed across others and left them in a state of perplexed amazement. While some companies might lose their chairmen and not see their share price take much of a beating, Coke would experience the opposite. Andrew Conway sat at his desk and wrote an unflattering assessment of Coke's prospects without Ivester. He had never written anything so negative about any company. And he did something he had never done in his career as a Coke analyst: He downgraded the stock. 'It's the equivalent of a major earthquake in Atlanta,' he said. The aftershocks rattled across Wall Street all day. Coke's share price, its hallowed measure of itself, suffered its biggest single-session drop in more than seventeen years.

Conway never stopped thinking about Ivester's departure. He saw it as something tragic, and also telling. He tacked the official announcement to the wall above his desk, where it would remain for years. It was the most momentous episode in the history of this company he had studied and admired for close to a decade, he believed, and he did not want to forget it.

Perhaps to contain the havoc, Coke also released its volume estimates for the fourth quarter shortly after announcing the news about Ivester. In true Coke tradition, a tradition begun under Goizueta, the estimates came three weeks before the end of the quarter. Coke said it was on track, with sales ahead of those for the third quarter. The stock, conditioned for so many years to pop up on the announcement, swung lower. Analysts were even more confused. Why, if the tide was turning, would Ivester decide to step down *now*? How could this have happened?

From Coke's front office, the spinning became more intense as the day wore on. A few more details were offered up. Doug Ivester, said a company spokesman, 'decided at the end of last week that it was time for fresh leadership at the Coca-Cola Company. He had some conversations with a few board members, they called a special meeting, and they reluctantly accepted his notice of retirement.'

Time for 'fresh leadership'? A 'special meeting'? Marc Cohen, an analyst for Goldman Sachs, held conference calls with his biggest clients but was at a loss to decipher what was happening in Atlanta. 'The explanation for his departure at this point in time for the reasons I've been offered seems incomplete,' he said when the market had closed. 'It strikes me as odd timing, if indeed the business has been repaired and is heading in a positive direction.'

If the point of unseating Ivester was to rescue the stock, it did not work. After reaching its yearlong high on the previous Friday, Coke's share price closed nearly four dollars lower on the news that Ivester would be leaving, and lost another five dollars the next day.

Don Keough was nowhere near Atlanta when all this took place. He was not in New York, either. It was the week of his annual shooting trip in England with his sons, and that was where he was, scaring up pheasant in the long grass of the Old World and pelting them with lead. He would not read the news on the ticker along with so many other people, and he would say later that it was several days after the fact before he learned that Ivester was leaving. Some of his associates were jubilant. 'We've been working on this for two years,' one of them blurted to another Coke executive, back in Atlanta.

Divining how Coke's board reached its decision was not a simple matter. Analysts grasped at straws. The Carl Ware situation hadn't helped Ivester, but then again, wasn't the business turning around? The vending machine that could change its prices had been a moment of embarrassment for the company, but what about all those more recent moments of pleasure, like the volume numbers starting to go up again? Ivester himself remained incommunicado.

'It was a series of things,' said one executive, who is still at Coke and has close ties to some of the most senior people. 'There were two big bungles: the vending machine that could raise prices, and Carl Ware. And then you had the bottlers, who had all been whispering that he was breaking them. So in the fall, the board put the ugly puzzle together.'

Keough, who worked so closely with Allen on other projects, would never take any credit for what happened to Ivester, though he would say without hesitation that he thought it was the right move for the company.

But to many people then working for Coke, Keough's close friendships with Allen and Buffett, not to mention Summerfield Johnston, all might have been instrumental in turning opinion against Ivester.

'There were enough problems with Ivester that you didn't have to have Keough,' Donald McHenry said. 'Clearly, there is a limit to your relationship with the bottlers. Clearly, it's just not wise to appear to be saying, "To hell with the regulators in Washington or in Europe, I'm going to get it done."'

When asked about Daft, Keough had nothing but praise. Daft was capable, responsive, businesslike, enthusiastic, he said. Sometimes he praised him at Ivester's expense. 'To be a dour, uptight person selling Coca-Cola is a contradiction in terms,' he told one interviewer.

At first, Keough stayed offstage. Gradually, though, he became more vocal and more visible at Coke once again. Before long, Daft announced that Don Keough would be returning as a 'senior adviser' to the company. He would continue to hold the post of chairman at Allen & Company as well. He split his time between Atlanta and New York, collecting no salary at either place but sharing in the bonuses at Allen and regaining perks, like a personal assistant and access to the corridors of power, at Coke. He began attending Coca-Cola board meetings once more.

Perhaps he saw himself as a knight riding to the rescue of the company he had loved for so long. Perhaps this was, for him, a long-awaited second act. But in any case, now Ivester's telephone had stopped ringing and Keough's rang all the time. Nearly seven years had passed since his final send-off on the green lawns beneath the Coke tower. Now, people couldn't help but notice he was back.

Some at the company were glad to see him. He represented the old style of doing things at Coke, a style in which pats on the back were prevalent. It was a style many of them had longed for under Ivester, when they felt the company had become chilly and impersonal and overly focused on the bottom line. 'He truly loves the company,' said Joe Wilkinson, a longtime admirer and former Coke executive, 'and he's got this incredible legacy, but he's adding to it.' At the same time, Wilkinson was reminded of the *Apollo 11* crew, and how Neil Armstrong, not Buzz Aldrin, got to be the first man to set foot on the moon. 'There's kind of a little bit of that with Keough,' he said. 'A little bit of "I should have been there first."'

A few weeks after Ivester stepped down, an article in *Fortune* described the meeting in Chicago and alluded to broad unhappiness with Ivester at the board level.

In the end, Ivester left no doubt that he had not left of his own free will. By the time he walked out of Coke's headquarters for good in February, he had demanded and received a severance package that took some people's breath away. He had been at Coke for twenty years, and he wanted to be paid for his work.

The package was worth more than $115 million in a combination of money to be paid immediately and over the course of Ivester's life. It included about $98 million worth of restricted stock – stock that he was not supposed to take title to until he reached the age of sixty-five – that he had accumulated in the years since he joined the company. He was cashing out, a good thirteen years earlier than anyone expected, and it would cost Coca-Cola money.

The severance gave him a handsome pension, at least $1.3 million a year for as long as he lived and covered the lifetime of Kay, his wife, as well. He would get to keep his laptop computer, his life insurance, his health insurance, and assorted other perks. In exchange, he had to agree not to work for another soft-drink company for the next seven years – a condition that people who knew Ivester and his love for the Coca-Cola Company found ridiculous. As one more token of their esteem, the board handed over the keys to his company car – an aging black Mercury Grand Marquis, which had been assigned to Ivester the year the Olympics came to Atlanta. It had driven him to Charlie Brown Airport, where Coke kept its fleet of Gulfstreams, and it had driven him home again. In it he had traveled the streets of Atlanta, on his way to meetings and public events, always looking for more opportunities to sell more Coca-Cola. It was his car, and he wanted to have it.

For some, the details of his severance package underscored the tragedy of the event. Ivester's upheaval 'was a knife in the back of a man who had been anointed by Roberto', said one former executive, 'and who was doing a good job'. To others it seemed an outrage, an excessive amount of money paid to someone to go away.

When Robert Woodruff left the Coca-Cola Company, essentially at the same time that he left the planet, every stick of furniture, right down to the crumbling vinyl chair pad beneath his desk, had to be preserved in honor of the man. His entire office had been moved from the twenty-fifth floor of the Coke tower down to a space on the twelfth floor, where it was painstakingly reassembled just as he had left it. Only one thing, really, was altered: Someone turned the pages of the paper calendar he kept, past the day that he had last been in the office, and didn't stop until they reached the page marked March 7, 1985. That was the day Woodruff died, and that was where the calendar would stay.

When Don Keough retired, he had a send-off that lasted for hours beneath the Atlanta sun, attended by hundreds, probably thousands, of Coke employees who demonstrated how much they hated to see him go. And when Roberto Goizueta died, life at the Coca-Cola Company had been suffused for weeks with sadness while people mourned the loss of a leader very few of them had met but most of them admired.

When Doug Ivester left the Coca-Cola Company, on a chilly

February afternoon, he did so practically alone. There was no big send-off party, no tears shed in his honor as he departed the Coke tower. No one cracked a bottle of champagne. Tenants in the complex in Atlanta's Buckhead section, where he set up his new office, would remember a dark-haired man puffing down the hall from the elevator bank, carrying carton after carton of papers, books, and personal effects by himself. 'Who is that?' one of them asked a friend after spotting him. The friend answered: '*That* is the former chairman of the Coca-Cola Company.'

About a month after the announcement that Ivester would be leaving, someone at Coke held a party to celebrate Daft's new role. The new millennium was only a few days old, and it had failed to bring the destruction of the world's computer networks and power grids that so many people feared.

A mood of nervous anticipation filled the air at the Coke party. Most of the top brass showed up. Don Keough was there. Ivester was not.

Chapter Nineteen

The Unscripted Part

WITHIN COKE, SOME PEOPLE rejoiced as Ivester's departure was announced. Over nearly twenty years at the company, he had made more than a few enemies, alienating people who saw him as cold, ruthless, arrogant, out of touch. There was a little sympathy when he left, but it was for themselves, not for him. 'It was sad to see it happen,' said one former executive, speaking of Ivester's departure and the downward spiral of the share price. People alternated between jubilation and despair. 'The stock would go down, and we'd be like, Yay! And then you'd think, oh, there goes my 401(k). People were rooting for him to fail, but it was at our expense.'

Like a few of the Coke directors, they thought getting rid of Ivester would mean the end of their troubles. They would find out that it was not so simple.

Ivester and Goizueta had added personnel during Coke's boom years as fast as they saw fit. Some of those people functioned as long-distance supervisors, checking up on the bottlers and the operations people who spent their time out in the hinterland, domestically or overseas. They had to approve budgets, advertising campaigns, initiatives, and programs of all kinds. Such tight control was seen as a good business practice, one that would eliminate waste and keep tabs on far-flung executives and their underlings. But at the same time it was almost too businesslike. It could be unyielding and autocratic, and many of the people beyond Atlanta hated that.

One of them was Doug Daft, accustomed as he was to doing his own thing in the field, whether it was China, Indonesia, or Hong Kong. Another was Keough, the consummate salesman, who had watched in dismay as the changes inside Coke threatened the identity, he felt, of the company he had helped to make great. It was not just the news that made the papers, the things that happened on Ivester's watch, that made the company look bad. It was the changing of Coke's way of doing business, from the model that Keough had helped to shape to one that bore Ivester's distinctive stamp. It had happened again and again in the company's history. Goizueta had remade the company the way he wanted to, and when he died Ivester proceeded to do what he thought would be best. He did not see the need to alter what Goizueta had left him, at least not in a radical way.

But as the business slowed, he realized that he would have to trim some jobs. As early as September 1998, as the Russian economic crisis hit, he and other senior people at the company – people with a sense of the numbers behind the public statements – realized that the Coke growth miracle had stalled.

They tried to address it. When they saw the collapse of the Russian ruble – and with it, most of Coke's sales in that country – combined with the Thai economic crisis, the Japanese recession, and the waning American, European, and Latin American demand for Coca-Cola, they tried to bring some of the buying, the hiring, and the investing to a stop. But stopping the Coke machine took time. It could not just screech to a halt; it could not be cut only in small ways, in ways that did not show. It took almost another year for the company to stop hiring people, opening factories, building plants. By that time there was even more damage to confront.

There was no alternative to the worst alternative, which was eliminating jobs – getting rid of people who worked for the Coca-Cola Company. It was an unpopular thought. In fact, it was practically unheard of at Coke.

It had happened within memory, on a very modest scale, when Coke's USA division decided to shed fifty or so people in 1990. The layoffs had had an immense impact on the other people who worked at the company, because people did not walk out of Coca-Cola, as a rule. They had to be carried out. In 1999, nearly ten years later, the USA layoff had not been forgotten. 'People were still talking about it,' one Coke executive remembered.

But increasingly, people at the top of Coke saw that the money-churning, can't-miss model upon which their company's fortunes depended needed replacing. Between the problems of the biggest bottlers, the weakening of the economy in so many places around the globe, and the increasing difficulty of selling Coca-Cola profitably, the company that Goizueta, Keough, and Ivester had built was in trouble.

Executives disagreed about what had gone wrong, and they disagreed about who was to blame, but they could not deny that the whole concept of the modern Coca-Cola Company needed an overhaul. Even for people whose job requirement was to put the most cheerful and positive spin on events, there was too much evidence.

It had been building since at least 1995, the last year that Coke's growth had seemed truly solid. Since then, there had been 'issues', as people in Atlanta liked to call them. The company had acknowledged that bottler transactions had helped its bottom line. It had more or less conceded that certain emerging markets were not going to grow indefinitely. And more recently, it had run into troubles in so many parts of the world where its business was believed to be strong that by the end of 1999, when fourth-quarter results would be compiled, virtually no one expected the Coca-Cola Company to hit the kinds of profit and volume targets it had set for the year in January.

Naturally, this was discussed only in secret. Within the four walls of the Coke tower, and during dinners in quiet corners of their clubs across the city, Coke management would acknowledge that it had to do something, and fast. But Coke did not alert Wall Street, the place where the company had done so well all along. Right through the end of 1999, many analysts were writing reports declaring that the worst was behind the Coca-Cola Company. But that was based solely on what the company had told them, and on the scraps of information they had been able to gather from supermarkets, bottlers, and other sources on their own. 'U.S. consumers continue to adapt to soft-drink price inflation and demand is generally recovering,' Marc Cohen, the beverage analyst for Goldman Sachs, had written in a note to investors in early December. Coke, he added, 'is ahead of the curve' versus Pepsi. Like the rest of the analysts, Cohen had been told nothing about the depths of the company's troubles.

Some of the biggest problems lurked within the bottling system. The Coca-Cola Enterprises model, so effective in the short run, had turned into an enormous drag on profits. The pattern of moving marketing support into the bottler to help drive the Coca-Cola agenda had seemed like a good idea, once, and was supposed to help sell Coca-Cola everywhere. But in the United States, and in other places, there was an oversupply of the soft drink. Cases were backing up, unsold, in supermarket storerooms and in the loading bays of bottling plants. A gray market abroad for American-made Coke was drawing off some of that, but Coke ran into criticism from its foreign bottlers, into whose markets these excess cans of Coke arrived. The bottlers kept ordering syrup, but some of the finished bottles and cans had no home.

Coca-Cola Enterprises, the prototype for the modern Coke bottling system, was only one of the drains on the Coca-Cola Company's finances. As the most developed anchor bottler in the most developed markets in the world, its problems seemed sure to spread to the other anchor bottlers as their markets matured, too. Take Coca-Cola Enterprises and multiply it – and its costs – by eleven, for all the anchor bottlers on the planet. Then you had a real nightmare, the dark side of the Coca-Cola bottler model that Ivester, Goizueta, and Keough had paraded so triumphantly before the world. Was there such a thing as too much Coke? They hadn't thought so. It had never occurred to them. They were serving a billion drinks a day, and people consumed forty-eight times that much worldwide. They expected to land an even bigger piece of the action.

Keough, meanwhile, told people he hadn't wanted to expand the Coca-Cola Enterprises magic to every last corner of the planet. He scoffed at Ivester's decision to do so, carried out after he was gone from the company. Ivester, Keough liked to say, took a good thing too far.

Now it looked as though he might be right. The sunny outlook under which that system had been created – believing in basically unlimited growth in the demand for Coke products – had darkened as the bottler network became difficult and expensive to sustain. The biggest bottlers were staggering under enormous loads of debt, taken on to acquire more franchises, to build more plants, to buy trucks and vending machines, and, in Coca-Cola Enterprises' case, to buy back their stock, when the market's interest waned. They remained partners of the Coca-Cola Company, but they looked like the ones who had gotten the short end of the stick.

No one could say how it had all gone so wrong, so deeply wrong, so quickly. 'We probably just went too far,' said one former executive. Said another: 'It was a good strategy, but it was too much, too fast.'

Some of the biggest bottlers were clamoring to get out. One anchor bottler, Fraser & Neave, which controlled bottling for several countries in Southeast Asia, had already bailed out. Carlsberg, in charge of Coca-Cola in the Scandinavian region, was also threatening to do so, complaining publicly that 'it is no longer profitable' to sell Coca-Cola. Most of the largest anchors, like Panamco, Amatil, and Coca-Cola Beverages, were limping from poor sales and debt overload. All of them had been pushed to expand according to the Coca-Cola Company's vision. With Coke the largest shareholder in all of them, they had little choice but to follow Coke-led plans for market dominance in all sorts of channels: the supermarket, the sports arena, the movie theater, the convenience store. But all of them also had other shareholders besides the Coca-Cola Company, and those shareholders were running out of patience. The idea that the bottlers could be valued on their cash flow was not sticking anymore; now investors were looking at return on invested capital, which at Coca-Cola Enterprises was about 6 percent. The bottler's executives tried to portray Coca-Cola Enterprises as an *improving* return-on-invested-capital stock. The market wasn't buying it, however.

There were still regulatory attacks on Coke as well, some of them initiated at Pepsi's suggestion, some of them unrelated to the archrival. Dawn raids by European officials on Coke offices and the offices of its big bottlers were becoming almost routine. The stock price slumped. The company looked bad.

By October 1999, when the senior management began meeting to discuss some kind of restructuring at Coke, so many things had gone wrong in the year already that a restructuring almost seemed attractive, as a way to change direction and, at the same time, write down some expenses. Bottling plants the company had bought up in India; new plants built ahead of demand in Russia; and thousands of vending machines partly or completely funded all over the world, particularly in Japan, made up the unfortunate legacy of a strategy that was no longer working. The product recall in Europe had cost millions, mainly in new advertising and promotions to get people to drink Coke again. Add to that the battered economies of so many big Coca-Cola markets, and the whole picture appeared desperately bleak. The steady march to the sea was over. Instead of posting another glorious year, Coke was about to record its worst performance ever.

With no end in sight, it was the people of the Coca-Cola Company – those thousands of employees who were not senior management but who had bought into management's notion of the company's growing stronger, along with its share price, by the day, and who had worked long hours and given up all kinds of other things to make the program succeed – who were going to have to pay.

Like Roberto Goizueta's shake-up of the company in 1981, the cutting seems to have started with a premise that Coke could be stripped to its essence, rethought, and then reintroduced to the world. Just as in 1981, there would be huge risks in what the executives were doing. But unlike Goizueta's plan, this was not about unlocking hidden value in the Coca-Cola Company. It was now about trying to hang on to the value that still remained.

'There were no goals of numbers of people on day one,' remembers one senior executive. 'It was, what's the right thing to do, and what do we have to do?' What will help the company, and what will benefit the shareholders? It would be an epic confrontation between two opposing ideas, the kind the Coca-Cola Company almost never had to have.

Doug Daft had heard some of the early discussions about reducing the head count, as had Jack Stahl, his colleague at the top of the hierarchy Ivester had put in place shortly before his resignation. So had a few others in senior management. None of them had anticipated huge cuts, and they were still trying to devise the strategy that would shape the job reductions. Would Coke be a pure marketing company, as some people thought it should be, with all its nonessential tasks removed to outside agencies, or would it continue as a company that had operations people, working with the bottlers day to day, along with marketers who could dream up more and better ways to get people to drink Coke?

As it turned out, marketing – the art of persuasion that had been Coke's great strength for more than a hundred years – would prevail. Under Daft, the company decreed it would dismantle much of what Ivester and Goizueta had put together in the 1990s, and in its place would emerge a smaller, nimbler Coca-Cola Company, where consumer desires could be met more quickly and profits monitored more efficiently, and the relationships that were so critical to selling Coke could be nurtured more effectively. It was an echo of the advice that Keough had given Ivester in his letter in July.

Whittling Coke to fit its new definition would not be easy, or painless. The man who would have to lead the company publicly through the process, from one Coca-Cola Company to another, was Daft.

By the middle of January he had come into his own a little more and at least no longer wobbled visibly on the job. Daft elicited sympathy from most people who met with him during those first weeks. He confessed he had been given no time to get used to the idea of being the top dog at Coke. He had never even been considered for the job until the still-secret machinations that removed Ivester vaulted him into the corner office. As time went on, he began to identify with Bilbo, the character from the movie *The Lord of the Rings* who, in the midst of chaos, has the all-powerful ring land improbably in his hands.

His first act, upon learning that chilly Friday night that he would succeed Ivester, was to track down his wife, Delphine, at home and beg her to cancel a trip she was planning to take to the West Coast to visit their daughter. 'Don't go,' Daft told her. His voice resonated with urgency, something that was out of character for him. 'This is one weekend when I'll need a prop.'

He had been discussing the Coca-Cola business in Japan with Ivester earlier in the day, following up after one of his frequent trips to the Far East. All day, Ivester had given his colleagues no hints that he would be leaving. When he called Daft into his office for a second time toward evening, he told him according to Daft, that he would be 'retiring' and that Daft had already been chosen to take his place. Daft all but panicked. *Do I or don't I accept?* he thought. Across the desk from him sat Ivester, the scion of Goizueta, the financial wizard who was supposed to take the Coca-Cola Company into the twenty-first century. Ivester understood the bottling system forward and backward. He could calculate complex transactions with business partners while standing on his head. He saw the world in crystal-clear terms as a place where there would always be new markets to sell Coke. He knew the customers, he had conceived of the latest ad campaign, he had been presenting strategy to the star-studded board of directors for two decades. If he had an obvious successor, it was Jack Stahl – *not* Doug Daft.

Daft had none of Ivester's credentials on his résumé. He was about to inherit a creation some felt he did not understand fully. *How in the world had he gotten himself into this?* He and Ivester sat in silence for a little while, each preoccupied with wildly different thoughts. And then Daft said to himself, *You must.* It was like winning the lottery, or getting into Harvard, or being invited to dinner at the White House. No matter how daunting or ill-fitting or guilt-inducing the circumstances, he told himself, you never turn away from that.

Keough stepped in to offer his help.

He would call himself a longtime fan of Daft's. Daft had reported to him in the 1980s and early 1990s, when Keough was president of Coke, and he had impressed Keough as someone who did his job quickly and quietly and, as Keough snorted, 'didn't have to write a six-page report about it afterward'. Ivester's succinctness had always bothered Keough. Daft's, for some reason, did not.

Keough wanted Daft to replace Ivester, and Daft was smart enough to realize that, after a move like that, he needed Keough. With Keough by his side, Daft believed he would have an ally who could help him handle the board, the press, and Coke's biggest investors. 'Everything I know about relationships, I learned from Don Keough,' Daft would say. Keough became a fixture at Coke events of all kinds, a presence on the phone even when he wasn't actually in the room.

Daft signaled early on that he intended to be a kinder, gentler chief executive. On his second day, he had his press office call up various reporters and offer them brief telephone time with him. The reporters, shocked by the ready access to the chairman of the Coca-Cola Company, all willingly rearranged their schedules for that afternoon. On the phone, Daft was cheerful and upbeat, reiterated his surprise at becoming the leader of Coke, and promised no sudden changes.

A few weeks later, he and the rest of the company's senior management were ready with their plan. James Chestnut had been working around the clock, along with Gary Fayard, the company's controller, and dozens of assistants. They had to get the numbers right and squeeze the Coca-Cola Company to fit its new definition. News of some kind of job cut had already seeped out of Atlanta. A few days earlier, Bill Pecoriello, a quick-thinking analyst then working for Sanford Bernstein, published a note saying that Coke was trying to remake itself into a kinder, gentler company – perhaps to make amends for the problems it had caused for itself in the recent past. Along with that, Pecoriello asserted, Coke planned to get rid of 'at least 2,000 jobs' and scale back its growth goals to more realistic levels.

The company refused to comment. It did announce in mid-January, however, that Jack Stahl would become Coke's president, succeeding Daft, when Daft formally took over as chairman in April. No longer would the president's office at Coke – the office that had meant so much to Keough – be left vacant. Daft made no cracks about not needing a filter. Barely settled in his own job, he rolled out the red carpet for Stahl, a man he had never worked with before and who had been groomed by Ivester.

Jimmy Williams, the director who had been charged with explaining Ivester's abrupt departure to the world, got to handle this development as well. 'You are going to see a more traditional CEO-COO relationship with a management team approach,' Williams told reporters. 'It's going to be an effective and a different approach.' He politely declined to compare that approach to Ivester's, saying only that every chief executive 'has to establish his own management style'.

But Williams mentioned nothing about the job cuts, which were in their final stages, and neither did anyone else.

Finally, on January 26, Daft did. Earlier that week, he summoned every Coke employee back from trips, meetings, and vacations. Everyone was told to be in their offices on Wednesday the twenty-sixth for an important company announcement. His plan called for not just job reductions but for a radical restructuring of the company, unprecedented in its sweep, scope, and effect on the people who made and sold Coca-Cola.

The public statement about the restructuring buried the real news deep inside a resolutely upbeat message. 'The Coca-Cola Company today announced a major organizational realignment that will put more responsibility, accountability and resources in the hand of the local business units in the more than 200 countries where the company does business,' the official release read. 'Specifically, this realignment will reduce the company's workforce around the world while transferring responsibilities from corporate to revenue-generating operating units.'

What it meant was this: Six thousand people at Coke would lose their jobs, most of them in the United States, and the vast majority of those in Atlanta, at the complex at the corner of North Avenue and Luckie Street. Ten thousand people worked for the Coca-Cola Company in the United States, and 3,300 of them were being fired. About 2,500 of those worked in Atlanta in the Coke tower. Another 20,000 people held jobs in other parts of the world, and 2,700 of them would have to go, too.

'This management team is committed to doing what is necessary to ensure a strong future for the Coca-Cola Company,' Daft said in announcing the cuts. 'We are equally committed to proceeding with care and sensitivity.'

The announcement shook Coke to its foundations, far more than the departure of Ivester or the death of Goizueta had. The people summoned to hear the news did not know what to think, other than that life as they knew it had just ended.

Their trauma began even before they set foot in the Coke tower that day. 'I pulled into the parking lot, and there was no room anywhere,' recalled one former executive. 'We had gotten a voice mail the day before saying all trips needed to be canceled, that everyone needed to be in the office.' As he nosed his car around the lot, searching for a place to put it, he felt a gloomy conviction that something enormous and bad was happening to his company. When he finally found a space, he went inside to learn that he would 'probably' lose his job, though it took weeks before the decision became final and he had to get out.

The plan to eliminate some jobs had been formed over time, starting when Ivester was still chairman and chief executive, but it accelerated and widened in the weeks leading up to the announcement. There had been vociferous disagreement among executives about how many jobs to eliminate, and in which departments. Outsourcing, or moving certain company functions to outside firms that could carry them out more efficiently and inexpensively, was an obvious way to reduce the head count at Coke. But the rest of the stripping, the cutting, the trimming – that was much harder. First there were discussions about what was wrong at Coke, then more discussions about how to make it right. Senior management spent much of its time behind closed doors, evaluating various proposals, always with an eye on the numbers: the numbers of people who would be leaving the Coca-Cola Company. With the stock price battered, the pressure grew to cut more jobs, not fewer. The company was being whittled back to its former size, the size it had been nearly a decade earlier when Don Keough and Roberto Goizueta were running things. Coke was stepping into a time machine, somehow convinced that it could go back to the way things had once been.

The layoffs were executed furiously at a company that had always taken pride in its execution. But there were so many of them that management could not keep up. People were supposed to be called in for meetings, one on one, with their supervisors and given the word and a chance to discuss it. Instead, some people heard through the grapevine that they were being eliminated, before anyone could tell them in person. Others got voice-mail messages, because they were posted abroad and did not come back to Atlanta for the announcement. Some people were placed 'on the block', without a clearly defined future. 'It was so sick,' said the executive who had trouble finding a parking spot. 'There was a three-person panel formed for me, to determine my future, and then I was sitting on a three-person panel to assess the grade below me. I hated every single minute of it.' It would be weeks before that executive found out his fate; his panel voted to get rid of him, keeping instead a man who was several years his senior.

The company offered early-retirement packages to some people, and then, to its African American employees, it offered something else. If they would agree to drop all future claims against the company – namely, any participation in the class-action discrimination lawsuit that Linda Ingram and her three co-plaintiffs were leading – they would be eligible for an 'enhanced' benefits package. If not, they would end up with the same offer being made to everyone else.

The black employees were confused. With chaos churning around them, they had to decide whether to stay involved with the lawsuit. Someone called Cyrus Mehri, the lead lawyer in the lawsuit. Soon an enraged Mehri was on the phone to Coke and to the judge overseeing the case.

By midmorning that Wednesday, weeping secretaries were filling cartons with their bosses' possessions and clearing out their own desks as well. Entire departments were dismantled, including the payroll department; its duties would be handled by an outside firm. The maintenance department, which took care of the buildings and grounds, would no longer exist; an outside company would handle that, too. A special group formed to handle technology operations for the millennium that had just occurred, a group pulled from various areas of the company, was told to pack up. The company had gotten through the millennium without a hitch. Now the people who had accomplished that were told they were no longer needed. Everything old-fashioned and familial about Coca-Cola – the notion of a company as more than just a collection of business decisions – that had not been eliminated under Goizueta or Ivester was being torn to pieces.

The shock traveled outside the gates of the complex and into the streets of Atlanta. People walking their dogs heard about it. Waitresses serving plates of chicken and biscuits at the OK Diner up in Buckhead, where so many Coca-Cola grandees lived, knew things had changed for them, too. The barbershops buzzed with gossip. Nothing like this had ever happened at Coke before.

It was fresh devastation for a company still grappling with the mysterious ejection of Ivester from the corner office. People at

Coke were still trying to figure out who Daft was. The job cuts gave him a permanent ugly nickname: Daft the Knife.

On the twenty-fifth floor, where senior management met to discuss Coke's future, people who worked as assistants and in other lower-level jobs had been aware that something like this was coming. In the public relations office, the executives had been briefed. They had been given their lines about why such a restructuring was the best thing for the Coca-Cola Company, and they rehearsed them. Then they got the word that several of them were being dismissed, too.

On all the other floors that made up the Coke tower, people moved around in shock on that January morning. Some of them felt sick to their stomachs. What had they done wrong? What had Coke done wrong?

The monitors still beamed at them from the elevator lobby, displaying the share price that, despite all the events of the last year, was still a respectable sixty-three dollars. After its plunge following Ivester's departure, the share price had climbed back up from the mid-fifties to the mid-sixties once again. Sure, it had been in the eighties at one point when Ivester was chairman. But many people, even at Coke, had considered that an inflated value for a stock that had split barely two years earlier, and they had been relieved when the price sank back to what they considered a more logical level. This was their company, the Coca-Cola they knew and loved.

All along, while they kept an eye on that share price, they had believed that what they were doing was right. It was certainly what they had been told. They had kept the share price at the forefront of everything they did. They had sold Coke, advertised Coke, created new ways to market Coke during all this time, and by all accounts everything was going fine. Maybe not spectacularly well, but fine. Business had cycles. Everyone knew that. What went up had to come down, and what was down would eventually rise again.

Many of them were told they could expect severance packages, use outplacement services, and rely on counseling to help them with what Coke called 'the transition'. But to many in the company's middle management who were fired, there was an added blow. They would lose their stock options: first the options that had not vested yet and then, as a practical matter for many people suddenly unemployed, the ones that could be exercised but only by paying out of their own pockets. Typically, a Coca-Cola employee who received options exercised them after a significant price rise had taken place. That way, they could buy and sell the options on the same day, with money left over from the transaction. That money was theirs to keep. But with the market price lower than the options' strike price, they would have had to borrow or use savings to purchase the stock. They didn't have much time.

For a company that had always used stock options to compensate its top people, this was one more jolt. 'We all got the royal screws put to us,' one person said. 'Those options that were vested were underwater. Then you had ninety days to exercise everything else. We didn't have jobs anymore, so how were we supposed to exercise everything in ninety days?'

The job cuts were bad news. But there was more to come.

The same morning, Coke released its full-year results, the ones so many people inside Coke had been dreading. And while new corporate chieftains often roll all kinds of bad news into their first earnings statements, both to rid themselves of unwanted baggage and to lower the bar for future comparisons, what came out of Coke that day was unparalleled for a company that had seemed to be so successful for so long.

There had been a new record set for volume, the statement said, with more than 16 billion cases of soft drinks sold in 1999, more than at any time in Coke's history. But at the same time, Coke said it would be taking massive write-downs, not only for the job cuts but also for unsavory practices like overselling concentrate to its bottlers and for the cost of factories and equipment in places like Russia and Japan that had not turned out to be good investments.

The concentrate situation was especially vexing. The record volume had been achieved, it appeared, by 'stuffing the pipeline', as one analyst called it, at least for the current year and maybe in other years as well. Coke's description of it was oblique. 'Throughout the past several months, the Coca-Cola Company has worked with bottlers around the world to determine the optimum level of bottler inventory levels,' the company's statement said.

'Based on this review, management of the Coca-Cola system determined that opportunities exist to reduce the level of concentrate inventory carried by bottlers in selected regions of the world, such as Eastern Europe, Japan, and Germany.' Some people found the numbers unbelievable; Coke had been assiduous in recent years about not overselling concentrate, and the thinking held that maybe this was one more way to lower expectations for the coming year.

The cost to Coke for the job cuts, which eventually totaled 5,200, came to $800 million. The cost of the write-downs came to virtually the same amount: another $813 million. Together, the two items sliced 31 percent off Coke's earnings for 1999 compared with 1998. 'It's not nothing,' hissed one analyst. 'It's not as if they were short a few million dollars. It's *$1.6 billion.*' Another $400 million or so in additional write-downs was also expected in the coming year, the result of bad investments in India. It would be a $2 billion hit to earnings, stretched over two fiscal years. Shortfalls of such catastrophic dimensions had not happened before, not to the Coca-Cola Company. It was the antithesis of the Goizueta vision and an upending of the Ivester strategy, and it left their successor, Doug Daft, with a lot of broken pieces with which to build his own vision.

The company warned that its performance in the current year wasn't going to be much better. The inventory reduction for concentrate would mean that Coke could expect between 11 cents and 13 cents less per share in earnings through the first half of 2000. Its earnings would lag even the lackluster performance of 1999.

Analysts on Wall Street who had sensed a change coming were stunned by what Coke revealed. This wasn't the Coca-Cola Company they knew. They hadn't been expecting nearly so many jobs to be cut. They hadn't guessed how badly the business had been doing. And if anyone hoped that by getting all the dismal news out into the open Coke would experience a bounce upward in its share price, they were in for another surprise. In contrast to other companies where news of restructuring indicated a turnaround, creating a burst of desire for the stock, Coke's announcement had the opposite impact.

Investors ran for the exits. More than 11 million shares changed hands on the day of the announcement, three times the usual trading volume. Coke's share price sank another $2.80, closing at $63.06. The day after the job cuts, the stock would fall another $3.50. The share price would keep drifting steadily downward for quite some time. This was not exactly the validation of Ivester's ouster, and of Daft's leadership, that the board was looking for.

Within Coke, the layoffs and the revelations scarred the people who left and soaked into the bones of those who remained. 'When you cut as wide and as deep as Coca-Cola cut, you are cutting a lot of talent out,' said one former executive, who was fired along with half of his department. 'And what that says to the remaining employees is, "It doesn't matter what kind of job I do. We're all susceptible." It is different, to be let go for whatever reason. Coke had never been through a layoff of that magnitude. It was cutting to the quick.'

The shocked atmosphere inside the company was replaced by outrage a few days later. The world of Coke promised by Coke's leaders for so many years disappeared.

'All they had been doing was pushing the numbers around,' said one employee, aghast after reading through the earnings report to try to make sense of the turmoil. 'They did not really create wealth.'

Everything came to an end in a torrent of pink slips and a revelation that the Coca-Cola Company was something separate from its image. For investors who had hoped the worst was over for Coca-Cola, it was the end of that illusion. For the executives and others who had grown up in the business with Goizueta and Keough and Ivester, it was a rude awakening from the dream they had all shared for two decades. For the people who were fired, it was the end of their belief in the Coca-Cola Company. The twenty-sixth of January would be the day their great faith in an American icon crumbled, the day the world they knew and counted on collapsed, the day their trust went up in smoke. They would talk about it for years to come, turning the years over in their minds, searching for clues that should have warned them that everything was not what they were being told it was. Everything that happened as the new millennium arrived redrew the image of their company – for them, the rest of Atlanta, and the rest of the world. 'It's like a death in the family,' said one. 'You move on, but you never really forget it.'

They roamed listlessly through their memories, looking for reasons to believe again. They wondered why this had all had to happen to them. Their sorrow was epic, and their souls filled with fury and desolation.

'It's all gone,' said Joe Wilkinson, a fifth-generation Atlantan who spent years parrying with politicians, competitors, and regulators on behalf of the Coca-Cola Company. 'They destroyed the company. It's like *Gone with the Wind*. Now, the old South needed to die. But there was nothing wrong with the Coca-Cola Company.'

Chapter Twenty

Always Coca-Cola

A FENG-SHUI EXPERT WALKED into the Coca-Cola Company one morning a few months after the layoffs, under contract to examine the building and make adjustments that would be harmonious and bring a change in the fortunes of the company.

The expert spent a lot of time on the twenty-fifth floor, where Goizueta had worked for sixteen years, where Ivester had worked for a little more than two, and where Doug Daft now had to pull the organization together. He pushed furniture around, checked the positions of pictures and mirrors, and tried other means of encouraging good *qi,* as the Chinese call it, which is the flow of positive energy through body and home. In the process, he removed some potted plants and told Doug Daft to take a table out of his office so there would be more open space. When he was finished, he declared the company's feng shui much improved and said he hoped things would be better from now on.

The company was reeling, and Daft would need all the help he could get. There was a lot he didn't know, and he readily admitted it. He needed a crash course on the complicated history between the company and its bottlers. He had never worked in the domestic Coca-Cola business, where those relationships were most intense. His frame of reference included Japan, China, and the Middle East, a series of markets that became part of the Coca-Cola universe far later and under completely different circumstances.

He needed to understand other markets, because Coke was counting on growth from all of them. He thought shifting some resources into developing new beverages – not the carbonated kind that were synonymous with Coke but other kinds, the ones Pepsi and other Coke competitors made – would help earnings. He immediately announced that the company would open four research centers around the globe, intended to formulate brand-new products that would be sold under the Coca-Cola Company banner. Then he announced a joint venture with Procter & Gamble, one that would turn over Coke's Minute Maid juices to P&G and allow Coke bottlers to put Pringles potato chips on their trucks. The analysts were confused by that one. But the board did not object. Daft also trumpeted plans to buy Sobe, a trendy noncarbonated-beverage business, and made a run at Quaker Oats, the owner of Gatorade, the top-selling noncarbonated drink in the country. He would change his mind or suffer setbacks on nearly all these projects.

He went out of his way to cure some of the most obvious problems afflicting Coke. By early January, he had persuaded Carl Ware to reconsider his retirement. On January 4, Daft proudly announced that Ware would become the company's executive vice president for corporate affairs, a far-reaching job that included working with governments as well as with the press and Wall Street. He got a 25 percent pay increase, and his bonus of $669,000 was nearly double his old salary. Ware, for his part, said the job itself had enticed him to return to Coke. 'This job is new, substantive, operational, and it goes beyond traditional corporate affairs,' he said. It held out promise and more. 'It seemed like such a good opportunity,' he added, 'that I could ill afford to pass on it.' He unpacked his boxes and prepared to settle in for a while.

Daft also made it clear to the company's lawyers that he wanted to get the racial-discrimination lawsuit behind him. It was part of Daft's strategy to prove that he was not Ivester, whose name was rarely uttered in the halls of the Coca-Cola Company now unless he was being blamed for something. Ivester had been made a scapegoat, in his absence, for everything bad that happened to the company, including events that transpired long after he was gone.

The lawsuit would not be easy to resolve. It had gotten even more complicated when Daft announced the thousands of job cuts that were supposed to turn Coke into a new kind of company.

Coke offered black employees a better severance package if they agreed not to pursue the lawsuit. But what the company did not reveal was that the two sides had been ordered to begin negotiations for a settlement of the case. The order, still a secret, had been issued in early January by Richard Story, the federal judge presiding over the case. Coke had agreed to the talks but had not set a date. Mehri had asked several times and been rebuffed. No talks had been held by the time the layoffs began.

And then up popped Larry Jones. He had access to a church in northern Atlanta with a large hall, capable of seating a hundred people or more. He volunteered that space for a meeting of the black employees, so they could discuss their alternatives. Between the lawsuit and the job cuts, many of them were feeling uninformed and especially vulnerable.

They had their meeting the weekend after the layoffs were announced. And on the following Monday, Jones got a call from his supervisor. Now it was his turn to be fired. He had to pack up and go immediately.

He would always believe that it was the direct result of the meeting he held. He was told otherwise, but he never changed his mind. The experience transformed him from a mild-mannered bureaucrat to a highly vocal organizer of African Americans at Coke. The company would not soon forget the name Larry Jones.

By early February, thanks to Mehri's lobbying, word was out: The lawsuit might be settled, and people shouldn't give up too quickly their right to take part in it. Jack Stahl, the new president of Coke, issued an unusual apology, stating that the company had not meant to make the process more difficult for its black employees.

Daft began trying to prove that the Coca-Cola Company was among the world's most supportive when it came to dealing with blacks, women, and other minority employees. He announced, over the first eight weeks of his tenure, that Coke would create a $1 billion fund to help black-owned businesses by granting contracts and investing in them; a program under which same-sex partners of people working at Coke would qualify for health benefits, just like spouses and children; and a new policy of 'casual Fridays', which Ivester was said to have resisted, would begin. Daft even instituted a new holiday, Founder's Day, which would be observed every May 8 in honor of John Pemberton's formulation of the first Coca-Cola. On Founder's Day, employees would be allowed to take the day off.

He made 'improving relationships' his personal motif, and with fanfare from the public relations office, he set off on a late-winter tour of Europe in which he met with regulators and other government officials. The targets of his campaign included Coke's old European Union nemesis, Karel van Miert – whom the company would hire as a motivational speaker before long.

Some relationships were more difficult to revive. Wall Street's regard for Coke ebbed over the company's continuing dull performance, and analysts called for Daft to lower Coke's volume and earnings targets. On April 4, 2000, Coke organized a meeting with analysts in New York, held at the Regent, a nineteenth-century building turned hotel that is a short stroll from the New York Stock Exchange. Lunch was served, buffet style, and then came a program of presentations by Coke management, including a forward look at the business for the current year. Everyone was eager to hear what Daft and his crew would say; the expectations about the expectations ran high. Surely the worst was behind them.

Into the ballroom crowded all the analysts, including veterans like Emanuel Goldman, who had flown overnight from San Francisco to take part. Jennifer Solomon, the Salomon Smith Barney beverage analyst who had spotted chinks in the Coca-Cola armor long before anyone at Coke would acknowledge that anything was less than perfect at the company, arrived in time for lunch. Andrew Conway was there, too. He had known Coke under Goizueta and Ivester. He wanted to know where it was headed.

They all perched on their chairs and waited for the critical information.

First, though, they were subjected to an extremely long discussion of Coke's marketing practices around the world. Local marketing, a favorite theme of Daft's, was highlighted in its many forms, from a bikini beach party in Chile to the company's sponsorship of a soccer tournament in Burkina Faso. The analysts shifted in the hotel chairs and shook their heads. What was this? Where was the information they had been promised? In one of its more bizarre decisions, the company aired a poorly edited, blurry film that showcased a school in the Chinese hinterland that had been paid for by Coke. The film showed Coke executives, one by one, inspecting the school: first Goizueta, then Ivester, and finally

Daft. All of them looked the same, hunched in uncomfortable Chairman Mao armchairs, the jet lag apparent as they sipped tea with their overtly enthusiastic Communist hosts.

Four hours dragged by. The analysts punched up share prices on their Palms. The stock market closed, as usual, at 4:00 P.M. And not long after that, as if by magic, Daft walked to the front of the room and announced Coke's volume targets for the coming year. The analysts pricked up their ears. Daft proudly declared that the targets were going to be roughly the same as before.

A palpable whoosh of disappointment, surprise, and disgust wafted from the audience. Daft looked unperturbed. 'We believe we can do five percent to six percent this year, and seven percent to eight percent over the long term,' he told them.

It was not reassuring to the analysts, who were already annoyed that they had been forced to sit through all the boring marketing talk before getting to the heart of the matter. They felt spun and used by the Coca-Cola Company. Most of them said they doubted that Coke could make those targets. Why didn't the company cut back its objectives, asked Jennifer Solomon during the question-and-answer period.

'We believe in it, it's achievable, and we've got the programs to do it,' Daft replied. 'We had to be honest with you.'

It was the beginning of a new relationship. By the end of the year, Coke had failed to reach Daft's targets.

Also in April, the company became a target — of an enormous public demonstration organized by Larry Jones and co-starring the Reverend Jesse Jackson. Jones was angry that the company had not moved faster to settle the discrimination lawsuit, which was nearly a year old. In March, he had begun organizing weekend rallies for black employees at which they would raise empty Coca-Cola cans, symbolizing how they had been left out of the company's success, and call on Coke to improve conditions at the company for people like them. By the end of March, Jones had organized a bus convoy that would make its way from Atlanta to Wilmington, Delaware, arriving just in time for Coke's annual shareholder meeting on April 19.

He ordered hats for everyone in his group; each one bore the slogan JUSTICE RIDE. He chartered buses; in the end, he filled only one. He met with Jackson, who had been busy with the lawsuit's plaintiffs, as well as with Cyrus Mehri and senior management from Coke. Jackson, too, planned to attend the shareholder meeting. There would be a showdown about race relations in Wilmington.

The night before, guests began gathering at the Hotel Dupont. The hotel staff was on tenterhooks, waiting for the protesters to arrive. Security, at Coke's direction, had been stepped up to the highest level. 'This is worse than the time the PLO came to town,' confided the maître d' in one of the hotel's restaurants, on April 18. Coke executives huddled behind the leatherbound menus and sent for extra bottles of merlot.

Jones's bus pulled in shortly before 9:00 A.M. It had stopped in Richmond, Virginia, and other points along the route, spending three days to get to Wilmington. At every stop, the riders were greeted with hugs and cheers and invitations to supper. Jones found it amazing. Such an outpouring of support, so many calls for Coke to do the right thing. He got teary just thinking about it.

He descended the steps of the bus, leading forty compatriots. Wearing their red caps, they took their seats in the theater as a group. When it was his turn to speak, Jones could hardly contain himself. He rose, walked to the microphone, and let loose with a volley of fire and brimstone, which was not exactly the kind of thing Coke shareholders were accustomed to hearing at the annual get-together.

He brought up the lawsuit, and then he brought up Carl Ware. He pointed out that when it came to blacks at Coke, 'in one hundred and fourteen years, you've only had one senior vice president. In one hundred and fourteen years, you only found one of us qualified? How long do we wait?'

His outrage peaked, and he wondered silently whether to call for a boycott. It was a tried-and-true method of getting an agenda through; no company wanted entire blocs of consumers refusing to buy its products, much less the bad publicity. So Jones went for it. He declared, 'We are *never* going to be anything but black employees.' And then his voice dropped, almost to a whisper, and he added: 'Let's stop buying Coca-Cola. Let's stop – buying – Coca-Cola!'

The applause threatened to swallow him up. He smiled, stepped aside, and found his way back to his seat. A few minutes later it was Jackson's turn to speak. His remarks were elegant, and vintage Jackson. He described himself as a Coca-Cola shareholder dismayed by developments over the past few months. He did not mention his various levels of involvement with Coke over the years.

He said he was disappointed by the board's lack of commitment to diversity, pointing out the near-total whiteness of the Coca-Cola directors themselves. '*Someone* has not gotten the message,' he thundered. He noted that Hispanics, some 27 percent of all Coke consumers, were not represented on the board. He raised doubts about the Coke lawyers, mainly from King & Spalding, who were handling the company's defense in the racial-discrimination lawsuit. 'Law bills are up, share price is down,' Jackson intoned. 'Coke will lose this case in a court of law but, worse, in the court of public opinion.' He did not call for a boycott, and afterward, several people saw him scolding Jones for raising the stakes.

Jones's boycott was largely left to him, and it made little impact. He arranged to have some Coke vending machines removed and replaced with Pepsi machines in Atlanta. He also brought a group of followers to New York City, two months after the shareholder meeting, and they stood on the concrete island in the middle of Times Square, holding up signs that said, NO JUSTICE, NO COKE. Trucks and taxicabs honked at them in apparent support. Coke did not call the police.

By the middle of June, Coke reached a tentative settlement of the lawsuit with Mehri, who had successfully kept Willie Gary off the case. Gary's efforts ran aground after Coke revealed that it was paying $5 million a year to be a major advertiser on his cable channel. Gary did win over two of the original four plaintiffs, after he promised he would get them more money than Mehri ever could.

The agreement came just before 4:00 P.M. as Mehri threatened to file a voluminous class-action brief against the company – filled, he said, with dozens of examples of discrimination. With Mehri's paralegal standing on the front steps of the federal courthouse in Atlanta awaiting the order to file the document as clerks inside got ready to close for the day, Coke agreed to pay more than $150 million in cash to its African American employees, including some who had already resigned. The board would be required to evaluate the company in terms of its progress on diversity every year, and new board members nominated would have to reflect diversity goals as well. An outside expert, Alexis Herman, was appointed to evaluate Coke's progress annually. The settlement, an average of $40,000 a person, totaled $192.5 million. It had turned out indeed to be bigger than Texaco.

'We had to fight over every concept,' Mehri said. 'It wasn't like a fistfight or a food fight. It was a battle of nerves.' Minutes after the settlement was announced, Willie Gary made an announcement of his own: On behalf of an entirely new group of former Coca-Cola employees, he was suing the company in federal court for $1.5 billion.

Trying to build up its beverage assortment, Coke bid more than $14 billion to acquire Quaker Oats, the owner of Gatorade. If it could buy Gatorade, Coke would edge ahead in the sports–drink category, and Daft had already vowed to push for more 'noncarbs', as they were known aboard Coke trucks. Pepsi had expressed interest in Quaker, and so had the Danone beverage company.

The price was settled, the terms were signed and sealed, and the champagne sat chilling in boardrooms in Atlanta and Chicago on the evening of November 21. Then someone at Quaker got an urgent phone call. The Coca-Cola board, after meeting for hours, had voted to scrap the deal.

The vote was unanimous, and the shock was palpable on Daft's face and everyone else's. He had believed he had the thing sewn up. He had even posed for pictures with Bob Morrison, his counterpart at Quaker.

When the markets opened the following day, Coke's stock sank more than 13 percent. After that, people inside and outside Coke began to ask a lot of questions. They felt the shooting down of the Quaker deal, which would have reinforced Daft's goal of improving volume by selling noncarbonated drinks as well as Coca–Cola, showed that Daft might not have the complete support of the board. The program to build a new Coca-Cola empire from noncarbonated drinks seemed to be in jeopardy, and maybe it had never really existed. The analysts trimmed their numbers again. They were still waiting for the lowering of Coke's targets, the lowering they thought was inevitable.

Winter came, and a new year, and with it more bleak results from Coke. By then the share price hovered between fifty and fifty-five dollars. Daft, however, received a bonus of one million stock options. In February 2001, Jack Stahl finished writing his president's letter for the annual report and then traveled to Naples, Florida, to address a convention where Coke and other companies always presented new products, strategies, and outlooks for the future.

People remarked that he seemed disconnected from the words he read from the speech he held in front of him. He looked tired and spent. 'I got the feeling he knew he would be a caretaker,' said one former Coke executive who heard him speak. 'He didn't seem fired up.'

This was *the president of the Coca-Cola Company*. The audience didn't know what to make of him. Surely, some of them thought, there is a new problem we don't know about. Yet.

Within a few weeks, Stahl left the company. No one at Coke suggested he was retiring. He was forty-seven years old. Evidently worried about more bad publicity, the company's lawyers required him to sign an agreement that prohibited him from saying anything 'disparaging' about Coke. He would keep silent on all matters Coca-Cola. About six months later, gone too was Charlie Frenette, who had been named head of Coke's operations in Europe a little more than a year earlier; like Stahl, he was dismissed and ordered, in writing, not to speak about his experiences at the company. Coke was investing in silence.

They were among those who were chosen by Ivester and then rejected under Daft. Ivester himself was enjoying life. No longer a part of the Coca-Cola Company, he remained involved in traditions that had long been treasured there. He was a director of Suntrust, the banking giant. The Emory University board asked him to stay even after he left Coke, so he did. He became vice chairman of the Robert W. Woodruff Health Sciences Center, the enormous medical system that included the hospital where Woodruff and Goizueta spent their final days.

He stayed in Atlanta, in the same house in the Buckhead neighborhood where so many of his neighbors were Coca-Cola men, too. But he bought a weekend place only a few miles from Woodruff's beloved Ichauway. He presided over twelve thousand acres, which he named Deer Run and where he could ride, entertain his friends, hunt quail, and take drives much as Woodruff had. There, as at Ichauway, the live oaks never lost their leaves, conveying a sense of permanent vigor to the land regardless of the season.

Shortly before Jack Stahl departed, Coke brought aboard an executive who was immediately named head of the Minute Maid–P&G joint venture. His name was Steve Heyer, and he had been hired away from Turner Broadcasting, part of the AOL Time Warner media empire. He came to Coke by way of Atlanta, where he had met Keough at the suggestion of Cathleen Black, another board member, who was the president of Hearst Magazines.

Heyer was passionate, feisty, ambitious, and an outsider. He understood brands and marketing, and he was unlike anything the world of Coke had seen in a very long time. He reminded some people of a young Don Keough. In one interview, he went out of his way to praise Keough by saying that he had come to work at Coke because he wanted to be around someone like him. His fondness for Keough, he would say, was immediate. 'The moment I got in my car, I called my mother and said, "I just met a guy who's really special. This is the kind of mentor I'd love to have,"' Heyer gushed in an interview with *Fortune*.

Not long after that, Daft brought Brian Dyson out of retirement to serve as a vice chairman. Dyson, blamed by some for New Coke and for Coca-Cola Enterprises' failings, suddenly found himself in power again. He was still a good friend of Keough's. He signed a contract that paid him $1.3 million in 2001, plus 900,000 stock options.

Within weeks, Heyer was seen as a contender for a top job, the presidency of Coke at the very least. He did everything he was told. He took on a variety of assignments; by the time he had been at the company a year, his portfolio included overseeing Coke sales in

South America – a job Keough had once had – and he had also been in charge of everything from advertising to syrup production. 'Heyer gets it,' said one industry expert excitedly. He seemed to be breathing new life into Coke.

Still, through all of 2001 and most of 2002, there was no president to take Stahl's place. Keough and his enormous personality remained aboard, his title still senior adviser to the Coca-Cola Company. When articles appeared asking whether Daft was truly in control, he would insist that he, not Keough, called the shots when it came to deals and major decisions, as well as minor ones. 'His understanding with me from the beginning is, you will give me your point of view and sometimes I pay attention to it, sometimes not,' he said in the summer of 2002.

In New York and Atlanta, Keough's phone rang constantly, and it was Keough whom many people interested in working at the Coca-Cola Company felt they should stop in and see. Keough would insist that he was not in charge. He didn't want a second chance at running Coke. He thought he had done a fine job the first time around. 'My ego doesn't need any more stroking,' he would say.

At the same time, Coke had been his professional arena for such a long time that, he acknowledged, 'there is no way I can fully separate myself from this company.' He believed that, and the proof of it was all over Coke. But it was not his doing, he insisted.

'The truth is, it is an institution in my life and I can't avoid it. The system wouldn't let me avoid it. I was the last man standing of an era, and people felt comfortable coming to me.'

He was still the chairman of Allen & Company. He helped deals get rolling – he knew lots and lots of people – and he jetted around the country, accepting awards such as Ad Man of the Year. He wanted to stay active, his friends said, and this was one way of doing that. Not bad for a guy who was seventy-six years old in the fall of 2002. He knew what he wanted. He wanted the Coca-Cola Company to be great.

Coke progressed on the new-product front. The company brought out Vanilla Coke, diet Coke with Lemon, and an energy drink called KMX. Later it made plans for a hot-coffee service, something Keough had worked on himself in the 1960s, and from the drawing board came a chocolate drink, a series of vitamin-fortified juices for the third world, and cans and bottles of lemonade.

But all that did little to help the share price, which fell below fifty dollars a share at the beginning of 2002 and sank lower, to forty and less, as the year wore on. Daft reduced the volume targets, finally, but it seemed to be too late to be of much help. The bloom was off the rose. Andrew Conway issued a report in 2002 that was mildly supportive but set a price target for the stock at fifty-seven dollars – still ten dollars below where it had been when Ivester resigned, three years earlier, and thirty dollars below its peak in 1998. Other analysts repeatedly questioned the volume growth Coke reported, asserting that much of it came from acquisitions and therefore was not 'real' growth.

The world had shifted, and the skeptics were in full cry. It was not a good time for the Coca-Cola Company, nor any company that was publicly traded. The bull market had been lassoed and dragged to a halt. Investors, once sure they would profit by buying stocks, felt cheated by all the companies – the WorldComs, the Enrons, the AT&Ts, the hundreds of dot-coms – that had promised so much but delivered far less. Business scandals erupted from back offices to corner suites. Money ebbed steadily from stocks that once could do no wrong. The Dow Jones industrial average, after peaking at more than 11,000 points, fell bit by bit to finish closer to 8,000 by the end of 2002.

Executives were accused of mismanagement, of excess, of shareholder deceit. Investigators swarmed across corporate America, turning up fraud after fraud.

Warren Buffett's Coca-Cola holdings had lost another $4 billion of their value by the end of 2002. During that summer, he persuaded the company to announce that it would expense its stock options – costing shareholders a couple of pennies per share but all in the interest of doing the right thing. Coke also said it would no longer give earnings guidance ahead of time. This was something that Donald McHenry had been urging for some time. 'There is a terrible temptation to manage earnings to meet a prediction you've made,' he said. A veil of rectitude appeared to be descending.

Two new board members were elected at the 2002 shareholder

meeting, which was held in April in New York as a gesture of support to the city after the terrorist attacks that destroyed the World Trade Center. The meeting itself was a nonstop showcase of entertainment, with performers like Jon Bon Jovi and Wynton Marsalis onstage, starting at nine o'clock in the morning. The new directors were Bob Nardelli, a former General Electric executive who had recently taken the top job at Home Depot, where Keough had once been a director; and Barry Diller, the entertainment mogul. Neither fulfilled the company's promise to diversify its board. Diller was more or less a stranger to Coke's chairman, but other people knew him.

'I've spoken to him a couple of times,' Daft would say. He had met Diller through Herbert Allen and Don Keough. Diller's picture still hung on the wall at Allen & Company, and Keough was a director of Interactive Corp., a media company that was a recent Diller creation.

Bottlers continued to be troubled. Coca-Cola Enterprises had put out a video in 2000 called *Your Local Bottler*. It included comments from John Alm, the chief executive, who at one point said: 'We are changing how we operate. What we're going to do is localize like we never have before.' Daft announced extra marketing support to the bottlers that year. It was apparently not enough to convince John Aide, the holdout in Tarpon Springs, Florida, to maintain the status quo. In October 2001, he sold his franchise – the last part of Florida to remain in an independent bottler's hands – to Coca-Cola Enterprises.

In 2002, Daft promised that a greater share of the profits the Coca-Cola System made would go to the bottlers. This was more fence-mending, meant to soothe the bottlers. It was also a piece of news that sent Coca-Cola stock plummeting to below thirty-eight dollars a share.

Bringing the company and the bottler together for the purpose of leading Coke back to its old dizzying heights was a reasonable objective, some said. Selling Coke to the world remained a simple proposition. 'It's not rocket science,' said Joe Wilkinson, who knew as much about it as anyone. 'It's one-on-one, in-the-trenches marketing. It's the old Frank Barron story.'

At the very end of 2002, just before Christmas, two of Coke's biggest bottlers announced that they would unite in a $3.6 billion merger. Panamco became part of Coca-Cola Femsa, which was based in Mexico and had continually turned in one of the best performances of any Coke anchor bottler. Panamco, on the other hand, had never overcome the burden of debt from its purchase of the Venezuelan bottler in 1997, and the merger eased things considerably for Panamco shareholders. Henry Schimberg was the vice chair of Panamco when the merger was announced. Allen & Company's investment bank arm, run by Herbert Allen's son, was one of Femsa's bankers on the deal. The younger Allen was also a Femsa director, named to the board in 2000.

At the end of the year, people who had once been part of Coke contemplated the company's slide and wondered when things would get better. 'There are two things that make that company great,' said one former executive, who spent his entire career at Coke. 'The brand Coca-Cola and the bottler system.'

Coke had tried to bring the bottlers in line, and that had backfired rather spectacularly. But the company still had the brand, and it was still the best-known brand in the universe.

By Christmas, it also had a president. Steve Heyer was moved up at last, and he praised Daft in his official acceptance speech. 'I feel really privileged and proud to be part of Doug's team,' he said in one interview. 'I came to the company because of Doug.'

Now the team that would shape the future of the Coca-Cola Company was complete. It included Keough, a relic of the old order; Daft, the accidental chairman; and Heyer, the new kid. They couldn't have come together at a more discouraging time. All around them the business world was in flames. The bull was dead. Entire industries that once seethed with promise lay in pieces, their leaders hauled before grand juries and their former glory gone to dust.

But the Coca-Cola Company would be different. The men of Coke were sure they could raise her up, bring back her lost prestige, restore the luster stolen by time and circumstance. They knew the formula. They had done it before. They would just have to do it again.

Epilogue: Nerve Tonic

IT WOULD TURN OUT TO BE much harder than they thought.

In the New Year that followed the assembly of the Keough, Daft and Heyer dream team, the Coca-Cola Company began to stumble. One stumble followed another, larger and more public each time, almost as if a curse had descended over cheerful, bright red Coke like a black cape.

The amount of Coca-Cola concentrate sold to bottlers grew by just 4 percent in the first quarter of 2003, and half that was from acquisitions the company had made at various times in the previous year. The share price tumbled nearly $3 in a single day, closing at a miserable $39.90 per share. Still, the company assured Wall Street that it was on the right track. It had everything in place, starting with the right executives, and it planned to improve profitability for not just itself, but its vast array of bottlers, too. It was a tall order even in the best of times.

The first quarter was still unfolding when, in March, came a serious fiasco. Another 1,000 people were fired from Coke, as a fresh effort to rid the company of its expenses got under way, and among them was a midlevel financial specialist named Matthew Whitley.

Whitley was unhappy over his treatment, and sued Coke for what he called an unfair dismissal. He claimed he had been fired for reporting fraudulent activity at Coke's fountain division, and gladly went into the specifics. Coke, he said, had rigged a marketing test in Richmond, Virginia, in which Coke was trying to prove the popularity of a product it called Frozen Coke. It was being offered to Burger King, a long-time Coke customer. The drink, a kind of slush made by combining Coca-Cola with crushed ice, would be sold only at Burger King's hundreds of restaurants if it met with Burger King's approval. It represented a major opportunity for the Coca-Cola Company to sell more of its concentrate to a giant fountain customer.

So getting Burger King's approval was critical. The test took place in 2000, not long after Daft took over from Doug Ivester. A man from Richmond with connections to local children's groups was recruited and paid $10,000 to take hundreds of boys and girls to Burger King, where they ordered 'value meals' that included Frozen Cokes. Burger King executives, impressed by the results they saw in Richmond, signed on to sell Frozen Coke, an exclusive product offered to them by the Coca-Cola Company, not only in Richmond but at scores of other restaurants as well.

In his lawsuit, Whitley sought $44.4 million in damages. Along with his assertions about the Burger King test, he said Coke's fountain division had also created slush funds, engaged in accounting fraud, manipulated its inventories. Another lawsuit, filed in 2000, had accused Coke of 'channel stuffing', or forcing more concentrate on its bottlers than they needed in highly profitable markets like Japan. Taken together with Whitley's claims, the company suddenly seemed wrongheaded.

The Burger King allegations dogged the company relentlessly. Coke had invested heavily to extend its contract with the fast-food chain in 1998, when Pepsi tried to take the business away with a sweet offer. Coke had promised various kinds of marketing help to Burger King, and that had helped beat back Pepsi's effort.

But no one had expected anything like this. When Burger King executives learned of Whitley's charges, they were irate. It would be some time before they got their audience with Coke's senior management. But there was nowhere for Coke to hide. By June, the company admitted that it had manipulated the Frozen Coke marketing test, and the following month it worked out a settlement of sorts with Burger King that included a payment of $21.1 million; few other details were forthcoming. A short time later, Coke announced that John Fisher, the head of the fountain division, would be leaving the company.

Some Coke veterans thought he should not be the only one to go. 'I was shocked the company did not immediately go down there and have a conversation with Burger King,' said a former senior executive, who resigned before the scandal erupted. 'It was counter to the ethics and values that I was trained with when I was there. As a person who spent 28 years with the company, I was shocked. And hurt.' To him, the company's general conduct before and after the incident came to light suggested 'something rotten at the core'.

Whitley eventually got a payday of his own. In October, Coke said it would settle with him for $540,000. About $300,000 of that would go to his lawyers. Neither side would comment further on the arrangement, but Coke did issue a statement saying that he had not been fired for reporting the fraud involving Frozen Coke. No, the company insisted, Whitley had actually been considered for not one but two new jobs during the March job cuts, but he had lost out to competitors who scored better than he did on various screenings.

Whitley went away, but his charges lingered over the company. They caught the attention of the Securities and Exchange Commission, flush with success after pursuing Martha Stewart and other high fliers of the moment. The S.E.C. launched an investigation into Coke's accounting. It began as dozens of companies were under intense scrutiny over the way they kept their books; accounting debacles involving Enron, MCI Worldcom, Adelphia Communications and other publicly traded giants had crowded newspaper headlines for months and turned once-docile investors into angry beasts. Now it was Coke's turn under the microscope. Soon the United States Attorney's office in Atlanta, working with the F.B.I., was interested, too. The company acknowledged that it was under investigation, and tried to move on. There were markets to conquer and dark sticky concentrate to sell. They had better things to do with their time.

But the channel-stuffing claims appeared to lead to Daft's door. The lawsuit filed in 2000 contended that Coke had faked its revenue, income and earnings forecasts by unloading unreasonable amounts of concentrate that its bottlers did not want or need. Cash incentives of up to $25 million were used to make the deals happen, the lawsuit said. When two Coke employees met with investigators, they reported that the questioning paid a great deal of attention to Daft's role. The company, though, rejected the claims about concentrate, saying they 'lack merit'.

All this time, Don Keough had kept busy. He remained a senior advisor to Daft, but his duties were gradually changing. In October, two events quietly occurred that would have an enormous impact on his future at Coke. Warren Buffett, still the biggest individual holder of Coca-Cola shares with about eight percent of the stock, named Keough to the board of Berkshire Hathaway, the conglomerate Buffett ran and from which his pronouncements about corporate ethics and business practices, as well as his investment choices, were the stuff of legend. At seventy-seven, Keough did not appear too old to contribute to Buffett's well-being, at least in Buffett's opinion. After all, Buffett himself was seventy-three.

And interestingly, Coke was about to change its long-time policy that required directors to step down at the age of seventy-four. With Buffett's birthday just around the corner, the Coca-Cola Company did away with that policy. Now the rule required directors who had passed that once-critical milestone to submit letters of resignation every year, which would be accepted or rejected by the company chairman as he saw fit.

The new rule worked well for Buffett, and Keough was pleased with it, too. Yet he was growing impatient with the rate of progress on other fronts at Coke. The share price was mired in the fifty-dollar range, well below its price when Daft took over. The company still struggled to get its advertising right. Cola sales were nothing to write home about. Morale had tanked with the first mass layoffs in early 2000, and had not improved. Very little had changed for the better at Coke, though Keough and others tended to blame other conditions, like the slumping economy and the weak stock market. In many ways, the company was worse off than it had been before the Age of Daft began.

The Coke employees who were questioned about Daft finished their meetings in January 2004. A month earlier, Daft had all but indicated publicly that his days were numbered. At a beverage conference in New York, he was asked whether management changes were imminent at Coke. 'I know what my own plans are,' he replied tersely. He would not elaborate.

Suddenly, on February 19th, he was out. Coke announced that he would retire at the end of 2004. It came as a surprise to many, since Daft was only sixty years old, but there was an even bigger surprise on its heels. Steven Heyer, the man apparently groomed to succeed him, the supposed heir handpicked by Keough and sent to work alongside Doug Daft, would not necessarily get the job. The Coke board said it would appoint a search committee to look at candidates inside and outside the company. It promised to make a decision as soon as possible.

The chairman of that search committee was Keough. In the blink of an eye, in the same meeting that determined the fate of Daft, he had been appointed a Coke director and put in charge of the all-powerful committee that would screen and select candidates to replace Daft. It was just like 1999, only this time his role was official when it came to determining who would lead the Coca-Cola Company.

Not everyone rolled out the red carpet for him. 'Coca-Cola's board appears to be moving in the wrong direction,' wrote John Faucher, a beverage analyst for JP Morgan. 'While Keough has long been a confidant of several board members, his appointment dramatically raised the board overlap metric and also increased the number of affiliated directors.' Keough, he pointed out, sat on boards controlled by three other Coke directors: Herbert Allen, Barry Diller and Buffett. A fourth director, Bob Nardelli, headed Home Depot, where Keough had been a director for years before being forced out by age.

Such criticism was easy for the directors to ignore. Seventy-seven years old, and holding the key to Coke's future, Keough at last was where he had always wanted to be. He wanted the new chairman and chief executive to be someone who could handle the Coca-Cola system, from front to back and sideways, too. The person had to understand the intricacies of the bottling business, along with its relationship to Coke, as well as the business of selling concentrate. He or she had to be smart and savvy and well-traveled, like Keough. And the person, whoever it was, had to know how to fix what so many people, inside and outside of Coke, now realized was broken. There needed to be a new spirit of enterprise at the company, a reason for people to come to work every day. The old promises had been scuttled, the ones about loyalty and rewards for hard work. A new Coca-Cola had emerged from the shards of the old one, and it was struggling for life. Someone out there had to be tapped to come in, do the job, get everything back on track again.

Why not Heyer?

He had been a superstar at Booz Allen, the consulting company, and then again at Turner Broadcasting in Atlanta, where he had caught Keough's eye in the first place. At Coke, he had risen faster than any outside hire in memory. He had rocketed from running a flimsy joint venture to being in charge of Coke sales across the Americas – Keough's onetime role. He had collected additional responsibilities along the way, like overseeing Coke's marketing, and just three years into the experiment his resume glowed redder than a Coca-Cola sign. Even more important to Wall Street, he had begun to patch the relationship between Coke and its bottlers – a relationship cracked in every direction by decades of abuse and mistrust. He had already been anointed, everyone thought; he had cleared every Atlanta hurdle, with room to spare. Rarely did a president of the Coca-Cola Company fail to become chairman, as long as time and circumstance did not get in the way, the way they once had for Keough.

The no-Daft-and-maybe-no-Heyer announcement threw analysts, reporters and investors into a panic. What was going on at the Coca-Cola Company? Once again, director Jimmie Williams was paraded before the crowd to answer their many questions. Heyer, he said, was a 'strong internal candidate'. However, the board would hire a search firm and look at many possibilities. Daft's exit, he insisted, had 'absolutely nothing' to do with the issues and investigations rocking the company.

'Everybody understood that in his mind, this was the time, and he'd prepared us for that,' Williams said.

People at Coke had their complaints about Heyer. Some of the secretaries called him 'the Devil'. He had a temper, and wasn't afraid to unleash it. But he was hardly the first Coke executive to be accused of that.

Daft, too, had his detractors. First considered a breath of fresh air after Ivester, he soon had a reputation for using his power relentlessly and erratically. 'There were constantly changing directions,' said a former senior executive, who spent two years answering to Daft as chairman. 'His management philosophy was, you appeal to people's own self-interests, of fear and greed. He would appear to be highly threatening at times, and then lavishly reward them at other times. It was: I am emperor, and they have to listen to what I say.'

Daft also had to live with the impact of the vast layoffs he ordered, whether they were his idea or someone else's. He was the leader at a time of trauma for Coke, and people who remained at the company were depressed. Their friends were gone, their company was roiled, and the flagging stock price didn't help, either. 'Big pieces of the organization got ripped out, and huge amounts of intellectual capital went into the Dumpster,' the former senior executive said. 'I don't think they ever realized what they lost. And people didn't trust him after that.'

Daft had collected generous payments for his role, though. He lived well, in an apartment Coke obtained for him at the Hotel Pierre in Manhattan, and he spoke now and then of opening a satellite headquarters in the city. He had never really liked Atlanta, and lived there only when he had to. He could afford multiple addresses: in addition to millions of dollars in salary and bonuses, he was awaiting a really enormous prize when he left Coke: one and a half million shares, written into his compensation as restricted stock. All he had to do was lift earnings to a certain level and the prize would be his. Even at Coke's sagging share price, he would gather in at least $60 million.

But now his days were coming to an end, and he had not made the target. He would have no say about who stepped into his shoes when he left, adding insult to injury. Even Ivester had been portrayed as someone who tapped his successor, even though that was not quite true. Heyer, for his part, said nothing about his own feelings.

It quickly became clear that Keough and his committee were after a different kind of superstar, a headliner from some other industry, something other than Coke. James M. Kilts, the chairman of Gillette, was a frequently mentioned name, along with Robert A. Eckert, the chairman of Mattel. Both had spent years in the food business; either could, conceivably, run the Coca-Cola Company. Coke needed someone who understood the business of marketing an old consumer product to a younger and more skeptical world. Even Jack Welch, the retired chairman of General Electric, seemed attractive to Keough; the story was that the wife of James Robinson, another Coke director, discussed the possibility with him at Welch's wedding reception.

Kilts was said to have turned the job offer down. Eckert, too, seemed less than thrilled. Welch, who Herbert Allen considered in the same league as Keough, said he was having too much fun, out of G.E. and into his third marriage, to think about taking on that particular job. The search firm Keough hired, Heidrick & Struggles, was coming up empty-handed. But there was one more source to tap, one that Coke and Keough had tapped plenty of times before. Sure enough, before the azaleas in Atlanta had shed their lush and profuse blossoms, Keough turned to the past to find someone who could lead the Coca-Cola of the future.

On May 4th, the Coca-Cola Company trumpeted the return of E. Neville Isdell, at various times a Coke executive and a bottling executive who had been retired since 2001. Isdell would become the new chairman and chief executive. In telephone interviews with reporters that day, the sixty-year-old Isdell was asked about his plans and priorities. Don Keough, connected on another line, interrupted several times to give his own opinions. In response to questions about other candidates, Keough insisted that Isdell, for all intents and purposes a Coke insider, had been the company's first choice all along. 'He was the first candidate we talked to,' he told one reporter, 'and the only one who was offered the job.'

Inside Coke, there was jubilation, the guarded sort. Of course they realized that Isdell was Keough's choice; of course they had seen how they'd fared under an earlier Keough choice. But there was still a sense of 'Happy days are here again,' as a former employee put it.

In his own remarks, Isdell described himself as willing to listen to Keough's advice. Ivester had not done that, to his peril. It was clear to observers of the beverage industry that no matter what his actual job title might be, Keough was a force to be reckoned with. 'Anyone who wouldn't listen to the wisdom of Don Keough,' Isdell intoned, 'is narrow-minded.'

He came to Coke at a time when the company was under

Federal investigation. He was returning to a place where he had worked for thirty-five years, first on the Coca-Cola side, and then, at the end, as a senior executive at a Coke anchor bottler called Coca-Cola Beverages. He had been there when the bottler was taken public on the London Stock Exchange in the summer of 1998. And he had seen all the hope drain out of that bottler as it confronted the war in the former Yugoslavia, the trail of economic wreckage left by the Russian ruble crisis, and the Coke recall in Belgium that reverberated across Eastern Europe. He had seen some very bad results, but had also helped craft a bigger bottler when Coca-Cola Hellenic merged with C.C.B. The management team from Hellenic took over, and Isdell retired to Barbados. It had taken a lot of persuasion – a lot of phone calls from Keough – to get him to leave the beach and come back to the chaos in Atlanta.

The other Coke directors believed they needed someone like him. They had discovered, to their dismay, that they almost couldn't give the job away. Where the Coca-Cola Company had been the envy of its peers in 1997, the year Goizueta died, these days it was a pitiful shadow of its former self. The directors themselves were coming under fire, for everything from their overlapping loyalties to the hefty severance packages they gave to departing executives. 'We want to see more independence on the audit panel,' Patrick McGurn, a prominent voice on shareholder interests, said that spring. There were links between Keough and Buffett, Keough and Allen, Keough and Diller. Buffett and Diller served together on the Washington Post Company's board. More troubling, no one on the board seemed willing or able to counter the influence of Coke's most powerful shareholder-directors – who now included Keough as well as Buffett and Allen.

There had been another dose of unfavorable publicity before Isdell's appointment became public. In April, someone at Coke leaked word that the company's general counsel, Deval L. Patrick, would be leaving. Patrick had been wooed by Coke in early 2001, away from the general counsel's post at Texaco. In the aftermath of the racial-discrimination lawsuit, Daft had wanted to make every possible visible effort to assure the world that all was well at Coke. Patrick arrived to a hero's welcome.

But he had evidently run afoul of someone. He quit, and Coke looked ham-handed. News reports suggested he had grown frustrated with Coke's executives and directors as he tried to resolve various legal battles at the company. Like Daft, he was supposed to stick around until the end of the year. Daft was long gone from the boardroom and the corridors of Coke; withering on the vine, he found more and more to do far from Atlanta.

With Isdell named, where did that leave Heyer? Some analysts expected him to run from Coke, but they hoped he would not. To them, he represented success on many levels, particularly when it came to the bottling system. For as much as Coke had tried to gain the upper hand in that critical partnership, the company kept losing out to the bottlers. So large was Coca-Cola Enterprises, by this time handling 80 percent of the Coke sold throughout the United States, that any sluggishness on its part could be devastating for Coke's sales figures. All over the world, the once-intoxicating notion of being able to sell as much concentrate as it wanted, at prices it alone controlled, was fading. Instead a clamor was growing, from Wall Street and from the bottlers themselves, to improve profits for the bottlers – or else. The Coca-Cola *bête noire* – the bottlers – showed no sign of submitting to Coke's vision.

Heyer, however, had begun to get a grip on that. Many bottlers liked him. He also understood how the Coca-Cola name had been all but forgotten by many younger consumers, and realized that it needed to be brought back to prominence through advertising and marketing.

'Heyer had a tremendous understanding of consumer value and how they needed to change consumers' perception of the brand,' John Faucher said. 'Is he the only person in the system who understands that? No. Would Coke be better off with Heyer? Yes, no question.'

But Coke would not get Heyer. On May 18, he had assured an audience that he would be staying on. Nevertheless, on June 9, only a month after Isdell ascended, Heyer left the company. He had no new job to report to. He clearly just wanted to leave. He got $24 million or so in severance for his three years at Coke, which drew fresh criticism of the company's policies. When Daft's severance package was revealed in August, he got far less, proportionally speaking: he lost the one and a half million shares that had been his in theory. He did, however, get to keep 200,000 shares of restricted stock, worth about $8 million.

In March, there had been another spectacular setback for Coke, one with haunting echoes of the history that had brought Coca-Cola into being. Coke had had a plan for some time to launch its Dasani bottled water in England, and with Coca-Cola Enterprises as its distributor, it did so in early 2004. The water was bottled, labeled and advertised across the United Kingdom as 'the purest water you can buy'. The English, with plenty of bottled water brands to choose from already, watched as Coke replaced the familiar with this unknown brand, Dasani, in shops and supermarkets across their land.

In most of Europe, bottled water meant spring water – either naturally bubbling or naturally flat, with little human interference involved. The water could be French, but it did have to be pure. People drank it for health reasons, and when they drank it, they expected it to have some sort of organic origin.

Dasani, though, was produced in England exactly the way it had been produced for years in the United States: ordinary tap water was filtered in a bottling plant, poured into bottles, and mixed with a copyrighted Coke formula of minerals like calcium chloride that Coke believed gave it a sharpened taste and gave consumers a reason to reach for Dasani.

The backfires came slowly at first. The English made fun of the fact that Dasani came from tap water, some of them angrily denouncing Coke for charging 95 pence per bottle. 'Taken for Plonkers', one headline blared, once the facts were known. 'Sidcup for 95p', gasped another, referring to the Sidcup water plant in Kent.

And the worst was still coming.

The minerals in Dasani produced a side effect when combined with that English tap water, as it turned out. The result was bromate, a cancer-causing substance, that was created as a byproduct of the calcium chloride added to the product. British law permitted a bromate level of 10 parts per billion, but testing found it was present at between 10 and 25 parts per billion in Dasani.

A massive uproar followed. Dasani was yanked from store

shelves, as newspapers, television commentators and what seemed like the entire British Empire crackled with indignation. Weeks after its launch, 500,000 bottles of Dasani were collected and destroyed; Coca-Cola Enterprises would later report that the recall cost it $37 million, and Coke would repay all but $5 million of that. Coke, however, maintained a stiff upper lip. 'We *chose* to take the product off the market,' a company executive would say.

The debacle was a huge setback for Coke's growth plans in Europe. No more bottled water in England, and none in France and Spain, either, where launches had been planned for the same year. As Isdell arrived, he had to take charge of a company that in many ways seemed to have lost its way. Many people interested in the fortunes of Coke began to wonder: just how much power would he have, when Keough or another director, unseen offstage, disagreed with his plans?

That was the central challenge for Isdell. He could dream up the best marketing in the world, assemble the finest team of executives Coke had ever seen and transform the growth rate from lackluster to spectacular. It wasn't all that difficult to do. But if he did not really have power – if, like his most recent predecessors, he lacked the ultimate authority to make important decisions – then he, too, would be taking early retirement. The company was a different place now. It seemed beaten, tired. Gone was the swagger, the self-assurance, and gone were thousands of employees who had made it work, for better or worse.

He could gather it up. He could turn it around. He would need time, and he would need space. And as had happened so many other times at Coke, no one would know how Coke's leader had fared until long after the hour was past.

'The potential is there,' said a former senior executive, a self-described optimist and veteran of Coke under Paul Austin, Roberto Goizueta, Doug Ivester and finally, Doug Daft. 'Can they get out of the way, to let it happen?'

Bibliography

I was fortunate to be able to interview dozens of current and former Coca-Cola employees and executives. Where possible, I have named them or identified them in the Notes section. Many people, even if they had left the company, were reluctant to speak on the record, citing fear of retribution through social channels, even if they no longer had to worry about repercussions at work. Where they are listed as anonymous, it is because I agreed to protect their identities. I did not include anything they said unless I could independently verify it.

The Coca-Cola Company cooperated with my research for this book by making its archivist, Phil Mooney, available to me. Phil took me on an amazing tour of the preservation of Robert Woodruff's office in the Coke tower in Atlanta and answered many questions I had about the history of Coca-Cola. Douglas Daft, Coke's chairman and CEO from December 1999 to February 2004, talked at length one summer morning in 2002 about his experiences since becoming chairman and about his childhood memories of Coke. Two of Coke's directors, Herbert Allen and Donald McHenry, also agreed to speak to me on the record. Many other executives and former executives shared their impressions and experiences but did not want to be identified by name or by role at the company.

Several former Coke bottlers, including Frank Barron, Dick Montag, and William Schmidt were extremely generous with their time, as was Summerfield Johnston, Jr. Emmet Bondurant II, the Atlanta lawyer who represented Schmidt and other bottlers in their long-running legal action against the Coca-Cola Company, and Tom Stanley of Houston, who represented independent bottlers of other soft drinks in a separate case against the company, provided invaluable background and insight. Cyrus Mehri patiently answered my questions about the racial discrimination lawsuit brought by current and former Coke employees against the company in 1999.

David Greising's book on Roberto Goizueta, *I'd Like the World to Buy a Coke,* and Frederick Allen's history of the company, *Secret Formula,* provided important information as well as fascinating detail. To understand the relationship between Goizueta and Robert Woodruff, as well as those among Woodruff and other Coke executives, I relied on interviews and on material in the Special Collections and Archives division of the Robert W. Woodruff Library at Emory University. The Vicksburg Foundation for Historic Preservation in Vicksburg, Mississippi, was also helpful to me in my quest for details about the earliest Coke bottler, Joseph Biedenharn.

These and other books and materials are listed below.

A. D. Puffer & Sons. *Soda-fountain catalog.* Boston: 1903.

Allen, Frederick. *Atlanta Rising.* Atlanta: Longstreet Press, 1996.

———. *Secret Formula.* New York: HarperCollins, 1994.

American Bottlers of Carbonated Beverages. *ABCB List of References to Authoritative Writings on the Carbonated Beverage Industry.* Washington, D.C.: American Bottlers of Carbonated Beverages, 1929.

———. *What Price Sugar.* New York: American Bottlers of Carbonated Beverages, 1929.

———. *1923 Yearbook.* New York: American Bottlers of Carbonated Beverages, 1923.

Andrews, Eliza Frances. *The War-Time Journal of a Georgia Girl, 1864–1865.* Chapel Hill, N.C.: University of North Carolina at Chapel Hill, 1996.

Bonham, Wesley A. *Modern Guide for Soda Dispensers.* Chicago: A. O. Ellison, 1897.

Bonnifield, Matthew Paul. *Oklahoma Innovator: the Life of Virgil Browne.* Norman, Okla.: University of Oklahoma Press, 1976.

Bottlers and Beverage Manufacturers Universal Encyclopedia. Chicago: Expositions Company of America, 1925.

Burge, Dolly Sumner Lunt, *A Woman's Wartime Journal: An Account* of the Passage over Georgia's Plantation of Sherman's Army on the March to the Sea, as Recorded in the Diary of Dolly Sumner Lunt (Mrs. Thomas Burge)* (electronic edition). Chapel Hill, N.C.: University of North Carolina at Chapel Hill, 1996.

Carter, Jimmy. *An Hour Before Daylight*. New York: Simon & Schuster, 2001.

Cheatham, Mike. *Your Friendly Neighbor*. Macon, Ga.: Mercer University Press, 1999.

The Coca-Cola Company: A Chronological History, 1886–1968. Atlanta: The Coca-Cola Company, 1968.

'The Coca-Cola Company Annual Report' Atlanta: The Coca-Cola Bottling Company, 1923, 1924, 1925, 1996, 1997, 1998, 1999, 2000, 2001, 2002.

Communauté Des Maitres Limonadiers, Marchands d'Eau-de-Vie, De la Ville, Fauxbourgs et Banlieue de Paris. *Statuts et Ordonnances*. Paris: Impr. de M. Rebuffe, 1716.

Dahl, J. O. *Soda Fountain and Luncheonette Management*. New York: Harper & Brothers, 1930.

Eberle, Eugene Gustave. *The Soda-Water Formulary*. Dallas: Texas Druggist Publishing Co., 1902.

Elliott, Charles Newton. *Mr. Anonymous*. Atlanta: Cherokee Publishing Company, 1982.

Enrico, Roger, and Jesse Kornbluth. *The Other Guy Blinked*. New York: Bantam Books, 1986.

Graham, Elizabeth Candler. *Classic Cooking with Coca-Cola*. Nashville: Celebrity Books, 1994.

———. *The Real Ones: Four Generations of the First Family of Coca-Cola*. Emeryville, Calif.: Barricade Books, 1992.

Greising, David. *I'd Like the World to Buy a Coke*. New York: John Wiley & Sons, 1998.

Hagstrom, Robert G., Jr. *The Warren Buffett Way*. New York: John Wiley & Sons, 1994.

Harrison, DeSales. *Footprints on the Sands of Time*. New York: Newcomen Society in North America, 1969.

Kahn, E. J., Jr. *The Big Drink*. New York: Random House, 1960.

Korab, A. E. *Technical Problems of Bottled Carbonated Beverage Manufacture*. Washington, D.C.: American Bottlers of

Carbonated Beverages, 1950.

Louis, J. C., and Harvey Yazijian. *The Cola Wars*. New York: Everest House Publishers, 1980.

Lowenstein, Roger. *When Genius Failed*. New York: Random House, 2000.

McHatton–Ripley, Eliza. *From Flag to Flag: A Woman's Adventures and Experiences in the South During the War, in Mexico and in Cuba*. New York: D. Appleton & Company, 1889.

MacMahon, Albert C. *MacMahon's Latest Recipes and American Soda Water Dispensers' Guide*. Chicago: Goodall & Loveless, 1893.

Navarro, Antonio. *Tocayo: A Cuban Resistance Leader's True Story*. Westport, Conn.: Sandown Books, 1981.

Oliver, Thomas. *The Real Coke, the Real Story*. New York: Random House, 1986.

Palmer, Carl J. *History of the Soda Fountain*. Soda Manufacturers Association, 1947.

Pendergrast, Mark. *For God, Country and Coca-Cola*. Second Edition. New York: Basic Books, 2000.

Priestley, Joseph, with introduction by Jack Lindsay. *Autobiography of Joseph Priestley*. Bath, England: Adams & Dart, 1970.

———. *Copies of Original Letters Recently Written by Persons in Paris to Dr. Priestley in America, Taken on Board of a Neutral Vessel*. London: J. Wright, 1798.

———. *Directions for Impregnating Water with Fixed Air,* forward by John J. Riley. Washington, D.C.: American Bottlers of Carbonated Beverages, 1945.

Riley, John J. *A History of the American Soft Drink Industry; Bottled Carbonated Beverages, 1807–1957*. Washington, D.C.: American Bottlers of Carbonated Beverages, 1957.

———. *Organization in the Soft Drink Industry*. Washington, D.C.: American Bottlers of Carbonated Beverages, 1946.

Schmidt, William, and Jan Schmidt. *The Schmidt Museum Collection of Coca-Cola Memorabilia,* Vol. I. Published privately.

Schofield, Robert E. *The Enlightenment of Joseph Priestley*. University Park, Pa.: Pennsylvania State University Press, 1997.

Sobel, Dava. *Longitude*. New York: Penguin Books, 1996.

Stoddard, Bob. *Pepsi-Cola, 100 Years*. Los Angeles: General Publishing Group, 1997.

Warner-Jenkinson Co. *Ice Cream, Carbonated Beverages, with a Short Introduction to the Study of Chemistry and Physics*. St. Louis: Warner-Jenkinson Mfg. Co., 1924.

Watters, Pat. *Coca-Cola: An Illustrated History*. Garden City, N.Y.: Doubleday, 1978.

White, Edward F. *The Spatula Soda-Water Guide*. Boston: Spatula Publishing Co., 1919.

Winschel, Terrence J. *Triumph and Defeat: The Vicksburg Campaign*. Mason City, Iowa: Savas Publishing Company, 1999.

Zyman, Sergio. *The End of Marketing as We Know It*. New York: HarperCollins, 2000.

Special Collections and Archives at the Robert W. Woodruff Library. Emory University, Atlanta.

Notes

Chapter One

2 nothing but Pepsi: Author interview, Warren Buffett, October 1998.

3 850 million . . . bottles a day: 'The Coca-Cola Company Annual Report', 1996, p. 49.

5 'to have everybody drink nothing but Coke': Author interview, Warren Buffett, October 1998.

Chapter Two

8 Bonnie Sinkfield story: author interview, Bonnie Sinkfield, June 2002.

10 'Have you ever seen a Coke bottler that wasn't rich?': Anthony Ramirez, 'It's Only Soft Drinks at Coca-Cola', *The New York Times,* May 21, 1990, section D, p. 1.

12 'than to push somebody's else': Palmer, *History of the Soda Fountain,* p. 25.

12 Brain tonic . . . nerve tonic: Asa G. Candler letterhead, 1894, Special Collections and Archives, Robert W. Woodruff Library.

12 five years later, sales topped 64,000 gallons: 'The Coca-Cola Company Annual Report', 1923, p. 7.

12 'in every state and territory': *The Coca-Cola Company: A Chronological History,* p. 1.

12 burrowing into the cliffs: Winschel, *Triumph and Defeat,* p. 151.

12 became a Coca-Cola syrup dealer: J. A. Biedenharn letter to Harrison Jones, Sept. 11, 1939. Collection of the Vicksburg Foundation for Historic Preservation, Vicksburg, Mississippi.

POP

13 'much to the satisfaction of the parties in charge': 'Soda Water,' *Harper's New Monthly Magazine,* August 1872, p. 345.

13 a reported $50,000: Palmer, p. 22.

14 began demanding state-of-the-art soda fountains: Ibid., p. 22.

14 'beyond all expectation': Ibid.

14 'why not bottle it for our country trade?': Biedenharn letter to Harrison Jones, Sept. 11, 1939.

14 a manufacturer in St. Louis: Wilbur G. Kurtz, Jr., 'Joseph A. Biedenharn', *The Coca-Cola Bottler,* April 1959, p. 97.

15 to Candler in Atlanta: Ibid., p. 191.

15 'we come off a wet floor and marked the floor': Deposition of E. R. Barber in 'Coca-Cola Bottling Company of Minnesota *v.* the Coca-Cola Company', February 12, 1957, p. 16, Special Collections and Archives, Robert W. Woodruff Library.

16 'something inexpensive that appealed strongly to the general public': Harrison, *Footprints on the Sands of Time,* p. 11.

16 aide to an Army assistant quartermaster: Franklin M. Garrett, 'Founders of the Business of Coca-Cola in Bottles', *The Coca-Cola Bottler,* April 1959, no page numbers given.

16 carbonated pineapple drink: Ibid.

17 accompanied by a third man: Harrison, *Footprints,* p. 14.

17 'didn't think much was going on': Garrett, 'Founders of the Business of Coca-Cola in Bottles', no page numbers given.

17 214,008 gallons in 1898: of 'The Coca-Cola Company Annual Report', 1924, p. 9.

18 'only to the most trusted employees since that time': 'Asa Griggs Candler', in *The Coca-Cola Bottler,* April 1959, p. 7.

18 'no one was permitted in this laboratory room': Ibid., p. 8.

19 the occasional ticket would still turn up: Elliott, *Mr. Anonymous,* p. 111.

19 such classics as 'Nearer, My God, to Thee': 1905 example, Special Collections and Archives, Robert W. Woodruff Library.

21 They attracted people: Cheatham, *Your Friendly Neighbor,* p. 99.

22 by the time he was twenty-one years old: Author interview, Summerfield Johnston, Jr., December 2002.

23 'a mighty short time': Deposition of E. R. Barber in 'Coca-Cola Bottling Company of Minnesota *v.* the Coca-Cola Company', p. 20.

23 couldn't agree on contract terms: Garrett, 'Founders of the Business of Coca-Cola in Bottles', no page number given.

23 in a motorboat, the *Josephine:* Watters, *Coca-Cola: An Illustrated History,* p. 75.

24 possible presence of foreign spies: World War II preparedness brochure, the Atlanta Coca-Cola Bottling Company, 1942, Special Collections and Archives, Robert W. Woodruff Library.

24 'the post office or the fire department': Kahn, *The Big Drink,* p. 75.

26 ratio of twenty to one: Author interview, Emmet J. Bondurant II, January 2002.

26 *if you need a good mule, we will lend you one:* Author interview, Summerfield Johnston, Jr., December 2002.

26 'Don't bother us unless you are a hustler': *The Coca-Cola Bottler,* April 1919, p. 18.

26 'brain and brawn that keeps everlastingly at it until it makes good': 'The Day's Work', in *The Coca-Cola Bottler,* September 1919, p. 24.

27 to 3,486,626 in 1909: 'The Coca-Cola Company Annual Report', 1924, p. 9.

27 His house included: Unbylined article in *The Atlanta Journal,* July 15, 1923; page number not given. Special Collections and Archives, Robert W. Woodruff Library.

28 belonged to Napoléon III: Bonnifield, *Oklahoma Innovator,* p. 192 (illustration).

28 'We're ready when you are': Author interviews, William and Jan Schmidt, April 2002.

28 banquet . . . began with crabmeat: 1959 souvenir copy, Special Collections and Archives, Robert W. Woodruff Library.

29 train marked COCA-COLA SPECIAL: John Shearer, 'Lettie Whitehead Evans Was Member of Coca-Cola Board', *Chattanooga News Free Press,* August 4, 1991, p. F 6.

29 a movie theater, and a swimming pool: Ned L. Irwin,

'Bottling Gold: Chattanooga's Coca-Cola Fortunes', 'Tennessee Historical Quarterly', 51, no. 4 (1992), p. 233.

30 feeling 'bilious and sick': 'The Bottle', *American Heritage,* June/July 1986, pp. 98–101.

30 'the rich, abundant life of its people': 'Merchandising Magic', *The Coca-Cola Bottler,* April 1959, p. 4.

31 By the end of 1915, Candler was gone: 'Asa Griggs Candler', in 1959 anniversary edition of *The Coca-Cola Bottler,* pp. 4–5.

32 'annihilated and destroyed': The Coca-Cola Bottling Company *v.* The Coca-Cola Company, 269 F. 796, 1920 USD. November 8, 1920, p. 16.

33 tough requirements for the rest of the world: Horatio Alger Society awards video, 1999, courtesy of the Horatio Alger Society, Washington, D.C.

33 to become an organist: Betsy Morris, 'Doug Is It', *Fortune,* May 25, 1998, pp. 70–84.

34 *I'll never get to go there:* Horatio Alger Awards essay, attributed to Douglas Ivester, 1999, courtesy of the Horatio Alger Society.

34 'It's a matter of when': Author interview, M. Douglas Ivester, October 21, 1998.

35 'I'm a CPA': Horatio Alger Awards essay, attributed to Douglas Ivester, 1999.

35 *then I'll be an accountant:* Ibid.

35 'to get a good job when I get out of school': Ibid.

37 He liked craps: Author interview, former Coca-Cola Company executive, January 2001.

37 'you don't *control* your distribution': Ibid.

38 'twenty-four hours a day, seven days a week': Speech to National Soft Drink Association by Douglas Ivester, October 1994.

39 called him a workaholic: 'Bulletin', University of Georgia, 1987.

40 He didn't like to drink: Author interview, former Coca-Cola Company executive, January 2001.

41 916 eight-ounce bottles: 'The Coca-Cola Company Annual Report', 1999.

42 'I know people who drink it morning, noon, and night': Author interview, Terri Corbett, October 2000.

43 'the liquid down people's throats was our business': Author interview, Frank Barron, Jr., November 2000.

43 'dad-gum accident': Ibid.

Chapter Three

48 green-and-white campaign-style buttons: Author interviews, various former Coca-Cola executives, 2001 and 2002.

48 three thousand people: Ibid.

49 'He bled Coca-Cola red': Author interview, George Marlin, March 2001.

49 'we don't sell funeral vaults': Donald R. Keough speech to Coca-Cola sales meeting, Coca-Cola Company video, 1974.

51 *than does any other executive in our company:* letter from Charles W. Duncan, Jr., to Robert W. Woodruff, November 6, 1970, Special Collections and Archives, Robert W. Woodruff Library.

51 the most mesmerizing: Keough speech to sales meeting, Coca-Cola Company video, 1974.

52 'what it appeared to be': Author interview, Ambassador Donald McHenry, April 2003.

53 'He was everywhere, all the time': Author interview, Roger Enrico, March 2003.

53 'the dispute didn't involve me': Author interview, former Coca-Cola Company executive, March 2003.

54 'I think about that . . . a lot': 'Coca-Cola Turns to Midlands for Leadership', *Omaha World-Herald Sunday Magazine,* March 14, 1982, p. 14.

57 Lupton . . . named his price: Greising, *I'd Like the World to Buy a Coke,* p. 140.

57 'This wasn't supposed to happen': Author interviews, former Coca-Cola Company executive and Coca-Cola bottler, 2000 and 2001.

61 'just about in tears listening to this guy': Author interview, George Marlin, July 2001.

61 'It was a factor that they offered': Author interview, Dick Montag, July 2001.

61 'The bottlers trusted Luke': Author interview, Emmet Bondurant II, January 2001.

62 'it sure would be a nice present': Author interview, former Coca-Cola bottling executive, May 2002.

62 'lulled into a position of trusting the Coca-Cola Company': Author interview, Emmet Bondurant II.

63 the last one . . . for $35 million in 1975: *Atlanta Journal,* August 22, 1975, Special Collections and Archives, Robert W. Woodruff Library.

64 'all this pressure from Coke to sell out': Author interview, Richard Larson, February 2001.

64 'rolled over and played dead': Author interview, Summerfield Johnston, Jr., December 2002.

65 'I suppose that was right': Ibid.

65 'if you don't do it our way': Author interview, former Coca-Cola Company executive, March 2001.

68 'other industries operating through franchised distributors': Memo from the deputy assistant attorney general, Antitrust Division, June 27, 1980, archives of the Jimmy Carter Library, Atlanta, Georgia.

68 'losses and defections to Kennedy and Anderson': Memo from Bob Malson to Stuart Eizenstat, June 30, 1980, archives of the Jimmy Carter Library, Atlanta, Georgia.

69 that it did not hinder competition: 'Jimmy Carter', *Public Papers of the Presidents of the United States:* 1334.

69 'not to promote the product': Author interview, Donald Keough, March 2001.

69 the twenty-seven dollars Goizueta had wanted: Greising, *Buy a Coke,* p. 154.

70 spouted a total of $1.18 billion in cash: Ibid.

70 'you either believe us or you don't': Ibid., p. 153.

70 'the proof of the vision': Melissa Turner, 'CCE Has Won Over the Skeptics', *The Atlanta Journal-Constitution,* November 18, 1987, section A, p. 16.

71 Tropicanas, which were Woodruff's favorite: assorted documents, Special Collections and Archives, Robert W. Woodruff Library.

71 'I'm a very lucky fifty-one-year-old': Letter from Donald Keough to Robert Woodruff, September 5, 1977, Special Collections and Archives, Robert W. Woodruff Library.

72 working the 6:30 A.M. Mass: 'Coca-Cola Turns to Midlands for Leadership', *Omaha World Telegram*, p. 12.

72 *sends you his very best wishes:* Letter from J. W. Jones to Donald Keough, 1971, Special Collections and Archives, Robert W. Woodruff Library.

72 *all of the best of human character:* letter from Donald Keough to Robert Woodruff, December 20, 1977, Special Collections and Archives, Robert W. Woodruff Library.

73 *dynamic American salesman:* letter from Bobby Wilkinson to Robert Woodruff, June 5, 1980, Special Collections and Archives, Robert W. Woodruff Library.

73 'under the banner of Roberto Goizueta': letter from Donald Keough to Robert Woodruff, September 9, 1980, Special Collections and Archives, Robert W. Woodruff Library.

74 the next president of the Coca-Cola Company: Author interview, former Coca-Cola executive, May 2001.

75 'Things just haven't worked out': Author interview, former Coca-Cola executive, July 2001.

75 'run for president and *be* president': Author interview, Herbert Allen, April 2003.

Chapter Four

76 oblivious to everything but the green light: Author interview, former Coca-Cola executives, June 2001 and March 2003.

78 'a serious Cuban': Author interview, Herbert Allen, April 2003.

78 'but anyway, I'm enjoying it': Roberto Goizueta, in speech to bottlers at one-hundredth anniversary of the Coca-Cola Company, May 9, 1986, Coca-Cola Company video.

78 'than I have already lost?': Author interview, former Coca-Cola Company executives, June 2002 and October 2002.

79 Don Quixote, windmill: Greising, *Buy a Coke,* p. 6.

80 the other student, Fidel Castro: Greising, *Buy a Coke,* p. 9, and author interviews.

80 'lack of work-day occupation': McHatton-Ripley, *From Flag to Flag,* p. 125.

81 El Carmelo: Navarro, *Tocayo,* pp. 121–22.

82 was instructed to begin a mission in Cuba: Bob Hall, 'Coca-Cola and Methodism', *Southern Exposure,* vol. 4, no. 3, p. 99.

82 'a steady customer and an advocate of the drink': Ibid.

82 'our commercial interests and our religious duty coincide': Ibid.

83 'every kind of industry on the island': 'Cuban News', in *The Coca-Cola Bottler*, May 1919, p. 16.

83 started work on the Fourth of July: Greising, *Buy a Coke*, pp. 1–4.

83 rusty marks: Greising, *Buy a Coke*, p. 19.

83 ransacked . . . ordered to alter the formula: Greising, *Buy a Coke*, pp. 20–21.

84 a soda called Sprite: Greising, *Buy a Coke*, p. 22.

86 $18,000 a year: Ibid., p. 25.

86 clothes . . . cared for: Ibid., p. 25.

87 'the Cuba that he knew no longer existed': Author interview, Coca-Cola executive, June 2002.

88 someone else's hat: Greising, *Buy a Coke*, p. 41.

89 With that knowledge came a promotion: Ibid., pp. 40–42.

89 death of their fourth child: Ibid., pp. 38–39.

89 it became difficult to get anyone to sign off on anything: Author interview, former Coca-Cola executives, February 2001 and May 2002.

92 'a franc compared to a bottle of Coke?': *The Coca-Cola Bottler*, February 1920, no page number given.

92 'wherever he is and whatever it costs': The Coca-Cola Company, *Chronological History*, p. 6.

93 a 'morale food' : Allen, *Secret Formula*, p. 250.

93 'Ship without displacing other military cargo': telegram from Eisenhower headquarters in North Africa, June 29, 1943, Special Collections and Archives, Robert W. Woodruff Library.

93 Ten billion bottles: Kahn, *The Big Drink*, p. 16.

93 By 1944, it was producing 750,000: Author interview, William Schmidt, April 2002.

94 sitting on a couch in the Oval Office: photograph of Robert W. Woodruff in preserved office at Coca-Cola Company headquarters, Atlanta, Georgia; and author interview, Coca-Cola Company executives, June 2002.

95 'mothered it into a giant': Elliott, *Mr. Anonymous*, p. 164.

95 larger than the one he had had before: Ibid.

95 'continued to operate as before': Ibid., p. 170.

95 office still held: visit to preserved office at Coca-Cola Company headquarters, Atlanta, Georgia, June 2002.

95 PREACHER DICK, FAITHFUL TO THE END: Correspondence between Joseph W. Jones and Morgan McNeel of the McNeel Marble Company, Marietta, Georgia, Special Collections and Archives, Robert W. Woodruff Library.

95 his 'connection with the Coca-Cola Company': Coca-Cola Company, *Chronological History*, p. 6.

96 'must pass through Atlanta': James Harvey Young, 'Three Atlanta Pharmacists', *Pharmacy in History*, vol. 31, no. 1 (1989), p. 16.

96 'can float and handle big enterprises': *The Coca-Cola Bottler*, October 1919, p. 16.

97 christening new aircraft with a bottle of Coca-Cola: Allen, *Atlanta Rising*, illustration 23.

98 'stolen' the event from them: Ibid, p. 240.

98 'Life, liberty, and the pursuit of thirst': 1926 Coca-Cola ad, Special Collections and Archives, Robert W. Woodruff Library.

98 'the Hydra-headed menace of Coca-Cola to our Puritan civilization': clipping from Uniontown, Kansas, *Cicerone*, March 21, 1929, Special Collections and Archives, Robert W. Woodruff Library.

99 'He must be a good friend of Woodruff's': Author interview, George Marlin, July 2001.

100 *It is supposed to be fresh:* Correspondence from Roberto Goizueta to Robert Woodruff, 1981, Special Collections and Archives, Robert W. Woodruff Library.

100 *he will never again be the same:* Correspondence from Donald Keough to Robert Woodruff, December 20, 1977, Special Collections and Archives, Robert W. Woodruff Library.

101 *Usually our guests are companionable:* Correspondence from Robert Woodruff to Dwight Eisenhower, December 1, 1948; and February 3, 1950, Special Collections and Archives, Robert W. Woodruff Library.

101 'people were forced to be informal': Author interview, former Coca-Cola Company executive, May 2002.

101 Nixon was dismissed: Allen, *Secret Formula,* pp. 325–26.

102 *I'm bathing in the largest bathtub I have ever seen:* Correspondence from Roberto Goizueta to Robert Woodruff, May 12, 1978, Special Collections and Archives, Robert W. Woodruff Library.

102 giant bouquet of red roses: Correspondence between Roberto Goizueta and Robert Woodruff, various dates in 1979, Special Collections and Archives, Robert W. Woodruff Library.

103 choice . . . between . . . pharmaceutical business or the entertainment business: author interview, former Coca-Cola Company executive, March 2001.

104 'that's a dangerous reality': Ibid.

104 Woodruff . . . made the motion: Author interview, Ambassador Donald McHenry, April 2003.

104 enormously rewarding: Author interview, Herbert Allen, April 2003.

104 'a very special, secret society': Description of Allen & Company in survey on Vault.com website, 2003.

104 'He's going to be in bed': Barry Rehfeld, 'Herbert A. Allen: Cashing In on Old Friends in High Places', *The New York Times,* August 15, 1993, Section 2, p. 4.

105 chattered endlessly about the box-office take: Author interview, former Coca-Cola Company executive, January 2001.

105 'a ridiculous amount of money': Author interview, Ambassador Donald McHenry, April 2003.

105 'It's show business': Author interview, Herbert Allen, April 2003.

108 'a great feeling of love': Author interview, William Schmidt, May 2002.

109 'We agreed to disagree': Ibid.

110 'Before we knew it, Bill was a pamphleteer': Author interview, Jan Schmidt, April 2002.

110 a sideshow to everything else that was going on inside the company: Author interview, former Coca-Cola Company executive, June 2002.

110 one that would cost Coke $30 million: Greising, *Buy a Coke,* p. 144.

111 more of its manufacturing income from patent medicines than any other city in the nation: Young, 'Three Atlanta Pharmacists', p. 16.

111 Grotto del Cano near Naples: Priestley, *Directions for Impregnating Water with Fixed Air,* p. xi.

112 some of the gas was captured as bubbles in the water: Ibid., p. 5.

113 *I shall have my reward:* Ibid., p. 3.

114 'never . . . imagined . . . you any harm': Priestley, *Autobiography of Joseph Priestley,* p. 29.

114 'some persons in power': Ibid., p. 30.

114 John Adams offered at one point to deport him: Ibid., p. 32, and Schofield, *The Enlightenment of Joseph Priestley,* p. 275.

114 'an innocent beverage': Palmer, *History,* p. 33.

115 block of ice: Eberle, *The Soda-Water Formulary,* p. 164.

115 Auto Smash: White, *The Spatula Soda-Water Guide,* p. 85.

115 expenses for syrup, ice cream, carbon dioxide, and ice: Bonham, *A Modern Guide for Soda Dispensers,* p. 10.

115 harmless analgesic: Young, 'Three Atlanta Pharmacists', p. 16.

116 *tired feeling, mental depression:* Graham, The Real Ones, p. 133.

116 *I did and was relieved*: Correspondence from Asa Candler to Warren Candler, April 10, 1888. Special Collections and Archives, Robert W. Woodruff Library.

117 advertised all over the country that he had done so: Young, 'Three Atlanta Pharmacists', pp. 19–20.

117 Kool & the Gang: Greising, *Buy a Coke,* p. 146, and various news accounts.

117 'Just like the one in *Animal House*': Author interview, Joseph Wilkinson, September 2002.

117 'a pure, vintage Coca-Cola marketing event': Author interview, former Coca-Cola executive, September 2002.

118 nearly 700,000 dominoes: Greising, *Buy a Coke,* p. 146.

118 *This is getting sacrilegious:* Author interview, George Marlin, July 2001.

118 gave him a thumbs-up: Ibid.

118 'Has there ever been a bigger industrial birthday party?':

Donald Keough in videotape of Coca-Cola Company centennial celebration, May 9, 1986, The Coca-Cola Company, Atlanta, Georgia.

118 singled out a bottler from southern Argentina: Ibid.

119 'an atmosphere of simple affection?': Ibid.

119 we're standing here holding hands: Ibid.

119 Lupton . . . had resigned: Courtesy of the Coca-Cola Company archives, Atlanta, Georgia.

120 'May all your luck . . . be good luck': Roberto Goizueta in centennial celebration videotape, May 9, 1986, the Coca-Cola Company, Atlanta, Georgia.

Chapter Five

121 'Don't tell anyone': Author interviews, William and Jan Schmidt, April 2002.

122 'This'll *never* sell!': Ibid.

123 'She keeps one by the bed': Debbie Newby, 'Coke – and Smiles – for Christmas: Spouse Surprises Cola-loving Wife with 100 Cases', *The Atlanta Journal-Constitution,* December 21, 1985, section C, p. 1.

123 'de-Coking' her car: Ibid.

125 was the winner: Author interview, Emmet Bondurant II, January 2002.

125 Some people poured Coke onto their windshields: Graham, *Classic Cooking with Coca-Cola,* p. 187.

125 Animal kingdom . . . drinking Coke: Kahn, *The Big Drink,* pp. 110–11.

127 5.32 pounds of cane sugar: 95 FRD 168, United States District Court for the District of Delaware (August 17, 1982), pp. 2–3.

127 'as that used in a highly charged soda water': Warner Jenkinson Manufacturing Company, *Ice Cream, Carbonated Beverages,* p. 73.

128 Goizueta . . . paid a visit to . . . Ichauway: Greising, *Buy a Coke,* p. 120.

129 used-bottle dealer: Louis and Harvey, *The Cola Wars,* p. 50.

131 'I know everything they're going to do': Author interview, George Marlin, July 2001.

131 'it would upset people': Author interview, Jennifer Solomon, July 2001.

131 *Thanks for the free advertising:* Allen, *Secret Formula,* p. 227.

132 research into what the consumer wanted: Nick Poulos, 'Goizueta: It's No Big Risk', *The Atlanta Journal-Constitution,* April 28, 1985, section K, p. 1.

133 'a more harmonious flavor': Richard W. Stevenson, 'Coke's Big Misjudgment', *The New York Times,* July 11, 1985, section D, p. 1.

134 'a disaster in the making': Author interview, Richard Larson, May 2001.

134 'What are those buses for?': Author interview, Larry Jones, February 2001.

134 'You didn't mess with the formula': Author interview, former Coca-Cola executive, May 2002.

134 *Maybe it could be something that puts us in a corner:* Author interview, Roger Enrico, March 2003.

135 'It wasn't any good': Ibid.

135 'put in a spinach filling': various news reports, 1985.

136 *putting toes on our ears or teeth on our knees:* Graham, *The Real Ones,* pp. 301, 302.

136 'like I was a Communist': author interview, Frank Barron, April 2002.

136 'just got creamed': author interview, Emmet Bondurant II, January 2002.

136 'I might have to change to Pepsi': Author interview, Asa Candler VI, June 2002.

136 'they will forget about old Coke': Stevenson, 'Coke's Big Misjudgment'.

136 *Dear Chief Dodo:* Stevenson, 'Coke's Big Misjudgment'.

137 Bob . . . drove as far as Tennessee: Newby, 'Coke – and smiles'.

137 'the largest increase on a monthly basis': Keith Herndon, 'Coca-Cola Says Americans Love New Taste', *The Atlanta Journal-Constitution,* June 6, 1985, section D, p. 1.

137 *The sorrow is knowing:* Graham, *The Real Ones,* p. 302.

137 *You have taken away my childhood:* Author interview, former Coca-Cola Company executive, March 2002.

139 'Big company admits it': Author interview, former Coca-Cola Company executive, June 2002.

139 'a little tiny piece of people's lives': Author interview, former Coca-Cola Company executive, March 2002.

140 'No one was happier than me': Author interview, Frank Barron, Jr., April 2002.

Chapter Six

141 'choice in the soft-drink marketplace': annual report of the Coca-Cola Company, 1985, p. 3.

141 'serendipitous, inadvertent, unplanned good luck': Author interview, Emmet Bondurant II, January 2002.

142 'how much some people like to second-guess . . . the Coca-Cola Company': *Beverage Digest,* April 28, 1995, p. 1.

142 'some things that the company wasn't prepared to do at that time': Zyman, *The End of Marketing as We Know It,* p. xx.

142 'sitting by his pool': *Beverage Digest,* April 28, 1995, p. 1

143 'It changed the way they looked at people': Author interview, Lauren Bryant, November 2000.

143 'challenge you, in a way that was as public as possible': Ibid.

144 'Coca-Cola . . . must be Coca-Cola, always': *Beverage Digest,* April 28, 1995, p. 2.

145 'increasing shareholder value over time': annual report of the Coca-Cola Company, 1987, p. 2.

145 'not to be satisfied with the growth that just came naturally': Author interview, former Coca-Cola Company executive, March 2002.

147 'he could not delegate the reputation of the company': Author interview, former Coca-Cola Company executive, August 2002.

147 'you feel good about it': Author interview, former Coca-Cola Company executive, April 2001.

148 'that which we have to offer': Elliott, *Mr. Anonymous,* p. 291.

148 *it was not because I didn't try:* Correspondence from Roberto Goizueta to Robert Woodruff, November 18, 1982, Special Collections and Archives, Robert W. Woodruff Library.

149 'they would never call him back': Author interview, Jennifer Solomon, July 2001.

149 *strong positive impact on the net earnings line:* Correspondence from Roberto Goizueta to a beverage industry analyst, December 1996.

150 'two bumps out of the stock price, instead of just one': Author interview, Coca-Cola Company executive, June 2002.

150 'Fatherland or death!': Navarro, *Tocayo,* p. 3.

151 'Breakfast is one of the most important meals': Author interview, former Coca-Cola Company executive, February 2001.

152 'If he didn't like you – he was mean': Author interview, Allan Kaplan, May 2002.

153 'to bring the stock price again up to $100': The Coca-Cola Company, *Special Progress Report,* June 4, 1986, p. 1.

154 'It was mind-blowing when you think about how consistent it was': Author interview, Jennifer Solomon, July 2001.

155 in a Pepsi-drinking household: Author interview, Ambassador Donald McHenry, April 2003.

155 'if it looks like a geriatric ward': Ibid.

156 Keough, however, sent William Allison: Various articles, *The Atlanta Journal-Constitution,* July–September 1981, Special Collections and Archives, Robert W. Woodruff Library.

157 'staff doesn't come up with these things on their own': Author interview, Ambassador Donald McHenry, April 2003.

157 he never left the room: Ibid.

158 'We'll establish a beachhead': Author interview, former Coca-Cola Company executive, April 2001.

159 'part of the wonderful scheme': Ibid.

159 'who don't know their own capital cities': The Coca-Cola Company, *Special Progress Report,* p. 9.

160 'you were afraid to sell': Author interview, Skip Carpenter, March 2001.

163 selling its soft drinks in Russia: Allen, *Secret Formula,* and various interviews with former Coca-Cola Company executives, 2001 and 2002.

164 'touched by the magic of Coca-Cola': Author interview, former Coca-Cola Company executive, June 2001.

166 'I didn't challenge myself or Mark': Author interview, Fredric Russell, May 2001.

166 admonished others . . . that they must never sell their stock: Author interviews, various former Coca-Cola Company executives, 2001–2003.

167 Goizueta would pay next to nothing in taxes: David Cay Johnston, 'Putting Aside $1 Billion While Making a Company Thrive', *The New York Times,* October 13, 1996, section 1, p. 36.

168 'it was all symbolic': Author interview, Herbert Allen, April 2003.

169 'He managed us very, very gently': Author interview, former Coca-Cola Company executive, March 2002.

170 applause four times: Jerry Schwartz, 'Coke's Chairman Defends $86 Million Pay and Bonus', *The New York Times,* April 16, 1992, section D, p. 1.

172 'they would invade them': Author interview, Emmet Bondurant II, January 2002.

173 'even truer than I thought it was going to be': Author interview, George Marlin, July 2001.

174 almost no incentive to do well: Author interview, Emanuel Goldman, December 2000.

175 'Advertising is like the icing on the cake': Author interview, Summerfield Johnston, Jr., December 2002.

177 'a control mentality': Ibid.

180 'They take what they need': Author interview, Richard Larson, February 2001.

180 'in practical terms, they can't pull it back': Author interview, former Coca-Cola Company executive, September 2002.

181 'the bottlers took twenty': Author interview, Andrew Conway, October 2002.

184 Enrico suspected something was up: Author interview, Roger Enrico, March 2003.

184 Cisneros . . . denied it: Ibid.

185 'the only dark spot on the Coca-Cola map': *Beverage Digest,* August 21, 1996, p. 1.

186 'a soft-drink monopoly': *Beverage Digest,* August 21, 1996, p. 2.

Chapter Seven

187 a much older man: Author interview, former Coca-Cola
    Company executive, November 2000.

188 'wherever Roberto was': Author interview, former Coca-
    Cola Company executive, April 2001.

190 looked very tired: Author interview, Andrew Conway,
    October 2002.

190 'a little fatigued': Ibid.

192 'Roberto thought it was a good idea, too': Author
    interview, former Coca-Cola Company executive, March
    2002.

192 'whatever you want': Author interview, former Coca-Cola
    Company executive, August 2003.

192 No, no: Ibid.

193 'Fantastic': Greising, *Buy A Coke,* p. 302.

Chapter Eight

194 a room downstairs: Author interview, former Coca-Cola
    Company executive, May 2001.

194 'I'd Like to Teach the World to Sing': Greising, *Buy a Coke,*
    p. 304.

195 'a good friend': *Beverage Digest,* October 24, 1997, p. 3.

195 colored badges: Author interviews, former Coca-Cola
    Company executives, 2000, 2001.

196 gross national product of Cuba: Chart prepared by the United
    States Conference of Mayors, 1998.

196 as seamless a transition: Thomas Stewart, 'America's Most
    Admired Companies: Why Leadership Matters', *Fortune,*
    March 2, 1998, pp. 70–101.

199 'sorcery that sells': Mark Weiner, 'We Are What We Eat',
    American Quarterly, June 1994, pp. 242–43.

200 'a very stable kind of personality': Author interview, former
    Coca-Cola Company executive, March 2001.

201 'actually they had done a pretty good job': Author interview,
    former Coca-Cola Company executive, April 2001.

201 'the meeting finished early': Author interview, consumer-
    products company executive, May 2001.

202 He wanted Ivester to listen: Author interview, Ambassador

Donald McHenry, April 2003.

202 'quality products than ever before': Speech by Douglas Ivester, October 28, 1998, New York.

203 'as intimidating as meeting the president of Coca-Cola': Author interview, former Coca-Cola Company executive, February 2001.

204 'a kind of cultish brainwashing': Author interview, former Coca-Cola Company executive, February 2001.

204 'It's all inbred': Author interview, former Coca-Cola Company executive, March 2001.

205 'the greatest enemy of the Coca-Cola Company': Nikhil Deogun, 'Ivester Alert: Advice to Coke People from Their New Boss: Don't Get Too Cocky', *The Wall Street Journal,* March 9, 1998, section A, p. 1.

205 he had been coached: Author interviews, former Coca-Cola Company executives, 2001, 2002.

206 'The language of a tyrant': Author interview, former Coca-Cola Company executive, February 2001.

207 until he was ready to declare that person his successor: Author interview, former Coca-Cola Company executive, August 2003.

208 'Size was all they cared about': Author interview, former Coca-Cola Company executive, March 2001.

209 they did not serve Coca-Cola products . . . if that was the case: Constance L. Hays, 'Julius R. Lunsford, 84, Trademark Law Expert', *The New York Times,* September 30, 1999, section C, p. 11.

210 'the intensity went over the edge': Author interview, Roger Enrico, October 2000.

210 'We will build a moat of Coca-Cola around the market': *Beverage Digest,* August 21, 1996, p. 4.

213 'There will never be a day care on this campus': Author interviews, former Coca-Cola Company executives, 2001, 2002

Chapter Nine

216 'crossed the line of death': Author interview, Roger Enrico, March 2003.

218 'consumers will turn on both of us': Author interview, Roger Enrico, October 2000.

218 'you're doing this because Pepsi is number one': Ibid.

220 'to say we need more': Author interview, John Bushey, September 1999.

220 'They believe that they are the only legitimate cola': Ibid.

221 to make him believe that his approach worked just fine: Author interview, former Wall Street beverage industry analyst, 1999.

223 No one doubted that he did indeed pursue it: Author interview, Rob Sharpe, November 2000.

225 'We want to see if we can stop this': Author interviews, Pepsico executives, November 2000.

225 Concentration . . . was not a good thing for France: Various newspaper articles, September 1998.

226 'The only place more arrogant than the Coca-Cola Company': Author interview, former Coca-Cola Company executive, December 1999.

226 still deep in the affairs of Coke: Author interview, Ambassador Donald McHenry, April 2003.

227 a parting courtesy from Goizueta: Author interview, former Coca-Cola Company executives, May and November 2002.

Chapter Ten

230 *the shares which you purchased in my name:* Correspondence from William Allison to Robert Woodruff, March 6, 1974, Special Collections and Archives, Robert W. Woodruff Library.

230 'greatest man-made cataclysm': Garrett, 'Founders of the Business of Coca-Cola in Bottles', p. 1.

230 'how to get it their religion': Mark Twain, as cited in Cheatham, *Your Friendly Neighbor,* p. 79.

231 'less than two weeks before U. S. Grant was named': Ibid.

232 'a pretty fundamental strategic shift': Author interview, Lauren Bryant, November 2000.

233 'We set our own course': Ibid.

236 It had been his idea: Author interview, former Coca-Cola Company executive, August 2003.

237 'diversification of its workforce': 'Preliminary Report to Doug Ivester Discussion Paper for a Diversity Management Strategy', submitted by Carl Ware, December 8, 1995, p. 2.

238 'ignored, overlooked or unacknowledged': Ibid., p. 3.

239 'well, why not?': Author interview, Linda Ingram, June 2001.

239 sent home to change: Author interview, former Coca-Cola Company executive, June 2001.

240 'am I in the fifties?': Author interview, Linda Ingram, June 2001.

240 'they didn't do anything': Ibid.

240 'all these thousands of conversations': Ibid.

241 'I just don't think we can be friends anymore': Ibid.

241 'the bag lady': Author interview, Larry Jones, February 2001.

242 'a lack of consciousness': Memo from Ingrid Jones to Doug Ivester, July 6, 1998.

243 'you just got moved': Author interview, Ambassador Donald McHenry, April 2003.

244 'not afraid of anything that you could do': Author interview, Linda Ingram, June 2001.

245 even bigger than Texaco: Author interview, Cyrus Mehri, April 2001.

246 'Everyone is treated equally badly here': Author interview, former Coca-Cola Company executive, March 2001.

246 in retaliation for her complaints: Ingram et al vs. The Coca-Cola Company, amended complaint (1999), p. 35.

246 white security officers did not have to do that: Ibid., pp. 36–37.

246 were paid more than she was: Ibid., pp. 34–35.

247 all there for the lawyer to see: Author interview, Cyrus Mehri, July 2000.

247 15.7 percent were African American: Ingram et al vs. The Coca-Cola Company, amended complaint, Exhibit B, p. 2.

248 median salary: Ibid., Exhibit E, p. 2.

Chapter Eleven

249 more money to be made in the restaurant business: Author interview, John Philis, May 2001.

252 'making millionaires out of so many people': Ibid.

253 rearranging routes, and cutting costs: Author interview, Frank Barron, Jr., November 2000.

254 'to our advantage to try to cooperate': Author interview, Dick Montag, June 2001.

255 'You must *never* compromise your ethics': Author interview, Albert Meyer, June 2001.

256 'tell us where Coke makes its money?': Ibid.

261 'the whole system must be healthy': Author interview, Jennifer Solomon, July 2001.

261 'How many businesses have that kind of margin?': Ibid.

261 'being negative on Coke': Ibid.

262 a former heavyweight boxing champion: The Coca-Cola Company, 'Special Progress Report', June 4, 1986, p. 3.

263 'the bottlers didn't want to give up bottling': Author interview, former Coca-Cola Company executive, October 2002.

265 'He's a crusader': Author interview, Frank Martin, August 2003.

266 franchise costs . . . ballooned: Coca-Cola Enterprises annual report, 1998, p. 31.

268 Ivester's holdings of Coke stock . . . compared with . . . shares of Coca-Cola Enterprises stock: proxy statement of Coca-Cola Enterprises, 1998, p. 12.

268 'give back just enough at the SG & A line': Author interview, Albert Meyer, June 2001.

269 'spent to drive the business forward': Author interview, Andrew Conway, March 2002.

270 'elephants with peashooters': Melody Petersen, 'Maybe Pepsi Has a Job for a Dogged Coke Critic', *The New York Times*, September 27, 1998, section 3, p. 2.

Chapter Twelve

272 'closer to seventy, seventy-five percent': Author interview, Jerry Dudley, July 2000.

272 'we have a deal with Coke right now': Ibid.

273 'No . . . they're doing it everywhere': Author interview, Tom Stanley, July 2001.

274 'places you couldn't even get to with a telegram': Ibid.

274 sales dropped 30 or 40 percent almost overnight: Ibid.

275 FISH FRY, NEXT LEFT: Author interviews, Bruce Hackett in 2000 and Tom Stanley in 2001.

275 would drop to his hands and knees: Author interview, Nelson Roach, July 2000.

276 'That's the culture of this company': Henry Schimberg, speech to Beverage Forum in New York, May 1999.

277 'without any regard for returns on invested capital': Author interview, Andrew Conway, June 2001 and March 2002.

277 'Now it's high-fructose corn syrup': Author interview, Jerry Dudley, July 2003.

279 'a minimum of 100 percent of total soft-drink space': 1998 marketing agreement between Coca-Cola Enterprises and U.S.A. Drug, submitted as exhibit during 2000 trial of HarMar Bottling Company et al vs. the Coca-Cola Company and Coca-Cola Enterprises, Texas State Supreme Court, Daingerfield, Texas.

279 'a beverage laboratory': Author interview, Lindsay Hutter, July 2000.

280 'It sort of devalues the category': Constance L. Hays, 'How Coke Pushed Rivals Off the Shelf', The New York Times, August 6, 2000, section 3, p. 1.

281 'tying everything together': Ibid.

281 'something we believed in': Author interview, Leslie Dudley, July 2000.

Chapter Thirteen

286 gliding to a perfect landing: Constance L. Hays, 'Keeping Schweppes Bubbling', The New York Times, April 4, 1999, section 3, p. 2.

288 'an unbridled exercise of dominant power': Author interview, soft-drink company executive, June 2002.

288 analysts and others paid more attention to the Cadbury acquisition: Constance L. Hays, 'Coke Warns of Poor Foreign Results as It Tells of Global Deal', The New York

Times, December 12, 1998, section C, p. 1.

289 'This is about freedom': Author interview, PepsiCo executive, December 2000.

289 'Coca-Cola should learn to respect the rules like everybody else': Neil Buckley, Betty Liu, and John Wilkinson, 'E.U. Takes Tough Line on Coke Deal', *The Financial Times,* April 29, 1999, section A, p. 1.

Chapter Fourteen

290 He decided to invite the younger man to lunch: Author interview, former Coca-Cola executive, April 2001.

292 'not about just giving access to us, but to everybody': Author interviews, PepsiCo executives, December 2000.

293 'better than anyone else': Ibid.

293 six times a day: Author interview, Douglas Daft, October 1998.

293 'and Zeus works for Pepsi': Author interview, Emanuel Goldman, March 1999.

295 'so troubling to me': Memo from Douglas Ivester to U.S.–based Coca-Cola Company employees, April 28, 1999, p. 1.

295 'help us determine what actions are appropriate': Memo from Douglas Ivester to U.S.–based Coca-Cola Company employees, May 25, 1999, p. 2.

295 'It's genteel': Author interview, Ambassador Donald McHenry, April 2003.

296 'You could count them on one hand': Author interview, Larry Jones, February 2001.

298 'Son, I am proud of you': Author interview, Coca-Cola Company executive, March 2001.

299 Jackson brought Willie Gary by to say hello: Author interview, Rev. Jesse Jackson, June 2000.

299 The kind of help that only Gary could provide: Ibid.

Chapter Fifteen

302 'We had to push them a little bit': Constance L. Hays et al, 'A Sputter in the Coke Machine', *The New York Times,* June 30, 1999, section C, p. 1.

303 'the purest of standard ingredients in the manufacture of my products': National Code of Ethics, in American Bottlers of Carbonated Beverages, *Yearbook,* p. 8.

303 to persuade people: Riley, *A History of the American Soft Drink Industry,* pp. 104–105.

304 bad for people: Ludy T. Benjamin, Jr., Anne M. Rogers, and Angela Rosenbaum, 'Coca-Cola, Caffeine and Mental Deficiency', *Journal of the History of Behavioral Sciences,* 27 (January 1991), p. 44.

304 a poison and a habit-forming drug: Ibid, p. 45.

305 'drowned in a bottle of Coca-Cola': Gary Alan Fine, 'Cokelore and Coke Law: Urban Belief Tales and the Problem of Multiple Origins', *Journal of American Folklore,* 92, numbers 363–66 (1979), p. 479.

305 'mental aversion . . . to ratty nourishment': Ibid.

305 desire for importance: Ibid., p. 481.

305 $20,000 in a case decided in 1969: Ibid.

306 'not serious': Author interview, former Coca-Cola Company executive, May 2001.

308 'among the highest in Europe': annual report, Coca-Cola Enterprises, 1998, p. 10.

309 'it is not harmful': author interview, Rob Baskin, June 1999.

309 'secret formula' was to blame: Author interview, former Coca-Cola Company executive, August 2003.

310 'You ought to get over there right away': Author interview, former Coca-Cola Company executive, March 2001.

310 Ivester was in Belgium: Author interview, former Coca-Cola Company executive, August 2003.

310 'It's the intuitive way to deal with it': Author interview, former Coca-Cola Company executive, December 2002.

310 'there just wasn't a problem': Author interview, former Coca-Cola Comapny executive, May 2002.

311 'they would have applauded him as he left': Author interview, former Coca-Cola Company executive, March 2001.

311 'You needed a czar': Author interview, former Coca-Cola Company executive, June 2002.

314 'The machinery breaks down': Author interview, former Coca-Cola Company executive, February 2001.

Chapter Sixteen

318 He would no longer be involved: Author interview, former Coca-Cola Company executive, October 2002.

318 Buffett – *not Keough:* Ibid.

318 He had several contacts at *Fortune:* Author interview, former Coca-Cola Company executive, June 2002.

318 'He was good at making people think they were important': Author interview, former Coca-Cola Company executive, October 2002.

320 He wanted to help: Author interview, former Coca-Cola Company executive, October 2002.

321 'Maybe somebody made a calculation error': Author interviews, Albert Meyer, 1999 and 2001.

322 'not parts that need copious refueling': Constance L. Hays, 'A Once-Sweet Bottling Plan Turns Sour for Coke', *The New York Times,* May 5, 1999, section C, p. 1

323 *we broke a lot of eggs:* Correspondence from Donald Keough to Douglas Ivester, July 22, 1999.

323 *hand-holder and baby-sitter:* Ibid.

325 no portrait or even a photograph of Keough: Author interview, former Coca-Cola Company executive, December 2002.

325 hated feeling irrelevant: Author interview, former Coca-Cola Company executive, December 2002.

326 *and crush it:* Correspondence from Donald Keough to Douglas Ivester, July 22, 1999.

326 doesn't want to see it fail: Author interview, former Coca-Cola Company executive, December 2002.

327 'ever did or could': Morris, 'Doug Is It', pp. 70–84.

328 'compared favorably with Roberto Goizueta one day': Patricia Sellers, 'Crunch Time for *Coke*', *Fortune,* July 19, 1999, p. 78.

330 'a few things we would have said a little differently': Ivester remarks to beverage analysts' meeting, July 15, 1999.

Chapter Seventeen

333 'How could I have let him down?': Author interview, former Coca-Cola Company executive, May 2002.

334 'You would say that Neville was the greatest speaker in the world': Author interview, former Coca-Cola Company executive, March 2002.

336 'encourages people to take in more and more liquids': Constance L. Hays and Donald G. McNeil, Jr., 'Putting Africa on Coke's Map', *The New York Times,* May 26, 1998, section D, p. 1.

336 'source of foreign exchange for exporter countries': Euripedes Alcantara, 'O Mundo Tem Sede', (The World Is Thirsty), *Veja,* October 20, 1999, p. 15.

336 'need to exercise and follow a balanced diet': Alcantara, 'O Mundo Tem Sede', p. 15.

336 Vend-All Nickel in Slot Vending Machine: Cheatham, *Your Friendly Neighbor,* pp. 99–100.

337 'tremendous asset to the Parent Company!': Cheatham, *Your Friendly Neighbor,* p. 104.

337 not until 1932 that the Coca-Cola Company . . . approved . . . vending machines: Coca-Cola Company, *Chronological History,* pp. 4–5.

337 'improved serving of the bottled product': Coca-Cola Company, Chronological History, p. 4.

337 'the front door of countless retail establishments': Ibid.

339 'The price just went up a dollar?': Editorial, 'Maybe the Heat Got to Em', *The Charlotte Observer,* October 29, 1999.

339 'This one is going to hurt us a little bit': Author interview, former Coca-Cola Company executive, May 2002.

339 'It'll blow over in a day or two': Ibid.

339 'a thousand cartoons': Ibid.

340 'being a role model for the business and for the rest of America': Author interview, Coca-Cola Company executive, June 2002.

341 'you need less hierarchy, not more': Douglas Ivester remarks at beverage industry analysts' meeting, July 15, 1999.

342 'I remember what Coke represented': Author interview, Douglas Daft, July 2002.

342 'You just don't do that in Japan': Author interview, Ben Kitay, April 2003.

344 'that black face, if you will': Author interview, Joseph

Wheeler, November 1999.

345 'smooth and successful transition of the leadership of the group': News release from the Coca-Cola Company, November 5, 1999, p. 1.

347 'our profitability is controlled by the Coca-Cola Company': Author interview, Richard Larson, March 2001.

348 'You're not going to sit there and just let it go down': Author interview, Summerfield Johnston, Jr., December 2002.

348 'I had a lot of discussions with everybody': Ibid.

349 'I can assure you that we don't control CCE': Author interview, Coca-Cola Company executive, June 2002.

Chapter Eighteen

351 Allen had said they'd meet him there: Author interview, former Coca-Cola Company executive, June and September 2002.

353 'the smoothness of the transition of leadership': The Coca-Cola Company proxy statement, March 1998, p. 21.

354 never even removed their overcoats: Author interview, former Coca-Cola Company executive, August 2003.

354 'I felt I had the obligation': Author interview, Herbert Allen, April 2003.

354 There had been no vote: Ibid.

354 'He didn't think he could run the company': Ibid.

354 told his wife, Kay, of his suspicions: Author interview, former Coca-Cola Company executive, August 2003.

355 without the consent of the rest of the board: Ibid.

356 'There weren't a lot of choices': Ibid.

356 'Doug wants to resign': Author interview, former Coca-Cola Company executive, October 2002.

357 Many of the directors were stunned: Author interview, Ambassador Donald McHenry, April 2003.

358 He had been present when Roberto Goizueta took his first trip to Ichauway: Correspondence from James Williams to Robert Woodruff, March 2, 1981, Special Collections and Archives, Robert W. Woodruff Library.

359 'The fellow is the right man at the right time': Constance L. Hays, 'Learning to Think Smaller at Coke', *The New York Times,* February 6, 2000, section 2, p. 1.

359 'I really don't know what was in people's minds': Author interview, Douglas Daft, July 2002.

360 'We've been working on this for two years': Author interview, former Coca-Cola Company executive, June 2002.

361 'in the fall, the board put the ugly puzzle together': Author interview, Coca-Cola Company executive, June 2002.

361 'I'm going to get it done': Author interview, Ambassador Donald McHenry, April 2003.

361 'a dour, uptight person selling Coca-Cola': Hays, 'Learning to Think Smaller at Coke', p. 1.

361 He began attending board meetings once more: Author interview, Ambassador Donald McHenry, April 2003.

362 'I should have been there first': Author interview, Joe Wilkinson, October 2002.

363 'a knife in the back': Author interview, former Coca-Cola Company executive, June 2002.

364 'the former chairman of the Coca-Cola Company': Author interview, Atlanta executive, 2000.

Chapter Nineteen

365 'but it was at our expense': Author interview, former Coca-Cola Company executive, February 2001.

366 'People were still talking about it': Author interview, Coca-Cola Company executive, June 2002.

367 'U.S. consumers continue to adapt': Marc Cohen, 'Beverage and Tobacco Lowdown', published by Goldman Sachs, December 6, 1999, p. 1.

368 Keough . . . hadn't wanted to expand the Coca-Cola Enterprises magic: Author interview, former Coca-Cola Company executive, March 2001.

369 'a good strategy, but it was too much, too fast': Author interview, former Coca-Cola Company executive, March 2001.

370 'what do we have to do?': Author interview, Coca-Cola Company executive, June 2002.

371 He began to identify with Bilbo: Author interview, Douglas Daft, July 2002.

371 'one weekend when I'll need a prop': Author interview, Ibid.

372 *You must:* Ibid.

372 'didn't have to write a six-page report': Hays, 'Learning to Think Smaller at Coke'.

372 'Everything I know about relationships, I learned from Don Keough': Author interview, Douglas Daft, July 2002.

374 'revenue-generating operating units': News release, the Coca-Cola Company, January 26, 2000.

374 'everyone needed to be in the office': Author interview, former Coca-Cola Company executive, May 2002.

375 'It was so sick': Ibid.

376 they were no longer needed: Author interview, former Coca-Cola Company executive, June 2002.

379 'It's *$1.6 billion*': Author interview, Marc Cohen, January 2000.

380 'It was cutting to the quick': Author interview, former Coca-Cola Company executive, June 2002.

380 'They did not really create wealth': Author interview, former Coca-Cola Company executive, May 2002.

381 'you never really forget it': Author interview, former Coca-Cola Company executive, May 2002.

381 'there was nothing wrong with the Coca-Cola Company': Author interview, Joe Wilkinson, June 2002.

Chapter Twenty

382 A feng shui expert walked into: Betsy McKay, 'Coke Leaving? No, but Feng Shui Thing Is True', *The Wall Street Journal,* October 18, 2000, section B, p. 1.

383 'I could ill afford to pass on it': Author interview, Carl Ware, January 2000.

387 'worse than the time the PLO came to town': Author interview, Hotel Dupont dining room host, April 2000.

388 saw him scolding Jones: Author interview, Larry Jones and others in attendance, June 2000.

389 'a battle of nerves': Author interview, Cyrus Mehri, August 2002.

390 'He didn't seem fired up': Author interview, former Coca-Cola Company executive, March 2002.

391 Steve Heyer: Author interview, beverage industry expert, May 2002.

391 'the kind of mentor I'd love to have': Patricia Sellers, 'Who's in Charge Here?' *Fortune,* December 24, 2001, p. 85.

392 'sometimes I pay attention to it, sometimes not': Author interview, Douglas Daft, July 2002.

392 'My ego doesn't need any more stroking': Author interview, Donald Keough, October 2002.

392 'there is no way I can fully separate myself': Ibid.

392 'people felt comfortable coming to me': Ibid.

393 'a terrible temptation': Author interview, Ambassador Donald McHenry, April 2003.

394 He had met Diller through Herbert Allen and Don Keough: Author interview, Douglas Daft, July 2002.

394 'It's the old Frank Barron story': Author interview, Joe Wilkinson, December 2002.

395 'The brand . . . and the bottler system': Author interview, former Coca-Cola Company executive, October 2002.

395 'I came to the company because of Doug': *Beverage Digest,* December 12, 2002, p. 1.

Epilogue

397 acquisitions the company had made . . . the previous year: Sherri Day, 'Cocoa-Cola Reports a profit, but Fails to Sway Investors', *The New York Times*, April 17, 2003, section C, page 2.

398 at scores of other restaurants as well: Sherri Day 'Coke Confirms Product Test Was Rigged,' *The New York Times*, June 18, 2003, section C, page 1.

398 created slush funds, engaged in accounting fraud: Sherri Day, 'Profits At Coke Climb 11% and Beat Analysts' Estimates', *The New York Times*, July 18, 2003, section C, page 5.

398 highly profitable markets like Japan: Sherri Day, 'Coke Employees Are Questioned in Fraud Inquiry', *The New York Times*, January 31, 2004, section C, page 1.

398 a payment of $21.1 million: Sherri Day, 'Coke to Pay Burger King $21 Million Over Rigged Test', *The New York Times*, August 13, 2003, section C, page 4.

399 'I was shocked. And hurt': Author interview, former Coca-Cola executive, July 2004.

399 'something rotten at the core': Ibid.

399 scored better than he did: Sherri Day, 'Coca-Cola Settles Whistleblower Suit for $540,000', *The New York Times*, October 8, 2003, section C, page 4.

399 the questioning paid a great deal of attention to Daft's role: Sherri Day, 'Coke Employees Are Questioned in Fraud Inquiry', *The New York Times*, January 31, 2004, section C, page 1.

400 'I know what my own plans are': Douglas N. Daft, question-and-answer session at *Beverage Digest* meeting in New York, December 8, 2003

401 'moving in the wrong direction': John Faucher, report on beverage companies, North America Equity Research, JP Morgan, May 28, 2004.

402 'he'd prepared us for that': Sherri Day, 'Coke's Chief Set to Retire at End of 2004', *The New York Times*, February 20, 2004, section C, page 1.

402 secretaries called him 'the Devil': Author interview, former Coca-Cola executive, January 2004.

403 'they have to listen to what I say': Author interview, former Coca-Cola executive, July 2004.

403 'people didn't trust him after that': Ibid.

404 'the only one who was offered the job': Claudia H. Deutsch, 'Coca-Cola Reaches Into Past for New Chief', *The New York Times*, May 5, 2004, section C, page 1.

404 'Happy days are here again': Author interview, former Coca-Cola executive, August 2004.

404 'Anyone who wouldn't listen to the wisdom': Claudia H. Deutsch, 'Coca-Cola Reaches Into Past for New Chief', *The New York Times*, May 5, 2004, section C, page 1.

406 'Yes, no question': Author interview, John Faucher, June 2004.

407 'Taken for Plonkers' . . . 'Sidcup for 95p':videotape of the British Broadcasting Corporation, *The Money Programme*, 'Coke's Water Bomb'. June 2004.

408 Coke would repay all but $5 million: *Beverage Digest*, August
     13, 2004.
408 'We *chose* to take the product off the market': British
     Broadcasting Corporation, 'Coke's Water Bomb'.
408 'Can they get out of the way': Author interview, former
     Coca-Cola executive, July 2004.

Acknowledgments

Iowe enormous thanks to dozens of people who did so much to make this book possible, including the following:

Bob and Laura Sillerman – for the Coca-Cola works of art, for the inspiration at the very beginning, for seeing me through this marathon and one more besides. Mikel, Joe, and Josie Witte, for mini-Cokes, encouragement, and help. Cait Murphy, a great reader. Lucia and David Greenhouse, Vicky and Wilson Neely, Sheila and Brian Murphy, Cathy Barnett and Tim Mayotte, Vance Thompson, Emily Remes and Craig Stewart, Dana Pollan and Mitchell Stern. Bev Bartow and Jim Stengel, for the big drink. Lori Bookstein, Myung-Hi and Chip Cody, and Anne and Austen Furse, for moral support and hospitality. Dr. Kerry Sulkowicz for help understanding types of leaders. Becky MacGuire, Mary McD. Murphy, Martha Murphy, Dr. Ellen Scherl, Steve Farley and Suzanne Worden, Margot Rosenberg, who insisted on going out to lunch, Janet Elder, who pointed me in the direction of a great library, and Joan Pope, computer consultant extraordinaire. And the late Richard F. Shepard, a good writer and a good friend.

My colleagues Alan Cowell, Craig Whitney, Melody Petersen, Steven Holmes, Jonathan Glater, Glenn Collins, Stuart Elliott, Greg Winter, and David Cay Johnston, for inspiration, irreverence, and their own fine articles about Coke. Anne Berryman, for all her help on stories from Atlanta, and David Dunlap, for directions to New York's Candler Building. Charles Conway, who has read much of this, Brent Bowers, a seasoned author who offered encouragement from start to finish, and Janny Scott, for talks over tea. Tom Redburn, Winnie O'Kelley, and Jim Schachter, for years of help with Coke coverage. Bruce Headlam and Kelley Holland, for their patience with this project when I was officially writing about something else. Robin Summers, Ken Meyn, and Judith Spindler, for time off and other forms of aid. Many thanks to my other editors at the *Times* over the years that I wrote about Coke: Alison Leigh Cowan, Jeff Cane, Judy Dobryzinski, Rick Gladstone, Pat Lyons, and Richard Teitelbaum, as well as the late Allen Myerson and David Rosenberg. And to all the *Times* copy editors: Harvey Dickson, Fred Brock, Joe Gemignani, Mickey Meece, and Dwayne Draffen, who worked on my news stories and made them readable, as well as Vicky Epstein and Dan Niemi, who put up with my idea of a deadline.

Thanks also to Phil Mooney, Kari Bjorhus, Sonya Soutus, and everyone at the Coca-Cola Company who helped me arrange interviews and gather information for the book, as well as to Dick Detwiler at PepsiCo. And to Rob Baskin, Linda Peek Schacht, Randy Donaldson, Ben Deutsch, Brad Shaw, Jon Harris, and Larry Jabbonsky, for their assistance during all the days when Coke and Pepsi were in the news.

Emmet Bondurant II, who knows the Coca-Cola Company and its vanished bottler system as well as anyone, patiently shared his wisdom with me. Tom Stanley of Houston also provided important help in researching this book, as did John Philis and Bob Karcher of the Lexington Candy Shop in Manhattan. Thanks also to the Penn Drug Company of Sidney, Iowa, who sent me a pen, and Kitchen Arts and Letters of Manhattan, where I finally tracked down a photograph of the oversized soda fountain displayed at the Centennial Exposition.

I thank the Coke bottlers who agreed to be interviewed, especially Frank and Anne Barron, Jan and Bill Schmidt, Dick Montag, and Summerfield Johnston, Jr. George Marlin and Joe Wilkinson, formerly of the Coca-Cola Company, provided all sorts of insights, as did many other former employees who didn't want to be identified. Doug Daft, former chairman and chief executive of the Coca-Cola Company, and other Coke executives spoke with me, on and off the record, for which I thank them. The members of the Coke board who agreed to interviews, Herbert Allen and Donald McHenry, provided valuable help as well.

Without libraries and librarians, this project would still be on the drawing board. For books, documents, and a quiet place to work,

I am grateful to Martin Elzy of the Jimmy Carter Presidential Library in Atlanta; Hilary Hardwick of the Atlanta History Center; the staff of the New York Public Library, and the staff of the Nantucket Atheneum; the staff of the New York Society Library, and the staff of the Chattanooga Public Library, Chattanooga, Tennessee. A special note of thanks to the staff of the Special Collections and Archives division of the Robert W. Woodruff Library at Emory University, who graciously wheeled in cart after cart of documents, letters, articles, and other artifacts that helped illustrate the history of the Coca-Cola Company and its bottlers. Thanks also to Nancy Bell of the Vicksburg Foundation for Historic Preservation, operator of the Biedenharn Candy Company and Museum of Coca-Cola Memorabilia, Vicksburg, Mississippi.

Enormous thanks to my agent, Amanda Urban, for taking my idea and turning it into a proposal, and then continuing to advise and support the project all the way through. And to my editor at Random House, Jonathan Karp, for his vision of what this book could be and all his help in getting there, over all the years it took.

I am grateful to Joe Lelyveld, for granting me a leave of absence from the *Times;* and to Glenn Kramon, the best kind of editor: kind, generous, willing to take a chance on a newcomer.

Thanks also to Albert Meyer for his insights into Coke's accounting; John Sicher, for access to the *Beverage Digest* archives and all kinds of knowledge; Ralph and Chris Crowley for the cook's tour of a modern bottling plant. And to the analysts who covered Coke, including Emanuel Goldman, most recently of ING Barings; Marc Cohen of Goldman Sachs; Andrew Conway of Morgan Stanley, then CS First Boston; Bill Pecoriello of Sanford C. Bernstein, then Morgan Stanley; John Faucher of JP Morgan; Daniel Peris, of Argus Research; Skip Carpenter of Thomas Weisel Partners; Jennifer Solomon, formerly of Salomon Smith Barney and Allan Kaplan, formerly of Merrill Lynch, for insight into Coke's relationship with Wall Street and their own evaluations of one secret formula or another. Thanks also to my children's teachers and to Sherma Samuel, Daphne Thompson, and Blanca Pelaez for all their help.

I also owe thanks to all the people who said they couldn't talk to me but found other people who could, and did.

My children deserve a standing ovation for their patience, love, and inspiration over the years that it took to complete this book. To my parents, thanks and love for their good example from the beginning, and my brothers, sister, in-laws, nieces, and nephews, for being part of the team.

Dedicated to my husband, John Hays, who is proof that some stories have happy endings. And to all the brave, everywhere.

About the Author

CONSTANCE L. HAYS has been a reporter for the Raleigh, North Carolina, *News & Observer,* and, since 1986, for *The New York Times,* where she covered the food and beverage industry for three years. She is married to John A. Hays, deputy chairman of Christie's. They live in New York City with their three children.

Index